No Exit

A volume in the series

CORNELL STUDIES IN SECURITY AFFAIRS

edited by Robert J. Art
Robert Jervis
Stephen M. Walt

A full list of titles in the series
appears at the end of the book.

No Exit

AMERICA AND THE GERMAN PROBLEM, 1943–1954

James McAllister

Cornell University Press

ITHACA AND LONDON

First published 2002 by Cornell University Press

Printed in the United States of America

Library of Congress Cataloging-in-Publication Data

McAllister, James, 1964–
    No exit : America and the German problem, 1943–1954 / James McAllister.
      p. cm.—(Cornell studies in security affairs)
    Includes bibliographical references and index.
    ISBN 0-8014-3876-4 (cloth : alk. paper)
    1. United States—Foreign relations—Germany. 2. Germany—Foreign relations—United States. 3. United States—Foreign relations—Europe. 4. Europe—Foreign relations—United States. 5. United States—Foreign relations—1945–1953. 6. Germany—Politics and government—1945–1990. 7. German reunification question (1949–1990). 8. World War, 1939–1945—Influence. 9. Balance of power—History—20th century. I. Title II. Series.
    E183.8.G3 M35   2001
    327.73043′09′044—dc21

2001003980

Cornell University Press strives to use environmentally responsible suppliers and materials to the fullest extent possible in the publishing of its books. Such materials include vegetable-based, low-VOC inks and acid-free papers that are recycled, totally chlorine-free, or partly composed of nonwood fibers. Books that bear the logo of the FSC (Forest Stewardship Council) use paper taken from forests that have been inspected and certified as meeting the highest standards for environmental and social responsibility. For further information, visit our website at www.cornellpress.cornell.edu.

Cloth printing   10 9 8 7 6 5 4 3 2 1

Contents

Acknowledgments

Contemporary international relations theorists often fail to appreciate how much their work owes to the founding fathers of the discipline. The day I arrived at Columbia University in the late 1980s was the same day that William T. R. Fox, the founder of the Institute of War and Peace Studies, passed away. I had never heard of Fox before that moment, but it is only now that I realize how much he has influenced my intellectual development. In his 1944 book *The Superpowers*, he attempted to address the puzzles and questions confronted in this book, and so, subsequently, did his many brilliant students, such as Kenneth Waltz, Glenn Snyder, and Warner Schilling. I believe that there is no better place to study international relations in the United States than Columbia's Institute of War and Peace Studies, and a good deal of the credit for this book rightly belongs to William T. R. Fox.

Having spent far too many years on the Institute's thirteenth floor, I find it impossible to list all of my colleagues for their support and advice, but I particularly thank J. Samuel Barkin, Marc Busch, James Davis, Daniel Drezner, Thomas Christensen, Drew Erdmann, Mikhail Hershkowitz, Martin Malin, Alan Russo, Randall Schweller, and Mark Sheetz. Harpreet Mahajan and the late Margaret V. Freund deserve special mention for their support. I also thank Stephen Peter Rosen and Samuel Huntington for allowing me the privilege of spending a year at the Olin Institute at Harvard in 1996–97.

All of the remaining credit for this book belongs to Richard Betts, Robert Jervis, and Marc Trachtenberg. There are very few things in life that can be stated with certainty, but these three scholars were nothing less than the academic equivalent of the 1927 New York Yankees. Virtually no political scientist except Robert Jervis would have allowed me the intellectual freedom and critical support necessary for the completion of this book. I owe him a debt that I can never hope to pay. Finding the proper words of acknowledgment for Marc Trachtenberg is just as difficult. My intellectual debt to Marc will be obvious to anyone who has read either *History and Strategy* or *A Constructed Peace.* He will always be my model of what a scholar should be, and his selfless integrity, conviction, and ideals I will attempt to convey to my own students. For their very perceptive comments on the final manuscript, I thank Robert Art, Roger Haydon, and an anonymous reader at Cornell University Press.

The final chapters of this book were completed at Williams College. The four years I have spent at Williams have been incomparable. I thank all of my colleagues in the political science department for their comments on various chapters of this book. One could not ask for better colleagues in international relations than Cheryl Shanks, Sam Crane, and Marc Lynch. As chair of the political science department, Michael MacDonald has been both a great adviser and a good friend. If I may draw on one final sports analogy, Michael is truly the Bill Walsh of Williams College, and he deserves much credit for the completion of this book. Finally, I thank Francis Oakley and the Oakley Center at Williams College for providing me with both financial support and a wonderful community of scholars during the final stages of revision.

The best part of completing this book is that my family will no longer have to ask how it is doing, as if it were a person in the final stages of life and close to death. I thank my sisters, Linda and Carol, for their support over the years. For nurturing an early interest in politics and supporting me in very hard times, I thank my parents, Maureen and Steve. The most powerful motivation I have had throughout the last decade has been the desire to one day present this book to my mother. It is to her that I dedicate this book.

Finally, I thank the person who has made these last few years the best ones of my life: my wife, Carrie.

J. M.

Williamstown, Massachusetts

No Exit

[1]

America, the German Problem, and the Bipolar Revolution

It is not given to human beings . . . to foresee or to predict to any large extent the unfolding course of events. In one phase men seem to have been right, in another they seem to have been wrong. Then again, a few years later, when the perspective of time has lengthened, all stands in a different setting.

Winston Churchill, 1940

Alexis de Tocqueville's famous nineteenth-century prophecy about the emergence of America and Russia as the two great powers in the international system was realized by the outcome of the Second World War. Although their forecasting skills were not quite as advanced as Tocqueville's, American military strategists anticipated the coming revolution in the global distribution of power long before the final collapse of Nazi Germany. In an analysis approved by the Joint Chiefs of Staff and sent to Secretary of State Cordell Hull in August 1944 that was intended to serve as guidance for postwar policy planning, General George Marshall urged the State Department to keep firmly in mind that America "will find a world profoundly changed in respect of relative national military strengths, a change more comparable indeed with that occasioned by the fall of Rome than with any other change occurring during the succeeding fifteen hundred years. . . . After the defeat of Japan, the United States and the Soviet Union will be the only military powers of the first magnitude."[1]

This book examines how American policymakers grappled, in both theory and practice, with the revolutionary changes in the distribution of power wrought by the Second World War. Many historians and international relations theorists have tended to assume, for quite understandable reasons, that the brute realities of power made the broad outlines of the postwar world relatively obvious to anyone not blinded by Wilsonian

---

[1] George Marshall to Cordell Hull, August 3, 1944, *Foreign Relations of the United States* (hereafter *FRUS*), 1944, vol. 1 (Washington, D.C.: U.S. Government Printing Office, 1966), 700. A complete list of *FRUS* volumes cited in this book, with their topical subtitles, can be found in the list of sources.

idealism or naive illusions about the nature of the Soviet Union. For example, Kenneth Waltz's influential revision of classical balance-of-power theory starts from the premise that America and the Soviet Union were bound to oppose each other simply due to their tremendous power: "In a bipolar world, each of the two great powers is bound to focus its fears on the other, to distrust its motives, and to impute offensive intentions to defensive measures."[2] However, the policy implications of the bipolar revolution were not so clear to those who tried to think about the future of world politics at the time. In his 1944 book *The Superpowers,* a fascinating attempt to assess the prospects for postwar peace and great power cooperation from a realist perspective, William T. R. Fox rejected the idea that anyone could possibly make "predictions" about the future of world politics solely on knowledge about the postwar distribution of power. Although one of Fox's primary purposes was to diminish the intellectual appeal of Wilsonianism and other utopian solutions to the dilemmas of politics in an anarchic international system, he was also attempting to reject the view that the United States and the Soviet Union were inevitably fated to be antagonists. "The high politics of our time would hold few mysteries for the man who could prove that these were the poles of political discord. His proof, however, would have to include demonstrations that the two strongest powers were necessarily bound to oppose each other and that there were only two such centers of power."[3]

Fox considered it a mistake to reach such pessimistic conclusions about the future precisely because of his analytical emphasis on the postwar distribution of power. The growth of Soviet power had potentially troubling implications for the long-term future of Europe, but the Soviet Union's tremendous devastation from the war would severely limit Stalin's short-term ability to pursue policies that might risk a general war with the Western powers. Although the Soviets might or might not seek to exert hegemony over much of Eastern Europe, Fox did not consider this the central issue of the postwar settlement in Europe because in his view Soviet control in the East did not threaten the security of the Western powers. It was also not an issue that the West would go to war to prevent. If the Soviets themselves were to initiate a general war in the immediate postwar period, Fox argued that their motivation would almost certainly

---

[2] Kenneth Waltz, "The Origins of War in Neorealist Theory," in *The Origin and Prevention of Major Wars,* ed. Robert I. Rotberg and Theodore K. Raab (Cambridge: Cambridge University Press, 1988), 52. Waltz's arguments about bipolarity can be found in Kenneth Waltz, "The Stability of a Bipolar World," *Daedalus* 93 (summer 1964): 881–909; and *Theory of International Politics* (New York: Random House, 1979).

[3] William T. R. Fox, *The Superpowers: The United States, Britain, and the Soviet Union—Their Responsibility for Peace* (New York: Harcourt, Brace, 1944), 98. Ironically, it was Waltz, a student of Fox's at Columbia University in the 1950s, who later put forward exactly this view of the postwar structure.

be defensive, based on the fear that the West was seeking "the political consolidation of Europe under anti-Soviet auspices."[4]

Although realists are often thought to advocate policies based on worst case assumptions about the capabilities of potential adversaries, Fox made exactly the opposite argument. If American policy toward the Soviet Union had to be based on the assumption of either postwar cooperation or conflict (which he acknowledged was a false dichotomy), Fox argued that the former would be the safer one to adopt: "As between the risk of acting as if the Soviet Union will be a trustworthy partner in maintaining peace and the risk of acting as if it will not, the lesser risk is clearly that based on the expectation of Soviet good faith. Otherwise, United States policy will facilitate the reconstitution of German power and the rebuilding of *Festung Europa* which we are just now laboriously and painfully dismantling."[5] Whether the great powers would be able to reach a cooperative settlement on the German question was the fundamental issue that would determine the future of world politics. Because of Germany's potential ability to tip the balance of power to one side or the other, Fox was under no illusions that a cooperative settlement between the Soviets and the Western powers would be easy to accomplish. Nevertheless, he certainly did not consider it impossible. Since it was obvious to him that neither America nor the Soviet Union could tolerate efforts to incorporate Germany into an exclusive sphere of influence without fatally damaging its national security, Fox argued that both sides would have to resist the temptation to include Germany in an alliance directed against the other. A great power war was one possible outcome of a competitive struggle to win the exclusive allegiance of Germany, but for Fox the more immediate danger was that the competition itself might lead to Germany's reemergence as an independent center of power. Indeed, Fox saw the common interest of the Western powers and the Soviet Union in preventing both a competitive struggle over the future of Germany and Germany's reemergence as an independent center of power as a primary reason why the Grand Alliance might survive the end of the Second World War:

> A "tripolar" system is not, however, beyond the realm of possibility. The assumption of bipolarity therefore needs to be explored, particularly if there is a possibility that Germany constitutes a potential third pole. The circumstance is at once perilous and hopeful. It is perilous because a rearmed Germany could again plunge the world into war; it is hopeful because, as we shall see, it gives both Moscow

[4] Ibid., 73–91 (quotation on 89).
[5] Ibid., 106.

and the West a very great incentive to agree on the solution of the German problem.[6]

One could not ask for a better road map to the central questions concerning the Cold War in Europe and postwar balance-of-power politics, or to the major themes of this book, than the one provided by Fox. The central question of the postwar world was and would remain the future of Germany. To see the struggle over Germany as merely a byproduct of the ideological antagonism between a capitalist America and a communist Soviet Union, or as just one of numerous issues of conflict, is a mistake. The German problem after 1945 was, as John Lewis Gaddis points out, a potent combination of two distinct but related concerns: "how to avoid the danger of a resurgent Germany itself, on the one hand, *and* the threat of a Germany on the wrong side in the Cold War, on the other."[7] Unless the sources of German economic power were to be completely and permanently destroyed, or Germany was to be permanently occupied and divided by the victor powers, there was no obvious escape from the dilemma: trying to resolve one potential German danger only increased the likelihood of being confronted with the other. A bipolar system without the problem of Germany might have been fairly safe and uncomplicated, but a bipolar system with the two great powers competing over the future of Germany was one of great danger and complexity.

This book has three major objectives, which are all very much interconnected. The first is to explain why America pursued the German policies that it did between 1945 and 1954. All of the agonizing choices, risks, and dilemmas concerning Germany that Fox foresaw in 1944 would haunt American policymakers throughout this period. The context of the German problem would change dramatically over time, but what remained constant was the reality that every policy choice might lead to war with the Soviet Union, strife within the Western alliance, or disastrous consequences in West Germany. Should the German problem be solved by keeping the country weak and disarmed? Was it possible to reach some sort of a cooperative settlement with the Soviet Union? Should Germany be divided or unified? Would creating a separate West German state lead to war with the Soviet Union? Should West Germany be rearmed, and how could this be accomplished in a way acceptable to countries that Nazi Germany had invaded and occupied less than a decade ago? Why American policymakers made the choices they did, and why they rejected other policy options, is what I seek to explain.[8] Like

---

[6] Ibid., 97–98.

[7] John Lewis Gaddis, *We Now Know: Rethinking Cold War History* (New York: Oxford University Press, 1997), 116.

[8] The historical literature related to the postwar German problem is continually growing. A work that has greatly influenced my own research on Germany and American foreign

other scholars concerned with questions related to Germany and the Cold War, I also examine the still hotly debated issue of whether there were "missed opportunities" for resolving the German question and the Cold War in Europe.[9]

WHAT WAS BIPOLARITY?

The second purpose of this book is to offer international relations theorists an alternative conceptualization of the structure of the postwar international system. No scholar has influenced how contemporary political scientists have thought about the postwar international system more than Kenneth Waltz. His transformation of the classical realism of Thucydides and Hans Morgenthau into a deductive and structural theory centered around the concept of polarity has provided the intellectual framework for many of the defining methodological and substantive debates in the field.[10] Waltz's arguments about the different properties of bipolar and multipolar systems continue to inspire heated debates over the future of Europe and American grand strategy after the Cold War.[11] Finally, much

policy is Marc Trachtenberg's *A Constructed Peace: The Making of the European Settlement, 1945–63* (Princeton: Princeton University Press, 1999). See also Thomas Schwartz, *America's Germany: John J. McCloy and the Federal Republic of Germany* (Cambridge: Cambridge University Press, 1991); Jeffrey M. Diefendorf, Axel Frohn, and Herman-Josef Rupieper, eds., *American Policy and the Reconstruction of Germany* (Cambridge: Cambridge University Press, 1993); Carolyn Eisenberg, *Drawing the Line: The American Decision to Divide Germany, 1944–49* (Cambridge: Cambridge University Press, 1996); Melvyn Leffler, "The Struggle for Germany and the Origins of the Cold War," Occasional Paper no. 16 (Washington, D. C.: German Historical Institute, 1996); and W. R. Smyser, *From Yalta to Berlin: The Cold War Struggle over Germany* (New York: St. Martin's Press, 1999).

[9] For discussions of "missed opportunities" see Deborah Welch Larson, *Anatomy of Mistrust: U.S.–Soviet Relations during the Cold War* (Ithaca: Cornell University Press, 1997); Ruud Van Dijk, "The 1952 Stalin Note Debate: Myth or Missed Opportunity for German Unification?" Working Paper no. 14, Cold War International History Project (May 1996); and Leffler, "The Struggle for Germany," 72–77.

[10] For broad overviews of the debates between neorealists and their major critics, see Robert Keohane, ed., *Neorealism and Its Critics* (New York: Columbia University Press, 1986); David Baldwin, ed., *Neorealism and Neoliberalism: The Contemporary Debate* (New York: Columbia University Press, 1993); Joseph Nye, "Neorealism and Neoliberalism," *World Politics* 40 (January 1988): 235–51; Stephan Haggard, "Structuralism and Its Critics: Recent Progress in International Relations Theory," in *Progress in Postwar International Relations*, ed. Emanuel Adler and Beverly Crawford (New York: Columbia University Press, 1991); and Robert Jervis, "Realism, Neoliberalism, and Cooperation: Understanding the Debate," *International Security* 24 (summer 1999): 42–63. For the distinction between classical realism and neorealism, see Kenneth Waltz, "Realist Thought and Neorealist Theory," *Journal of International Affairs* 44 (spring–summer 1990): 21–37; Randall L. Schweller and David Priess, "A Tale of Two Realisms: Expanding the Institutions Debate," *Mershon International Studies Review* 41 (May 1997): 1–33; and Benjamin Frankel, ed., *Realism: Restatements and Renewal* (New York: Frank Cass, 1996).

[11] See Karl W. Deutsch and J. David Singer, "Multipolar Power Systems and International Stability," *World Politics* 16 (April 1964); and Richard Rosecrance, "Bipolarity, Multipolarity,

of the best scholarship in security studies and international political economy since 1979 has been influenced by Waltz's theoretical framework, commonly known as neorealism or structural realism.[12]

Stripped to its bare foundation, Waltz's theoretical argument is simple, elegant, and deductive. The post-1945 international system differed from all of its predecessors because for the first time in modern history only two states could be classified as great powers. For Waltz, international systems of two great powers have vastly different properties and dynamics from those of multipolar systems. Bipolar systems are more stable than multipolar systems for two primary reasons. First, in a bipolar world great powers balance each other primarily by "internal" rather than "external" means: they rely on their own military capabilities rather than on alliances or the capabilities of allies.[13] According to Waltz, the greater emphasis on internal means of balancing is the "defining difference" between a multipolar and a bipolar system. Internal balancing is a less uncertain and more efficient process than external balancing, and Waltz posits that this reduction of uncertainty is a crucial element in explaining why bipolar systems are more stable and less war-prone than multipolar systems.[14]

The second core hypothesis that Waltz advances concerns the relationship between polarity and the freedom of action enjoyed by the alliance

---

and the Future," *Journal of Conflict Resolution* 10 (September 1966): 314–27; John Lewis Gaddis, "The Long Peace: Elements of Stability in the Postwar International System," *International Security* 10 (spring 1986): 99–142; Steven Van Evera, "Primed for Peace: Europe after the Cold War," *International Security* 15 (winter 1990/91): 33–40; Dale C. Copeland, "Neorealism and the Myth of Bipolar Stability: Toward a New Dynamic Realist Theory of Major War," *Security Studies* 5 (spring 1996): 29–89; and William C. Wohlforth, "The Stability of a Unipolar World," *International Security* 24 (summer 1999): 5–41. For an extension and development of Waltz's emphasis on polarity focused on the question of alliance behavior, see Glenn H. Snyder, *Alliance Politics* (Ithaca: Cornell University Press, 1997).

[12] For examples of excellent research in the area of security studies based to a greater or lesser extent on Waltz's theoretical framework, see Barry R. Posen, *The Sources of Military Doctrine* (Ithaca: Cornell University Press, 1984); Stephen Walt, *The Origins of Alliances* (Ithaca: Cornell University Press, 1987); and Thomas J. Christensen and Jack L. Snyder, "Chain Gangs and Passed Bucks: Predicting Alliance Patterns in Multipolarity," *International Organization* 44, no. 2 (spring 1990): 137–68. A full listing is too lengthy to include here, but a good sense of Waltz's impact on the field can be found in Stephen Walt, "The Renaissance of Security Studies," *International Studies Quarterly* 35 (1991): 211–39; and Colin Elman, "Horses For Courses: Why Not Neorealist Theories of Foreign Policy?" *Security Studies* 6 (autumn 1996): 7–51. For research in international political economy influenced by neorealism, see Joseph M. Grieco, *Cooperation among Nations* (Ithaca: Cornell University Press, 1990); Joanne Gowa, "Bipolarity, Multipolarity, and Free Trade," *American Political Science Review* 83 (1989): 1245–56; and Gowa, *Allies, Adversaries and International Trade* (Princeton: Princeton University Press, 1994).

[13] Waltz defines internal balancing efforts as "moves to increase economic capability, to increase military strength," and external balancing efforts as "moves to strengthen and enlarge one's own alliance or to weaken and shrink an opposing one." See Waltz, *Theory of International Politics*, 118.

[14] Ibid., 168–69 (quotation on 168).

leader in bipolar systems. In contrast to multipolar systems, where Waltz argues that alliance leaders must take seriously the views and preferences of major allies in order to prevent their defection, the essential irrelevance of allies to the balance-of-power process in bipolar systems allows the alliance leader to pursue its own strategy without making concessions to allies.[15] The historical example that Waltz cites as a general model of alliance relations in bipolar systems is America's willingness to coerce and pressure its closest allies during the Suez Crisis of 1956, which he contrasts with Germany's alleged inability in a multipolar world to resist a similar fait accompli on the part of Austria-Hungary during the July Crisis of 1914.[16] For Waltz, the two cases vividly illustrate the essential difference between alliance dynamics in bipolar worlds, where the alliance leader can ignore the concerns and preferences of its allies because the possibility of their defection to the opposing coalition is irrelevant to the overall balance between the superpowers, and alliance dynamics in multipolar worlds, where alliance leaders must go along with allies because their own security depends on maintaining the cohesion of the alliance. Waltz sets out the structural logic for the greater freedom of alliance leaders under conditions of bipolarity in the following passage:

> The gross inequality between the two superpowers and the members of their respective alliances makes any realignment of the latter fairly insignificant. The leaders' strategy can therefore be flexible. In balance-of-power politics old style, flexibility of alignment made for rigidity of strategy or the limitation of freedom of decision. In balance-of-power politics new style, the obverse is true: Rigidity of alignment in a two-power world makes for flexibility of strategy and the enlargement of freedom of decision.[17]

Despite all of the attention paid to Waltz's theoretical framework, it has gone largely unnoticed that neither of these hypotheses is supported by the historical evidence of the only structurally bipolar system that has existed in the modern era.[18] Waltz's hypothesis about the primacy of internal over external balancing under conditions of bipolarity receives very

---

[15] Ibid., 167–70.

[16] Many historians and political scientists would question whether Waltz's example accurately captures the alliance relationship between Germany and Austria-Hungary in 1914. See Jack Levy, "Preferences, Constraints, and Choices in July 1914," *International Security* 15 (winter 1990/91): 151–86.

[17] Waltz, *Theory of International Politics*, 169–70.

[18] For scholarly arguments that do note the disparities between the theory of bipolarity and the history of the Cold War, see R. Harrison Wagner, "What Was Bipolarity?" *International Organization* 47 (winter 1993): 77–106; and Richard Ned Lebow, "The Long Peace, the End of the Cold War, and the Failure of Realism," in *International Relations Theory and the End of the Cold War*, ed. Lebow and Thomas Risse-Kappen (New York: Columbia University Press, 1995), 23–56. For a much more elaborate and pathbreaking

little support from the historical record of how the Truman administration consistently made the tradeoff between the two balancing strategies from 1947 up to the outbreak of the Korean War in June 1950. Every sector of the administration, including the military establishment, supported the decision to invest resources in the external buildup of Western European power through Marshall Plan aid rather than in the internal buildup of American military power.[19] The Marshall Plan, the formation of NATO, and the restoration of the power of West Germany were the core elements of the Truman administration's balancing strategy between 1947 and 1950, and all three of these policies are examples of external balancing. Even when officials such as Secretary of Defense James Forrestal began to agitate for greater military expenditures after the start of the 1948 Berlin crisis, Truman and Marshall continued to give priority to the restoration of West German and Western European economic power. Despite the deterioration of American-Soviet relations throughout this period, Truman kept the defense budget basically constant and was even considering reductions on the eve of the Korean War. In 1949 Secretary of State Dean Acheson was struggling to get through Congress the Military Assistance Program, which sought an allocation of $1.4 billion to help rearm the Western European allies; Truman was simultaneously ordering the Defense Department to cut almost $2 billion from a military budget that many already considered thoroughly inadequate.[20] In contrast to what one would expect from Waltz's argument, the Truman administration chose to balance the Soviet Union primarily by external rather than internal means. Even after the Korean War and the adoption of NSC 68, which reflected a move toward a much greater buildup of American military

---

work on systems theory that analyzes both the strengths and weaknesses of Waltz's approach, see Robert Jervis, *Systems Effects: Complexity in Political and Social Life* (Princeton: Princeton University Press, 1997), esp. 92–124.

[19] See, for example, Robert Pollard, "Economic Security and the Origins of the Cold War: Bretton Woods, the Marshall Plan, and American Rearmament, 1944–50," *Diplomatic History* 9 (summer 1985): 271–89; and Robert Jervis, "The Impact of the Korean War on the Cold War," *Journal of Conflict Resolution* 24 (December 1980): 563–92. For the military establishment's support of putting resources into the restoration of European power, see Melvyn Leffler, "The American Conception of National Security and the Beginnings of the Cold War," *American Historical Review* 89 (April 1984): 371. For an excellent account of the Truman administration's approach to what Waltz would call internal balancing, see Michael Hogan, *A Cross of Iron: Harry S. Truman and the Origins of the National Security State, 1945–54* (Cambridge: Cambridge University Press, 1998).

[20] For Forrestal's unsuccessful efforts to persuade Truman and Marshall on the merits of increasing the defense budget, see Warner R. Schilling, "The Politics of National Defense: Fiscal 1950," in *Strategy, Politics, and Defense Budgets,* ed. Schilling, Paul Y. Hammond, and Glenn H. Snyder (New York: Columbia University Press, 1962), 1–266; Townsend Hoopes and Douglas Brinkley, *Driven Patriot: The Life and Times of James Forrestal* (New York: Alfred A. Knopf, 1992), 415–21; and Steven L. Rearden, "Frustrating the Kremlin Design: Acheson and NSC 68," in *Dean Acheson and the Making of U.S. Foreign Policy,* ed. Douglas Brinkley (New York: St. Martin's Press, 1993), 159–75.

power than had previously been contemplated, it is hard to see any clear preference given to internal rather than external balancing because the Truman administration also placed much greater emphasis after Korea on the rearmament of its Western European allies. Greater internal balancing after 1950 was matched by greater external balancing.

Waltz's hypothesis concerning alliance dynamics in bipolar systems also receives little empirical support. Does the Suez model represent the *general* pattern of U.S.–Western European alliance relations, or is it instead an exception to the rule? Both the Truman and the Eisenhower administrations were far more sensitive to the concerns and preferences of allies than Waltz's theory suggests.[21] In policy questions related to Germany in the 1940s and early 1950s, relations between the United States and its Western European allies bear little or no resemblance to the dynamics of the Suez crisis. For example, officials such as Lucius Clay, military governor for Germany, and George Kennan often wished or assumed that America's German policy need not consider the views and preferences of France, Great Britain, and West Germany, but the historical record does not support the idea that America could unilaterally set policies on important issues.[22] More important, it is hard to accept Waltz's central premise that American policymakers in this period viewed the possible realignment of any of its allies to the opposing coalition as "fairly insignificant." Indeed, it is precisely because the defection of either West Germany or France to the opposing coalition was viewed as a potential major catastrophe that American policymakers could not even think about constructing alliance relations on the model of Suez.

The key question, of course, is why American policymakers in the 1940s and the early 1950s acted exactly opposite to the way in which

---

[21] Explaining the big influence of small allies on alliance leaders is the task that Thomas Risse-Kappen tackles in his book *Cooperation among Democracies: The European Influence on U.S. Foreign Policy* (Princeton: Princeton University Press, 1995). Risse-Kappen is correct in pointing out that allies had a much greater influence on U.S. foreign policy than one would expect from neorealist theory. See also Mary N. Hampton, "NATO at the Creation: U.S. Foreign Policy, West Germany, and the Wilsonian Impulse," *Security Studies* 4 (spring 1995): 610–56. In her pathbreaking work on East Germany and the Berlin Crisis, Hope Harrison has shown that Soviet relations with weaker allies did not conform to the expectations of Waltz's framework. See Hope Harrison, "The Bargaining Power of Weaker Allies in Bipolarity and Crisis: The Dynamics of Soviet–East German Relations, 1953–61" (Ph.D. diss., Columbia University, 1994).

[22] On important issues such as the London program of 1948 and the North Atlantic Treaty of 1949, let alone the German rearmament question, concessions were made by both parties throughout the negotiations. For a contemporary acknowledgment of this pattern in America's German policy, see the CIA analysis of the London program, "France's German Policy," December 29, 1948, box 255, Presidential Secretary's File (hereafter PSF), Harry S. Truman Library (hereafter HSTL). For examples of U.S. concessions to its allies in the negotiations over NATO, see Alan K. Henrikson, "The Creation of the North Atlantic Alliance," *Naval War College Review* 33 (May–June 1980): 4–39.

Waltz suggests alliance leaders should act under conditions of bipo-larity.[23] The answer is that American policymakers perceived a qualitatively different postwar structure than the one put forward in Waltz's *Theory of International Politics*. Waltz's arguments about the primacy of internal bal-ancing and the freedom of action enjoyed by the alliance leader in bipolar systems do not follow simply from the fact that there are only two great powers in the international system, but also from the absence of any po-tential third great power in the system. Drawing on small group theory, Waltz argues that "with more than two parties, hostility and fear may lead A and B to seek the support of C. If they both court C, their hostility and fear increase. When a group narrows to just two members, choice dis-appears. On matters of ultimate importance each can deal only with the other. No appeal can be made to third parties. A system of two has unique properties."[24] Every argument that Waltz makes in *Theory of International Politics* is an elaboration or extension of this basic logic. It is this absence of a potential third power able to tip the balance to one side or the other that explains why Waltz argues that great powers must concentrate on the buildup of their own military power rather than on the construction of al-liances and on increasing the power of their allies.[25]

One can certainly admire what Waltz set out to do in *Theory of International Politics*, particularly his efforts to develop a more deductive and consistent version of classical realist theory. Nevertheless, his theore-tical bipolar system bears little resemblance to the actual historical system that came into being in 1945. The problem is not that Waltz's theoretical framework cannot accommodate the role of ideas or the importance of in-stitutions, as many critics of neorealism maintain. Instead, the problem is that Waltz's theory makes it impossible to understand the politics of power in Europe after 1945. Even before the Cold War began, it was ap-parent to everyone that the defection or conquest of Germany by one side or the other would tilt the balance of power decisively. Whether we label America A and the Soviet Union B or vice versa, it is clear that both sides viewed Germany as C. Whether one dates the start of the bidding to Stalin's reassurances to the German people that he favored unity rather than dismemberment in 1945, or to Secretary of State James F. Byrnes's

---

[23] The question of whether Waltz's theory can be used or tested as a theory of foreign policy is one that is hotly debated by international relations theorists. It is much less of an issue for those studying American foreign policy after 1945 because Waltz's "hypotheses" concern the behavior of alliance leaders or polar powers, which means they are hypotheses about the foreign policy of the United States. For the most recent debate over this issue, see Kenneth Waltz, "International Politics Is Not Foreign Policy," and Colin Elman, "Cause, Effect, and Consistency: A Response to Kenneth Waltz," both in *Security Studies* 6 (autumn 1996): 54–61.

[24] Waltz, *Theory of International Politics*, 174.

[25] For the importance Waltz places on the absence of third parties in explaining the nature of a bipolar world, see *Theory of International Politics*, 169–70, 174.

Stuttgart speech of September 1946, both the Soviet Union and the United States thought it was critical to seek the support and adherence of Germany. Indeed, much of the history of the 1940s and early 1950s can be seen as desperate efforts by both sides to secure the allegiance of Germany. As R. Harrison Wagner correctly points out, "If it had been generally accepted that a shift of West Germany from the side of the United States to the Soviet Union would not 'tilt the balance of power,' it seems unlikely that the Cold War would have occurred."[26]

Rather than view the postwar system as bipolar, we should view the structure of the early postwar international system as a "latent tripolar system." The belief that Germany represented a potential third power whose defection or allegiance would determine the overall balance of power, as well as the closely related belief that a united Western Europe could eventually emerge as a third center of power, exerted a dominant influence on American foreign policy after it became clear that there would be no cooperative settlement of the German problem. For the most part, the Cold War in Europe in the late 1940s and early 1950s was not a direct competition about the relative power of the United States vis-à-vis the Soviet Union. If all that mattered in thinking about the postwar balance of power were the relative capabilities of the United States and the Soviet Union, as neorealist logic suggests, policymakers would not have been alarmed—the Soviet Union could never hope to redress the enormous gap in relative capabilities by its own internal efforts. As one CIA review of the world situation in 1949 noted, "The security problems of the US and the USSR do not primarily lie in their direct relation to each other but rather in the relations of each to third states, groups of states, or geographical regions."[27] What was crucial to both sides, and what drove great power politics in this period, was the struggle to determine the future orientation and alignment of both West Germany and Western Europe.

Following the realist tradition represented by scholars such as Aaron Friedberg and William Wohlforth, this book adopts a perceptual approach to the question of determining how the distribution of power influenced both the course of American foreign policy and the Cold War in Europe in the 1940s and early 1950s. Unless one is willing to make the assumption that structural forces exert effects on great power behavior independently of perceptions, it is essential to incorporate perceptions of power as an independent or intervening variable in any analysis focused on the distribution of power. The primary justification for employing such an approach is well stated by Wohlforth: "If power influences the

---

[26] Wagner, "What Was Bipolarity?" 88.
[27] CIA o-49, January 19, 1949, box 251, PSF, HSTL.

course of international politics, it must do so largely through the perceptions of the people who make decisions on behalf of states."[28] This basic
insight will certainly not come as any surprise to diplomatic historians,
but international relations theorists have increasingly lost sight of it in recent years. Decades of deductive theorizing and quantitative research into
the concept of polarity have treated the distribution of power almost exclusively as an "objective" feature of the international system which exists
independently of how strategists and statesmen think about power in
given historical periods. Although there is nothing inherently wrong with
either deductive or quantitative approaches to the study of the distribution of power, the obvious lack of progress in resolving debates over polarity suggests that these approaches need to be supplemented by more
historical and perceptual approaches.[29]

This book argues that a perceptual/historical approach is particularly
necessary because none of Waltz's testable hypotheses about the behavior
of alliance leaders or U.S.–Western European alliance relations under
conditions of bipolarity stands up to the historical evidence. This is far
from a minor point. Waltz's primary thesis about the stabilizing properties of bipolar systems is based on the validity of these hypotheses.
Although this should be an important finding, my main point is that the
larger failure of neorealist theory is not that its testable hypotheses are un-
supported but rather that the framework itself makes it impossible to understand what the Cold War in Europe was all about, or exactly how the
postwar structure influenced balance-of-power politics, American foreign
policy, and U.S.–Western European alliance relations in the 1940s and
1950s. Both the distribution of power and the condition of anarchy, the
main elements of neorealist theory, are crucial to understanding the dy-

[28] See Aaron L. Friedberg, *The Weary Titan: Britain and the Experience of Relative Decline,
1895–1905* (Princeton: Princeton University Press, 1988); William C. Wohlforth, *The Elusive
Balance: Power and Perceptions During the Cold War* (Ithaca: Cornell University Press, 1993);
Wohlforth, "The Perception of Power: Russia in the Pre-1914 Balance," *World Politics* 39
(April 1987): 353–81; and Thomas J. Christensen, "Perceptions and Alliances in Europe,
1865–1940," *International Organization* 51 (winter 1997): 65–97. For an excellent assessment
of these and other related works in the realist tradition, see Gideon Rose, "Neoclassical
Realism and Theories of Foreign Policy," *World Politics* 51 (October 1998): 144–72. The question of whether treating perceptions of power rather than "objective" power constitutes a
departure from realism is discussed in Jeffrey W. Legro and Andrew Moravcsik, "Is
Anybody Still a Realist?" *International Security* 24 (fall 1999): 5–55. As important as these and
other abstract questions are to some international relations theorists, this book does not take
a position on this question. In general, I believe that scholars who emphasize either the importance of objective or perceived power qualify as realists. Scholars such as Waltz and
Wohlforth may differ on this question, but they still share far more with each other than they
do with other schools of thought, such as constructivism or liberalism.

[29] For overviews of debates related to the concept of polarity, see Joseph L. Nogee,
"Polarity: An Ambiguous Concept," *Orbis* 18 (winter 1975): 1193–1224; Alan Ned Sabrosky,
Polarity and War: The Changing Structure of International Conflict (Boulder, Colo.: Westview
Press, 1985); and Charles W. Kegley Jr. and Gregory A. Raymond, *A Multipolar Peace? Great
Power Politics in the Twenty-First Century* (New York: St. Martin's Press, 1994).

namics of the postwar international system—but they are crucial in ways much different from what Waltz leads us to expect.

Of course, a perceptions-of-power/historical approach inevitably moves the burden of the research toward inductive theorizing and extensive archival research. For those scholars primarily interested in discovering broad generalizations about the distribution of power, a perceptions-of-power approach will have very limited appeal. In addition, as Wohlforth concedes, such an approach may have limited appeal because it "reduces the scholar to the level of the decision-maker: rather than issuing all-knowing pronouncements on the invisible structures to which hapless statesman must react, the scholar shuffles humbly after the statesman, sharing his flawed view of power, perhaps repeating his mistakes. Many realists will not accept these limitations."[30]

I argue that following American statesmen of the 1940s and 1950s in their efforts to understand and deal with the revolutionary structural changes brought about by the Second World War can be a productive enterprise for international relations theorists. Like Waltz, American statesmen believed that the changes in the distribution of power wrought by the Second World War constituted nothing less than a fundamental revolution in the history of the modern state system. Unlike Waltz, American statesmen were less than clear about what these changes in the distribution of power implied for U.S.–Soviet relations, American foreign and national security policy, and the future of Germany and Europe. Understanding how American policymakers resolved the challenges posed by the new configuration of power that emerged in 1945 continues to spark interesting and productive debate among diplomatic historians.[31] The recent release of Soviet and Eastern bloc documents has greatly influenced how historians now think about the Cold War, and it should also lead political scientists to test and revise leading theories.[32]

Neorealists have little to lose by devoting more attention to rigorous historical research that traces the effects of the distribution of power at

---

[30] William C. Wohlforth, "Realism and the End of the Cold War," *International Security* 19 (winter 1994/95): 91–129 (quotation on 127).

[31] Many of these debates have revolved around Melvyn Leffler's magisterial study of American national security policy during the Truman administration and John Lewis Gaddis's *We Now Know*. See Robert Jervis, "The End of the Cold War on the Cold War?" *Diplomatic History* 17 (fall 1993): 651–60; Lynn Eden, "The End of U.S. Cold War History? A Review Essay," *International Security* 18 (summer 1993): 174–207; and Marc Trachtenberg, "Melvyn Leffler and the Origins of the Cold War," *Orbis* (summer 1995): 439–55.

[32] For the neglect of the new Cold War history by international relations theorists, see William Wohlforth, "A Certain Idea of Science: How International Relations Theory Avoids the New Cold War History," *Journal of Cold War Studies* 1 (spring 1999): 39–60. Of course, it is a mistake to believe that there is now any "final" history of the Cold War due to the new documentation. See Melvyn Leffler, "The Cold War: What Do We Now Know?" *American Historical Review* 102 (April 1999): 501–24.

both the systemic and national levels. Historians have largely ignored neo-realist theory in conducting their own research, but Paul Schroeder, one of the few historians who has examined the fit between theory and evidence, recently concluded that "the kind of approach involved in neo-realist theory renders it [history] incomprehensible. It obstructs new insights and hypotheses, leads scholars to overlook or explain away large bodies of inconvenient facts, flattens out vital historical distinctions."[33] Historians should be obvious alliance partners for political scientists concerned with the role of power and the search for security in international affairs, but this alliance will never be consummated if neorealists do not devote more attention to studying the role of power and structure in concrete historical circumstances.[34] Arguments by political scientists to the effect that historians do not understand neorealist theory or the kinds of empirical evidence that would falsify neorealist theory may or may not be correct, but they often come perilously close to suggesting that the theory itself is immune from empirical falsification.[35] If neorealists do not want what Imre Lakatos called a "degenerating research program," in which the disparity between theory and evidence is increasingly explained away by variables outside the purview of the theory, they need more theoretically informed historical research before deciding whether neorealist theory itself needs to be amended or discarded.[36]

This book argues that the primary reason for the disparity between neorealist theory and the historical evidence of the early postwar period can be attributed to Waltz's use of the concept of bipolarity to measure the

[33] Paul Schroeder, "Historical Reality vs. Neo-Realist Theory," *International Security* 19 (summer 1994): 108–48 (quotation on 148).

[34] An encouraging sign of greater interaction between political scientists and diplomatic historians is the recent symposium in *International Security* exploring areas of consensus and divergence between the two disciplines. See Colin Elman and Mirium Fendius Elman, "Diplomatic History and International Relations Theory," 5–21; Jack Levy, "Too Important To Leave to the Other: History and Science in the Study of International Relations," 22–33; Stephen H. Haber, David Kennedy, and Stephen D. Krasner, "Brothers under the Skin: Diplomatic History and International Relations," 34–43; and John Lewis Gaddis, "History, Theory, and Common Ground," 75–85, all in *International Security* 22 (summer 1997).

[35] See the correspondence between Colin Elman and Miriam Fendius Elman and Paul Schroeder, "History vs. Neo-realism: A Second Look," *International Security* 20 (summer 1995): 182–95. For a discussion of issues related to falsifying or confirming neorealist theory, see Robert Keohane, "Theory of World Politics;" and Kenneth Waltz, "A Response to My Critics," both in *Neorealism and Its Critics*, ed. Keohane, 170–75, 334–35.

[36] For Lakatosian arguments that scholars should continue to rely on neorealist theory until a better theory is developed, see Elman, Elman, and Schroeder, "History vs. Neorealism: A Second Look"; and Ethan Kapstein, "Is Realism Dead? The Domestic Sources of International Politics," *International Organization* 49 (autumn 1995): 751–74. For a contrasting assessment of neorealism from a Lakatosian perspective, see John A. Vasquez, "The Realist Paradigm as a Degenerating Research Program: An Appraisal of Neotraditional Research on Waltz's Balancing Proposition," *American Political Science Review* 91 (December 1997): 899–912. For defenses of neorealism see the responses that follow Vasquez's essay by Kenneth Waltz, Thomas Christensen and Jack Snyder, the Elmans, Randall Schweller, and Stephen Walt, 913–35.

overall distribution of power in the international system. As Edward Mansfield points out, employing the concept of polarity to explain patterns of behavior in the international system requires the acceptance of two major and very debatable assumptions: "(1) nonpolar major powers are unimportant for the purposes of determining the international distribution of power; and (2) polar powers are equally powerful or asymmetries of power among them are of little consequence for explaining patterns of international outcomes."[37] Mansfield is correct in arguing that scholarly efforts to classify the distribution of power for given periods should move away from these two assumptions. Understanding American foreign policy during the formative period of the Cold War requires an understanding of both short- and long-term assessments of Soviet capabilities, as well as the importance policymakers attributed to the actual and potential capabilities of nonpolar major powers, particularly the capabilities of Germany and Western Europe.

International relations, of course, cannot be reduced to the distribution of power. But power remains a very good place to start. This book suggests that international relations theorists would be better served by the conception of the postwar structure advanced by William T. R. Fox in 1944 rather than the one popularized by Waltz. There are two important reasons why scholars, particularly those sympathetic to neorealism, should view the early postwar system as one of latent tripolarity rather than one of bipolarity. First, the concept of latent tripolarity enables us to understand the importance and centrality of the postwar German question in a way that the concept of bipolarity cannot. Second, the concept of latent tripolarity provides a much better fit with the historical evidence of America's balancing strategies, the intense struggle over Germany, and the general pattern of U.S.–Western European alliance relations during the formative period of the Cold War. Waltz's theory of bipolarity strongly suggests that America should have been a unilateral, isolationist power that devoted all of its resources to the buildup of its military power rather than a multilateral, internationalist power that devoted significant attention and resources to its allies. Viewing the early postwar system as one of latent tripolarity enables us better to understand why American strategists devoted great resources to external balancing and were constrained by the preferences and concerns of the Western European allies.

---

[37] See Edward D. Mansfield, *Power, Trade, and War* (Princeton: Princeton University Press, 1994), 12–13. For a powerful argument about the need for international relations theorists to adopt more precise specifications about the distribution of power in given historical periods, see Randall L. Schweller, "Tripolarity and the Second World War," *International Studies Quarterly* 37 (March 1993): 73–104; and Schweller, *Deadly Imbalances: Tripolarity and Hitler's Strategy of World Conquest* (New York: Columbia University Press, 1998).

NO EXIT: THE DEVELOPMENT OF THE
"PERMANENT" AMERICAN MILITARY PRESENCE

The third purpose of this book is to explain the development of the "permanent" American military presence in Europe and its relationship to the German question and the future of Europe. Scholars all too often assume that, given the realities of power or the historical "lessons" of the interwar period, everyone immediately understood that American military forces were in Europe on a permanent basis after the Second World War. For example, drawing heavily on Waltz's theoretical framework, John Mearsheimer argues that "the European state system abruptly shifted from multipolar to bipolar after 1945. Three factors were responsible: The near-complete destruction of German power, the growth of Soviet power, and the permanent commitment of American power to the Continent."[38] Yet the historical record shows that American policymakers from Franklin Delano Roosevelt to Dwight Eisenhower strenuously tried to avoid having the future of Europe dependent on a permanent U.S. military presence on the continent. The perception of a lasting presence was lacking on both sides of the Atlantic in the 1940s and early 1950s. America's overarching goal after 1947 was to create a united Western Europe that could contain Germany and balance against the Soviet Union without a permanent U.S. military presence. The creation of a united Western Europe, it was thought, would bring into being a power bloc equivalent to the United States and Soviet Union and transform a latent tripolar system into an actual tripolar system. American military forces would no longer be necessary in Europe after the structure of the system was transformed.

A Europe without a permanent U.S. military presence is unthinkable today, but the idea that European stability would be permanently ensured by American military forces was just as unthinkable in the 1940s and 1950s. Roosevelt made it very clear throughout the Second World War that he envisioned the rapid withdrawal of U.S. forces from the continent after the war. His famous statement at the Yalta Conference in February 1945 that American forces could not be expected to stay in Europe for more than two years only confirmed what he had repeatedly told both Churchill and Stalin.[39] FDR's firm conviction that European stability could not rest on the permanent presence of American military forces was reflected in the postwar military and political planning that had been carried out by his administration during the war. As Deborah

[38] John Mearsheimer, "Back to the Future: Instability in Europe after the Cold War," *International Security* 15 (summer 1990): 26.

[39] See Warren Kimball, *The Juggler: Franklin Roosevelt as Wartime Statesman* (Princeton: Princeton University Press, 1991), 83–105; and John Lamberton Harper, *American Visions of Europe* (Cambridge: Cambridge University Press, 1994), 77–131.

Larson points out, "Anticipating no conflict with the Soviet Union or other European powers, the Joint Chiefs did not even consider locating permanent bases in Europe."[40] State Department planners also assumed an eventual American withdrawal from Germany. As one official noted in a July 1945 memorandum concerning the postwar treatment of Germany, "If the safety of the world, so far as Germany is concerned, is to be entrusted to the occupation of Germany and the policing of Germany to prevent her from rearming or preparing to rearm, *the policing and occupation must be permanent.* Permanent occupation of Germany by the Allies, and particularly by the United States, is inconceivable."[41] Roosevelt's attraction to draconian plans for Germany, such as the Morgenthau Plan, which called for the deindustrialization of Germany, were heavily influenced by his conviction that the German problem could not be solved by a permanent American occupation. America's later obsession with Western European unity was also rooted in the belief that the German problem and the long-term maintenance of a European balance of power could not be solved by a permanent American military presence.

It could be argued that this assumption of an eventual American withdrawal from Europe was simply a product of wartime illusions about the possibilities of postwar cooperation with the Soviet Union, and that the adoption by the Truman administration of strategies of containment established a "permanent" American military presence in Europe.[42] However, it is hard to square this argument with the fact that not even George Kennan, the American official most associated with the concept of containment, drew this conclusion. In his memoirs, Kennan wrote that his first objective in Europe was "the correction of the great geopolitical disbalance to which the outcome of World War II had led."[43] After this goal was accomplished, Kennan's second objective "was to get us as soon as possible out of the position of abnormal political-military responsibility in Western Europe which the war had forced upon us. I had no confidence that a *status quo* dependent on so wide an American commitment could be

---

[40] Deborah Welch Larson, *Origins of Containment: A Psychological Explanation* (Princeton: Princeton University Press, 1985), 3.

[41] Memorandum by the Central Secretariat, July 12, 1945, *FRUS, 1945, The Conference of Berlin (Potsdam),* vol. 1, 501.

[42] The two classic studies of the Truman administration's national security policies in this period are John Lewis Gaddis, *Strategies of Containment: A Critical Appraisal of Postwar American National Security Policies* (New York: Oxford University Press, 1982); and Melvyn P. Leffler, *A Preponderance of Power: National Security, the Truman Administration, and the Cold War* (Stanford, Calif.: Stanford University Press, 1992).

[43] George F. Kennan, *Memoirs, 1925–50* (New York: Atlantic, Little, Brown, 1967), 463. For Kennan, correcting the "geopolitical disbalance" meant creating a third independent center of power in Western Europe. See Harper, *American Visions of Europe,* 183–232; and John Lewis Gaddis, "The United States and the Question of a Sphere of Influence in Europe, 1945–49," in *Western Security: The Formative Years,* ed. Olav Riste (New York: Columbia University Press, 1985), 60–91.

an enduring one. Such bipolarity, I thought, might do for a few years; it could not endure indefinitely."[44] Walter Lippmann, often considered to be the other great American realist of the postwar era, shared Kennan's belief that a lasting European settlement could and should be one that could be maintained without American military forces on the continent.[45]

Kennan was always something of a maverick and an independent thinker within the Truman administration, but his well-known policy differences with his State Department colleagues in 1948–49 over whether the United States should seek a general settlement in Germany that would remove American and Soviet forces from central Europe was largely a dispute over timing, not one of basic principles. Even his most vigorous opponents at the time, such as Secretary of State Acheson, did not believe that the signing of the North Atlantic Treaty or the creation of the Federal Republic of Germany in 1949 would lead to the establishment of a permanent American presence on the continent. When asked by a senator during hearings whether the North Atlantic Treaty would mean that the United States was "going to be expected to send substantial numbers of troops over there as a more or less permanent contribution to the development of their capacity to resist," Acheson replied, "The answer to that question, Senator . . . is a clear and absolute no."[46] As Timothy Ireland points out in his book *Creating the Entangling Alliance*, "It is important to realize that, until the creation of the NATO structure and the assignment of U.S. ground forces to that organization, none of the American policies for Europe, as revolutionary as they were, implied permanent American involvement in continental affairs."[47]

Ireland is correct about U.S. policies up to the signing of the North Atlantic Treaty, but he mistakenly suggests that the sending of additional ground forces and the appointment of Eisenhower as Supreme Commander of the Allied Powers in Europe in December 1950 finally resolved the question of America's permanent involvement in European affairs. This was certainly not Eisenhower's assessment, either during his term as Supreme Commander or during his presidency. Indeed, Eisenhower based his entire strategic conception on the idea that the primary purpose

---

[44] Kennan, *Memoirs, 1925–50*, 464.

[45] See Walter Lippmann, *The Cold War: A Study in U.S. Foreign Policy* (New York: Harper & Brothers Publishers, 1947). Since Kennan and Lippmann are often portrayed as the primary antagonists in the debate over the direction of postwar foreign policy, their agreement on this central issue is very significant.

[46] Dean Acheson, *Present at the Creation: My Years in the State Department* (New York: W. W. Norton and Company, 1969), 285. No solid evidence rebuts Acheson's claim in his memoirs that his answer was "deplorably wrong . . . But it was not intended to deceive." For the most recent biography of Acheson, see James Chace, *Acheson: The Secretary of State Who Created the American World* (New York: Simon & Schuster, 1998).

[47] Timothy Ireland, *Creating the Entangling Alliance* (Westport, Conn.: Greenwood Press, 1981), 183.

of stationing additional American troops on the continent was to rapidly reduce the amount of time it would take the Western European allies to be able to defend themselves. His own estimates about when American forces could be completely removed from Europe were in the range of five to ten years.[48] Eisenhower wanted ten or twelve American divisions sent to Europe as quickly as possible, but he believed that their presence in Europe should be considered temporary: "Of course, we should not plan on keeping our divisions there forever. Once the Europeans build up an adequate force, and get some reserves trained, the Americans can come home."[49] As Marc Trachtenberg points out, during the founding period of NATO, the "permanence" of the American presence in Europe was neither assumed by the United States nor taken for granted by the Western European allies:

> During the crucial formative period in the early 1950s, everyone wanted a permanent American presence in Europe—everyone, that is, except the Americans themselves. It is hard to understand why the intensity and persistence of America's desire to pull out as soon as she reasonably could has never been recognized, either in the public discussion or in the scholarly literature, because it comes through with unmistakable clarity in the *Foreign Relations* documents.[50]

As this book will show, statements revealing the American desire to eventually withdraw its forces from Europe were not idle musings but a primary influence on American grand strategy and U.S.–Western European relations throughout the early period of the Cold War. The most important area in which this desire was translated into policy, of course, was in America's fervent support and direct sponsorship of Western European integration. Scholars, particularly neorealists, often tend to portray Western European integration as something outside of, and not important to, the high politics of the early Cold War. This reflects the belief that the states of Western Europe were in a sense liberated from

---

[48] See Robert Art, "A Defensible Defense: America's Grand Strategy After the Cold War," *International Security* 15 (spring 1991): 23; and Eisenhower to Edward James Bermingham, February 28, 1951, in *The Papers of Dwight David Eisenhower: NATO and the Campaign of 1952*, ed. Louis Galambos (Baltimore: Johns Hopkins Press, 1980), 76–77. As in so many other areas, Marc Trachtenberg's emphasis on this element of Eisenhower's thought has been pathbreaking. See *A Constructed Peace*, 147–282.

[49] Notes of a Meeting at the White House, January 31, 1951, *FRUS*, 1951, vol. 3, 456. According to Matthew Connelly's notes of the meeting, Eisenhower said, "The U.S. does not have to stay in Europe if we build it up and we should not. It should be remembered that it is a long way from Russian bases to Western Europe." See Connelly, Notes of Cabinet Meeting on January 31, 1951, box 1, Matthew Connelly Papers, HSTL.

[50] Marc Trachtenberg, "The Nuclearization of NATO and U.S. Western European Relations," in *History and Strategy* (Princeton: Princeton University Press, 1991), 167.

the perils of anarchy and the security dilemma.[51] Although this interpretation is a plausible one for much later periods of the Cold War, it was clearly not true during the late 1940s and early 1950s. For American policymakers, Western European unity was the "skeleton key" that would permanently end the German problem and enable the region to become a third great center of power able to stand on its own without U.S. military forces continually serving as either a "pacifier" or "protector."[52] Creating a unified and supranational Western Europe was seen as the crucial element in transforming both the anarchic nature of the classical European state system and restoring the basis of an indigenous power balance on the continent.

This argument suggests the need to revise what has become the common historical wisdom about the ultimate goals of American foreign policy toward its Western European allies during the formative period of the Cold War. Scholars such as Melvyn Leffler and Geir Lundestad have argued that America was intent on preventing the emergence of a "third force" or an independent center of power on the continent. According to Leffler, "Neither an integrated Europe nor a united Germany nor an independent Japan must be permitted to emerge as a third force or a neutral bloc."[53] Although it is true that American officials did not want a neutral Western Europe or, needless to say, a united Western Europe actively opposed to the United States, they did want a Western Europe strong enough to defend itself externally against the Soviet Union and internally against either a divided or united Germany. If exerting American control over the states of Western Europe and preventing the emergence of independent power blocs were goals of critical importance, it is hard to explain the great attraction for the creation of European institutions that might have brought about exactly the situation that Washington ostensibly feared.

PLAN AND OVERVIEW OF THE BOOK

The historical period covered in this book ranges roughly from the beginning of American postwar planning in 1943 to the end of the German rearmament crisis in 1954. Chapter 2 examines Roosevelt's wartime diplo-

---

[51] Christopher Layne, "The Unipolar Illusion: Why New Great Powers Will Arise," *International Security* 17 (spring 1993): 41. For an elaboration of the argument about bipolarity's supposed effect on politics within Western Europe, see Waltz, *Theory of International Politics*, 70–71.

[52] Thomas A. Schwartz, "The 'Skeleton Key'—American Foreign Policy, European Unity, and German Rearmament, 1949–54," *Central European History* 19 (1986): 369–85.

[53] Leffler, *A Preponderance of Power*, 17; and Geir Lundestad, *"Empire" by Integration: The United States and European Integration, 1945–1997* (New York: Oxford University Press, 1998), 4, 54–57.

macy and his core assumptions about the postwar world. FDR's diplomacy and American postwar planning are understood in light of his primary postwar objective, which was to create a European order that could be stable without a permanent American military commitment. For Roosevelt, eliminating European concerns about the revival of Germany was the crucial element in eliminating balance-of-power politics on the continent, preserving the wartime alliance with the Soviet Union, and creating a stable European order. If the states of Western Europe no longer had to worry about the revival of German power, they would not have to devote their energies to building up their armaments and forming alliances to balance against Germany. If the Soviet Union no longer had to worry about a revival of German power, it might be prepared to moderate its control over the states of Eastern Europe and accept a settlement which would allow these states a much greater degree of freedom in their internal affairs. The American president's enthusiasm for the dismemberment of Germany into several states and his initial support for the Morgenthau Plan were reflections of this overall strategy. Although the causal arrows went both ways, FDR's plans for Germany were also strongly influenced by his conviction that a lasting European settlement could not rely on a lengthy U.S. occupation.

Chapter 3 examines the collapse of the wartime alliance. Roosevelt's hopes for the postwar world were already in serious trouble at the time of his death due to the bitter controversy with the Soviet Union over the composition of the postwar Polish government. However, neither President Truman nor Secretary of State Byrnes were anxious to allow the fate of Poland or Eastern Europe to disrupt the cohesion of the Grand Alliance. The critical question for American policymakers at the Potsdam Conference in July 1945 was the future of Germany, not the fate of Eastern Europe. Questions about the future of Germany were fought out among the allies in the context of the complex issue of reparations, which emerged as the central issue, as it had after the First World War. Already growing increasingly suspicious of the Soviet Union and skeptical about the ability of the great powers to collectively run Germany as a single economic unit, Byrnes negotiated a reparations settlement which economically divided the country into western and eastern zones of occupation. Although some scholars have viewed Byrnes's approach to the German question as an early application of "atomic diplomacy," his primary intent in negotiating the reparations settlement was to prevent future conflicts among the allies over Germany by giving the Soviets a free hand to run their zone as they saw fit. Byrnes's corollary assumption, of course, was that the Soviet Union would not have any influence in the western zones or in any plans that might develop for international control of the Ruhr.

The nature of the Potsdam settlement that Byrnes negotiated with the Soviets—a division of Germany into western and eastern spheres—was bound to cause difficulties primarily because its true meaning was less than clear in the eyes of either the American occupation authorities in Germany or the French, who had been excluded from the conference. General Lucius Clay, a true believer in Roosevelt's vision of a cooperative postwar European system, believed that his mission was to preserve the wartime alliance, run Germany as a single economic unit through the creation of central administrations, and get the country on its feet and off the backs of American taxpayers as quickly as possible. All of Clay's objectives in Germany were vehemently opposed by the French. Uncertain about the duration of the American military presence in Europe, the French were unwilling to go along with the creation of central German administrations which they viewed as the first step in a process that would result in the reestablishment of a united Germany.

The French more or less won their battle with Clay over the establishment of central German administrations. The State Department never placed its considerable weight behind Clay's recommended policy of coercing the French to go along with the creation of central administrations. Byrnes did not go along with Clay's strategy primarily because the French determination to keep the Soviets out of the western zones meshed perfectly with his own preferences. By the time of his famous Stuttgart speech in September 1946, Byrnes had made it clear that he was now willing to openly compete with the Soviets for the allegiance of the German people. Rather than ending balance-of-power politics in Europe, as FDR hoped to do, American policy was now directed toward winning the struggle for Germany.

Chapter 4 examines initial U.S. efforts to restore an indigenous balance of power in Europe between 1947 and 1949. No longer even remotely interested in Germany's unification or in weakening its potential power, the Truman administration sought to integrate West Germany into a united Western Europe. The long-term objective was to create a Western Europe fully capable of containing the Soviet Union—and Germany—without American forces on the continent. But even in the context of a divided Germany, American policymakers still had to overcome French concerns about the future implications of restoring the economic potential of the western zones of Germany. For many influential American strategists and policy advisors, particularly Kennan and John Foster Dulles, the only long-term solution to the structural problem of German power was the creation of a supranational Western Europe. Although the intent of the Marshall Plan was precisely to encourage Western Europe to move progressively in this direction, American policymakers could not wait until supranational institutions were in place before taking steps to revive the economy of the western zones of Germany. Indeed, by the beginning of 1948 both American occupational authorities and the State Department were already pushing for the creation of a separate West German state.

[22]

The adoption of the London program in May 1948 was a direct challenge to the Soviet Union, and the outbreak of the Berlin crisis a month later dramatically highlighted all of the immediate dangers and risks inherent in the restoration of German power.

The Berlin crisis raised a central question about the course of American foreign policy since Potsdam: Should the division of Germany be pushed through to its ultimate conclusion, or would America be better served by striking a deal with the Soviet Union that would remove all occupation forces from Germany? George Kennan was one of the few policymakers on either side of the Atlantic who thought that the West should explore the possibility of a settlement with the Soviet Union regarding Germany. Despite the fact that American intelligence analysts believed there was a good chance that the Soviets would be receptive to a deal very much on Western terms, both the State Department and General Clay rejected Kennan's arguments and proceeded with the establishment of the Federal Republic of Germany in May 1949. Whether the Soviets were actually interested in a deal over Germany is beside the point; the Western powers themselves were simply not interested in establishing a unified and neutral Germany.

Restoring a balance of power in Europe meant restoring West German power, but for obvious reasons it was politically impossible to do this without maintaining some restrictions over West Germany. Nevertheless, convincing the West Germans to throw their lot in with the West after 1947 meant that the occupation regime would have to be steadily abandoned, as would burdensome restrictions on the country's actual and potential economic resources. The inevitable result of such an approach would be that West Germany would once again attain a powerful position in Europe. American policymakers were acutely aware of how much France would seek to slow down the restoration of West German power, but they did not feel that it was in the interest of either France or the West more broadly to maintain onerous restrictions on West Germany. Efforts to do so would only encourage the rise of nationalist or neutralist sentiment in West Germany and put pro-Western democratic statesmen like Konrad Adenauer on the defensive. For American policymakers, the only viable way to reconcile the competing interests of France and West Germany in the long term was through the gradual surrender of sovereign authority to supranational European institutions. American statesmen did not have blueprints for how and when this process would or should occur, but the French proposal for the creation of a European Coal and Steel Community (ECSC) in May 1950 was exactly the type of supranational institution that U.S. policymakers believed was essential to Europe's future.

The United States strove to apply the ECSC model to security affairs and attempted to form the European Defense Community (EDC) as the institutional framework within which the rearmament of West Germany could take place.[54] Chapter 5 examines this effort. The Truman administration's determination to restore an indigenous European balance of power after 1947 implicitly suggested that at some point in the future West Germany would be allowed to rearm and contribute to the defense of Western Europe. Military officials were eager to hasten the process of rearming West Germany. However, prior to the outbreak of the Korean War, American political officials did not advocate German rearmament because they recognized that it would put at risk all of the progress made in reconciling France and West Germany. Dean Acheson's decision to abandon his previous opposition to German rearmament after Korea would spark the longest and most consequential crisis in the history of the Atlantic Alliance.

How could the United States convince the French to accept West German rearmament as long as there were no guarantees of a permanent American military presence in Europe? Although the Truman administration could have easily persuaded the rest of the Atlantic alliance to support the direct admission of West Germany to NATO, it eventually decided to throw its support behind the French plan for the creation of a supranational European army. I argue that there were two primary reasons why American policymakers came to support the creation of the supranational EDC by the summer of 1951. The first is that influential policymakers such as David Bruce and John McCloy effectively argued that the supranational EDC solution represented the only way to reconcile legitimate French fears with West Germany's insistence that it would only rearm on a nondiscriminatory basis. West Germany would not accept discriminatory conditions in an alliance of sovereign states such as NATO, but it would accept restrictions within a European institutional framework whose rules applied equally to all of its members, including France. Unlike NATO, The EDC seemed to offer a solution to both the short-term impasse over West German rearmament, as well as a golden opportunity

---

[54] Given the fact that the establishment and ratification of the European Defense Community was undoubtedly Washington's single most important objective in one of the most crucial periods of the Cold War, it is remarkable how little scholarly attention it has received. Many scholars, particularly political scientists, still rely on pre-archival and now vastly outdated works such as Ralph McGeehan's *The German Rearmament Question* (Urbana, Ill.: University of Illinois Press, 1971); Daniel Lerner and Raymond Aron, *France Defeats the EDC* (New York: Praeger, 1957); and Edward Fursdon, *The European Defense Community: A History* (New York: St. Martin's Press, 1980). In addition to Schwartz's biography of McCloy, useful sources for studying the EDC include David Clay Large, *Germans to the Front: West German Rearmament in the Adenauer Era* (Chapel Hill: University of North Carolina Press, 1996); Saki Dockrill, *Britain's Policy for West German Rearmament, 1950–55* (Cambridge: Cambridge University Press, 1991); and Ronald W. Pruessen, "Cold War Threats and America's Commitment to the European Defense Community: One Corner of a Triangle," *Journal of European Integration History* (spring 1996): 51–69.

to recast the political future of Europe by placing French and German military affairs under the control of a supranational institution.

The second reason why the EDC solution triumphed over the NATO solution is that Eisenhower put his considerable authority behind the EDC. The Achilles heel of plans for a European army was the fact that military officials had always viewed them as unworkable; Eisenhower's support decisively silenced all criticism of the plan on this basis. Eisenhower came to support the EDC primarily because he saw it as the solution more likely to enable Western Europe to emerge as an integrated unit able to permanently defend itself without an American military presence on the continent. Despite the fact that the Eisenhower conception of the EDC was intended to accomplish exactly what the French feared most—the withdrawal of American military forces—the EDC treaty was signed by in May 1952 by France, West Germany, Italy, and the members of the Benelux Economic Union (Belgium, the Netherlands, and Luxembourg).

Few objectives in the postwar era were ever accorded the importance that American policymakers attributed to the ratification of the EDC treaty. But neither Dulles's threats of "agonizing reappraisal" nor greater support for French efforts in Indochina proved to be enough to overcome French concerns about German rearmament and the EDC, and the treaty was not ratified. After May 1952, the French increasingly sought stronger and more explicit guarantees about the future presence of American and British forces on the continent, which revealed their basic concern that the institutional framework of the EDC could not contain and control West Germany. Although the American desire to create a Western European order that could solve the German problem and contain the Soviet Union is understandable, such a solution was not possible less than ten years after the Second World War. In the context of the 1950s, the transformation of Western Europe from a Hobbesian state of nature to a pluralistic security community could only be based on the permanent presence of American troops on the continent as a pacifier of national rivalries.

Is a permanent American military presence in Europe still necessary or desirable? Should America now encourage Europe to assume greater responsibility for its own security affairs? Is the creation of a European "third force" in the American national interest? The concluding chapter of the book examines the relevance of the early postwar period for contemporary issues and the central questions that will confront American policymakers in the future.

[2]

Wartime Diplomacy and Postwar Plans

The laws of history and geography will compel these powers to a trial of strength, either military or in the fields of economics and ideology. These same laws make it inevitable that both powers should become enemies of Europe. And it is equally certain that both these powers will sooner or later find it desirable to seek the support of the sole surviving nation in Europe, the German people.

Adolf Hitler, April 1945

Leaving aside the despicable nature of the source, many historians and international relations theorists would not quarrel much with the logic behind Hitler's prophecy. Wartime alliances usually do collapse after the defeat of the common opponent, and an alliance between two states with radically different social systems would seem to have even less chance of surviving the defeat of a common adversary. Believing that the Grand Alliance would survive after the war would seem to require extra doses of Wilsonian ideology and naiveté about Stalin, qualities that Franklin Delano Roosevelt and some of his advisors are often thought to have possessed in abundance.[1] Even without factoring in the conflicting nature of the respective states, it is easy to see why Kenneth Waltz argues that "contrary to the expectations of such an experienced statesmen as President Franklin D. Roosevelt, realist theorists would surely have predicted the collapse of the allied coalition upon the morrow of victory."[2]

This chapter examines American wartime diplomacy and postwar planning during the Second World War. What is truly remarkable about the vast majority of American forecasting about the postwar world is the

---

[1] For bitter critiques of FDR's wartime diplomacy and his relationship with Stalin, see Robert Nisbet, *Roosevelt and Stalin: The Failed Courtship* (Washington, D.C.: Regnery Gateway, 1988); and Amos Perlmutter, *FDR and Stalin: A Not So Grand Alliance* (Columbus: University of Missouri Press, 1993). Hitler's prophecy about future U.S.–Soviet rivalry is quoted in Schweller, *Deadly Imbalances: Tripolarity and Hitler's Strategy of World Conquest* (New York: Columbia University Press, 1998), 182.

[2] Kenneth Waltz, "A Response to My Critics," in *Neorealism and Its Critics*, ed. Robert Keohane (New York: Columbia University Press, 1986), 333–34.

general absence of worst-case assumptions about the future of U.S.–Soviet relations. Optimism about the future of postwar relations was certainly not limited to Roosevelt and a small group of naive Wilsonians.[3] Neither realists nor top military officials, the two groups one would suspect to be most likely to see the future in terms of the laws of geography, history, and power, were particularly gloomy about the future of the alliance. Although the Joint Chiefs of Staff (JCS) acknowledged a real possibility that the Grand Alliance could collapse after the war, they generally thought that the major issues between the United States and the Soviet Union could be worked out.[4] In a report forwarded to the JCS in March 1945, just two months before the end of the war in Europe, the leading academic realists in the United States strongly cautioned against drawing the conclusion that the Grand Alliance was doomed: "Even though history may abound with instances in which 'the allies of today' proved to be 'the enemies of tomorrow,' it would be criminal folly to jettison our wartime alliance in the moment of victory in the mistaken belief that war with the Soviet Union is 'inevitable.'"[5] Acknowledging that the United States could not make concessions that would threaten its national security or vital interests, these academics argued that "there is almost no other concession which it can afford not to make to assure Soviet collaboration in the maintenance of security."[6]

There are several reasons why even tough-minded realists and military officials resisted fatalism and worst-case reasoning about the future of the Grand Alliance well into 1945. First, even if Stalin and the Soviet Union had the most ambitious objectives in postwar Europe, America would still possess an overwhelming preponderance of power for a number of years.

---

[3] Even with the partial opening of Soviet archives, we still have far less information about how the Soviets viewed the postwar world. It is interesting to note that lower-level Soviet diplomats such as Maisky, Litvinov, and Gromyko were optimistic about the survival of the Grand Alliance. See Vladimir O. Petchanov, "The Big Three after World War II: New Documents on Soviet Thinking about Postwar Relations with the United States and Great Britain," Working Paper no. 13, Cold War International History Project (September 1999); and Aleksei M. Filitov, "Problems of Post-War Construction in Soviet Foreign Policy Conceptions during World War II," in *The Soviet Union and Europe in the Cold War, 1943–53,* ed. Francesca Gori and Silvio Pons (New York: St. Martin's Press, 1996), 3–22. For a much darker view of Stalin's postwar designs, see R. C. Raack, *Stalin's Drive to the West: The Origins of the Cold War* (Stanford: Stanford University Press, 1995).

[4] As William Emerson points out, on the question of how to deal with potential Soviet aggressiveness, the views of FDR and the JCS were the same. See William Emerson, "Franklin Roosevelt as Commander-in-Chief," *Military Affairs* 22 (winter 1958): 181–207.

[5] See JCS, "A Security Policy for Postwar America," Info Memo 382, March 29, 1945. I thank Marc Sheetz for providing me with a copy of this document. The authors of the document included many of the founding fathers of the American study of international relations, including Frederick S. Dunn, Edward M. Earle, William T. R. Fox, and Arnold Wolfers. For a good discussion of their argument, which has largely been ignored by scholars, see Melvyn Leffler, *A Preponderance of Power: National Security, the Truman Administration, and the Cold War* (Stanford, Calif.: Stanford University Press, 1992), 11.

[6] JCS, "A Security Policy for America," 5.

Because the two strongest states in the system would not be equivalent powers, there was no compelling need for American policymakers to act on fears which might not turn out to be real. Moreover, the fact that the Soviet Union was almost certain to be one of the two strongest powers in the postwar world for many years provided a very real incentive to establish amicable relations. Second, realists argued that as much as America might like to see democratic regimes established in Eastern Europe, there was a general acceptance from 1943 on that this was not a very crucial issue for U.S. security. Third, realists recognized that Germany would be the crucial issue of the postwar peace settlement and that America certainly could not accept total Soviet control over Germany. Yet, even this issue did not seem irresolvable. In short, Roosevelt's optimism about the prospects of the Grand Alliance was not out of line with the views of realists or military planners.

Of course, the American president did bring some rather specific views and assumptions to American planning for postwar Europe which were of crucial significance. FDR never deviated from the belief that a viable postwar order could not be based on a permanent American military presence on the continent. Order and stability in Europe would have to be maintained without America serving as a permanent night watchman and pacifier. Making that task even more difficult was the fact that he was unwilling to countenance the establishment of a new balance of power based on the strength of the states of Central and Western Europe. Such a strategy would have inevitably involved the restoration of German power, which was totally anathema to Roosevelt's thinking. His long-term goal was to alter the balance-of-power dynamics of the European state system primarily by eliminating Germany's central place in that system. His support for the Morgenthau Plan and the dismemberment of Germany was a function of his belief that Germany was the primary disrupter of European stability and the taproot of alliances, arms buildups, and spheres of influence.

APPEASEMENT AND THE POSTWAR BALANCE OF POWER

The German invasion of the Soviet Union in June 1941 offered great hope for the United States and Great Britain, but it also raised the difficult question of how America should respond to potential Soviet territorial demands in postwar Europe. As Mark Stoler points out, American policymakers were "in the unenviable position of having to aid an ally to achieve victory, while fearing that victory would lead to a menacing expansion by that ally."[7] Even before the German attack, American officials

---

[7] Mark Stoler, "The 'Second Front' and American Fear of Soviet Expansion, 1941–43," *Military Affairs* 39 (October 1975): 136.

were concerned that the British would attempt to appease Stalin by formally recognizing the Soviet annexation of the Baltic republics.[8] Well aware of the problems that might emerge from open recognition of the fruits of the Molotov-Ribbentrop Pact, Assistant Secretary of State Adolf Berle urged Roosevelt to openly declare that the United States would not make any commitments relating to postwar territorial settlements.[9] The Atlantic Charter, signed by FDR and Churchill at Placentia Bay in August 1941, was designed to head off any definitive settlements involving territorial arrangements until after the defeat of Germany. The provision that the parties "desire to see no territorial changes that do not accord with the freely expressed wishes of the peoples concerned" clearly ruled out the type of arrangements sought by Stalin from the British before the German invasion.[10]

Yet Stalin did not accept the belief that the Atlantic Charter should stand in the way of British recognition of the Soviet Union's borders prior to the German invasion—a point he made very clear to British Foreign Secretary Anthony Eden during December 1941 negotiations in Moscow for a formal alliance treaty. Without a clarification of where Great Britain stood on postwar questions, Stalin warned that he could not develop any trust toward his Western partners. Eden was in a difficult position in negotiations with Stalin right from the start because both his own government and the United States had warned him in advance that he must adhere to the Atlantic Charter's provisions. Deprived of all diplomatic flexibility on the territorial questions that Stalin insisted must be settled prior to the signing of any treaty, Eden could do little more than listen to the Soviet leader's views about how postwar Europe should be organized. When the British War Cabinet refused Eden's request to reconsider the prohibition on territorial agreements, Eden had no choice but to leave Moscow without concluding a treaty.[11]

---

[8] Berle Memorandum, June 19, 1941, in the Adolf A. Berle Diary, 1937–71, reel 6 (Hyde Park, N.Y.: Franklin D. Roosevelt Library and National Archives and Records Services Administration, 1978). (Hereafter the Roosevelt Library is referred to as FDRL.)

[9] Memorandum to the President, July 9, 1941, Adolf A. Berle Diary, reel 6.

[10] For the provisions of the Atlantic Charter, see *Foreign Relations of the United States, 1941*, vol. 1 (Washington, D.C.: U.S. Government Printing Office, 1958), 367–69. For FDR's concerns about the dangers of negotiating territorial settlements at this time, see Warren F. Kimball, *Forged in War: Roosevelt, Churchill, and the Second World War* (New York: William Morrow and Company, 1997), 95–99.

[11] The British reaction to Stalin's demands can be followed in Lloyd Gardner, *Spheres of Influence: The Great Powers Partition Europe, from Munich to Yalta* (Chicago: Ivan R. Dee, 1993), 107–16; Gabriel Gorodetsky, *Stanford Cripps' Mission to Moscow, 1940–42* (Cambridge: Cambridge University Press, 1984), 270–88; Stephen Merritt Miner, *Between Churchill and Stalin: The Soviet Union, Great Britain, and the Origins of the Grand Alliance* (Chapel Hill: University of North Carolina Press, 1988), 150–225; and Anthony Eden, *The Reckoning* (Boston: Houghton Mifflin Company, 1965), 336–52. For Stalin's conception of postwar Soviet security requirements as revealed to Eden in December 1941, see Albert Resis,

Eden was unwilling to accept this judgment as final and immediately sought to reverse the policy upon his return to London. His opposition to the restrictions imposed by the Atlantic Charter marked the beginning of what would become a perennial debate over how to overcome Stalin's suspicions of the West in a manner consistent with Western interests. In his memoirs, Eden argued that adhering to the Atlantic Charter's provisions in this specific case was a mistake because it was "prudent to tie the Soviet Union to agreements as early as possible" since Stalin might later be in a position to expand much further into Europe.[12] However, as Stephen Miner and others have argued, Eden's real reasons for accepting Stalin's demands in 1941–42 were based on the logic of appeasement rather than realpolitik.[13] Eden's primary objective was to change Stalin's suspicious views about Great Britain in order to make him a willing partner in the preservation of postwar European stability. Stalin's demands, according to Eden, only made sense as a test of the Western powers because he obviously knew that the Allies would not attempt to dislodge him from the contested territories if he was in possession of them. Since recognition of the Soviet frontiers at the time of the German invasion had no practical significance, Eden felt that adhering to the "exaggeratedly moral" American position on postwar arrangements made little sense. Moreover, it was a dangerous position because it obviated any possibility of forging closer relations with Stalin during the war. Gaining Soviet trust would be "a lengthy and laborious process" and one which he felt "must start now and not wait until the war is over."[14]

For different reasons, American officials were hostile to all of the arguments invoked by the British in favor of an Anglo-Soviet treaty. U.S. Secretary of State Cordell Hull accepted the validity of Eden's objective—gaining the trust of the Soviet government—but he disagreed with the idea that recognizing the 1941 frontiers was the best or the only way of accomplishing it. Starting with the Harriman-Beaverbrook mission of September 1941, Hull and Roosevelt had been committed to the idea that prompt and generous lend-lease deliveries to Russia should be the "test" of American goodwill toward the Soviet Union.[15] Other officials, such as John Winant, the American ambassador to Great Britain, questioned Eden's underlying

"Spheres of Influence in Soviet Wartime Diplomacy," *Journal of Modern History* 53 (September 1981): 417–39.

[12] Eden, *The Reckoning*, 370.

[13] Miner stresses the appeasement theme throughout *Between Churchill and Stalin*. See also Lothar Kettenacker, "The Anglo-Soviet Alliance and the Problem of Germany, 1941–45," *Journal of Contemporary History* 17 (1982): 435–58.

[14] Memorandum of Conversation by Welles, *FRUS*, 1941, vol. 3, 518.

[15] Hull to FDR, February 4, 1942, *FRUS*, 1942, vol. 3, 504. As George Herring points out, FDR never wavered from the belief that lend-lease was not to be used for bargaining purposes with the Soviet Union. See George C. Herring, "Lend-Lease to Russia and the Origins of the Cold War," *Journal of American History* 61 (June 1969): 93–114; and John D. Langer, "The Harriman-Beaverbrook Mission and the Debate over Unconditional Aid for the Soviet Union, 1941," *Journal of Contemporary History* 14 (1979): 463–82.

assumption that Stalin would be satisfied with the mere restoration of his 1941 borders. Since Stalin's postwar objectives might be much more extensive than the ones he was putting forward, Winant argued that it would be better to take a firm attitude from the beginning.[16]

U.S. Undersecretary of State Sumner Welles objected to the British arguments for a quite different reason. After hearing British Ambassador to the Soviet Union Lord Halifax outline the logic behind the Anglo-Soviet Treaty, Welles told him that he "could not conceive of this war being fought in order to reconstruct the shoddy, inherently vicious, kind of patchwork world order which the European powers had attempted to construct during the years between 1919 and 1939." Regardless of how important Soviet cooperation was to the war effort, or how badly the Baltic states had governed themselves in the interwar period, they were independent republics which should not be turned over in a secret agreement to the Soviet Union. According to Welles, the thinking behind British justifications for the Anglo-Soviet Treaty was very reminiscent of the logic pursued by Chamberlain during the Munich crisis of 1938.[17]

Welles's arguments against the Anglo-Soviet Treaty were based on more than simply "exaggerated moralism" and principled opposition to appeasement. The British justified the Anglo-Soviet Treaty by pointing to the advantages of having the Soviet Union in a better position to balance the Germans after the war.[18] This justification of the treaty was not compelling to Welles because he thought that Germany should be partitioned after the war, making it much easier for the victor powers to control. The nineteenth century confederation of German states should be the model for the postwar period because a federated Germany "had been no menace to the rest of Europe or the rest of the world. It had not been until Prussia had obtained a complete domination over all of the other German states that the danger to the world had arisen."[19] According to Welles, President Roosevelt also rejected the British claim that Soviet control of the Baltics would be necessary for postwar balancing against a resurgent Germany. If Germany was going to present the same type of threat as it

---

[16] Enclosure by Winant, "British Soviet Negotiations," February 4, 1942, *FRUS*, 1942, vol. 3, 510.

[17] Memorandum of Conversation by Welles, February 20, 1942, *FRUS*, 1942, vol. 3, 519–20.

[18] As Miner points out, in his memoirs Eden left out all of the justifications he used for the Anglo-Soviet Treaty concerning the merits of having Russia in a better position to balance Germany after the war. The sections that Eden left out of his memoirs related to Germany can be found in *FRUS*, 1942, vol. 3, 517–18. See Miner, *Between Churchill and Stalin*, 197–98.

[19] Memorandum of Conversation by Welles, *FRUS*, 1942, vol. 3, 520. After he left the administration, Welles popularized his harsh views on the postwar treatment of Germany in his best-seller *The Time For Decision* (New York: Harper & Row Publishers, 1944), 336–61. As his most recent biographer points out, Welles thought that harsh treatment of Germany would make it possible to avoid Soviet annexation of the Baltics and a subsequent U.S.–Soviet conflict. See Benjamin Welles, *Sumner Welles: FDR's Global Strategist* (New York: St. Martin's Press, 1997), 339.

had in the past, then there might be a need for the measures suggested by the British. But Roosevelt was not willing to make this assumption. In a statement that reveals a great deal about how he hoped solving the German problem would solve all of the other problems in postwar Europe, FDR indicated that the "nature of the security which should rightly be accorded to the Soviet Union would depend upon the type of Germany which would be established at the end of the war."[20]

Not surprisingly, the unwillingness of Roosevelt and other officials to go along with the Anglo-Soviet Treaty is often portrayed as an exemplar of the influence of Wilsonian idealism on American diplomacy.[21] However, Roosevelt and officials such as Berle and Welles were well aware that a victorious Soviet Union would surely exert a preponderant influence over the foreign affairs of much of Eastern Europe. Welles and Berle were the most vigorous defenders of the principles of the Atlantic Charter, but they also accepted the fact that great powers had both the ability and the propensity to exert influence over the foreign policies of smaller states on their borders. As early as February 1942, Berle acknowledged that Eastern Europe "will be dominated by someone—either Russia or Germany, in the sense of being within the shadow of an over-mastering military power." In his view, this was an acceptable fact of life under certain conditions and with certain limits. The primary condition was that although the Soviets had a right to make sure that states on their borders did not provide a threat to their security, they did not have a corresponding right "to dictate the method of life, cultural development and type of civilization to be enjoyed by these countries. . . . This is indeed the chief distinction which exists between a power which seeks world domination and a power which does not."[22]

The historical model that Berle and Welles envisioned for Soviet relations with Eastern Europe after the war was adopted from Roosevelt's "Good Neighbor" policy toward Latin America. In return for foregoing the right to thoroughly dominate the internal affairs of smaller states, American policymakers accepted the idea that the Soviets had a legitimate right not to face a hostile cordon sanitaire in Eastern Europe after the war. How the Good Neighbor or "open" spheres of influence policy was intended to function can be seen in discussions between State Department and Polish government exiles in London in early 1942.[23] On the one hand,

---

[20] Memorandum of Conversation by Welles, *FRUS*, 1942, vol. 3, 521.

[21] See Lynn Etheridge Davis, *The Cold War Begins: Soviet-American Conflict over Eastern Europe* (Princeton: Princeton University Press, 1974), 11–37; and Henry Kissinger, *Diplomacy* (New York: Simon & Schuster, 1994), 405–9.

[22] Berle diary entry, February 5, 1942, in *Navigating the Rapids, 1918–71: From the Papers of Adolf A. Berle*, ed. Beatrice Bishop Berle and Travis Beal Jacobs (New York: Harcourt Brace Jovanovich, 1973), 401.

[23] For the Good Neighbor model, see Warren Kimball, "Baffled Virtue . . . Injured Innocence: The Western Hemisphere as Regional Role Model," in *The Juggler: Franklin*

Roosevelt and the State Department opposed Polish plans for a postwar confederation in Eastern Europe, largely because of the belief that these plans would be met with great hostility from the Soviet Union.[24] However, although the concept of open spheres of influence led the United States to oppose Polish plans simply because they might appear threatening to the Soviet Union, the same logic also made it illegitimate in their eyes for the Soviets to erect an iron-clad security zone in Eastern Europe. Again, ending the German problem was viewed as the way to ameliorate any perceived Soviet security need for total control over the internal affairs of Eastern Europe states. As Welles explained to General Sikorski, the leader of the London Poles, "if Germany were disarmed the Soviet Union would not have to provide the type of barrier between Germany and the Soviet Union which it previously had to contemplate."[25] Since the specific details of solving the German problem could obviously not be resolved until after the war, it is understandable why the United States wished to defer questions concerning postwar security arrangements in Eastern Europe.

President Roosevelt vigorously supported Welles and Berle in their opposition to the Anglo-Soviet Treaty, but it is clear that he did not oppose the treaty for the same reasons. Although open spheres on the pattern of U.S.–Latin American relations might have been a worthy and achievable objective, FDR was unwilling to allow the question of postwar borders to prevent the establishment of amicable relations with the Soviet Union. He remained opposed to the Anglo-Soviet Treaty for reasons of domestic politics, but he also let Soviet Ambassador to Washington Maxim Litvinov know that he would not oppose the Soviet claims at the end of the war. According to Litvinov's record of the conversation, the American president did not envision "any difficulties regarding our border desires after the war. . . . He himself had always thought it had been a mistake to separate provinces from Russia after the war and he thought Wilson had also been opposed to this. And therefore he assures Stalin in a personal way that he absolutely agrees with us."[26] Shortly after Roosevelt's meeting with Litvinov, Berle recorded in his diary that the president told him "he would not particularly mind the Russians taking quite a chunk of territory; they might have the Baltic Republics, and eastern Poland, and even

Roosevelt as Wartime Statesman (Princeton: Princeton University Press, 1991), 107–25; and Welles, *Time For Decision*, 332–34. On the concept of "open" spheres of influence, see Eduard Mark, "American Policy toward Eastern Europe and the Origins of the Cold War, 1941–46: An Alternative Interpretation," *Journal of American History* 68 (September 1981): 313–35.

[24] Memorandum of Conversation by Welles, March 4, 1942, *FRUS*, 1942, vol. 3, 113.

[25] Memorandum of Conversation by Welles, March 6, 1942, *FRUS*, 1942, vol. 3, 114.

[26] Hugh Phillips, "Mission to America: Maksim M. Litvinov in the United States, 1941–43," *Diplomatic History* 12 (spring 1988): 268. See also Perlmutter, *A Not So Grand Alliance*, esp. 255, 275.

perhaps Bukovina, as well as Bessarabia."[27] Clearly, from an early point in the war, FDR was not very disturbed about the prospects of Soviet territorial expansion into these areas.

An alliance crisis over the terms of the Anglo-Soviet Treaty was eventually avoided in May 1942 when the Soviets agreed to sign the treaty without the secret protocol.[28] The Berle-Welles approach was to convince Stalin that he could gain security without bolshevizing Eastern Europe. However, William Bullitt, the former U.S. ambassador to the Soviet Union, argued that only containment would prevent the Soviets from dominating Eastern Europe after the war. Asked by Roosevelt in late 1942 to study the problem of postwar civil administration, Bullitt submitted a report that had little to do with the assigned topic but one that directly challenged Roosevelt's primary assumptions about the postwar world. The main thrust of Bullitt's analysis was to urge FDR to resist supporting what he called Britain's "Balance of Impotence" policy on the continent.[29] Consciously or not, Bullitt was criticizing the president's "grand design" for the postwar world, elements of which Great Britain fully opposed.[30] Leaving aside the title that Bullitt attached to those views, he did accurately capture the thinking behind FDR's "Four Policemen" concept.[31] He correctly noted that the assumption underlying FDR's wartime diplomacy was the belief that Soviet policy was driven by mistrust of the West and that this mistrust could be overcome by measures such as Lend-Lease and the opening of a second front. In Bullitt's view, these assumptions misjudged the nature of the adversary because Soviet policy was driven by offensive motives. Unless faced with strong opposition, Soviet power would move into the vacuum created by the destruction of Germany after the war. For Bullitt, as it would be for later American strategists, the long-term solution to the problems posed by the Soviet Union was the establishment of an integrated and armed Europe. The short-term solution was to have American and British forces set up a second front in the Balkans

---

[27] Berle diary entry, April 30, 1942, in *Navigating the Rapids,* ed. Berle and Jacobs, 412.

[28] The most compelling explanation for the switch is that FDR offered the Soviet Union the opening up of a second front in 1942, an objective far more important to the Soviets than a formal treaty on the fate of the Baltic states. See Mark Stoler, *The Politics of the Second Front* (Westport, Conn.: Greenwood Press, 1977), 34–45.

[29] Orville H. Bullitt, ed., *For the President Personal and Secret: Correspondence between Franklin D. Roosevelt and William C. Bullitt* (Boston: Houghton Mifflin Company, 1972), 575–94. For background on the Bullitt–FDR relationship, see Lloyd C. Gardner, *Architects of Illusion* (Chicago: Quadrangle Books, 1970), 3–54.

[30] Most notably, the British opposed FDR's insistence that France should be disarmed after the war. See Memorandum by Harry Hopkins, March 15, 1943, *FRUS, 1943,* vol. 3, 17. In addition to the more comprehensive research of Kimball and Harper, a useful source on FDR's "grand design" is Willard Range, *Franklin D. Roosevelt's World Order* (Athens: University of Georgia Press, 1959).

[31] The "Four Policemen" concept was outlined by FDR in conversations with Molotov in May and June 1942. See *FRUS,* 1942, vol. 2, 566–83.

rather than in Western Europe, which he thought would prevent the Soviet Union from occupying much of Europe at the end of the war.[32]

Three years after the war, Bullitt revealed to *Life* magazine the president's response to his memorandum. According to Bullitt, Roosevelt recognized the logic behind his argument but was unwilling to follow his advice on how to prevent Soviet domination of Europe.[33] Roosevelt recalled how during the First World War Wilson had rejected his advice based on a "hunch" and told Bullitt that this time around he was going to gamble on more optimistic assessments of Stalin. Although there is no record of the meeting other than Bullitt's, his account in *Life* rings true. In a series of interviews with Forest Davis in 1943 and 1944 published in the *Saturday Evening Post*, Roosevelt revealed much of his thinking about the nature of the postwar world. As Davis noted, and as the president wanted him to know and publicize, his focus at the time was "not with aspirations toward a better world such as he articulated in the Four Freedoms and with Winston Churchill, in the Atlantic Charter, but with the cold, realistic techniques, or instruments, needed to make those aspirations work. This means that he is concentrating on power; dealing with problems of power politics in contrast to what the pundits describe as welfare politics."[34] Acknowledging that he was gambling in his assessment of Stalin, FDR suggested that reassurance rather than confrontation was the core element of his postwar diplomacy. What emerges from a careful reading of the Davis interview is Roosevelt's belief that the power realities of the postwar world left him little choice but to place his bets on winning Stalin's trust before the war ended. In fact, as he told journalist Edgar Snow shortly after the article was published, he was not really gambling at all, since "our alternative was to begin right then preparing for World War III." Unlike in 1918, when the United States was the "rising colossus," the Second World War would result in the Soviet Union rising to "a power level alongside the English speaking democracies."[35] Since neither Great Britain nor the United States could move permanently into the power vacuum created by the defeat of Germany, Roosevelt implied that

---

[32] Bullitt, *For the President*, 576–99.

[33] William C. Bullitt, "How We Won the War and Lost the Peace," *Life*, August 30, 1948, 94. FDR obviously did not reject the Bullitt thesis out of hand because he asked Eden what he thought about it during a meeting in March 1943. Eden was also unconvinced by Bullitt's argument and his policy prescription. See Memorandum of Conversation by Welles, March 16, 1943, *FRUS*, 1943, vol. 3, 19–24.

[34] See Forrest Davis, "Roosevelt's World Blueprint," *Saturday Evening Post*, April 10, 1943, 20–21, 109–11 (quotation on 20); and Davis, "What Really Happened at Teheran," *Saturday Evening Post*, May 13 and May 20, 1944. The Davis articles were based on personal interviews with the President and were approved for publication by the White House. FDR himself thought that the articles were "exceedingly good and exceedingly fair." See FDR to Forrest Davis, June 14, 1944, FDRL, Official File 4287.

[35] Edgar Snow, *Journey to the Beginning* (New York: Random House, 1958), 343.

he had little choice but to attempt to win the Soviet Union over to postwar cooperation with the Western powers.

Roosevelt's views after 1943 reflected the reality that, in contrast to 1941–42, when the basic survival of the Soviet Union could not be taken for granted, the Soviets would emerge from the war vastly strengthened in both absolute and relative terms. The decisive Soviet victory at Stalingrad made the Bullitt strategy of containment appear even less feasible and desirable.[36] Other officials held the president's position that it was essential to establish better U.S.–Soviet relations as soon as possible. The contrast between these two approaches can be seen in a memo sent to Harry Hopkins, administrator of the Lend-Lease program, by Major General J. H. Burns in December 1942. According to Burns, "If the Allies are victorious, Russia will be one of the three most powerful countries in the world. For the future peace of the world, we should be real friends so that we can help shape world events in such a way as to provide security and prosperity."[37] Two of Burns's specific suggestions for improving relations with the Soviet Union would become important elements of U.S. wartime diplomacy during 1943. First, he recommended holding a bilateral conference between Stalin and Roosevelt that would exclude any role for Churchill. Although the bilateral meeting never took place, FDR persistently pursued this objective throughout the year.[38] The president's attempt to exclude Churchill marked the beginning of persistent American efforts to avoid the appearance of "ganging up" with the British against the Soviets. Second, Burns recommended the appointment of a top-flight ambassador to the Soviet Union loyal to the concept that Russia must be treated as a "real friend." The replacement of Ambassador William Standley with Averell Harriman in the summer of 1943 reflected the increased importance Roosevelt placed on closer U.S.–Soviet relations.[39]

---

[36] See Warren Kimball, "Stalingrad: A Chance for Choices," *The Journal of Military History* 60 (January 1996): 89–114. A further complication to adopting a tougher strategy after Stalingrad was the fear that Stalin might seek a separate peace with Germany. These fears were not groundless, as Vojtech Mastny has shown. See Vojtech Mastny, "Stalin and the Prospects of a Separate Peace," *The American Historical Review* 77 (December 1972): 1365–88.

[37] Major General J. H. Burns, memorandum, "Importance of Soviet Relationships and Suggestions for Improving Them," December 1, 1942, President's Soviet Protocol Committee, box 18, FDRL. According to Edward Bennett, FDR seriously considered appointing Burns ambassador to the Soviet Union in 1943. See Bennett, *Franklin D. Roosevelt and the Search For Victory* (Wilmington, Del.: Scholarly Resources, 1990), 43.

[38] Setting up such a meeting was the main objective of Joseph Davies's trip to Moscow in May 1943. See Elizabeth Kimball Maclean, "Joseph E. Davies and Soviet-American Relations, 1941–43," *Diplomatic History* 4 (winter 1980): 73–93.

[39] For Harriman's views of U.S.–Soviet relations, which were more optimistic in 1943 than they would be later, see Deborah Welch Larson, *Origins of Containment: A Psychological Explanation* (Princeton: Princeton University Press, 1985), 76–77; and Harriete L. Chandler, "The Transition to Cold Warrior: The Evolution of W. Averell Harriman's Assessment of the U.S.S.R's Polish Policy," *East European Quarterly* 10 (1976): 229–45.

American assessments of postwar Soviet power in 1943 reinforced the belief that every possible effort should be made to maintain the wartime alliance past the defeat of Nazi Germany. Quoting from a "very high level United States military strategic estimate," Burns provided Hopkins with a memorandum on the eve of the Quebec Conference which contrasted Russia's collapse in the First World War with her present role as the "decisive factor" in the defeat of Nazi Germany. The memo stated that after the defeat of the Axis states Russian military power could not be balanced by the other European states and that her "post-war position in Europe will be a dominant one. With Germany crushed, there is no power in Europe to oppose her tremendous military forces."[40] Assessments of the postwar balance in Europe had tremendous implications for both short- and long-term decisions in 1943. Contrary to the popular belief that only Churchill and the British military thought about strategy from a political perspective, the American insistence on concentrating military forces in Western Europe was greatly motivated by postwar political considerations.[41] First, concentrating American and British forces in the Balkans—the political strategy urged by Bullitt—would not be perceived by Stalin as a fulfillment of the long-delayed pledge of a second front, thus further alienating him from the Allies. Second, an attack in the Balkans could not achieve its stated objective: the prevention of the Soviet Union from dominating Eastern Europe.[42] Indeed, it was for precisely this reason that State Department officials urged Cordell Hull to refrain from endorsing Bullitt's proposals on the eve of the Quebec Conference:

> Our friends in the War Department tell us that such an attempt [preventing the Soviet Union from regaining its June 1941 borders] would be sheer military fantasy; that the United States and the United Kingdom are not in a position successfully to oppose the Soviet Union in Eastern Europe if Germany is defeated. In short, the only way Mr. Bullitt's suggestion could actually be implemented

[40] The Executive of the President's Soviet Protocol Committee (Burns) to the President's Special Assistant (Hopkins), August 10, 1943, *FRUS, 1943, Conferences at Washington and Quebec*, 625. In his memoirs, Averell Harriman recalled that at the Quebec Conference, "Hopkins had been impressed by the argument of the Joint Chiefs of Staff that Russia was going to be the dominant power in Europe after the war." See W. Averell Harriman and Elie Abel, *Special Envoy to Churchill and Stalin, 1941–46* (New York: Random House, 1975), 224.

[41] See Stoler, *Politics of the Second Front;* Eric Larrabee, *Commander in Chief: Franklin Delano Roosevelt, His Lieutenants and Their War* (New York: Harper & Row Publishers, 1987); and Emerson, "Franklin Roosevelt as Commander-in-Chief," 203–7.

[42] See Stoler, *Politics of the Second Front*, 97–123. The Bullitt strategy of getting Western forces further east into Europe is usually associated with Winston Churchill. However, at this point in the war Churchill was not advocating this military strategy and concern about the Soviets was not his primary reason in 1943 for contesting the American approach to the Second Front. See Tuvia Ben-Moshe, "Winston Churchill and the 'Second Front': A Reappraisal," *The Journal of Modern History* 62 (September 1990): 503–37.

would be by means of a coalition between the United States, United Kingdom and the German military forces."[43]

The political logic behind the American military strategy to launch a second front in Western Europe is set out in a remarkable paper prepared for the JCS by Geroid T. Robinson of the Research and Analysis Division of the Office of Strategic Services.[44] According to Robinson, concentrating Anglo-American forces in Western Europe was the only military option that would protect the fundamental American interest of preventing any single power from dominating the European continent. This objective did not conflict with the "minimum" Soviet aim of restoring their June 1941 borders and establishing "friendly" governments in all of the neighboring states. However, it did conflict with the possible "maximum" aim of extending Soviet control throughout all of Europe. The problem facing American diplomacy, according to Robinson, was "to make a settlement on minimum terms so attractive, and a settlement on maximum terms so costly (even to Soviet forces that will be much stronger on the continent than the forces of Britain and America combined) that at least our own fundamental aims would be realized."[45] Regardless of Soviet postwar intentions, the best course for American strategy would be to combine the second front in Western Europe with efforts aimed at reaching workable compromises with the Soviets. In Robinson's view, "The policy of compromise will produce results of great value, if it proves workable. If it breaks down, the open rivalry that then develops will be no sharper than it would have been if no compromise had been attempted, and the large Anglo-American force on the continent will be in the best possible position to deal with the Russians."[46]

To be sure, the strategy of concentrating American military forces in Western Europe essentially wrote off any possibility of militarily influencing events in Eastern Europe. By the summer of 1943, however, neither President Roosevelt nor the JCS had any faith that Soviet domination

[43] Memorandum by John Hickerson for Cordell Hull, August 10, 1943, Records of the Office of European Affairs (Matthews-Hickerson File), 1934–1947 (Washington, D.C.: National Archives and Records Service, 1982), reel 2. A recent study suggests that the "soft white underbelly" strategy favored by Bullitt and Churchill was indeed a fantasy that might have facilitated Soviet movement into Europe rather than impeded it. See Thomas M. Barker, "The Ljubljana Strategy: Alternative to Anvil/Dragoon or Fantasy?" *The Journal of Military History* 56 (January 1992): 57–86.

[44] See Office of Strategic Services, "Strategy and Policy: Can America and Russia Cooperate," August 20, 1943, Records of the Joint Chiefs of Staff, Part 1, 1942–45: The Soviet Union, reel 1 (Frederick, Md.: University Publications of America, 1981).

[45] Office of Strategic Services, "Strategy and Policy," 7–12 (quotation on 12). Robinson, later the founder of the Russian Institute at Columbia University, maintained this basic perspective toward Eastern Europe well after the war. For a discussion of his later views, see Robert Messer, "Paths Not Taken: The United States Department of State and Alternatives to Containment," *Diplomatic History* 1 (fall 1977): 297–319.

[46] Office of Strategic Services, "Strategy and Policy," 15.

of the region could be prevented through the use of American military power. A JCS paper of September 18, 1943, stated: "the Soviet Union would be able to impose whatever territorial settlements it desired in Central Europe and the Balkans."[47] FDR revealed essentially the same views in a conversation with Cardinal Spellman. According to Spellman, FDR said that the Soviet Union would control Finland, the Baltic States, the Eastern half of Poland, and Bessarabia after the war and that nothing could be done to prevent it: "There is no point to oppose these desires of Stalin, because he has the power to get them anyhow. So better give them gracefully."[48] This is exactly what Roosevelt did at the Teheran Conference in November 1943 when he let Stalin know that the United States would not oppose the reincorporation of the Baltic states into the Soviet Union and the redrawing of the Soviet-Polish border around the Curzon Line.

Subsequent American assessments of the postwar balance reiterated the same basic analysis contained in the memorandum Burns provided to Hopkins in the summer of 1943. A report by the Office of Strategic Services (OSS) in May 1944 viewed the rise of Russian power and the de-cline of British power as one of the most important long-term conse-quences of the war. Russia's exhaustion and devastation at the end of the war would provide the United States and Great Britain with a strong bar-gaining position in the short term. Anglo-American superiority in Europe, however, was essentially seen as a "wasting asset" that would di-minish over time: "By the test of potential military effectiveness in Europe, every one of the *long-term* factors just mentioned (geographic lo-cation, population curve, economic trend, dynamic will) is more favor-able to Russia than to the British Empire or even to the United States."[49] Maintaining the wartime alliance in Germany and elsewhere with "an ex-panding and dynamic power" (the Soviet Union), a "developing but es-sentially satisfied power" (the United States), and "a power that shows symptoms of decline" (the British Empire) would not be easy, but the main conclusion of the OSS report was that both the United States and

[47] JCS 506, as discussed in Maurice Matloff, *Strategic Planning for Coalition Warfare, 1943–44* (Washington, D.C.: Department of the Army, 1959), 292.
[48] Robert I. Gannon, *The Cardinal Spellman Story* (New York: Doubleday & Company, 1962), 223. In an earlier meeting with representatives from the Commission to Study the Bases of a Just and Durable Peace in March 1943, FDR warned that the Soviets would, if nec-essary, seize disputed territories by force. According to John Foster Dulles, who was present at the meeting, "He indicated fear lest too much 'idealism' in these matters should lead to a rejection of collaboration as a permanent principle." See Memorandum of Conference with the President at the White House on Friday, March 26, 1943, box 22, John Foster Dulles Papers, Seeley-Mudd Library, Princeton University.
[49] Office of Strategic Services, "Russian Aims in Germany and the Problem of Three-Power Cooperation," in O.S.S./State Department Intelligence and Research Reports: The Soviet Union, Part 6 (Washington, D.C.: University Publications of America, 1977).

Great Britain would have to make a dedicated effort to reach firm agreements with the Soviet Union before the end of the war.[50]

JCS assessments of the postwar balance also provided support for Roosevelt's policy of attempting to maintain the Grand Alliance. Their basic assessment of the postwar distribution of power is spelled out at length in JCS 838/1, the document that would serve as military guidance for the State Department until the Potsdam Conference in July 1945.[51] According to Admiral William Leahy, the "outstanding fact" that should be taken into consideration in postwar planning was "the recent phenomenal development of the heretofore latent Russian military and economic strength . . . a development which seems certain to prove epochal in its bearing on future politico-military international relationships, and which has yet to reach the full scope attainable with Russian resources."[52] Even with American intervention on the side of Great Britain, Russian power in Europe would be so great that the United States "might be able to successfully defend Britain, but we could not, under existing conditions, defeat Russia. . . . We would find ourselves engaged in a war which we could not win even though the United States would be in no danger of defeat and occupation."[53] Since any future war in Europe would find Great Britain and the Soviet Union on opposite sides, Leahy argued that the United States should "now and in the future, exert its utmost efforts and utilize all its influence to prevent such a situation arising and to promote a spirit of mutual cooperation between Russia, Britain, and ourselves."[54]

The most thorough analysis of the future of Europe prepared before the February 1945 Yalta Conference was an OSS report written with the help of leading Soviet specialists from the State Department, including Charles Bohlen, Llewellyn Thompson, and Eldridge Dubrow. The report, entitled "Capabilities and Intentions of the USSR in the Postwar Period,"

[50] Office of Strategic Services, "Russian Aims in Germany." Like an earlier OSS paper, the general conclusion was that there was still cause for optimism about postwar cooperation with the Soviets in Germany. See Office of Strategic Services, "Will the Soviet Union Be Willing to Participate in a Joint Military Occupation and a Joint Military Government in Germany," September 23, 1943, in O.S.S./State Department Intelligence and Research Reports: The Soviet Union, Part 6.

[51] On the origins of JCS 838/1, see Walter Poole, "From Conciliation to Containment: The Joint Chiefs of Staff and the Coming of the Cold War, 1945–46," *Military Affairs* 42 (1978): 12–16; and Mark Stoler, "From Continentalism to Globalism: General Stanley D. Embick, the Joint Strategic Survey Committee, and the Military View of American National Policy during the Second World War," *Diplomatic History* 6 (summer 1982): 303–21.

[52] Excerpt from letter of Admiral Leahy, May 16, 1944, *FRUS, 1945, The Conferences at Malta and Yalta,* 107. The version published in the Yalta volume contains the entire letter to Hull.

[53] Excerpt from letter of Admiral Leahy, 108. It is worth noting that the original formulation was more emphatic; "we could never defeat Russia." The addition of the qualifying phrase "under existing conditions" was put in by Leahy, who thought it "inadvisable for such a statement to be made officially by the Joint Chiefs of Staff." See, 162nd Meeting of the Joint Chiefs of Staff, in Records of the Joint Chiefs of Staff, Part 1, 1942–45: Meetings, reel 2 (Frederick, Md.: University Publications of America, 1980).

[54] Excerpt from letter of Admiral Leahy, 108.

has been described by Eduard Mark as "the most comprehensive statement of postwar Soviet foreign policy yet attempted."[55] In addition to its
examination of Soviet foreign policy, the paper provides an insightful
analysis of American perceptions of the short- and long-term relative
power positions of the United States and the Soviet Union on the eve of
Yalta. Largely due to the devastation of their economy, the OSS argued,
the Soviets would probably keep their military expenditures at the 1938
level in order to increase their economic power in the future. At the end of
the war in Europe, the Russian military and economic position vis-à-vis
the West would be weaker than "at any time thereafter," a fact the OSS
believed the Soviet Union could not help but recognize. Due to these two
factors, the report predicted that "Russia will have neither the resources
nor, so far as economic factors are governing, the inclination, to embark
on adventurist foreign policies which, in the opinion of Soviet leaders,
might involve the USSR in a conflict or a critical armament race with the
great Western powers."[56]

The long-term analysis of relative capabilities, however, presented a
much less optimistic picture for the West. Part of the reason why the
Soviets would seek to avoid conflict with the West in the short term was
their belief that "throughout a period of considerable length, the population and the economic and military capabilities of the USSR will increase
more rapidly than those of any other power.... Otherwise stated, the
Soviet leaders almost certainly believe that time is working with them." In
the future, the increase in Soviet capabilities would provide Moscow with
much greater freedom of action in Europe. By the time the postwar period
of occupation was over, the Soviets would have strong reason to believe
that the distribution of power in Europe would favor them in any conflict
with the Western powers.[57]

These assessments of the postwar distribution of power show, first,
that American officials who were most knowledgeable about the emerging postwar structure did not conclude that the emerging bipolar structure would inevitably lead to hostility between the United States and the
Soviet Union. What the Soviets could do with their power at the end of
the war—dominate Eastern Europe—was not something that the United

---

[55] "Capabilities and Intentions of the Soviet Union in the Postwar Period," January 5, 1945,
in O.S.S./State Department Intelligence and Research Reports: The Soviet Union, Part 6, reel
4. For the background of this paper, see Eduard Mark, "October or Thermidor?
Interpretations of Stalinism and the Perception of Soviet Foreign Policy in the United States,
1927–47," *American Historical Review* 94 (October 1989): 937–62 (quotation on 950). See also
JCS, "Estimate of Soviet Post-war Capabilities and Intentions," Info Memo 374, Records of
the Joint Chiefs of Staff, Part 1, 1942–45: The Soviet Union, reel 1.

[56] "Capabilities and Intentions of the USSR in the Postwar Period," reel 4. The JCS thought
that these factors would be moderating influences on Soviet foreign policy until at least 1952.
See Poole, "From Conciliation to Containment," 12.

[57] "Capabilities and Intentions of the USSR in the Postwar Period," reel 4.

States could prevent. More importantly, analysts hardly suggested that Soviet control over much of Eastern Europe was something the United States needed to prevent in order to protect its own interests on the continent. The long-term assessments of Soviet power did suggest that there was reason for concern, but the potential for any serious security threat to the fundamental interests of the United States was far from imminent. Second, analysts of the postwar structure generally refrained from offering anything more than general policy implications for either the short- or long-term future of Europe, yet it is easy to see how their assessments tended to lead away from a diplomacy based on confrontation and worst-case scenarios. A tough approach toward Soviet aims in Eastern Europe before the end of the war would be futile and counterproductive because it would not alter the fact, as Roosevelt would later point out, that Stalin "had the power" to do what he wanted in the region. Since the United States would have plenty of time to move toward a confrontational policy if and when the Soviets appeared to be threatening core American interests, there was very little reason to reach any definitive and possibly premature conclusion about whether the Soviets would in fact become a threat to the United States. As Roosevelt told his son Elliot shortly after the Teheran Conference, "Maybe the Soviet Union will get strong in Europe. Whether that's bad depends on a whole lot of factors."[58]

OCCUPATION ZONES AND
AMERICAN MILITARY FORCES IN EUROPE

In his 1943 book *U.S. Foreign Policy: Shield of the Republic*, Walter Lippmann wrote that "our grand objective must be a settlement that does not call for a permanent American military intervention to maintain it."[59] Although President Roosevelt often spoke of his grand objectives in far loftier and idealistic terms, such as ending balance-of-power politics once and for all, Lippmann's statement perfectly captures what the president was really aiming for in both his wartime diplomacy and postwar planning. Roosevelt's thoughts on the subject of America's postwar role in Europe surfaced most clearly during his meetings en route to the Teheran Conference with the JCS over occupation zones and postwar bases. During his discussions with George Marshall and other top military officials, FDR made it absolutely clear that he did not envision or want anything more than a temporary military role on the continent. Despite the fact that America was to be one of the Four Policemen of the postwar

---

[58] Elliot Roosevelt, *As He Saw It* (New York: Duell, Sloan, and Pearce, 1946), 185.
[59] Walter Lippmann, *U.S. Foreign Policy: Shield of the Republic* (Boston: Little, Brown and Company, 1943), 146.

world, the beat that its military forces would patrol excluded continental Europe. As he told Stalin during the Teheran Conference, "England and the Soviet Union would have to handle the land armies in the event of any future threat to the peace."[60] An absolute unwillingness to contemplate the stationing of American ground forces in Europe before the emergence of any threat to the peace continued to be Roosevelt's position throughout the Yalta Conference.

Roosevelt's views about America's military role in postwar Europe emerged during a discussion of Rankin C, which was essentially a contingency plan for a rapid invasion of the continent in the event of a sudden German collapse. Although the Bullitt strategy for placing troops as far east as possible was rejected, both the president and his military advisors believed it was crucial to have American forces in Germany to meet the Soviets at the earliest possible moment. FDR was all in favor of moving forces to the continent as quickly as possible if Germany showed signs of capitulating before the start of the planned invasion of Western Europe, but what bothered him about Rankin C was its placement of American forces in southern Germany during the postwar occupation.[61] Although Marshall and his other military advisors tried to convince him that the location of the American zone was a result of logistical factors, Roosevelt did not believe logistics were the real reason. In his view, the attempt to place American forces in the southern part of Germany represented an effort on Churchill's part to entangle the United States in a postwar commitment to France that the president was determined to avoid.[62]

There is little evidence that the controversy over occupation zones reflected any British scheme, but it did reflect a long-standing dispute between Roosevelt and the British over the postwar status of France. The reconstitution of a strong France after the war, a fundamental aim of British policy, was of little interest to FDR. To the contrary, the president was determined to make sure that France remained an irrelevant player in the postwar world by keeping the country disarmed and stripping it of colonies. Regardless of his well-known personal hostility to General de Gaulle, FDR's views on France's postwar role would have generated conflict with any leader determined to restore French power and influence.[63] For both Roosevelt and Admiral Leahy, an occupation of the southern

---

[60] Roosevelt-Stalin Meeting, November 29, 1943, *FRUS*, 1943, *The Conferences at Cairo and Teheran*, 531.

[61] See William M. Franklin, "Zonal Boundaries and Access to Berlin," *World Politics* 16 (October 1963): 1–31.

[62] Minutes of the President's Meeting with JCS, November 19, 1943, *FRUS*, 1943, *Conferences at Cairo and Teheran*, 256.

[63] For FDR's views on de Gaulle and France's postwar role, see Mario Rossi, *Roosevelt and the French* (Westport, Conn.: Praeger, 1993); Julian G. Hurstfield, *America and the French Nation, 1939–45* (Chapel Hill: University of North Carolina Press, 1986); and Milton Viorst, *Hostile Allies: FDR and Charles De Gaulle* (New York: MacMillan Company, 1965).

zone of Germany was unacceptable primarily because it might entangle the United States in postwar French politics. In Leahy's view, postwar disorder and the possibility of revolution in France meant that "we should definitely get out of France as soon as possible. We should accept any difficulties in order to get out of France at the earliest possible time."[64]

Churchill was unwilling to follow Roosevelt's lead on the issue of France's postwar status—given the rise of Russian power and the destruction of German power.[65] In Churchill's view, "It was important to recreate a strong France, whatever we might think about French desserts or the probable difficulty of achieving our purpose. For the prospect of having no strong country on the map between England and Russia was not attractive."[66] The revival of France was particularly necessary since Churchill was rightly skeptical about America retaining a military presence on the continent for very long after the war. Even though he hoped that America would in some way be involved in the postwar policing of Europe, Churchill argued that he "could not easily foresee the United States being able to keep large numbers of men indefinitely on guard in Europe. If such an experiment were tried he could not believe it would last for more than one Presidential election."[67]

Roosevelt's concern about getting "roped" into an unwanted European sphere of influence led to a lengthy dispute that would last until September 1944. Despite the best efforts of Churchill and his own military officials, FDR refused to change his position on the matter of occupation zones. Arguments made by the JCS related to the difficulties involved in switching occupation zones at the end of the war were rejected because the president felt that there was no reason why British and American forces could not play "leapfrog" all day after the defeat of Germany.[68] Even arguments made by Churchill that occupying the southern zone might make it easier for French forces to replace American forces in Germany fell on deaf ears.[69] If Churchill wanted to restore French power, FDR insisted that he could not and should not ask the United States for help; "Do please don't ask me to keep any American forces in France. I just cannot do it! I would have to bring them all back home. As I suggested before, I denounce and protest the paternity of Belgium, France, and Italy."[70]

[64] Minutes of Meeting with the JCS, November 19, 1943, *FRUS, 1943, Conferences at Cairo and Teheran,* 255.

[65] See Francois Kersaudy, *Churchill and De Gaulle* (London: William Collins, 1981).

[66] C-297/1, May 28, 1943, in *Churchill and Roosevelt: The Complete Correspondence,* ed. Warren Kimball (Princeton: Princeton University Press, 1984), 2:223.

[67] Ibid.

[68] See Minutes of Meeting between the President and the JCS, February 21, 1944, Records of the Joint Chiefs of Staff, Part 1, 1942–45: Meetings, reel 1.

[69] C-589, February 23, 1944, in Kimball, *Churchill and Roosevelt,* 2:747.

[70] Roosevelt to Churchill, February 29, 1944, *FRUS,* 1944, vol. 1, 189.

Roosevelt's position on occupation zones in Germany was crucial since it also represented the formal American position in negotiations within the European Advisory Commission (EAC). Shortly before sending his cable to Churchill, FDR sent the American representative to the EAC, John Winant, a more complete list of his reasons for insisting on the northern zone. Two of these reasons are particularly worth noting because they reveal Roosevelt's thinking about the purpose of American forces in Europe. First, FDR argued that the main American objective on the continent was not solving internal problems in Southern Europe but "eliminating Germany as a possible and even probable cause of a third world war."[71] Second, and more importantly, Roosevelt argued that Churchill was mistaken to view the question of occupation zones as one involving long-term British security concerns. After the occupation was completed, the president believed that the British could work out any security arrangements in Germany that they thought were necessary: "The United States will be only too glad to retire all its military forces from Europe as soon as this is feasible."[72]

The question of occupation zones in Germany was not settled until the Quebec Conference of September 1944, when Roosevelt finally agreed to accept U.S. occupation of the southern zone. Since his primary reason for rejecting the southern zone had been his concern about getting too involved in postwar European affairs, it is worth speculating about whether his shift in thinking reflected increasing doubts about postwar Soviet intentions and a corresponding acceptance of the need for a long-term presence of American forces in Europe. In his classic study of Roosevelt's foreign policy, the historian Robert Dallek argues that the decision to accept the southern occupation zone did indeed reflect much more than a belated recognition of the logistical difficulties involved in switching zones: "What FDR left unsaid, however, was his conviction that America's presence in a southwestern zone bordering Austria, Czechoslovakia, and France would considerably increase the possibility of a long-term role for American ground forces in Europe."[73]

This argument suggests that Roosevelt was moving away from the idea of a rapid troop withdrawal from Europe, as well as from some of his basic concepts about the postwar world, but the evidence does not support Dallek's conclusion. First, if the president had reached such an important decision, it seems likely that he would have given Churchill some indication of his rationale for agreeing to switch zones. However, as

---

[71] The Acting Secretary of State to Winant, February 26, 1944, *FRUS*, 1944, vol. 1, 184.

[72] Ibid. See also *FRUS*, 1944, vol. 1, 223–24, 232.

[73] Robert Dallek, *Franklin D. Roosevelt and American Foreign Policy, 1932–45* (New York: Oxford University Press, 1979), 476. For a similar criticism of Dallek's thesis, see John Lamberton Harper, *American Visions of Europe* (Cambridge: Cambridge University Press, 1994), 102–4.

Fraser Harbutt points out, Churchill left Quebec more uncertain than ever about America's future presence on the continent. According to Harbutt, the period after the conference "stands out as the single period when [Churchill] accepted and worked toward a postwar order based on the likelihood of separate postwar European and American arenas."[74]

The best evidence of Churchill's underlying doubts about America's postwar commitment to Europe can be seen in his behavior at the Moscow Conference of October 1944, where he sought to reach solid "percentage" arrangements that would delimit Anglo-Soviet spheres in Europe. When Stalin brought up the need for a long-term occupation of Germany, Churchill was quick to respond that he "did not think that the Americans would stay very long."[75] Churchill's behavior cannot provide a guide to what Roosevelt was thinking, but it is hard to believe that a statesman so concerned with the question of an American withdrawal from the continent would not have recognized that FDR had changed his thoughts on this issue.

The more compelling evidence against Dallek's thesis is that after the Quebec Conference, Roosevelt continued to make the same arguments against policing France and withdrawing from Europe that he had made from the beginning of the dispute over occupation zones. In his correspondence with Churchill, FDR was still unwilling to make any promises about rearming France after the war and added, almost gratuitously since Churchill had not raised the subject, "You know, of course, that after Germany's collapse I must bring American troops home as rapidly as transportation problems will permit."[76] Not surprisingly, Churchill was very upset with Roosevelt's position and all that it implied for the future of Europe:

> If after Germany's collapse you "must bring the American troops home as rapidly as transportation problems will permit" and if the French are to have no equipped postwar army or time to make one, or to give it battle experience, how will it be possible to hold down Western Germany beyond the present Russian occupation line? We certainly could not undertake the task without your aid and that of the French. All would therefore rapidly disintegrate as it did the last time. I hope, however, that my fears are groundless.[77]

---

[74] Fraser J. Harbutt, *The Iron Curtain: Churchill, America, and the Origins of the Cold War* (New York: Oxford University Press, 1986), 74.

[75] Cited in the minutes of the Moscow Conference printed in Joseph Siracusa, "The Meaning of Tolstoy: Churchill, Stalin, and the Balkans," *Diplomatic History* 3 (fall 1979): 452.

[76] R-649, November 18, 1944, in Kimball, *Churchill and Roosevelt*, 3:394.

[77] C-825, November 19, 1944, in Kimball, *Churchill and Roosevelt*, 3:388–89.

President Roosevelt's determination to stay out of postwar European affairs went far beyond the question of occupation zones. In many respects, continental Europe was the regional exception to the "expansive" conception of American national security that evolved during the Second World War.[78] Although both Roosevelt and the JCS sought and acquired military bases in many remote spots around the globe throughout the war, bases were not sought in continental Europe.[79] The neglect of Europe in American postwar military planning was not an accident. Far too busy running the war to devote much time and effort to working out the details of America's postwar commitments, the JCS delegated the task of postwar base planning to the Joint Strategic Survey Committee (JSSC). The head of the JSSC was General Stanley D. Embick, a continentalist and Anglophobe. As Mark Stoler points out, Embick's basic view of postwar security "was based on the belief that a self-sufficient United States need not concern itself with Europe after the war, that its wartime strategy and postwar security did not need to be tied to British continental and imperial interests, and that there was no inherent conflict between wartime or postwar Soviet and American interests."[80]

Roosevelt's desire to stay out of postwar European affairs meshed well with Embick's base plans. In the meetings with the JCS on the way to Teheran, FDR approved Embick's postwar base recommendations with some slight modifications in favor of retaining bases in Iceland and the Azores. JCS document 570/2, which remained the basis for postwar military planning until the end of the war, reflected the president's regional conception of postwar security in which each of the Four Policemen would be primarily responsible for specific areas. The key assumption of JCS 570/2 was that "U.S. interests will be primarily the Western hemisphere, and the central Pacific to the Far East."[81] As Michael Sherry notes, the JCS plans "followed the traditional geographic orientation of American military policy toward hemisphere defense and the Pacific. In so doing they reflected FDR's outlook and the Joint Chiefs' own apparent

---

[78] Michael S. Sherry, *Preparing for the Next War* (New Haven: Yale University Press, 1977); and Melvyn Leffler, "The American Conception of National Security and the Beginnings of the Cold War, 1945–48," *American Historical Review* 89 (April 1984): 346–81.

[79] See the excellent dissertation by Elliot Vanveltner Converse, "United States Plans for a Postwar Overseas Military Base System" (Ph.D. diss., Princeton University, 1984); and Richard A. Best, *"Co-operation" With Like-Minded Peoples: British Influences on American Security Policy, 1945–49* (New York: Greenwood Press, 1986), 51–68.

[80] Stoler, "From Continentalism to Globalism," 320–21. For an excellent discussion of Embick and the Joint Chiefs of Staff, see Mark Stoler, *Allies and Adversaries: The Joint Chiefs of Staff, the Grand Alliance, and U.S. Strategy in World War II* (Chapel Hill: University of North Carolina Press, 2000).

[81] JCS 570/2, cited in Converse, "United States Plans for a Postwar Overseas Base System," 47.

lack of anxiety over possible conflict with Germany, the Soviet Union, or other European powers."[82]

The individual military branches developed their postwar plans in accordance with Roosevelt's desires. The Army Air Force (AAF), partly because it did not see how the Soviet Union could become a threat due to its lack of strategic airpower, did not have a long-term plan for Europe.[83] Interestingly, the AAF did plan on large deployments in Asia to guard against a resurgent Japan, but planned nothing comparable in Europe to guard against a renewed threat from Germany. The explanation for this apparent anomaly, as Elliot Vanveltner Converse points out, is that "President Roosevelt, in approving JCS 570/2, had, in effect, indicated to the military that Europe would be outside the American sphere."[84] The Navy, which had always looked to the Pacific more than the Atlantic, also had no difficulty accepting FDR's strategic guidance. As Vincent Davis notes, "The President's policy was quite congenial to the Navy Planners. They still had their eyes firmly focused to the west across the Pacific, ready to continue the neglect of Europe which characterized their thinking for fifty years before World War II."[85] Like the AAF, the Navy did not envision the Soviet Union as a postwar threat because of its weak naval forces. Even though Secretary of the Navy James Forrestal was in the forefront of those warning about a possible postwar Soviet threat, naval planning as late as April 1945 reflected a "continuing indifference to postwar Europe."[86]

The conflict with the British over occupation zones in Germany and the general direction of postwar military planning during the Second World War call into question some of the major themes of the historiography of postwar American foreign relations. Efforts to explain America's postwar military presence in Western Europe as a result of the "lessons" of the interwar period or as an obvious consequence of geopolitical realities seem compelling until one looks at how policymakers actually thought about

---

[82] Sherry, *Preparing for the Next War*, 45–46.

[83] Converse, "United States Plans for a Postwar Overseas Base System," 70. For the failure of the AAF to see the Soviet Union as a potential enemy because of its primitive air force, see Perry Smith, *The Air Force Plans for Peace* (Baltimore: Johns Hopkins Press, 1970), 51–53. See also John Lewis Gaddis, "The Insecurities of Victory: The United States and the Perception of Soviet Threat after World War II," in Gaddis, *The Long Peace: Inquiries into the History of the Cold War* (New York: Oxford University Press, 1989), 20–47.

[84] Converse, "United States Plans for a Postwar Overseas Base System," 72. As early as April 1943, FDR told William Hassett that after the war "the United States will see to the protection of the Americas, leaving the peace of Europe to Great Britain and Russia." See William D. Hassett, *Off the Record with F.D.R.* (New Brunswick: Rutgers University Press, 1958), 220.

[85] Vincent Davis, *Postwar Defense Policy and the U.S. Navy, 1943–46* (Chapel Hill: University of North Carolina Press, 1970), 79.

[86] Ibid., 114. For Forrestal's views during his time as Secretary of the Navy, see Townsend Hoopes and Douglas Brinkley, *Driven Patriot: The Life and Times of James Forrestal* (New York: Alfred A. Knopf, 1992), esp. 128–214.

these issues during the war. No one could or did argue with the geopolitical premise that America's basic national security interest after the war would be the prevention of any single power from dominating Eurasia. However, this specific goal did not lead Roosevelt to place any importance on keeping U.S. ground forces in Europe and it did not lead American military planners to argue for the construction of bases on the continent. It is commonplace to argue that the lessons of the interwar era and Pearl Harbor revolutionized the American conception of national security, yet what is truly remarkable about American military planning during the Second World War is how little those two events actually seem to have influenced either Roosevelt's views or those of military planners concerning postwar European security.

ROOSEVELT AND THE GERMAN QUESTION

Few issues absorbed the time and energy of State Department planners more than the postwar treatment of Germany. No less than six departmental committees were formed to handle the numerous questions related to this concern.[87] By 1943 the overwhelming consensus of State Department planners was that the central goal of American policy should be to integrate a disarmed but united Germany into the world economy.[88] The partition or dismemberment of Germany was rejected because of the belief that it would never be accepted by the German people and because it would disrupt the economic stability of Europe as a whole.[89] Very conscious of the lessons of the early interwar period, State Department planners believed that ultimately the postwar order would have to satisfy the basic needs and desires of the German people.

President Roosevelt's thinking about the German question ran in an entirely different direction than the State Department's. Where State

[87] See Harley Notter, *Postwar Foreign Policy Preparation, 1939–45* (Washington, D.C.: Department of State, 1950), 554–60.

[88] The best summary of State Department plans for postwar Germany is the paper "The Treatment of Germany," prepared by the Committee on Postwar Programs and published in *FRUS, 1943*, vol. 1, 53–72. See also Bruce Kuklick, *American Policy and the Division of Germany* (Ithaca: Cornell University Press, 1972); Paul Hammond, "Directives for the Occupation of Germany: The Washington Controversy," in *American Civil Military Decisions*, ed. Harold Stein (Montgomery: University of Alabama Press, 1963), 350–415; and Carolyn Eisenberg, *Drawing the Line: The American Decision to Divide Germany, 1944–49* (Cambridge: Cambridge University Press, 1996), 14–70.

[89] See the document "Germany: Partition," August 17, 1943, in Notter, *Postwar Foreign Policy Preparation*, 554–57. In a September 1943 letter and memo to FDR, Hull wrote that "imposed partition would be little short of disaster both for Germany and for us." See his "Comment on the Proposals Advanced by the Hon. Gerard Swope on the Treatment of Germany," box 16, John H. Backer Papers, Low Library, Columbia University. The Backer Papers are largely composed of archival documents related to Germany collected by the late historian.

Department planners were very concerned about designing a postwar order that could eventually be voluntarily accepted by the Germans after a period of occupation, FDR placed no importance on what the German people would or would not accept as a reasonable settlement after the war. Although the policy of "unconditional surrender" was largely designed to reassure the Soviet Union that neither the United States nor Great Britain would negotiate a compromise peace with the Nazis, it was also seen by Roosevelt as a way to avoid establishing any explicit or implicit criteria, such as Wilson's Fourteen Points, about how the Germans were to be treated by the allies after the war.[90]

What the policy of unconditional surrender specifically implied for the treatment of postwar Germany was not something Roosevelt wanted to be openly discussed or clarified. Whenever he was asked for clarification of what the doctrine meant in specific terms, FDR always responded with a Civil War analogy: Lee was made to surrender to Grant unconditionally, but he was then treated fairly and his men were allowed to keep their horses. In other words, after they surrendered, the German people would receive fair treatment from the Allies.[91] However, FDR made a critical distinction between the German people and the German nation. For example, in April 1944 he rejected a JCS proposal to modify the unconditional surrender policy because it suggested that the unity of Germany would be preserved after the war. The president was certainly unwilling to reassure the Germans on this point. As he told Leahy, "Please note that I am *not* willing at this time to say that we do not intend to destroy the German nation."[92]

All of Roosevelt's thinking suggests that he did indeed intend to destroy the German nation by breaking up the unity established by Bismarck in the nineteenth century. In his conversations with Eden in May 1943, FDR indicated that he hoped that the partition of Germany would occur as a result of a spontaneous separatist movement within the country after the war. But if such a movement did not occur, FDR and

[90] Unconditional surrender remains one of FDR's more controversial policies. For a critical view, see Anne Armstrong, *Unconditional Surrender* (New Brunswick: Rutgers University Press, 1961). A more positive assessment can be found in John L. Chase, "Unconditional Surrender Reconsidered," *Political Science Quarterly* 80 (June 1955): 258–79; and A. E. Campbell, "Franklin Roosevelt and Unconditional Surrender," in *Diplomacy and Intelligence during the Second World War*, ed. Richard Langhorne (Cambridge: Cambridge University Press, 1985), 219–41.

[91] As Steven Casey points out, FDR did make some efforts to reassure the German people that he would only hold Nazi leaders responsible for the war. See Steven Casey, "Franklin D. Roosevelt, Ernest 'Putzi' Hanfstaengl and the 'S-Project', June 1942–June 1944," *Journal of Contemporary History* 35 (July 2000): 339–59.

[92] Memorandum by FDR to the JCS, April 1, 1944, *FRUS*, 1944, vol. 1, 502. For the military's opposition to unconditional surrender, largely based on the belief that it would prolong the war, see Brian Villa, "The U.S. Army, Unconditional Surrender, and the Potsdam Proclamation," *Journal of American History* 63 (June 1976): 66–92.

Eden both agreed that "under any circumstances, Germany must be divided into several states, one of which must, over all circumstances, be Prussia."[93] Sumner Welles, one of the few State Department officials who favored the partition of Germany, reflected FDR's thoughts on the matter when he told Eden on the following day that a unified Germany was to be avoided under all circumstances. According to Welles, "we had learned by experience that the urge of militaristic pan-Germanism was so potent a force as to make any united Germany a very dangerous factor in the world whether it was ostensibly governed by a communist regime, or by a socialist or by a liberal democratic."[94]

Roosevelt was willing to concede that partition might not be a viable solution, but he thought that State Department arguments against partition were exaggerated.[95] The lack of any meeting of the minds between FDR and Hull over the postwar treatment of Germany was dramatically revealed by their opposing stances in meetings with Soviet officials in late 1943. At the Moscow Conference of October 1943, Hull conveyed the impression to the Soviets that the U.S. government had not yet reached any consensus on the partition of Germany, but FDR conveyed exactly the opposite impression the following month by presenting at Teheran a proposal for partitioning the Reich into five separate states, with the Ruhr and the Saar being placed under international control. If nothing else, the Teheran Conference undoubtedly increased Roosevelt's support for the partition of Germany because Stalin indicated that he too was in agreement with the policy.[96]

Neither the president nor the State Department were very concerned about resolving their differences over the postwar treatment of Germany until August 1944 when Treasury Secretary Henry Morgenthau Jr. forced the issue to the surface. Ironically, given the notoriety his plans would later achieve, there is little indication that Morgenthau paid much interest to the German question before this point.[97] Angry and disappointed by a State Department document that he read during a flight to London, Morgenthau pursued the question of postwar planning for Germany with both American and British officials during his stay. Conversations with John Winant and Phillip Mosely, the key American members of the EAC, confirmed his suspicion that State Department planning for Germany was

[93] Memorandum by Hopkins, March 15, 1943, *FRUS*, 1943, vol. 3, 16.

[94] Memorandum of Conversation by Welles, March 16, 1943, *FRUS*, 1943, vol. 1, 21.

[95] Memorandum of Conversation with FDR, October 5, 1943, *FRUS*, 1943, vol. 1, 542.

[96] For the contrast between the views of FDR and Hull regarding Germany, see "Summary of the Proceedings of the Seventh Session of the Tripartite Conference," October 25, 1943, *FRUS*, 1943, vol. 1, 629–32; and "Tripartite Political Meeting," December 1, 1943; and Bohlen Minutes, 553–555, *FRUS*, 1943, *Conferences at Cairo and Teheran*, 596–604. For an excellent account of the diplomacy of Moscow and Teheran, see Keith Sainsbury, *The Turning Point* (New York: Oxford University Press, 1985).

[97] John Morton Blum, *Roosevelt and Morgenthau* (Boston: Houghton Mifflin, 1970), 566–67.

proceeding on the assumption of unity rather than partition, as well as on the premise that Germany would be reintegrated into the world economy.[98] Eden also played a major role in stoking Morgenthau's anger by showing him the minutes of the Teheran Conference, where the Big Three clearly leaned in the direction of dismemberment.

Morgenthau's ignorance of the policy process in Washington (not to mention the well-established views of the State Department on the German question) is obvious because he went directly to Hull to protest what he saw as Winant's blatant disavowal of the plans discussed by the Big Three at Teheran. Hull was undoubtedly telling the truth when he stated that he had not been permitted to look at the minutes of the meetings at Teheran, but he was certainly misleading in not making it clear to Morgenthau that Winant was following State Department preferences established long before Teheran.[99] Roosevelt's initial reaction to Morgenthau's report of his trip to England was rather noncommittal. Always dismissive of the EAC, he was not very concerned about the fact that they were not developing plans for Germany in accordance with Teheran. According to Morgenthau, his reaction was "Give me thirty minutes with Churchill and I can correct this."[100] Morgenthau had a greater impact on the president when he showed him excerpts from the army's plans for military government in Germany. FDR immediately demanded the recall of the handbook because of what he saw as its "soft" treatment of Germany:

> It gives me the impression that Germany is to be restored just as much as the Netherlands or Belgium, and the people of Germany brought back as quickly as possible to their pre-war estate. . . . It is of the utmost importance that every person in Germany should realize that this time Germany is a defeated nation. . . . Too many people here and in England hold to the view that the German people as a whole are not responsible for what has taken place—that only a few Nazi leaders are responsible. . . . The German people as a whole must have it driven home to them that the whole nation has been engaged in a lawless conspiracy against the decencies of modern civilization.[101]

Roosevelt's correspondence around this time shows that Morgenthau had made an impression on him by raising concerns that the State Department and the army were contemplating a liberal peace for Germany. On August 21, 1944, he wrote to Senator Kenneth McKellar: "It is amaz-

---

[98] John Chase, "The Development of the Morgenthau Plan through the Quebec Conference," *Journal of Politics* 16 (1954): 324–59; Blum, *Roosevelt and Morgenthau,* 566–70.
[99] Morgenthau Diary, August 18, 1944, Book 763 (microfilm), FDRL.
[100] Morgenthau Diary, August 19, 1944, Book 763, FDRL.
[101] FDR cited in Dallek, *FDR and American Foreign Policy,* 472–73.

ing how many people are beginning to get soft in the future terms of the Germans and Japs. I fear it is going to be real trouble to us next year or the year after."[102] A few days later he wrote to Queen Wilhemina of the Netherlands that there were two schools of thought in regard to Germany, an altruistic and a tough school: "Most decidedly I belong to the latter school, for though I am not blood-thirsty, I want the Germans to know that this time at least they have definitely lost the war."[103]

The Morgenthau Plan has found few defenders and many critics, but it is not too difficult to provide a rational explanation for the emphasis Morgenthau placed on transforming Germany away from an economy based on heavy industry toward one based on agriculture.[104] Since war potential is largely a function of economic capability, Morgenthau sought to eliminate Germany's economic ability to wage or threaten war in the future. His plan, understandable in light of the experience of the interwar period, started from the premise that international controls could easily erode over time and that a future Germany would then be able to reverse the verdict of the war. Through a combination of partition and deindustrialization, Morgenthau was seeking additional insurance against the possible breakdown of international controls over Germany.

Morgenthau mistakenly thought that the proponents of a "soft" peace for Germany were largely inspired by the idea of turning her into a bulwark of containment against the Soviet Union. His own plan, of course, was also based on rather specific assumptions about the need to reduce German power in order to preserve good relations with the Soviets after the war. One of the more interesting papers in the Morgenthau collection at Hyde Park is a paper prepared by one of Morgenthau's associates, Arthur Goodhart. Entitled "The Situation in Europe in Twenty Five Years," Goodhart concluded that Germany might once again have a powerful position in Europe by 1970 unless it were partitioned and steps were taken to eliminate its war potential. Attempting to preserve German power as a hedge against a possible Russian threat to Europe was viewed as a policy that would lead to the collapse of the alliance:

> The surest way of making the U.S.S.R. militant would be by threatening her with a strong Germany. It was fear of a strong Germany which probably caused Stalin to enter into the 1939 pact, and fear of a strong Germany in 1970 might have a similar result. It is therefore

---

[102] FDR to Senator Kenneth McKellar, August 21, 1944, Personal File 3715, FDRL.

[103] FDR to Queen Wilhemina, August 26, 1944, in *F.D.R. His Personal Letters, 1928–45*, ed. Elliott Roosevelt (New York: Duell, Sloan, and Pearce, 1947), 2:1535.

[104] See Warren Kimball, *Swords or Ploughshares: The Morgenthau Plan for Defeated Nazi Germany* (Philadelphia: J. B. Lippincott Company, 1976); John Snell, *Wartime Origins of the East-West Dilemma over Germany* (New Orleans: Hauser Printing, 1959), 64–93; and Eisenberg, *Drawing the Line*, 14–70.

my belief that the U.S.S.R will not be a menace either to the U.S.A., Great Britain, or France unless she is driven to such a course by fear of Germany.[105]

Nevertheless, rational assumptions and concerns about alienating the Soviet Union cannot obscure the elements of irrationality and vengeance underlying the Morgenthau Plan. The foundation of the plan was the belief that there had to be a "complete shutdown of the Ruhr." How the people of these areas were supposed to survive was of no concern to Morgenthau: in his view they could be either evacuated en masse or be kept alive by rations from army soup kitchens. Although even his associates at the Treasury Department originally protested that the whole idea of flooding the Ruhr mines and turning the area over to agriculture was impractical and inhumane, Morgenthau never moderated his views on the subject.[106] None of the more moderate suggestions found their way into Morgenthau's "Program to Prevent Germany from Starting a World War III," which FDR would later endorse at the Quebec Conference.

Morgenthau's agitation resulted in the formation of a Cabinet Committee on Germany composed of Hull, Stimson, Morgenthau, and Hopkins. The main antagonists were Morgenthau and Stimson, with Hull and Hopkins providing tacit support for Morgenthau's plan simply by not speaking out against it. Roosevelt was largely silent during the meetings, but he declared himself in favor of making Germany a primarily agricultural country and agreed with Morgenthau's central thesis that it was a fallacy that Europe needed a strong, industrial Germany.[107] In a series of eloquent letters sent to FDR before the Quebec Conference, Stimson sought to reverse the growing trend in favor of the Morgenthau Plan, calling it a "crime against civilization itself" and "an open confession of the bankruptcy of hope."[108] Although the president would later tell Stimson that he had no idea how he could have put his initials on the Morgenthau Plan, there is really no mystery at all in accounting for his actions. Roosevelt signed on to the plan because it embodied his own predisposition to treat postwar Germany harshly and it was very compatible with a policy of reassurance toward the Soviet Union. Finally, although the connection is rarely noted, FDR was undoubtedly attracted to the last sen-

[105] "The Situation in Europe in Twenty-Five Years," Morgenthau Diary, September 23, 1944, Book 774 (microfilm), 94–102, FDRL.

[106] For White's objections to parts of the plan, see Morgenthau Diary, September 4, 1944, Book 768, FDRL.

[107] These debates can be followed in *FRUS, 1944, The Conference at Quebec*, 77–144.

[108] Henry Stimson and McGeorge Bundy, *On Active Service in Peace and War* (New York: Harper & Brothers, 1947), 577–78; and Stimson to FDR, September 5, 1944, *FRUS, 1944, Conference at Quebec*, 98–100.

tence of the Morgenthau Plan: "Under this program United States troops could be withdrawn within a relatively short time."[109] Indeed, given all of the elements of the Treasury Department proposals that meshed with his own views about the future of Europe, the real puzzle would have been if Roosevelt had shown no interest in the Morgenthau Plan.

Morgenthau's victory over Stimson and the State Department, however, did not last very long. The substance of the plan was quickly leaked to the press by its opponents and the public reaction to it was hostile. Less than six weeks away from the presidential election, Roosevelt clearly did not want controversy over postwar plans for Germany.[110] Moreover, despite Churchill's endorsement of the plan at Quebec, the War Cabinet immediately withdrew its support from any postwar treatment of Germany along the lines specified in Morgenthau's plan. Even the Soviets, correctly recognizing that Morgenthau's plan would make it impossible to collect large reparations from current production, made it known to State Department officials that "Mr. Morgenthau's type of thinking was not acceptable to the Soviet government."[111]

Roosevelt never again gave his support to any proposals for Germany resembling the Morgenthau Plan. After the Quebec fiasco he consistently gave his tacit approval to the postwar plans for Germany developed by the State Department. However, the plans he supported were always ambiguous combinations of softness and toughness open to vastly different interpretations. It was exactly this kind of ambiguity that FDR now wanted. On one plan presented to him in November 1944, an observer noted, "what he liked about it particularly was that it did not dot all the i's and cross all the t's. There are many questions that must be left for future determination, since we have no way of knowing what we shall find in Germany."[112] While the State Department aimed at reintegrating Germany into the world economy, Roosevelt thought it might be better to ban the country from exporting goods to the rest of the world.[113] Most important, ignoring all of the State Department arguments against partition, the president would continue to voice his support for the partition of Germany at Yalta.

[109] Henry Morgenthau Jr., *Germany Is Our Problem* (New York: Harper & Brothers, 1945), 4.

[110] Both Kimball and Dallek believe that domestic politics largely accounts for FDR's quick reversal on the Morgenthau Plan. See Kimball, *Swords or Ploughshares*, 41–44; and Dallek, *The American Style of Foreign Policy* (New York: Alfred A. Knopf, 1986), 146–47.

[111] Memorandum of Conversation by Leo Paslovsky with A. A. Sobolev, September 28, 1944, *Records of the Office of European Affairs*, reel 15.

[112] Memorandum by Paslovsky, November 15, 1944, *FRUS, 1945, The Conferences at Malta and Yalta*, 170.

[113] FDR to Hull, December 4, 1944, *FRUS, 1945, The Conferences at Malta and Yalta*, 174.

YALTA, POLAND, AND THE ORIGINS OF THE COLD WAR

Abstract planning for the postwar world took a backseat to diplomacy at the Yalta Conference of February 1945. Despite the later notoriety attributed to the diplomacy of Yalta, Roosevelt and the majority of officials who accompanied him to Yalta left the meeting very optimistic about the future of the Grand Alliance. According to Harry Hopkins, "The Russians had proved that they could be reasonable and farseeing and there wasn't any doubt in the minds of the President or any of us that we could live with them peacefully for as far into the future as any of us could imagine."[114] Whatever private doubts Roosevelt may have had about the future of the Grand Alliance after Yalta, he kept them to himself when he delivered what turned out to be his final address to Congress on March 1, 1945. The Yalta agreements, the president told the American public, "ought to spell the end of the system of unilateral action, the exclusive alliances, the spheres of influence, the balances of power, and all the other expedients which have been tried for centuries—and have always failed."[115]

Conflict over the terms of the Yalta settlement on Poland, however, quickly eroded much of the optimism that had existed within the American delegation at the end of the Yalta Conference.[116] On April 23, less than two weeks after Roosevelt's death, President Truman expressed American disapproval of Soviet conduct in Poland by delivering a harsh reprimand to Foreign Minister Molotov. Declaring that Soviet-American relations could not be conducted on the basis of a "one way street," Truman warned the Soviet foreign minister that strict adherence to the Yalta agreements provided the only possible foundation for postwar cooperation.[117] Critics of FDR's wartime diplomacy, both within and out-

[114] Cited in Robert E. Sherwood, *Roosevelt and Hopkins* (New York: Harper & Brothers, 1948), 870. See also Edward R. Stettinius Jr., *Roosevelt and the Russians: The Yalta Conference* (Garden City, N.Y.: Doubleday, 1949); and Charles Bohlen, *Witness to History* (New York: W. W. Norton, 1973), 200–1. Only Admiral Leahy claims to have left the conference with some reservations about the future consequences of Yalta. See William D. Leahy, *I Was There* (New York: Whittlesey House, 1950), 323.

[115] Address to Congress Reporting on the Yalta Conference, March 1, 1945, in *The Public Papers and Addresses of Franklin D. Roosevelt* (New York: Harper & Brothers, 1950), 13:586. Journalist Edgar Snow, who met with the president two days after the speech, recalls that FDR rejected all of his arguments and doubts about the Soviet Union's willingness to implement the Yalta agreements. See Edgar Snow, "Fragments from FDR: Part II," *Monthly Review* 8 (March 1957): 402.

[116] See *FRUS*, 1945, vol. 5, 110–361; Davis, *The Cold War Begins*, 202–41; and Geir Lundestad, *The American Non-Policy towards Eastern Europe, 1943–47* (New York: Humanities Press, 1975), 197–202.

[117] The exchange between Truman and Molotov can be found in *FRUS*, 1945, vol. 5, 256–58. Truman's account, which exaggerates the toughness of his remarks, can be found in Harry S. Truman, *Year of Decisions* (Garden City, N.Y.: Doubleday & Company, 1955), 80–82. See also Wilson Miscamble, "Anthony Eden and the Truman-Molotov Conversations, April 1945," *Diplomatic History* 2 (spring 1978): 172–85; and Melvyn Leffler, "Adherence to

side of the administration, were greatly encouraged by Truman's decision to force the issue of Soviet compliance with the terms of Yalta. After hearing about the exchange from Secretary of State Edward Stettinius, Senator Arthur Vandenberg Jr. wrote in his diary, "This is the best news in months. FDR's appeasement of Russia is over."[118]

Some historians accept Vandenberg's belief that Truman deliberately set out in his meeting with Molotov to reverse the direction of Roosevelt's wartime diplomacy.[119] Others believe that Truman was an unwitting victim of FDR's use of Wilsonian rhetoric, which obscured the true nature of his predecessor's realpolitik diplomacy toward the Soviet Union in Eastern Europe. For example, Daniel Yergin argues that although FDR was a "renegade Wilsonian" willing to compromise his principles in the interests of great power cooperation, Truman's approach toward Poland reflected an unfortunate shift toward Wilsonianism in its purest form: "The American leaders no longer simply found dictatorship abhorrent; they felt *responsible* for what happened all over the world. They were gripped again by messianic liberalism, the powerful urge to reform the world that has been called Wilsonianism."[120] Intentionally or not, both perspectives suggest that Truman's retreat from Roosevelt's recognition of a Soviet sphere of influence in Poland plays a crucial role in accounting for the rapid transition from the Second World War to the Cold War.

Assessing the meaning and significance of the Truman-Molotov meeting, as well as the overall importance of the transition from Roosevelt to Truman, is important because conflict over Poland is traditionally considered to be the issue which began the unraveling of the Grand Alliance.[121] There are two relevant questions which must be answered before reaching any firm conclusions about the Truman-Molotov exchange. First, was Truman actually departing from his predecessor's course by placing too much importance on the Polish question as a "test-case" and "symbol" of postwar U.S.–Soviet relations? Second, how would Roosevelt likely have reacted in the event of continued Soviet intransigence over Poland? Examining both of these questions suggests that the Truman-Molotov exchange has been greatly exaggerated by scholars seeking to demonstrate

---

Agreements: Yalta and the Experiences of the Early Cold War," *International Security* 11 (summer 1986): 88–123.

[118] Arthur H. Vandenberg Jr., *The Private Papers of Senator Vandenberg* (Boston: Houghton Mifflin, 1952), 176.

[119] Diane Shaver Clemens, "Averell Harriman, John Deane, the Joint Chiefs of Staff, and the 'Reversal of Cooperation' with the Soviet Union in April 1945," *International History Review* 14 (May 1992): 221–40; and Gar Alperovitz, *Atomic Diplomacy: Hiroshima and Potsdam*, rev. ed. (New York: Penguin Books, 1985), 67–81.

[120] Daniel Yergin, *Shattered Peace: The Origins of the Cold War and the National Security State* (Boston, Mass.: Houghton Mifflin, 1977), 84.

[121] See Louis Halle, *The Cold War as History* (New York: Harper & Row, 1967), 55–65; and Winston Churchill, *Triumph and Tragedy* (Boston: Houghton Mifflin Company, [1953] 1981), 320.

the importance of the transition from Roosevelt to Truman in accounting for the onset of the Cold War.

To be sure, it is fairly safe to conclude that FDR would not have administered a crude warning to Molotov in the manner Truman delivered it at the White House. Landing a "straight one-two to the jaw" was simply not a part of Roosevelt's diplomatic repertoire in handling problems with the Soviet Union. Even Averell Harriman, who at the time was advocating the adoption of a harder line toward the Soviet Union, regretted the blunt way in which Truman attempted to get his message across to Molotov. In his memoirs, Harriman would later recall: "I did regret that Truman went at it so hard because his behavior gave Molotov an excuse to tell Stalin that the Roosevelt policy was being abandoned. I regretted that Truman gave him the opportunity. I think it was a mistake, though not a decisive mistake."[122]

However, leaving aside considerations of style and timing, Truman's unwillingness to accept the Soviet position on Poland was very consistent with the substance of Roosevelt's position after Yalta. Indeed, contrary to the popular consensus that Truman was tougher on the Polish question, a persuasive argument can be made that FDR would have been more likely to turn the dispute into a serious "test-case" of postwar U.S.–Soviet relations. Unlike Truman, who had no knowledge of the complex history of allied diplomacy over the Polish question, Roosevelt was far more sensitive to the implications of Soviet noncompliance with the Yalta accords. After years of reassuring Stalin that they acknowledged his legitimate interests in Poland, both FDR and Churchill wanted some indication that the Soviet leader was eventually going to permit a free and sovereign Poland, subject to the limitation that any future government also had to be "friendly" to the Soviet Union. The extent to which Poland was to be free and sovereign can be debated, but Roosevelt was clearly unwilling to accept an outcome totally imposed by Stalin. For FDR, Poland may not have mattered very much in and of itself, but it mattered as a test of Stalin's intentions and of his willingness to show some restraint in an area in which both the United States and Great Britain had signaled that they were unwilling to accept a unilateral settlement.

Roosevelt's and Churchill's real interest in the Polish question has been partially obscured by the complexities of wartime diplomacy and the often brutal way that both leaders dealt with the London Poles before Yalta.[123] Believing that Stalin's primary concern was to establish the

---

[122] Harriman and Abel, *Special Envoy to Churchill and Stalin*, 454.

[123] In addition to the *FRUS* series, see the extensive collection of documents published by the General Sikorski Institute, *Documents on Polish-Soviet Relations, 1939–45* (London: W. H. Heinemann, 1967); and Antony Polonsky, ed., *The Great Powers and the Polish Question, 1941–45* (London: Orbis Books, 1976). See also Piotr S. Wandycz, *The United States and Poland* (Cambridge, Mass.: Harvard University Press, 1980), 236–306.

Curzon Line as the future boundary between Poland and the Soviet Union, both statesmen urged the London Poles to accept the Soviet stance before their already weak bargaining position deteriorated even further. As early as January 1944, Churchill warned Polish Premier Stanislaw Mikolajczyk that the consequence of failing to accept the Curzon Line might ultimately be the total loss of Poland's independence.[124] The unwillingness or the inability of Mikolajczyk to convince the majority of the London Poles to agree on the Curzon Line, with corresponding territorial compensation for Poland in the west, had exactly the results Churchill and Roosevelt feared. Stalin's commitment to the Lublin Poles steadily increased over time and, despite pleas from both Churchill and FDR to refrain from doing so, the Soviet Union recognized the Lublin group as the provisional government of Poland at the end of 1944.

It is understandable that many scholars have assessed Roosevelt's efforts on behalf of the London Poles at Yalta through the prism of his earlier behavior, which was indeed overwhelmingly sympathetic to the aims of the Soviet Union. However, transferring his pre-Yalta lack of support over Poland's border claims to the question of the composition and nature of the postwar government overlooks the vast difference between the two issues. In contrast to many other Eastern European questions, Anglo-American support for the Curzon Line was not founded solely on a recognition that the Soviets "had the power" to do as they pleased. During his meetings with Stalin in October 1944, Churchill told the Soviet leader that if he were faced with any domestic opposition to accepting the Curzon Line, he would "say it was right, fair and necessary for the safety and future of Russia. If some General Sosnowski objected it would not matter because Britain and the United States thought it right and fair."[125] Churchill stated exactly the same views to the London Poles throughout 1944.[126] Although Roosevelt hoped that the Soviets might make a concession or two in favor of Poland, he also agreed with the basic fairness and legitimacy of the proposed border settlement.[127]

[124] See especially documents 83, 96, and 257 in *Documents on Polish-Soviet Relations*, 2:144–49, 165–71, and 450–57. Churchill always maintained that the whole problem posed by the Lublin Poles could have been averted by early concessions over the Curzon Line. See document no. 318, February 27, 1945, in *Documents on Polish-Soviet Relations*, 2:535.

[125] See the transcript of the Moscow meetings published in Siracusa, "The Meaning of Tolstoy: Churchill, Stalin, and the Balkans, October 1944," 445. Churchill continued to support Soviet territorial claims at Yalta: "I have always considered that after all Russia has suffered in fighting Germany and after all her efforts in liberating Poland her claim is one founded not on force but on right." See, Matthews Minutes, *FRUS, 1945, Conferences at Malta and Yalta,* 678.

[126] For Churchill's efforts to put pressure on the London Poles, see Sir Llewellyn Woodward, *British Policy in the Second World War* (London: Her Majesty's Stationery Office, 1971), 3:161–68.

[127] FDR thought that the territory Poland was to receive in the west more than made up for the concessions in the east: "Now East Prussia is bigger than the disputed area in the Ukraine and has a coastline on the Baltic of course. It's much richer territory than the Polish

Stalin's parallel efforts to justify the legitimacy of the Lublin group as the sole government of Poland, however, were consistently rejected by both Roosevelt and Churchill. Shortly before the Yalta Conference, FDR informed Stalin that America would not recognize the Lublin group because of the lack of "any evidence either arising from the manner of its creation or from subsequent developments to justify the conclusion that the Lublin Committee as at present constituted represents the people of Poland."[128] The American president's behavior at Yalta suggests that he continued to hold this view. During his private meeting with Stalin, Roosevelt did not take the opportunity, as he did at Teheran and in other previous meetings with Soviet diplomats, to indicate to Stalin that his "official" position in support of a sovereign and independent Poland did not reflect his private views. FDR said that free elections were the "crux" of the matter and he made it clear that he did not view such elections as merely a way to satisfy American public opinion. He told Stalin: "I want this election in Poland to be beyond question. It should be like Caesar's wife. I did not know her but they said she was pure."[129] To be sure, Roosevelt sought to gloss over the difficulties caused by the Soviet Union's evident determination to maintain the Lublin Poles in power. However, far too much emphasis has been placed on his willingness to substitute the vague Declaration on Liberated Europe for the creation of a European High Commission, or his statement that it was only a question of "wording" that separated the Western powers from the Soviet Union on the Polish question. In the final analysis, the fact remained that only Stalin could grant or withhold a free and sovereign Poland; precision in the wording of agreements and the establishment of enforcement mechanisms would be worthless if Stalin was intent on exercising exclusive control over Poland. Roosevelt's purpose at Yalta was undoubtedly to demonstrate to Stalin that it was in the Soviet Union's larger interest to exercise self-restraint over Poland. In all likelihood, FDR left Yalta unsure of how far Stalin would attempt to stretch the accords on Poland, and Stalin left Yalta unsure about how far he could stretch the accords without destroying the alliance. Although he had numerous opportunities to retreat from the Anglo-American position on the need for a more fundamental reorganization of the Polish provisional government, FDR steadfastly re-

---

Ukraine. . . . So if what Stalin wants is to get these noblemen's estates and give the Poles East Prussia in exchange there shouldn't be any objection to that, should there?" Cited in Snow, "Fragments from FDR: Part II," 400–1. For Stalin's views on Poland's postwar borders, see R. C. Raack, "Stalin Fixes the Oder-Neisse Line," *Journal of Contemporary History* 25 (1990): 467–88.

[128] Roosevelt to Stalin, December 30, 1944, *FRUS, 1945, Conferences at Malta and Yalta,* 224.

[129] Sixth Plenary Meeting, February 9, 1945, *FRUS, 1945, Conferences at Malta and Yalta,* 848, 854.

fused to accept what he called a "thinly disguised continuance" of the Lublin government.[130]

At the time of his death on April 12, 1945, FDR was probably uncertain about the future of Poland and the larger question of whether his "great gamble" on the Soviet Union would ultimately succeed or fail. What settlement he would have accepted over Poland, or how he would have dealt with the Soviets, cannot be answered with any definitiveness. After the arrival of the Cold War, scholars on both the Right and Left seized on isolated statements or cables sent during his final weeks to demonstrate either that he was an early cold warrior or that his faith in a postwar U.S.–Soviet partnership remained as strong as ever. Neither argument should be taken very seriously. His final cable to Churchill perfectly captures both his own uncertainty about the future course of American policy and the ambiguous legacy he left to his successors: "I would minimize the general Soviet problem as much as possible, because these problems, in one form or another, seem to arise every day, and most of them straighten out, as in the case of the Berne meeting. We must be firm, however, and our course thus far is correct."[131]

TRUMAN TAKES COMMAND

Determining whether American policy should continue to minimize the Soviet problem to the extent possible or continue the firm stance over Poland would have been a formidable challenge for an experienced and knowledgeable statesman. Unfortunately, Truman possessed neither experience in foreign affairs nor knowledge about the hidden assumptions and objectives of Roosevelt's wartime diplomacy.[132] During his brief tenure as vice-president, Truman was uninvolved in any high-level discussions of foreign affairs and his personal relationship with FDR was virtually nonexistent. As he later described the experience to his daughter, "I was at cabinet meetings and saw Roosevelt once or twice in those months. But he never did talk to me confidentially about the war, or about foreign

---

[130] See FDR to Stalin, April 1, 1945, *FRUS, 1945*, vol. 5, 195. At the same time, however, FDR was still satisfied with the basic agreement over Poland. In a March 1945 letter to Thomas Lamont, the president criticized the American people for thinking they have the "right to lay down the law in idealistic but not always workable terms," and for "living in the age of innocence" when it came to international affairs. See FDR to Thomas Lamont, March 29, 1945, Personal File 70, FDRL.

[131] Cited in Winston Churchill, *Triumph and Tragedy*, 398. For a good discussion of the numerous problems involved in drawing solid inferences from all of FDR's final cables, see Kimball, *The Juggler*, 179–80.

[132] For a good discussion of Truman's views about world politics prior to April 1945, see Wilson Miscamble, "The Evolution of an Internationalist: Harry S. Truman and American Foreign Policy," *Australian Journal of Politics and History* 23 (August 1977): 268–83; and Larson, *Origins of Containment*, 126–44.

affairs, or what he had in mind for the peace after the war."[133] Truman
pledged himself to the achievement of Roosevelt's postwar goals, but he
seems to have been aware from the start that his predecessor's diplomacy
was more complicated than he and the American public had been led to
believe. His suspicions can be seen in the way he immediately latched
onto the belief that James F. Byrnes would make an ideal secretary of state
because he was the keeper of the secrets of Yalta.[134] Truman's relationship
with Joseph E. Davies, the former U.S. ambassador to the Soviet Union,
can also be attributed to his search for advisers who knew the inside story
of FDR's wartime diplomacy. The irony, of course, is that neither Byrnes
nor Davies knew much more than Truman about the complexities of
Roosevelt's diplomacy.

On the eve of the opening meeting of the United Nations, the last thing
Truman wanted was an open confrontation with the Soviet Union over
Poland. It is for this reason that his first cable to Churchill on the subject
adhered to the same tactical line that Roosevelt had taken during his final
weeks. Truman did not retreat from the Anglo-American position on
Poland, but he wanted Churchill to refrain from making a speech before
the House of Commons blaming the Soviet Union for the deadlock before
another private effort was made to resolve the issue directly with Stalin.
Like his predecessor, Truman wanted to avoid an open confrontation because of (1) his belief that publicity would not be in the best interest of the
Poles and (2) the negative effects confrontation would have on the
prospects for postwar collaboration with the Soviet Union.[135]

Molotov's visit to Washington prior to the UN meeting provided the
last opportunity for private diplomacy over Poland, but the gap between
the two sides was simply too great for a settlement. Stalin's decision to
sign a treaty of friendship with the Lublin Poles during Molotov's visit
sent a strong message that the Soviet Union was not going to back down
in order to reach a settlement, a message that Molotov quickly confirmed
during extensive meetings with Stettinius and Eden.[136] After consulting
with Averell Harriman and other top advisors, Truman also decided to
stand firm on Poland. Although warning that the West was faced with a
"barbarian invasion of Europe," Harriman told Truman that he was not

---

[133] Margaret Truman, *Harry S. Truman* (New York: William Morrow & Company, 1973),
358.

[134] Truman told a critic of his choice of Byrnes for Secretary of State that "I'm doing it . . .
because I think it's the only way I can be sure of knowing what went on at Yalta." Cited in
Robert Messer, *The End of an Alliance: James F. Byrnes, Roosevelt, Truman, and the Origins of the
Cold War* (Chapel Hill: University of North Carolina Press, 1982), 70. For further discussion
of the complexities of the Truman-Byrnes partnership, see the most recent biography of
Byrnes by David Robertson, *Sly and Able: A Political Biography of James F. Byrnes* (New York:
W. W. Norton, 1994).

[135] Truman to Churchill, April 13, 1945, *FRUS*, 1945, vol. 5, 211–12.

[136] The minutes of the meetings are printed in *FRUS*, 1945, vol. 5, 237–51.

pessimistic about arriving at workable arrangements with the Soviet Union because the United States would have considerable leverage to influence its behavior after the war. Harriman's confidence in a "firm but friendly" strategy toward the Soviet Union was undoubtedly attractive to Truman because it implied that he did not have to choose between standing firm over Poland and potentially breaking up the Grand Alliance. Washington could not expect to get 100 percent of its wishes, but Truman told Harriman that the Soviets needed the United States more than the United States needed the Soviet Union and that he expected to get 85 percent of what he wanted.[137]

Truman's faith in a tough strategy toward the Soviet Union was very superficial, however, and he retreated from it when it failed to live up to his expectations. First, Stalin quickly gave the new president a harsh lesson in percentages by failing to retreat an inch from his position on Poland. The subsequent turn to public diplomacy at the UN meeting, where Stettinius refused to permit the seating of the Lublin Poles, proved to be no more successful than private diplomacy in breaking the impasse. Second, Truman's initial attempt at laying the groundwork for the application of Harriman's economic leverage strategy—revising the terms of the Lend-Lease agreements—turned into a fiasco when overzealous officials interpreted it far more strictly than intended. The uproar over the cut-off of Lend-Lease aid, combined with the overall deterioration in U.S.–Soviet relations, led Truman to abruptly reverse course after his first month in office. Overriding opposition from Byrnes and other State Department advisors, Truman dispatched Harry Hopkins to Moscow and Davies to London in order to stem the further dissolution of the Grand Alliance. Hopkins and Davies, the two advisors most closely associated with Roosevelt's cooperative approach, both conveyed the message that Truman remained committed to the policies of his predecessor.[138]

The decision to send Hopkins to Moscow was an explicit return to the style of Rooseveltian diplomacy. Indeed, Soviet expert Charles Bohlen recommended the idea to Harriman after concluding that if Roosevelt were still alive he would have sent Hopkins to meet with Stalin.[139] Truman, who had already considered sending Davies as his personal envoy to Stalin, agreed to send Hopkins instead. Although Hopkins did not have detailed negotiating instructions, Truman wrote in his diary that

[137] Ibid., 231–34.

[138] The most controversial explanation for the abrupt reversal of course is laid out in Alperovitz's *Atomic Diplomacy*. Alperovitz argues that Truman's decision to pursue a more conciliatory course was motivated by the belief that American interests would be better served by a "delayed showdown" at Potsdam rather than an "immediate showdown" in May. The Hopkins Mission, in his view, was a bridge strategy that would keep open American options until the atomic bomb had been tested. See Alperovitz, *Atomic Diplomacy*, 1–60.

[139] Bohlen, *Witness to History*, 215.

he told Hopkins "he could use diplomatic language, or he could use a baseball bat" as long as he conveyed to Stalin the message that the United States intended to adhere to the Yalta agreements and expected the Soviet Union to do the same.[140] Given Hopkins's role as the architect of Lend-Lease aid and his close identification with FDR's policy of furthering U.S.–Soviet cooperation, Truman surely knew that Hopkins was going to choose the first approach in his efforts to restore amicable relations with Stalin.

Although their conversations in Moscow covered a range of issues that were producing tension within the alliance, Hopkins's primary purpose was to settle the Polish question once and for all.[141] Hopkins emphasized to Stalin that the United States had no real interests in Poland and no commitment to the London Poles, and that both Roosevelt and Truman had always anticipated that the Lublin Poles would constitute a majority in any reorganized Polish provisional government. Repeatedly, he suggested to Stalin that the real problem was not Soviet behavior, but the unfortunate effect this behavior was having on American public opinion.[142] As Truman's diary indicates, Hopkins was only voicing his own lack of concern over the merits of the Polish settlement:

> He said he'd go, said he understood my position and that he'd make it clear to Uncle Joe Stalin that I knew what I wanted—and that I intended to get it—peace for the world for at least ninety years. That Poland, Rumania, Bulgaria, Czechoslovakia, Austria, Yugoslavia, Latvia, Lithuania, Estonia et al. made no difference to U.S. interests only so far as World Peace is concerned. That Poland ought to have a "free election," at least as free as Hague, Tom Pendergast, Joe Martin, or Taft would allow in their respective bailiwicks. . . . Uncle Joe should make some sort of jesture [*sic*]—whether he means it or not to keep it before our public that he intends to keep his word.[143]

The Hopkins mission represented a return to the style of Rooseveltian diplomacy, but it also represented a substantive reversal of FDR's final position on Poland. At Yalta, Roosevelt had told Stalin that he wanted

---

[140] Truman Appointment Sheet, May 19, 1945, printed in *Off the Record: The Private Papers of Harry S. Truman*, ed. Robert Ferrell (New York: Harper & Row Publishers, 1980), 31.

[141] See George McJimsey, *Harry Hopkins: Ally of the Poor and Defender of Democracy* (Cambridge, Mass.: Harvard University Press, 1987), 377–88; Bohlen, *Witness to History*, 215–24; and Harriman and Abel, *Special Envoy to Churchill and Stalin*, 459–75.

[142] The discussions between Hopkins and Stalin related to Poland are published in *FRUS*, 1945, vol. 5, 299–338.

[143] Truman diary entry, May 23, 1945, box 333, PSF, Harry S. Truman Library (hereafter HSTL). This entry speaks volumes about Truman's alleged commitment to "messianic liberalism." In his memoirs, Truman remembered the comment about the baseball bat but failed to include his views on elections in Eastern Europe.

elections in Poland to be as pure as Caesar's wife. Perhaps more realistically, Truman was now willing to settle for the considerably lesser standards of Boss Hague and Tom Pendergast.[144] On the more immediate issue of the composition of the provisional government, Truman was also willing to make substantial concessions to Soviet views. Since April 7, 1945, Stalin had been advocating the adoption of the "Yugoslav precedent" as a model for the reorganization of the Polish government. Generally interpreted as providing approximately 80 percent of the cabinet ministries to the Lublin Poles, the Yugoslav precedent had been emphatically rejected by the West as the basis of a settlement. At his second meeting with Hopkins, Stalin made it clear that he remained committed to the ratio established in Yugoslavia and that only four cabinet ministries out of a possible twenty could be occupied by the non-Lublin Poles.[145]

Hopkins's subsequent success in breaking the deadlock over Poland had little to do with his powers of persuasion and everything to do with the fact that he tacitly accepted the Yugoslav precedent.[146] Knowing in advance that the number of non-Lublin Poles was to be strictly limited, Stalin was then fairly conciliatory in accepting Western candidates for inclusion in a reorganized Polish provisional government. Under the shadow of a Soviet show trial of sixteen Polish leaders arrested the month before, the various factions reached agreement on the composition of a provisional government. The Western-backed Poles accepted the deal, but with few illusions about their prospects. As Harriman noted, "In frankness I must report that this settlement has been reached because all the non-Lublin Poles are so concerned over the present situation in Poland that they are ready to accept any compromise which gives some hope for Polish independence and freedom."[147] The final balance sheet on Truman's handling of the Polish question is summarized quite well by Eduard Mark:

> Indeed, for all the brave rhetoric the new president permitted himself in the first weeks of his accession, virtually his first act in relation to Eastern Europe was to accept what Roosevelt had vowed he would not: in return for Stalin's renewed promise to permit free

[144] Truman was far from alone in adopting this standard. Believing that there was no way to prevent Soviet domination of Poland, Leahy hoped it would be "possible to give to the reorganized Polish Government an external appearance of independence." Byrnes had a similar standard. See Leahy, *I Was There*, 352; and Messer, *The End of an Alliance*, 79.

[145] Memorandum of Second Conversation at the Kremlin, May 27, 1945, *FRUS*, 1945, *Potsdam Conference*, vol. 1, 40.

[146] For more positive assessments of the Hopkins mission, see Davis, *The Cold War Begins*, 238; and Lundestad, *The American Non-Policy towards Eastern Europe*, 202–4.

[147] *FRUS*, 1945, vol. 5, 354. This was certainly the attitude of Stanislaw Mikolajczyk, whom the West viewed as the most important leader of the London Poles. See Joanna Hanson, "Stanislaw Mikolajczyk: November 1944–June 1945," *European History Quarterly* 21 (January 1991): 39–73.

elections, the United States had recognized a "thinly disguised continuance" of the Lublin regime as the interim government of Poland.[148]

Not surprisingly, Truman's assessment of the Polish settlement was far more positive since his primary objective was to improve relations with Stalin. After hearing from Hopkins on the developments in Moscow, Truman told Henry Morgenthau that he was "the happiest man in the world over what I have been able to accomplish."[149] At a June 1945 press conference, Truman attributed the success of the Hopkins mission to "a very pleasant yielding on the part of the Russians" and argued that it was proof that "if we keep our heads and be patient, we will arrive at a conclusion, because the Russians are just as anxious to get along with us as we are with them."[150] Truman's diary entry for June 7 expressed his renewed sense of optimism about the prospects for postwar cooperation: "I'm not afraid of Russia. They've always been our friends and I can't see any reason why they shouldn't always be."[151] The frequent contrast in the literature of Truman as the tough opponent of Stalin and Roosevelt as the craven appeaser certainly does not fit the record of the final conclusion of the Polish question.

THE DAVIES MISSION AND THE
WITHDRAWAL OF FORCES FROM THE SOVIET ZONE

Truman's optimism about the postwar world reached its height at the time of the Hopkins mission. Conversely, this period represented the nadir of Churchill's own outlook on the course of events. Despite his long and close relationship with Hopkins, Churchill did not share Truman's assessment of the Polish settlement. Although acknowledging that Hopkins had been successful in breaking the post-Yalta impasse, the prime minister saw little reason to celebrate since the agreements were "no advance on Yalta" and represented little more than "a milestone in a long hill we ought never have been asked to climb."[152] More important, the Hopkins mission served as further confirmation that America and

[148] Mark, "American Policy toward Eastern Europe," 327. For a similar judgement, see Robert James Maddox, "Truman, Poland, and the Origins of the Cold War," *Presidential Studies Quarterly* 17 (May 1984): 41.

[149] Cited in Terry H. Anderson, *The United States, Great Britain, and the Cold War, 1944–47* (Columbia: University of Missouri Press, 1981), 71.

[150] June 13 press conference, in *Public Papers of the Presidents of the United States* (Washington, D.C.: U.S. Government Printing Office, 1961), 123.

[151] Truman's June 7 diary entry, published in Ferrell, *Off the Record*, 44. For Truman's public statements reflecting a similar optimism, see Larson, *The Origins of Containment*, 184–86.

[152] Churchill, *Triumph and Tragedy*, 506.

Britain continued to have vastly different perspectives about how to deal with the emergence of Soviet power in Europe. The June 11 diary entry of Viscount Alanbrooke, chief of the imperial general staff, illustrates the sharp contrast between Churchill's and Truman's outlook in the aftermath of the Hopkins mission:

> Winston gave a long and very gloomy review of the situation. The Russians were farther west in Europe than they had ever been except once. They were all powerful in Europe. At any time that it took their fancy they could march across the rest of Europe and drive us back into our island. They had a two-to-one superiority over our forces, and the Americans were returning home. The quicker they went home, the sooner they would be required back here again. He finished up by saying that never in his life had he been more worried by the European situation than he was at present.[153]

Churchill's pessimism was a result of many different factors, but Truman's decision to send Joseph Davies to explain his views to the British prime minister was certainly a contributing factor. If Truman had consciously searched for a special envoy whose purpose was to strengthen all of Churchill's fears and suspicions about American postwar policies in Europe, it is doubtful whether he could have improved upon his choice of Davies.[154] At the time of Davies's visit to London in late May 1945, Churchill was anxiously awaiting a decision by Truman on the date of a meeting between the Big Three. Churchill's hope was that an early meeting with Stalin would enable the West to exploit the bargaining leverage provided by the presence of American and British forces 120 miles within the Soviet zone of occupation. After the withdrawal of forces, the Western position would be hopeless, but Churchill believed that there was still time to negotiate from a position of strength. In his view, the powerful bargaining chip provided by the location of the Western armies should be maintained "until we are satisfied about Poland and also the temporary character of the Russian occupation of Germany. . . . If they are not settled before the United States armies withdraw from Europe and the Western world folds up its war machines, there are no hopes of a satisfactory solution and very little of preventing a third world war."[155]

[153] Arthur Bryant, *Triumph in the West: A History of the War Years Based on the Diaries of Lord Alanbrooke, Chief of the Imperial General Staff* (New York: Doubleday & Company, 1959), 358.

[154] For background on Davies and his relationship with Truman, see Elizabeth Kimberley Maclean, *Joseph E. Davies: Special Envoy to the Soviets* (Westport, Conn.: Praeger, 1992), esp. 133–49.

[155] See Churchill, *Triumph and Tragedy*, 424–507 (quotation on 439); Tony Sharp, *The Wartime Alliance and the Zonal Division of Germany* (Oxford: Clarendon Press, 1973), 142–64; and Woodward, *British Foreign Policy in the Second World War*, 3:571–79.

Davies, who had just recently been awarded the "Order of Lenin" by Stalin, was not sent to London to debate the merits of Churchill's bargaining strategy. The purpose of his visit was to make it crystal clear that Truman was not going to support any Anglo-American front directed against the Soviet Union. In his presentation of Truman's views, Davies emphasized the president's desire for continued unity among the Big Three and for the need to avoid any appearance of "ganging up" on the Soviet Union. Indeed, not only would there be no prior meeting of the two Western leaders before the conference with Stalin, as Churchill had earlier suggested. Davies actually informed the prime minister that the president desired to meet with Stalin alone before any meeting of the Big Three. Throughout the rest of their discussion, Davies defended Soviet policies as the result of either a legitimate difference of interpretation about the Yalta agreements or a legitimate response to Anglo-American behavior that Stalin viewed as threatening. Declaring himself to have been "shocked beyond words to find so violent and bitter an attitude" toward the Soviet Union, Davies suggested that Churchill's own anti-Soviet attitudes were one of the major causes of tension within the alliance.[156]

Discerning Truman's intentions regarding both the short- and long-term role of American forces in Europe was clearly Churchill's most important concern during his meeting with Davies. Repeatedly, he emphasized the dire consequences that would follow from an American troop withdrawal. At one point during their conversation, Churchill bluntly asked Davies, "Are you trying to say for the President that the U.S. is withdrawing from participation in European affairs?" Davies replied that he had no authority to say anything on this particular issue, but he did offer Churchill his personal opinion that American forces would shortly be ordered to return to their assigned zone in Germany, and that it was hard to foresee a long-term role for American forces in Europe: "So far as holding large armed forces indefinitely in Europe in the present state of public opinion, no president would be sustained by the country in such a decision, now or for some time to come."[157]

To state the obvious, the Davies mission was a complete diplomatic disaster. Highly concerned about even the appearance of a possible Western threat to the Soviet Union, Davies was totally oblivious to Churchill's legitimate concerns about the potential threat that the Soviet Union posed to postwar Europe. Davies stated that Truman wanted to achieve a "balanced tripod of power" in the postwar era, yet he tacitly assigned Great Britain to a distinctly junior status by proposing that Churchill accept a bilateral meeting between Stalin and Truman. Since Truman had sent

---

[156] Davies's report to Truman on his conversations with Churchill can be found in *FRUS, 1945, Potsdam Conference*, vol. 1, 64–78 (quotation on 70).
[157] Ibid., 73.

Davies to London to officially represent his views, Churchill was entirely justified in thinking that Davies was accurately conveying the thoughts of the president.

How well Davies actually reflected the views of the president during the meeting with Churchill remains an open question. Truman's later account of the Davies mission is highly contradictory. On the one hand, he wrote in his memoirs that Davies "had represented my position and the policy of the United States with accuracy, carrying out instructions with exceptional skill."[158] On the other hand, Truman argued that he had never contemplated meeting with Stalin prior to a meeting of the Big Three. However, if the latter claim is true, then Davies carried out his instructions with truly exceptional incompetence because he managed to convince both Churchill and Eden that Truman wanted to arrange a prior meeting with Stalin.[159] Since there is a great deal of evidence that indicates Truman was at least considering a meeting with Stalin prior to a more general meeting of the Big Three, it seems fair to conclude that Davies was accurately reflecting the president's views to Churchill.[160]

Truman was also probably being less than candid when he later recalled his views on the maintenance of American forces in Europe. In his memoirs, the president wrote that when Davies related Churchill's fears of an American troop withdrawal from Europe he "interrupted Davies to say that I had no such thing in mind, that we would withdraw only the troops we could spare from Europe for our war in the Pacific. We were committed to the rehabilitation of Europe, and there was to be no abandonment this time."[161] None of the other officials present at Davies's oral briefing to Truman on June 6 recorded in their memoirs any stirring declaration about maintaining American forces in Europe. More important, there were no cables to Churchill from Truman reassuring him that there was to be no "abandonment" this time around. If Davies had badly misrepresented Truman's views on this subject, it seems likely that Truman would have taken steps to reassure Churchill that he had been misrepresented. Regardless of what Truman's actual views were at this time, any attempt to reassure Churchill on this issue would have been overshadowed by his decision on June 12 to go ahead—as Davies had predicted—

[158] Truman, *Year of Decisions*, 261. See also June 7 diary entry in Ferrell, ed., *Off the Record*, 44.

[159] Unsure that he had understood Davies correctly on the issue of a bilateral meeting, Churchill specifically asked Eden to confirm that his understanding of the proposal was correct. See Eden, *The Reckoning*, 624.

[160] Leahy confirms that Davies was sent to London to discuss the proposed meeting between Truman and Stalin. See Leahy, *I Was There*, 379. In addition, both Henry Wallace and Charles Bohlen recalled that Truman was interested at the time in arranging a prior meeting with Stalin. Although Maclean does not reach a clear conclusion on the issue, she leaves little doubt that Davies was under the impression that he had the authority to propose a bilateral meeting between Truman and Stalin. See Maclean, *Envoy to the Soviets*, 147–48.

[161] Truman, *Year of Decisions*, 262.

with the withdrawal of American forces from the Soviet occupation zone in Germany.

Nothing reveals the vastly different perspectives on the future of Europe held by Churchill and leading American officials more than the dispute over withdrawal from the Soviet zone. After having repeatedly failed to convince Eisenhower and the JCS of the merits of meeting Soviet forces as far to the east as possible, Churchill viewed the presence of Western forces in the Soviet zones as the last chance to negotiate a favorable postwar settlement. All of the elements of Churchill's "Iron Curtain" speech of March 1946, including the specific phrase, can be found in his cables to Truman during the last months of the war. American statesmen would find the analysis compelling in 1946, but during the spring of 1945 no one in a position of authority shared his assessment that withdrawal from the Soviet zone constituted anything resembling what Churchill later described as a "fateful milestone for mankind."[162]

What accounts for the divergence between Churchill and leading American officials in the closing months of the war? One of the most popular answers is that Churchill was a Clausewitzian who thought in terms of postwar political objectives. On the other hand, Americans such as Eisenhower thought exclusively in terms of military victory and of keeping to the letter of agreements.[163] Eisenhower often portrayed his differences with Churchill in this way, but many historians have argued persuasively that political considerations played an important role in the general's decisions during this period. As Stephen Ambrose points out, Eisenhower's decision not to take Berlin and Prague cannot be understood solely, or even primarily, in military terms:

> For his part, Eisenhower was eager to show the Russians such good will. This was the real reason, above all others, that Eisenhower left Berlin and Prague to the Russians. For all his constant insistence on "military" rather than "political" factors, he avoided the two capitals for the most obvious of political reasons—to please the Russians. . . . Nothing, he felt, would have gotten American-Russian relations off to a worse start than to engage in a race for Berlin. He wanted to work with the Russians, not compete with them.[164]

---

[162] Churchill, *Triumph and Tragedy,* 528.

[163] See Bernard Brodie, *War and Politics* (New York: Macmillan Publishing, 1973), 36–45. For an excellent review of Eisenhower's relationship with Churchill and other British military officials, see Theodore Draper, "Eisenhower's War," in *A Present of Things Past* (New York: Hill and Wang, 1988), 3–66.

[164] Stephen Ambrose, *Eisenhower* (New York: Simon and Schuster, 1983), 401. For an opposing view which emphasizes purely military considerations, see Forrest Pogue, "Why Eisenhower's Forces Stopped at the Elbe," *World Politics* 4 (April 1952): 356–68.

The decision to withdraw from the Soviet zone was based on the same rationale. Just as capturing Berlin was not considered to be an objective worth the cost in American lives since it was eventually going to be turned over to the Soviets, Eisenhower saw little point in holding up the withdrawal of American forces for bargaining purposes. All that would be accomplished through Churchill's strategy would be to increase Soviet suspicions of the West, which is exactly what the leading figures on the American side of the withdrawal decision wanted to avoid in May–June 1945. Eisenhower, Lucius Clay, and Harry Hopkins—the three leading advocates of an immediate withdrawal from the Soviet zone—were all adherents of Roosevelt's belief that breaking down Soviet mistrust of the West was the key to establishing postwar cooperation. Eisenhower's views on postwar cooperation in May 1945 were very simplistic: "The more contact we have with the Russians, the more they will understand us and the greater will be the cooperation.... It should be possible to work with the Russians if we follow the same pattern of friendly cooperation that has resulted in the great record of Allied unity demonstrated first by AFHQ [Allied Force Headquarters] and subsequently by SHAEF [Supreme Headquarters, Allied Expeditionary Force]."[165] Clay was also a true believer in Roosevelt's approach to postwar cooperation with the Soviets. During his stopover in Germany after the Hopkins mission, Charles Bohlen noted that Clay "advanced a theory, which was by that time all too familiar to me, that the key to getting along with the Soviets was that you had to give trust to get trust."[166]

The persistence of belief in the possibility of postwar cooperation with the Soviets and differing views about the ways to achieve this cooperation primarily explain why Churchill's assessment in May–June 1945 were dismissed by the Truman administration. Neither Eisenhower nor Clay were blind to the possibility that ultimately it might not be possible to cooperate with the Soviets in governing postwar Germany. Indeed, both of them cabled Washington in early June, before a final decision on withdrawal had been reached, that serious thought should be given to planning tripartite arrangements for the postwar occupation of Germany based on the three western zones and a separate Soviet zone.[167] However, until it was conclusively demonstrated that cooperation with the Soviets

---

[165] Harry C. Butcher, *My Three Years with Eisenhower* (New York: Simon and Schuster, 1946), 855. Like FDR, Eisenhower operated from the premise that Soviet cooperation would be determined by Western actions. See Eisenhower, *Crusade in Europe* (Garden City, N.Y.: Doubleday & Company, 1948), 438.

[166] Bohlen, *Witness to History*, 222.

[167] See Eisenhower to Joint Chiefs of Staff, June 6, 1945, in *The Papers of Dwight David Eisenhower: Occupation, 1945*, ed. Alfred D. Chandler and Louis Galambos (Baltimore: Johns Hopkins Press, 1978), 136; Jean Edward Smith, *Lucius D. Clay: An American Life* (New York: Henry Holt, 1990), 258; and *FRUS*, 1945, vol. 3, 331.

would fail, both Eisenhower and Clay wanted to make a serious effort at establishing four-power arrangements for administering Germany. Since the Soviets had refused to permit the establishment of the Allied Control Council until a date for withdrawal was set, Eisenhower and Clay, as well as Hopkins, all urged Truman to accept the Soviet terms, which he did on June 12, 1945.

CONCLUSION

Overall, the evidence suggests that Truman did not reverse Roosevelt's basic course in the period before the July 1945 Potsdam Conference. After a brief flirtation with a deterrence strategy in his first few weeks, Truman ultimately fell back on his predecessor's strategy of seeking to preserve the wartime coalition with the Soviet Union. On both of the substantive issues that threatened the maintenance of the Grand Alliance before Potsdam—Poland and the withdrawal of American forces from the Soviet zones—Truman chose to pursue a course which ameliorated tensions with the Soviet Union and preserved the potential for amicable postwar relations. Churchill was willing to imperil the maintenance of the wartime coalition by immediately confronting Stalin with an Anglo-American bloc, but Truman was not yet willing to risk the perception that the Western powers were ganging up on the Soviet Union. According to Henry Kissinger, Truman's actions before Potsdam show that he, like FDR, was not ready "to face the geopolitical realities victory had wrought, or to jettison Roosevelt's vision of a world order governed by Four Policemen."[168]

Kissinger is correct about Truman's unwillingness to abandon the main objectives of Roosevelt's policies in the last months of the Second World War, but his larger point is inaccurate. The idea that American policymakers during the Second World War did not face up to "geopolitical realities" is frequently asserted but is simply not true. The geopolitical reality that Roosevelt faced during the war was that a strong Soviet Union was needed to defeat Nazi Germany and that an allied victory inevitably meant that Stalin would have the power to do what he wished in Eastern Europe after the war. Churchill told the London Poles in November 1944 that "the brutal facts could not be overlooked. He could no more stop the Russian advance than stop the tide coming in. It was no use saying something which would only make the Russians more angry . . . ."[169] The fact that Churchill in 1945 was now willing to overlook or ignore the brutal

---

[168] Kissinger, *Diplomacy*, 433.
[169] Cited in David Carlton, *Churchill and the Soviet Union* (Manchester: Manchester University Press, 2000), 111.

facts about the Soviet Union and Eastern Europe that he knew very well in 1944 does not make him the hero of the story. Neither postwar American security nor the balance of power in Europe turned on the fate of Eastern Europe, and it is hard to fault either Roosevelt or Truman for not pursuing a more confrontational policy over these issues. If either president had pursued the tougher course implied by Kissinger and other historians, it is quite possible that a different set of historians would be castigating them for ignoring the "geopolitical realities" of an inevitable Soviet domination of Eastern Europe.

[3]

One German Problem or Two?

By partitioning Germany, the Allies solved the "German problem" that had given rise to two world wars in the space of twenty-five years. The structural effect of the division of Germany was to transform the volatile tripolar system into a stable but very competitive, bipolar world.

Randall Schweller, 1998

In the great power politics of multipolar worlds, who is a danger to whom, and who can be expected to deal with threats and problems, are matters of uncertainty. In the great power politics of bipolar worlds, who is a danger to whom is never in doubt. This is the first big difference between the politics of power in the two systems.

Kenneth Waltz, 1979

The future of Europe in 1945 looked much more uncertain to American and Western European policymakers than it appears to contemporary international relations scholars armed with neorealist theory and hindsight. Few people doubted that the structure of Europe and the international system had been greatly transformed as a result of the war, but virtually every other fundamental question about the future of Europe was shrouded in layers of doubt and uncertainty. Two of the most important questions for Western Europeans concerned America's future presence on the continent and the future of Germany. Would America keep its military forces in Europe for a lengthy period of time to counterbalance Soviet power in Europe? Most European observers in 1945 were rightly skeptical that America would remain on the continent for very long after the war. Neither Roosevelt nor Truman had given much support to the idea that America would stay in Europe for any substantial period; in fact, they had encouraged the opposite idea. The issue of Germany also raised a whole series of questions for which the answers were not obvious. Was a unified or divided Germany more conducive to lasting European peace and stability? Would the Western powers and the Soviet Union be able to agree on the future organization and status of Germany? What course should the Western powers pursue if they were unable to reach a tolerable settlement with the Soviet Union over Germany? The questions on the minds of Western statesmen in 1945 were fairly obvious ones, but there was no consensus on the answers.

The volatile tripolar system of the late 1930s was not immediately transformed into a stable bipolar system in 1945 because the question of how powerful and how independent Germany would be was not resolved as a result of the war—and would remain unresolved for nearly two decades. German power had been devastated by the war, but this did not by any means settle the question of how powerful it would be in the future. America and Russia were clearly the two dominant powers, but both the future of Europe and U.S.–Soviet relations would turn on whether the problem posed by German power could be resolved in such a way that no one would challenge its basic legitimacy. In this respect, the major problem faced by Western policymakers after the Second World War was little different than the one they had faced after the First World War. The problem was not German power as it stood in 1918 or 1945, but how powerful Germany would be ten or twenty years later. Of course, the ascendancy of the Soviet Union in 1945 made solving the problem of German power in Europe much more complicated, but the latter problem would have existed even without the former.

The persistence of the German problem after the Second World War suggests that it is misleading to view the early postwar world as a bipolar system as theorized by Kenneth Waltz.[1] Even before the war ended, Western statesmen knew that they were confronted with two interconnected problems of power, a Soviet and a German one. Reflecting the way that France approached the postwar world from the very beginning, Foreign Minister Georges Bidault explained to American policymakers in 1948 that "the Western democracies are faced with (1) an eventual threat, which is Germany; (2) an actual threat, which is the Soviet Union; (3) an immediate threat which is Soviet action in Germany."[2] American and British officials might have disagreed with Bidault's ordering of the threats, but they too accepted the real nature of all three. As early as 1946, Duff Cooper, the British ambassador to France, analyzed the volatile and complex nature of the postwar structure in very similar terms to Bidault. After noting that neither America nor Great Britain could be counted on to occupy Germany indefinitely, he pointed out that "Germany is weak today. She was weak in 1919, but in ten years she had much of her strength and in twenty years she was the greatest power in the world." The emergence of Soviet power was an important change from 1919, according to Cooper, but this change presented the Western powers with "two dangers instead of one. The first danger is that Germany will herself grow strong enough to repeat her attacks on civilisation. The second danger is that Germany will sink

---

[1] See chapter 1.

[2] Caffery to Secretary of State, June 29, 1948, *Foreign Relations of the United States, 1948,* vol. 3 (Washington, D.C.: Government Printing Office, 1974), 142–43.

into a satellite of Russia which will then become the most formidable power the world has ever seen."[3]

This chapter examines the collapse of the Grand Alliance and the origins of the Cold War struggle over Germany. During the Second World War, American postwar planners believed that an open competition between the United States and the Soviet Union for the hearts and minds of the German people would be a disaster for both sides. But less than eighteen months after the German surrender, the first real American bid for the loyalty of the German people came in a September 1946 speech at Stuttgart by Secretary of State James F. Byrnes. In the first major statement of America's postwar German policy, Byrnes sought to counter the Soviet Union's efforts to portray itself as the sole defender of German unity and prosperity by officially declaring that the United States would oppose the separation of either the Ruhr or the Rhineland from Germany, as well as the maintenance of any controls that would subject these areas to outside domination or manipulation. Byrnes also suggested that Germany's borders in the east had not been finalized and that some changes might still be made to the boundary with Poland. In addition, the Stuttgart speech contained the first high-level disavowal of Roosevelt's statement at Yalta that American forces would not be maintained on the continent for more than two years after the war. Although the Stuttgart speech contained some harsh words and unpalatable policies for the Germans, Byrnes went a long way toward distancing the Truman administration from the legacy of the Morgenthau Plan and the popular perception that America would quickly withdraw from Europe.[4]

Byrnes's speech was warmly approved by the American occupational authorities and by the German people. But even observers who felt that Soviet behavior in Germany provided a strong justification for the speech believed that Byrnes had also embarked on a potentially dangerous course at Stuttgart. Byrnes's open appeal to German nationalism, Eugene Rostow argued, was nothing less than "the most dangerous idea in the world" and "a step towards national disaster."[5] Despite all of the obvious difficulties that had emerged among the victor powers since the end of the war, Rostow maintained that the United States, the Soviet Union, and Western Europe continued to share a common interest in reaching a cooperative solution to the German problem. In fact, Rostow suggested that the Western powers had the greater interest in avoiding an all-out contest

---

[3] Duff Cooper to Foreign Office, March 1, 1946, published in *Die Ruhrfrage 1945/46 und die Entsehung des Landes Nordrhein-Westfalen*, ed. Rolf Steininger (Düsseldorf: Droste Verlag, 1988), 538.

[4] The Stuttgart speech is reprinted in U.S. State Department, *Germany, 1947–49: The Story in Documents* (Washington, D.C.: Government Printing Office, 1950), 3–8.

[5] Eugene Rostow, "The Partition of Germany and the Unity of Europe," *The Virginia Quarterly Review* 23 (winter 1947): 20.

for the allegiance of Germany because "if German life remains a tug of war between us and the Russians, the Russians, and above all the Germans, will almost surely win."[6] Arguing that the Stuttgart speech was "preparing the ground for political disaster," Walter Lippmann shared Rostow's belief that the West could not and should not make Germany a part of any anti-Soviet coalition in Europe. In his view, "Applied to Germany, the policy of containment is a booby trap, constructed by men who do not understand the politics of power."[7]

Historical judgments about the Stuttgart speech and the origins of the Cold War in Europe are often based on the belief that the Potsdam settlement reflected a sincere American commitment and desire to cooperatively run Germany as a single economic and political unit with the Soviet Union; debates then generally turn on the question of why four-power control collapsed and which of the participants was primarily to blame.[8] However, framing the issue in this way obscures the real nature of the German settlement negotiated by Byrnes with the Soviets at Potsdam. As many British and American officials recognized at the time, Byrnes negotiated a reparations agreement with the Soviet Union that essentially treated the western and eastern zones of Germany as two separate countries. The nature of the agreement was not an accident. Byrnes's guiding assumptions at Potsdam were that a capitalist United States and a communist Soviet Union were bound to come into conflict if they tried to run Germany as an integrated and united entity, and that a clear economic boundary separating the two zones would be more conducive to peaceful relations. As Marc Trachtenberg argues, rather than setting up the basis for a future partnership in Germany, Byrnes was really seeking to establish the terms for an "amicable divorce" at the Potsdam Conference.[9]

Why did the friendly division of Germany become transformed into the hostile division reflected in Byrnes's Stuttgart speech? A large part of the answer is to be found in the fact that Byrnes sought to obscure the reality of a settlement which was based on separate zones with language and provisions designed to foster the illusion that Potsdam had preserved the unity of Germany. Byrnes might have preferred to draw a clear line across Germany, but the Potsdam Protocol certainly did not draw such a clear line. While not at all suggesting that the hostile division of Germany

[6] Ibid.

[7] Walter Lippmann, *The Cold War: A Study in U.S. Foreign Policy* (New York: Harper & Brothers Publishers, 1947), 46, 48.

[8] This is one of the main purposes of Carolyn Eisenberg's *Drawing the Line: The American Decision to Divide Germany, 1944–49* (Cambridge: Cambridge University Press, 1996), esp. 7, 484–93. For a good analysis of the strengths and weaknesses of Eisenberg's attempt to place primary blame on the United States, see Charles Maier, "Who Divided Germany?" *Diplomatic History* 22 (summer 1998): 481–88.

[9] Mark Trachtenberg, *A Constructed Peace: The Making of the European Settlement, 1945–63* (Princeton: Princeton University Press, 1999), 15–34.

resulted solely from American policy, or that different American policies might have led to a better outcome, it was Byrnes more than anyone else who consistently took the lead in dividing Germany both during and after Potsdam. First, he failed to put any serious pressure on the French throughout 1945–46 to go along with the creation of central administrations in Germany. Whether such pressure would have averted the division of Germany is far from certain, but it surely contributed to the process of division. Second, Byrnes explicitly authorized Lucius Clay's reparations stop of May 1946, which denied the Soviets important benefits they had obtained from the Potsdam agreement. Third, in July 1946 Byrnes pushed for the merger of the British and American zones of occupation, a move which marked a major step toward formalizing the division of Germany. Although Byrnes may not originally have wanted the division of Germany to become a source of hostility and tension between the great powers, he preferred division on any terms to a united Germany that would allow the Soviets any real influence in the western zones.

THE GERMAN QUESTION AFTER YALTA

President Roosevelt's dismissal of the value of detailed postwar planning before American military forces assumed control of Germany was vindicated at the end of the fighting in Europe. Shocked by the extent of the devastation they found in Germany, Clay and his advisors believed that the punitive focus of the American occupation directive, JCS 1067, represented an obstacle to ameliorating the real and immediate problems they confronted in Germany. Well aware that the U.S. Army would bear the brunt of domestic criticism for widespread suffering and chaos in Germany, as well as the high costs of the occupation, Clay immediately began calling for a revision of JCS 1067: "I think that Washington must revise its thinking relative to destruction of Germany's war potential as an immediate problem. . . . retribution now is far greater than is realized at home."[10] Clay's financial advisor, Lewis Douglas, was even more emphatic about the inadequacies of JCS 1067: "This thing was assembled by economic idiots! It makes no sense to forbid the most skilled workers in Europe from producing as much as they can for a continent which is desperately short of everything!"[11]

The Office of Military Government for Germany, United States (OMGUS) appraisal of the situation was moderate in comparison with some of the other reports Truman received from visitors to Germany dur-

---

[10] Clay to McCloy, April 26, 1945, in *The Papers of Lucius Clay*, ed. Jean E. Smith, 2 vols. (Bloomington: Indiana University Press, 1974), 1:8.

[11] Robert Murphy, *Diplomat among Warriors* (Garden City, N.Y.: Doubleday & Co, 1964), 251.

ing his first few months in office. "There is a complete economic, social and political collapse going on in Central Europe," Assistant Secretary of War John McCloy reported to Truman in late April, "the extent of which is unparalleled in history unless one goes back to the collapse of the Roman Empire, and even that may not have been as great an economic upheaval."[12] After their tour of Germany in May 1945, Senator Burton Wheeler and his staff told a member of the American reparations delegation, "Unless we move fast on German reconstruction, there will be a German wide revolution, with more war and the spread of communism. . . . Unless we [start] building up Germany fast, we will have to keep the U.S. Army here for decades, or turn it all over to the Russians."[13] Wheeler and his staff also believed that the tremendous devastation would make it impossible for Germany to pay reparations: "Germany is so destroyed that 'not a thing' can be expected in reparations. If we try to take anything out Germany will need food, supplies, and everything to prevent starvation and suffering and the demand will fall on us."[14]

The behavior of Soviet military forces within their zone of occupation greatly contributed to the overall impression of chaos and anarchy in Germany. The existence of highly organized "trophy teams" with detailed instructions to dismantle and ship back to the Soviet Union everything from pianos to entire factories increased fears that postwar Germany would become dependent on massive outside assistance from the United States.[15] In addition, the fact that the Soviets were clearly attempting to exploit a window of opportunity in order to increase their overall share of reparations from Germany raised serious questions about the prospects for running the country as a single economic unit. Harriman described Soviet behavior as neither "surprising" nor "reprehensible," but he also cited it as proof that the Soviets were going to act unilaterally

---

[12] Cited in Harry S. Truman, *Year of Decisions* (Garden City, N.Y.: Doubleday & Company, 1955), 102. See also Kai Bird, *The Chairman: John J. McCloy, the Making of the American Establishment* (New York: Simon & Schuster, 1992), 233–38.

[13] Luther Gulick to Edwin Pauley and Isador Lubin, "Talk With Senator Wheeler," May 27, 1945, White House Central Files, Confidential Files, box 2, Harry S. Truman Library (hereafter HSTL).

[14] Ibid. After his own meeting with Wheeler and several other senators who had toured the continent, and still very happy with the settlement over Poland, Truman privately ridiculed their belief that "the European world is at an end and that Russia is a big bad wolf." See Truman diary entry, July 7, 1945, in *Off the Record: The Private Papers of Harry S. Truman*, ed. Robert Ferrell (New York: Harper & Row Publishers, 1980), 48.

[15] See Norman M. Naimark, *The Russians in Germany: A History of the Soviet Zone of Occupation, 1945–49* (Cambridge, Mass.: Harvard University Press, 1995), 166–70; Vassily Yershov, "Confiscation and Plunder by the Army of Occupation," in *Soviet Economic Policy in Post-War Germany*, ed. Robert Slusser (New York: Research Program on the USSR, 1953), 1–11; and Barbara Ann Chotiner and John W. Atwell, "Soviet Occupation Policy toward Germany, 1945–49," in *U.S. Occupation in Europe after World War II*, ed. Hans A. Schmitt (Lawrence: Regents Press of Kansas, 1978), 45–63.

within their zone of occupation in Germany.[16] Kennan went even further and argued that the State Department should simply give up on the idea of negotiating a reparations plan based on the treatment of Germany as a single economic unit and plan for a "simple horse trade: How much are we going to make available to the Russians from our zones, and what price are we going to demand for it?"[17] Kennan may still have been far removed from the foreign policy elite of Washington at this time, but his thoughts on reparations closely paralleled the approach Byrnes would take at Potsdam.

To a very great extent, the future of Germany after Yalta came to be focused on the question of reparations. Yalta had established a very ambiguous framework for addressing an inherently complex subject. Although one often finds references in the historical literature to a solid agreement on the part of the United States and the Soviet Union to extract twenty billion dollars in reparations from Germany, with ten billion allocated to the Soviet Union, the final wording of the protocol explicitly stated that this sum was only to be considered as a "basis for discussion."[18] Great Britain refused to accept even this level of commitment, but the United States was willing to go along with the Soviet proposal subject to the all-important qualification expressed in the final protocol. Although Soviet negotiators undoubtedly viewed the inclusion of a specific sum in the protocol as a victory that might provide them with leverage in future negotiations, they were also well aware that the figure did not represent a sacrosanct commitment. After hearing Churchill explain that the War Cabinet was worried that Germany might not be able to pay such a large amount of reparations, even Stalin minimized its significance: "The experts may be right, but all they were preparing was a figure to be used as a basis for discussions—it could be reduced or increased by the Commission in Moscow."[19]

Very little significance should be attributed to the fact that the United States and the Soviet Union signed the Yalta reparations protocol without the concurrence of Great Britain. The records of the plenary sessions show that the fundamental division at Yalta was between the two Western powers and the Soviet Union. When Stalin advanced arguments for ex-

[16] Harriman to Secretary of State, April 6, 1945, *FRUS*, 1945, vol. 3, 1190–92.

[17] See Kennan to Secretary of State, May 3, 1945, and Kennan to Secretary of State, May 14, 1945, both in *FRUS*, 1945, vol. 3, 1203–5, 1211–13 (quotation on 1212).

[18] The reparations protocol is published in *FRUS*, 1945, *The Conferences at Malta and Yalta*, 978–79. As in the case of Poland, the ambiguity of the Yalta reparations protocol has provided a field day for scholarly disagreement. For arguments that emphasize the importance of the twenty-billion-dollar figure, see Robert Messer, *The End of an Alliance: James F. Byrnes, Roosevelt, Truman, and the Origins of the Cold War* (Chapel Hill: University of North Carolina Press, 1982), 48–49; and Melvyn Leffler, "Adherence to Agreements: Yalta and the Experiences of the Early Cold War," *International Security* 11 (summer 1986): 103–5.

[19] *FRUS*, 1945, *Conferences at Malta and Yalta*, 902.

tracting large amounts of reparations from Germany, both Churchill and Roosevelt responded that they would not repeat the mistakes of the inter-war reparations experience. The United States had lent over ten billion dollars to Germany after the last war in order to enable it to pay reparations, Roosevelt explained to Stalin, and the American taxpayer had been stuck with the bill after Germany defaulted on repayment. Although he would willingly support any Soviet claim to reparations, FDR immediately qualified this commitment by saying that "the Germans should be allowed to live in order that they might not become a burden on the world. . . . He concluded that he was in favor of extracting the maximum in reparations from Germany but not to the extent that people would starve."[20] In short, as long as the United States would not have to directly or indirectly finance Germany's payment of reparations, Roosevelt was in favor of letting the Soviets remove everything possible for their own reconstruction needs. How the tradeoff would be made if and when Soviet reparations claims came into conflict with America's desire to avoid subsidizing the Germans was an issue that FDR clearly wanted to postpone for after the war.

Avoiding the perceived mistakes of the interwar reparations settlement provided a common objective for American officials as the war came to an end. As John Gimbel points out, "Among the many issues that divided American policy planners for Germany in 1944–45, one agreement in principle stands out: The United States should avoid the mistakes it had made after World War I."[21] Although he desired a "hard peace," Truman later wrote in his memoirs, "we remembered that after 1919 Germany was so enfeebled that only American money made it possible to pay the reparations that had been imposed."[22] After hearing Robert Murphy, the U.S. political adviser on German affairs, voice his concern that the American government might once again wind up paying for the occupation and subsidizing Germany's payment of reparations, Admiral Leahy reassured him that he had little to worry about because Truman's thoughts were exactly the same: "That danger is uppermost in the President's mind, too. I have heard him say that the American people foolishly made big loans to Germany, and the money was used to pay reparations. When the loans were defaulted, American's were left holding the bag. The President says he is determined not to let that happen again."[23]

[20] Ibid., 622.

[21] John Gimbel, *The Origins of the Marshall Plan* (Stanford, Calif.: Stanford University Press, 1976), 54. The best discussion of how perceptions and misperceptions of the interwar reparations experience influenced American policymakers can be found in John H. Backer, *The Decision to Divide Germany* (Durham, N.C.: Duke University Press, 1978), esp. chaps. 1–3.

[22] Truman, *Year of Decisions*, 307.

[23] William D. Leahy, *I Was There* (New York: Whittlesey House, 1950), 270.

Truman's determination to avoid paying for German reparations can be seen in his decision to replace Isador Lubin as the chief American representative on the Allied Reparations Commission. A statistician appointed by Roosevelt in March 1945, Lubin was very sympathetic to the Treasury Department's conception that reparations claims should be satisfied through a policy of extensive deindustrialization in Germany. After reading a draft statement on reparations prepared by Lubin, Emile Despres described it as "the most extreme statement which I have yet seen of the Treasury doctrine with respect to economic treatment of Germany."[24] Never sympathetic to the basic philosophy of the Morgenthau Plan, Truman wanted someone closer to his own views to handle what he described as "the most important job in America as of this moment."[25] Clearly anticipating conflict rather than cooperation with the Soviet Union over reparations, Truman chose Edwin Pauley to lead the U.S. delegation in Moscow because he wanted "a tough bargainer, someone who could be as tough as Molotov."[26] If nothing else, Pauley more than lived up to his reputation for toughness in the preliminary negotiations over reparations. According to Richard Scandrett, a dissenting member of the American reparations delegation in Moscow, Pauley and his staff were far more interested in being tough than in negotiating an amicable reparations agreement with the Soviet Union. Pauley and his staff were so enraged by the evidence of how thoroughly the Soviets had looted their occupation zone that staff meetings were devoted primarily to figuring out ways of making them account for what had already been taken from Germany. In Richard Scandrett's opinion, one shared by many historians, Pauley's real purpose during the Moscow negotiations was to set the stage for a reversal of the Yalta framework on reparations.[27]

As noted above, judgments about whether Pauley was attempting to reverse the meaning and spirit of Yalta depend entirely on what aspect of the protocol is emphasized. Pauley could and did justify his preference for discussing German reparations in available machinery and goods,

[24] Despres to Clayton, March 24, 1945, *FRUS*, 1945, vol. 3, 1181. Lubin's statement can be found on 1179–1181.

[25] See Isador Lubin Oral History, 1957, Columbia Oral History Project (hereafter COHP), 85; and Isador Lubin Oral History, 1976, HSTL. Truman did not explicitly refer to Lubin's views in justifying his decision, but it is hard to believe that State Department opposition to Morgenthau did not play some role in the decision. See also Truman, *Year of Decisions*, 235–36.

[26] Truman, *Year of Decisions*, 308.

[27] Richard Scandrett, "Summary of Procedure of Allied Commission on Reparations," August 1945, box 16, Backer Papers, Columbia University. (Scandrett's original papers can be found at Cornell University.) Scandrett's opinion of how greatly Soviet looting affected Pauley's views on reparations is confirmed by British sources. See Playfair to Hall-Patch, July 30, 1945, in *Documents on British Policy Overseas* (hereafter *DBPO*), series 1, vol. 1, *The Conference at Potsdam, 1945* (London: Her Majesty's Stationery Office, 1984), calendar no. 440i.

rather than in specific dollar amounts, as fully consistent with the spirit of Roosevelt's position at Yalta.[28] His unwillingness to negotiate a specific sum was also quite consistent with FDR's conviction that the final solution to German questions should be postponed until the situation on the ground was clarified. Finally, Pauley was also consistent with the Yalta protocol when he insisted that any reparations plan had to be based on the "first-charge" principle, the issue which contributed the most to the impasse with the Soviet Union.[29] The first-charge principle mandated that revenue from German exports would first have to cover the costs of necessary imports into Germany, the occupation, and German consumption before any allocations could be made for the purposes of reparations.[30] American and British insistence on the adoption of the first-charge principle reflected the determination of both powers to avoid subsidizing the payment of reparations to the Soviet Union.[31] According to Pauley, it was only on this basis that "pure" reparations could be extracted from Germany, as opposed to "fictitious reparations which come out of your pocket or ours."[32]

Not surprisingly, Pauley was unable to persuade the Soviets of the virtues of the first-charge principle. In the event of a conflict between paying for essential imports into Germany and the payment of reparations, Maisky maintained that the latter consideration should be accorded the greater priority. Despite Pauley's attempts to demonstrate that the Americans and the Soviets had a common interest in the adoption of the first-charge principle, there was simply no getting around the fact that the Western powers and the Soviet Union did not share common interests over reparations. The primary interest of both the United States and Great Britain was to avoid being faced with a situation in which their own resources would be devoted to both the maintenance of the German population and the payment of reparations to the Soviet Union. Conversely,

---

[28] See Pauley to Secretary of State, July 7, 1945, *FRUS, 1945, Potsdam Conference,* vol. 1, 530–31.

[29] The "first-charge" principle can be found in State Department briefing papers prepared for the Yalta Conference. See "Reparation and Restitution Policy toward Germany," January 16, 1945, *FRUS, 1945, Conferences at Malta and Yalta,* 193–97.

[30] According to Pauley's formula, R (current reparations) = P (German production) - (O + C + I), with O standing for occupation costs, C for German consumption, and I for imports. See Pauley to Maisky, July 13, 1945, *FRUS, Potsdam Conference,* vol. 1, 547. For a more comprehensive discussion of the economics of Pauley's reparations formula, see Bruce Kuklick, *American Policy and the Division of Germany* (Ithaca: Cornell University Press, 1972), 130–40.

[31] The first-charge principle was reiterated throughout the instructions provided to Pauley by the State Department. See *FRUS, 1945,* vol. 3, 1222–27. The British reparations delegation shared the same basic principles. For an excellent study of the British viewpoint on reparations by a participant in the Moscow negotiations, see Alec Cairncross, *The Price of War* (New York: Basil Blackwell, 1986), 1–99; and John Farquharson, "Anglo-American Policy on German Reparations from Yalta to Potsdam," *English Historical Review* 112 (1997): 904–26.

[32] Pauley to Maisky, July 13, *FRUS, 1945, Potsdam Conference,* vol. 1, 547.

because they wanted to obtain the maximum amount of reparations possible, the Soviets undoubtedly did not care whether reparations were "pure" extractions from indigenous German resources or "fictitious" reparations financed by American and British taxpayers. The Western formula, no matter how economically sound it might be, would likely have denied the Soviets immediate or substantial reparations. By the start of the Potsdam Conference, after weeks of negotiations in Moscow, the Western powers and the Soviet Union were as far apart as ever on the basic principles of a reparations settlement.

BYRNES AND THE POTSDAM SETTLEMENT

During the war Roosevelt, Stalin, and Churchill had all indicated that they were somewhat sympathetic to the idea of partitioning Germany in one way or another, but by the time of the Potsdam Conference in July 1945, none of the great powers was openly willing to associate itself with this position. Despite Stalin's open rejection of partition in the aftermath of the German surrender, it is still far from clear what kind of Germany the Soviet leader wanted or expected would come into existence. In his meetings with East German communists in June 1945, Stalin indicated that there would be "two Germanys—despite all the unity of the allies." But since Stalin also told the East Germans that they should oppose British and American plans for dismemberment and aim for a united Germany, it is not surprising that historians have reached no consensus over Stalin's perspective on the German question in 1945.[33] Whether Stalin preferred having an eastern zone under total Soviet control—with no corresponding say or influence in the western portions—to a united Germany which he could not reasonably expect to control completely cannot currently be settled by documentary evidence. Which course was logically more congruent with his interests is also difficult to determine

[33] Stalin's comments as recorded by Wilhelm Pieck, cited in Wilfried Loth, "Stalin's Plans for Post-War Germany," in *The Soviet Union and Europe in the Cold War, 1943–53*, ed. Francesca Gori and Silvio Pons (New York: St. Martin's Press, 1996), 24. Pieck's notes have been one of the major new sources on Soviet policy toward Germany. Some scholars interpret them to mean that Stalin was intent on using a divided Germany as a secure base to ultimately control all of Germany. For this view, see R. C. Raack, "Stalin Plans His Post-War Germany," *Journal of Contemporary History* 28 (January 1993): 53–73; and John Lewis Gaddis, *We Now Know: Rethinking Cold War History* (New York: Oxford University Press, 1997), 116. For an argument based on Pieck's notes which suggests Stalin essentially was willing to accept a parliamentary regime for a united Germany, see Wilfried Loth, *Stalin's Unwanted Child: The Soviet Union, the German Question, and the Founding of the GDR* (New York: St. Martin's Press, 1998). Finally, Trachtenberg believes that the notes suggest that Stalin accepted the fact that Germany was going to be divided and that he did not seriously expect to see a unified Germany. See Trachtenberg, *A Constructed Peace*, 30.

because both scenarios had their advantages and disadvantages from the Soviet perspective.

Viewed purely as an intellectual proposition about the most desirable future of Germany, American policymakers almost unanimously favored a united rather than a partitioned Germany. Roosevelt's death eliminated the influence of those at the highest levels who supported the formal partition of Germany. Fervent supporters of FDR's primary objective of maintaining friendly postwar relations with the Soviet Union, such as Lucius Clay and Robert Murphy, rejected his belief that a partitioned Germany would make it easier to preserve the Grand Alliance and would be more compatible with long-term European security. The State Department, as it had throughout the war, continued in the months before Potsdam to state the case against partition and a spheres-of-influence settlement. Partition did not represent a viable solution to the German problem because it would lead to disputes among the victor powers, would hamper the economic rehabilitation of Europe, and would never be accepted as legitimate by the German people.[34] Even OSS analysts, who were very concerned about Soviet motives and the postwar balance of power, still thought that a neutral, united Germany represented a better solution to the German problem than partition.[35]

America's policy toward Germany at the Potsdam Conference, however, was not going to be made by OMGUS or the State Department. The central figure in determining American policy at Potsdam was clearly Secretary of State Byrnes. Much like Roosevelt, Byrnes did not rely very much on his subordinates for advice and did not have much time or patience for abstract theoretical debates. Judging from the documentation found in the *Foreign Relations of the United States* series and his personal papers, Byrnes did not engage in lengthy discussions with his subordinates about the German problem prior to Potsdam. Indeed, British documents on Potsdam often provide more revealing glimpses into Byrnes's thinking than do American documents. The main thrust of the evidence, however, suggests that Byrnes was deeply committed to a solution of the German problem based on separate Western and Soviet zones. If any single statesman should be credited or blamed for taking the first deliberate step toward formalizing the division of Germany, the award would clearly have to go to Byrnes rather than Stalin or officials in the British Foreign Office. In contrast to Byrnes, both the British and the Soviets, for different reasons, fought against the idea of treating Germany in terms of separate economic zones.

---

[34] *FRUS, 1945, Potsdam Conference,* vol. 1, 456–61.
[35] "Problems and Objectives of United States Policy," April 2, 1945, with enclosing memorandum from William J. Donovan to Truman, May 5, 1945, Rose Conway File, box 15, HSTL.

Byrnes had two central concerns at Potsdam concerning Germany: keeping the Russians out of the western zones of Germany and undoing the connection between reparations and the treatment of Germany as a single economic unit. His interest in establishing clear limits to the extension of Soviet power and influence in Germany by the start of Potsdam can be seen in the firm opposition of the American government to any form of international control of the Ruhr. The Big Three had engaged in tentative discussions about postwar control of the Ruhr as early as the Teheran Conference, yet neither Byrnes nor Truman were willing to even discuss Soviet proposals at Potsdam.[36] Among the many reasons for the United States to oppose international control of the Ruhr, any such arrangement would inevitably lead to an undesirable extension of Soviet power into the heart of Western Europe, a point emphasized by the State Department and the Joint Strategic Survey Committee (JSSC).[37] At a very basic level, the origins of postwar containment in Europe can be seen in the unwillingness of Byrnes and Truman to consider Soviet proposals for international control of the Ruhr. The heart of Germany's industrial potential would be controlled exclusively by the West, without the participation of the Soviet Union.

Byrnes's desire to keep the Soviets out of the affairs of the western zones can be seen even more clearly in his plan for zonal reparations, which he proposed at Potsdam. American and British thinking on reparations prior to Potsdam had always conceptualized reparations within the context of the treatment of the German economy as a single economic unit. In a radical departure, Byrnes now proposed that the Soviets and the Western powers draw reparations solely from their own zones. Economic relations between the zones would largely consist of trading excess German industrial capacity from the west for food from the east. But the idea that a zonal reparations plan was consistent with the treatment of the German economy as a single unit was rightfully seen as a contradiction in terms—no matter how much the difference was minimized by the

---

[36] In *I Was There*, Admiral Leahy suggests that support for international control of the Ruhr was part of Truman's agenda at Potsdam, but all of the evidence from the conference supports the opposite conclusion. See Leahy, *I Was There*, 390, 428. Before turning over Walter Brown's diary notes to State Department historians in 1954, Byrnes made corrections in the margins of the diary in order to make it clear that he did not agree with, and never intended to present, any proposals for the internationalization of the Ruhr at Potsdam. See W. B.'s book, July 16, 1945, folder 54 (1) and folder 602, Byrnes Papers, Clemson University. To be sure, as Robert Messer points out, any conclusions drawn from the Byrnes Papers should be qualified because of the fact that Byrnes went out of his way to modify the records in order to emphasize his anticommunist credentials. Nevertheless, in this instance Byrnes's behavior at Potsdam is consistent with his comments on Brown's diary notes.

[37] "The Disposition of the Ruhr," *FRUS, 1945, Potsdam Conference*, vol. 1, 587. In addition to bringing the Soviets into Western Europe, the JSSC also argued against internationalization of the Ruhr because it "might well require larger United States commitments in the areas internationalized and for longer periods of time." See *FRUS, 1945, Potsdam Conference*, vol. 1, 595–96.

Americans. Sir David Waley, the leading British Treasury official concerned with the reparations issue at Potsdam, recognized that American advocacy of a zonal plan stemmed precisely from the belief that "the Russian zone will inevitably be treated as a separate economic unit and that however undesirable it may be to draw a line across the middle of Germany, this is bound to happen and it is unrealistic to make a bargain except on a basis that assumes it will happen."[38]

British officials at the Treasury and the Foreign Office were very perceptive in recognizing that Byrnes's zonal reparations plan virtually guaranteed a divided Germany, and it was precisely for this reason that they were vigorously *opposed* to the plan. According to Waley, "The most disturbing feature of the new American solution of the reparations problem was its implication that the U.S. government had abandoned hope of successful co-operation with the Russians in administering Germany as a single economic unit."[39] The British Foreign Office also viewed the Byrnes plan as a disaster because "however much we may safeguard the principle of economic unity on paper, the American plan, if followed as the Americans appear to understand it, will from the outset make it impossible to administer Germany as a unit."[40] Often viewed as more skeptical of the possibilities of postwar cooperation with the Soviets, the British were more reluctant than the Americans to make a deal at Potsdam based on the assumption that Germany would not be run as a single economic unit.

For the most part, British negotiators at Potsdam strove to eliminate what they viewed as the worst features of Byrnes's zonal reparations plan. For example, long after the Soviets and Americans had agreed to drop the first-charge principle, the crucial element in any unified treatment of Germany, British officials fought to have it reinstated. According to British Foreign Secretary Ernest Bevin, if the Big Three dropped the first-charge principle it would "cut across the agreement to treat Germany as a whole economy. It would divide Germany into three zones."[41]

---

[38] Memorandum by Sir D. Waley, August 2, 1945, in *DBPO*, series 1, vol. 1, 1259. As Waley noted, with the exception of Clay and Eisenhower, the rest of the American delegation thought it was "quite unrealistic" to believe that Germany was going to be treated as a single economic unit. See Waley to Eady, July 28, 1945, in *DBPO*, series 1, vol. 1, calendar 440i.

[39] "Note of Third Staff Conference with Prime Minister and Foreign Secretary," July 31, 1945, in *DBPO*, series 1, vol. 1, 1053. See also John Farquharson, "The Essential Division: Britain and the Partition of Germany, 1945–49," *German History* 9 (February 1991): 23–45; and Cairncross, *The Price of War*, 94–95.

[40] FO 934/1/4(34), "Reparation and German Economic Unity," July 31, 1945, in *DBPO*, series 1, vol. 1, 1071. This paper was prepared in the hope that "something may be saved from the wreckage" brought on by the American plan.

[41] *FRUS*, 1945, *Potsdam Conference*, vol. 2, 521. By the time Attlee and Bevin arrived at Potsdam, the British had decided to accept the zonal framework as long as it was modified to protect the first-charge principle and the treatment of Germany as a single economic unit. In a revealing commentary about the respective positions of the Big Three at Potsdam, Bevin drew encouragement from the fact that "The Russians were clearly willing to consider proposals for treating Germany as an economic whole, as was shown by their latest proposals

Indeed, virtually right up to the moment when the Big Three finally reached agreement on the reparations question, Waley continued his efforts to persuade Byrnes that the merits of a zonal plan were more than outweighed by the fact that it would lead to the consolidation of a divided Germany.

> I did my best to convince Byrnes that his system of swaps is utterly inconsistent with the idea of treating Germany as a single economic unit. I said that the peasant in Brandenberg who sells his potatoes to Berlin has to be paid by receiving boots and shoes from Berlin and cannot be paid by Russia receiving steel plant. I pointed out that if a line is drawn across the middle of Europe, so that there is a frontier with Russia on one side and the Western Powers on the other side, this has an importance far transcending reparations.[42]

British perceptions of the reparations settlement are important because of what they reveal about American attitudes toward the Soviet Union and the future of Germany. Even before Churchill and Eden left Potsdam on July 25 in order to find out the results of the recent elections, Byrnes made it clear that British views on Germany were of limited importance to him. Indeed, Byrnes did not even discuss the zonal reparations plan with the British before presenting it to Molotov on July 23. Despite the fact that the British controlled the resources of the Ruhr, Byrnes would repeatedly propose deals to Molotov without any prior consultation with the British. As Alec Cadogan noted in his diary, the numerous ways in which the British were slighted at Potsdam suggested that it would be more accurate to refer to the "Big 2 1/2" rather than the Big Three.[43] Attempts by the British to convince Byrnes to abandon his plan were unsuccessful.

For quite different reasons than the British, the Soviets were also not immediately receptive to a zonal reparations plan. Regardless of how extensively the Soviets removed goods and machinery from their own zone, it was highly unlikely that reparations on the scale they expected could be satisfied solely from within the eastern zone. It is precisely for this reason that Molotov was far from subtle in signaling his willingness to make significant concessions on reparations in order to preserve Soviet access to the western zones. After hearing Byrnes's proposal for a zonal reparations

---

for including in the Statement of Political Principles a passage about the need for some central German administration." See "Note of Third Staff Conference," in *DBPO*, series 1, vol. 1, 1053.

[42] Sir D. Waley to Sir W. Eady, July 31, 1945, in *DBPO*, series 1, vol. 1, 1050.

[43] See David Dilks, ed., *The Diaries of Sir Alec Cadogan, 1938–45* (New York: G. P. Putnam and Sons, 1971), 778. For an excellent discussion of how British views were ignored by the Americans, see Farquharson, "Anglo-American Policy on Reparations," 904–26.

settlement on July 23, Molotov immediately set out to reassure him that Stalin "strongly favored an overall plan for reparations" and that he "would be quite prepared to consider reducing their reparations claims."[44] During a meeting later in the day, Molotov proved his willingness to negotiate on the basis of the Yalta protocol by offering to deduct two billion dollars from Soviet claims in order to eliminate any difficulties caused by unauthorized removals from the eastern zone.[45]

The key to understanding American diplomacy at Potsdam lies in recognizing that Byrnes did not want to strike a deal based on the unified treatment of the German economy, regardless of how much the Soviet Union was willing to reduce its reparations claims. Widely regarded as a "fixer" and acknowledged to be one of the shrewdest negotiators in American politics, Byrnes could not have missed Molotov's willingness to make serious concessions on virtually every element involved in the reparations question.[46] If a diplomat as experienced in international affairs as Molotov was willing to reduce Soviet claims by over two billion dollars in less than one hour of informal discussions, it should have been fairly obvious that he was prepared to reduce the amount even further in later stages of the bargaining process. However, the question of how far the Soviet Union might ultimately have been willing to reduce its claims in order to achieve a unified reparations settlement is really a moot point because Byrnes repeatedly made it clear that he was only willing to negotiate within the context of his zonal reparations plan.

Why was Byrnes so committed to the adoption of a zonal reparations plan? The answer is not at all obvious. After all, a fundamental tenet of State Department planning up to the Potsdam Conference was the conviction that all of Germany must be treated as a single economic unit. Even economic arrangements between the three western zones were opposed by the State Department because "it would tend toward the establishment of an economic wall between Eastern and Western Germany, and, probably between Eastern and Western Europe."[47] The Soviet insistence on the fixed sum of twenty billion dollars presented a serious obstacle to an agreement, but less than three weeks before Potsdam the State

---

[44] *FRUS,* 1945, *Potsdam Conference,* vol. 2, 275.

[45] Ibid., 295–98.

[46] In addition to addressing the amount of reparations, Molotov put forward compromise proposals related to the first-charge principle and implied that the Soviets were willing to modify their extremely broad definition of what constituted "war booty." See ibid., 274–75, 279–81, 810. In what would have been a very significant concession, there is even evidence that Stalin attempted to convince the Polish leaders to reduce their claims on German territory in order to improve his own hand concerning reparations. See Vojtech Mastny, *Russia's Road to the Cold War: Diplomacy, Warfare, and the Politics of Communism, 1941–45* (New York: Columbia University Press, 1979), 299–300.

[47] See the Briefing Book Paper, "Policy Toward Germany," *FRUS,* 1945, *Potsdam Conference,* vol. 1, 441.

Department had instructed Pauley that a figure between twelve and fourteen billion, with half of all available reparations allocated to the Soviet Union, represented a realistic starting point for negotiations. The reduction of the overall Soviet claim to eight billion dollars, and Molotov's indication that he would be willing to reduce the claim even further, would appear to have put the two sides well within the range of a settlement.[48] Although there were possible merits to a zonal reparations plan, Byrnes's proposal ran a very great risk of establishing a de facto partition of Germany—as British officials repeatedly pointed out.[49]

Byrnes himself always maintained that he went to Potsdam in favor of reaching an overall reparations settlement and that he only reluctantly abandoned this position when faced with the reality that the Soviets had stripped their zone, unilaterally assigned part of it to Poland, and persisted in advancing an outrageous definition of war trophies.[50] This may indeed have been the case, but there is simply no evidence to suggest that Byrnes made any effort toward salvaging a unified reparations framework during the first week of the conference. If Soviet behavior was only "reluctantly" forcing him to abandon a unified plan, then it is surely a puzzle why he took no steps to warn Molotov of the inevitable consequences of Soviet conduct before putting forward his zonal plan, and why he maintained his own inflexible position after the Soviets demonstrated a willingness to negotiate on both the principles and the amounts of a settlement.[51] Whether a different approach on Byrnes's part would have resulted in an acceptable unified plan is far from certain, but it is not beyond the realm of possibility that the Soviets might have been willing to abandon exclusive control of their zone for an acceptable reparations agreement.[52]

The primary reason Byrnes pushed for a zonal reparations plan at Potsdam ultimately must be attributed to his intuitive belief that a unified plan would lead to endless conflicts and disagreements between the United States and the Soviet Union. Unlike many British and American officials, Byrnes did not approach the reparations question from a predominately economic perspective. Byrnes was probably well aware that

[48] Ibid., 519.

[49] State Department officials who did not attend the Potsdam Conference, such as Charles Kindleberger and Willard Thorp, also viewed Byrnes's plan as one that would result in a divided Europe. See Kuklick, *American Policy and the Division of Germany*, 162.

[50] See *FRUS, 1945, Potsdam Conference*, vol. 2, 295–97; James F. Byrnes, *All in One Lifetime* (New York: Harper & Brothers, 1958), 301; and the memo of a conversation between Byrnes and Senator Warren Austin published in Thomas G. Patterson, "Potsdam, the Atomic Bomb, and the Cold War: A Discussion with James F. Byrnes," *Pacific Historic Review* 41 (May 1972): 225–30.

[51] For an excellent example of alternative courses that Byrnes could have pursued if he had been interested in a unified plan, see the recommendations made by Phillip Mosely to Will Clayton, July 22, 1945, *FRUS, 1945, Potsdam Conference*, vol. 2, 850–52.

[52] See Farquharson, "The Essential Division," 26–27.

the desire of the Soviets for large-scale reparations could be exploited in exchange for their acceptance of Western economic principles, but he also seems to have recognized that an agreement negotiated under these circumstances would have been both worthless and counterproductive for both parties. What the Soviets conceded under duress at Potsdam they would later seek to take back by reinterpreting or evading the letter of the agreement. According to Isador Lubin, Byrnes simply did not have any faith in the Soviet Union's willingness to adhere to an agreement on reparations: "They wanted to take what they could take anyway, so he said, 'To hell with it. What's the use of trying to figure out, who, where, and so on.' So we said everything beyond a point to the East you get, everything in the West we get and if we want to give you something from the west, we'll negotiate on it."[53]

The fact that a zonal reparations plan led in the direction of a divided Germany did not really matter to Byrnes because he clearly thought division to be a likely outcome regardless of the position he adopted. The great advantage of a zonal plan was that it would make it easier for both the United States and the Soviet Union to maintain amicable relations by avoiding potential sources of conflict. This was the essence of the argument he made to the Soviets throughout Potsdam. Noting all of the factors that stood in the way of a unified plan, Byrnes told Molotov that he was "very much afraid that the attempt to resolve these conditions in practice would lead to endless quarrels and disagreements between the three countries at a time when unity between them was essential."[54] When Molotov demanded to know if the United States was openly repudiating the Yalta agreements, Byrnes stated that the Yalta framework should be abandoned because any attempt to carry it out "would be a constant source of irritation between us, whereas the United States wanted its relations to be cordial and friendly as heretofore." Indeed, as he explained to Molotov on July 27, the preservation of friendly relations was the most important reason for adopting a zonal plan: "What had impressed him [Byrnes] the most—it was more important than the money involved—was the desire to remove any source of irritation between our two governments."[55]

It is easy to dismiss Byrnes's statements about preserving friendly relations as pure diplomatic pabulum, particularly since he was concerned about reducing the amount of reparations that the Soviet Union could expect to get out of the western zones, but the evidence does not support this interpretation. As Robert James Maddox points out, "Reparations was one of the few issues for which the failure to gain agreement would

---

[53] Lubin Oral History, COHP, 90.
[54] *FRUS, 1945, Potsdam Conference*, vol. 2, 274.
[55] Ibid., 430.

have worked to the advantage of the United States—the bulk of German industry lay in the western zones."[56] If Byrnes's only purpose was to deny the Soviets reparations from the western zones, he could have simply terminated the negotiations or postponed them to a later date. In addition, Byrnes could have indirectly denied the Soviets any reparations from the western zones by simply allowing his negotiators to squabble endlessly over the first-charge principle, the definition of restitution and war booty, and a host of other issues. The fact that he did not take either approach supports the interpretation that Byrnes sincerely wanted to reach an amicable reparations settlement that both the United States and the Soviet Union could willingly accept.

Often overlooked in discussions of the Byrnes reparations plan is the fact that a zonal approach had some very attractive features for the Soviet Union. First, Byrnes promised the Soviets a totally free hand to remove whatever they wanted from their own zone: "what was available in the Soviet zone would concern neither the British, French nor United States and they would not, therefore, be interfering in that determination."[57] When Molotov said that he understood the American proposal to mean that the Soviets would only be entitled to a fixed percentage from their own zone, Byrnes quickly corrected him; "The Secretary replied that this was not quite accurate, since in the first place the Soviet Union would take what it wished from its zone."[58] Second, Byrnes assured the Soviets that their share of reparations would be delivered regardless of economic conditions in the western zones: "If the Soviets agreed to his plan they would have no interest in exports and imports from our zone. Any difficulty in regard to imports and exports would have to be settled between the British and ourselves. The Soviets would get their percentage regardless of what happened to us."[59] Finally, in return for agreement on the reparations proposal, Byrnes agreed to accept the previously rejected Soviet claims for more extensive cessions of German territory to Poland.

Reaching the final settlement on reparations, however, required Byrnes to depart from a strictly zonal arrangement. These changes would later wind up providing the basis for the 1946 conflict over reparations. As the plan was originally conceived, economic exchanges between the eastern and western zones would largely consist of barter deals in which industrial plant from the Ruhr would be exchanged for food and raw materials of equivalent value from the Soviet zone. The Soviets had no objection in principle to a "system of swaps," as long as they were also provided with an additional and fixed amount of equipment from the Ruhr as compen-

---

[56] Robert James Maddox, *From War to Cold War: The Education of Harry S. Truman* (Boulder, Colo.: Westview Press, 1988), 98.

[57] *FRUS, 1945, Potsdam Conference*, vol. 2, 487.

[58] Ibid., 475.

[59] Ibid., 491.

sation for the fact that their zone had a lesser percentage of Germany's remaining wealth. The Soviet position was based on the Yalta provision that they were entitled to half of all available reparations from Germany. Byrnes and Pauley asserted that the eastern zone contained 50 percent of Germany's remaining wealth, but if it did not, then it logically followed that the Soviets were entitled to some form of compensation from the western zones if they adopted the American plan.

The Soviet insistence that their zone had only 42 percent of Germany's remaining wealth added a serious complication to negotiations for a purely zonal settlement.[60] Privately, Will Clayton, assistant secretary of state, acknowledged to the British reparations team as early as the evening of July 24 that in order to strike a bargain with the Soviets he was eventually willing to concede that the eastern zone had only 45 percent of Germany's remaining wealth and that, therefore, the Western powers should be willing to provide a certain percentage of equipment from the Ruhr as compensation.[61] Although the documentation on the internal American discussions is very incomplete, it is clear that Pauley and Harriman openly resisted Clayton's approach. After a meeting with Byrnes on July 29, Clayton wrote a memo that set out why the Soviets were correct in maintaining that there was a disparity in the distribution of the wealth remaining in the eastern and western zones. More important, Clayton told Byrnes that the Soviets should be permitted to have a voice in determining what equipment was removed from the Ruhr: "I feel that any decision to exclude them from any participation in the distribution of the heavy equipment of the Ruhr as reparation would be considered by the Russians as a reversal of the Yalta and Moscow position, since no Allied understanding would be necessary to enable them to get reparations from their own zone."[62]

Choosing between the conflicting positions held by Pauley and Clayton could not have been an easy decision for Byrnes. The Pauley stance would have denied the Soviets any voice at all in economic affairs in the western zones, which is what Byrnes wanted. It is for this reason that Byrnes's first reaction was to side with Pauley and preserve the clarity of a strictly zonal settlement. Despite the fact that Clayton had just recommended to him that he accept the idea that the Soviets were legitimately entitled to some amount of compensation from the western zones, Byrnes continued to maintain his previous line that the eastern zone had 50 percent of Germany's remaining wealth. Actually, he attempted to go even further by telling Molotov for the first time that "percentage figures fixed at Yalta were no

[60] Record of Meeting on German Reparations held at the Cecilienhof, July 24, 1945, in *DBPO*, series 1, vol. 1, 665.

[61] Memorandum by Sir W. Monckton, July 24, 1945, in *DBPO*, series 1, vol. 1, 617.

[62] See Clayton to Byrnes, July 29, 1945, *FRUS*, 1945, *Potsdam Conference*, vol. 2, 900–1 (quotation on 901). Pauley's disagreement with Clayton's views can be found on 917.

more agreed to except as a basis of discussion than had been the actual amounts of reparations."[63] Perhaps inadvertently, Truman quickly dashed the already slight prospects Byrnes had of establishing this line of argument by stating that he wished to see the Soviets receive 50 percent of all the available reparations from Germany.

Byrnes was now faced with the prospect of holding out for a pure zonal settlement or bargaining with the Soviets on the basis of Clayton's proposal, and he decided to side with Clayton. On July 30, Byrnes conceded the issue of compensation when he put forward a proposal that provided the Soviet Union with a certain percentage of industrial machinery from the Ruhr "free and clear." He also sweetened the deal by accepting the Western Neisse as the provisional German-Polish border. Over the course of the next two days, the Big Three haggled over the specific percentages and finally agreed that 15 percent of the capital equipment available in the western zones deemed to be unnecessary for the German peacetime economy should be exchanged for food and other raw materials from the east, and that an additional 10 percent of unnecessary capital equipment should be provided to the Soviet Union without any corresponding payment. With the most difficult of all questions settled, the Potsdam Conference ended with the semblance of a great power agreement on Germany.

Virtually all historians agree that the zonal reparations settlement was a very significant step toward a divided Germany. The controversial question about Potsdam is whether Byrnes and other American officials were aware of the fact that the zonal plan would lead to this outcome. Interestingly, both revisionist and orthodox scholars reject the idea that Byrnes and Truman were aware of the long-term implications of the zonal reparations plan. Drawing heavily on the open door theory of William Appleman Williams, Bruce Kuklick argues that Byrnes and other American officials "did not clearly see that they had gone a long way in dividing Germany; they thought the Russians would eventually come around."[64] After noting that Molotov was well aware that a zonal reparations plan undermined the principle of a unified treatment of Germany, John Lewis Gaddis argues that neither Byrnes nor Truman shared a similar awareness: "But the President and his secretary of state, preoccupied with their immediate goal of minimizing American responsibilities in Europe, failed to see or chose to ignore the long-range implications of their own policy."[65]

There is some evidence to support the idea that Byrnes may have failed to recognize the long-term implications of the zonal plan. If Byrnes in-

[63] Ibid., 474.
[64] Kuklick, *American Policy and the Division of Germany*, 160.
[65] John Lewis Gaddis, *The United States and the Origins of the Cold War, 1941–1947* (New York: Columbia University Press, 1971), 241.

tended his zonal plan to have a broader application than simply reparations, it seems logical that he would have at least explored the possibility of abandoning prior plans for the establishment of central administrations and other arrangements which required active cooperation between the Soviets and the Western powers. Indeed, if Byrnes's objective was to reduce potential sources of friction and tension between the United States and the Soviet Union, he should have been the first to recognize that the creation and management of central administrations would have been a never ending source of potential future conflict. However, there is no evidence that Byrnes ever contemplated abandoning plans for central administrations at any point during the Potsdam Conference. More than once, Byrnes explained to Molotov that "under his scheme nothing was changed in regard to overall treatment of German finance, transport, foreign trade, etc."[66]

There is also no direct evidence that would allow us to rule out the possibility that Byrnes may have sincerely thought that central administrations could potentially serve as counterbalancing factors to a zonal reparations settlement. Nevertheless, before accepting the idea that Byrnes was confused or ignorant about the consequences of his own plan, it should be noted that he had an overwhelming political interest in conveying the impression that he was against the partition of Germany. Both the State Department and the War Department were in favor of preserving a united Germany. Clay and Eisenhower were also in favor of giving the Allied Control Council (ACC) every possible chance to preserve the wartime alliance in Germany. By supporting central administrations, Byrnes may have simply wanted to put himself on record in favor of common policies in order to deflect possible criticism from those within the U.S. government who were already critical of the zonal reparations plan. More important, with Stalin having already publicly voiced his support for German unity, Byrnes may have wanted to guard himself against the possibility of later being blamed for the division of Germany. In short, although it is possible that Byrnes may have had some residual faith in four-power control of Germany, or that he was simply hedging his bets, the fact that he supported central administrations at Potsdam can also be explained in terms of purely tactical considerations and political expediency.

Nevertheless, the preponderance of evidence suggests that Byrnes was well aware of the likely outcome of Potsdam and that his goal was to establish the basis for a friendly division of Germany. By focusing on issues such as central administrations and the text of the conference protocol, he intentionally conveyed a misleading impression of ambivalence. Most of the general political and economic principles for the postwar treatment of Germany had been developed before Byrnes put forward his zonal plan

---

[66] See *FRUS, 1945, Potsdam Conference,* vol. 2, 275, 474.

and they survived partly through inertia and a lack of interest. For understandable reasons, both Byrnes and Molotov had suspended discussions over general economic principles for Germany until progress had been made on the more pressing matter of reparations. It was not until July 31, after the basic outlines of the zonal plan had been settled, that the Big Three returned to the question of economic principles. In a move that reflected his intuitive understanding of the reparations deal he had arranged with Molotov, Byrnes's first motion was to delete the entire paragraph related to the first-charge principle from the final protocol.[67] Stalin was more than willing to go along with the motion, but Bevin refused because the Foreign Office felt that this "would be admitting failure to treat Germany as an economic unit."[68]

Bevin and the Foreign Office were absolutely correct about the larger implications of dropping paragraph 19, but its retention in the final protocol made no sense when Byrnes had already negotiated a deal that provided the Soviets with a totally free hand to do what they wanted in their zone. The dispute over the wording of paragraph 19 lasted all the way to the end of the conference and, in the end, the differing views of the British and the Americans were simply papered over. With Byrnes and Truman already determined to leave Potsdam on August 1, American negotiators simply did not want to argue any more about general economic principles. A memorandum prepared by Waley the day after the conference shows very clearly why the true meaning of Potsdam should never be sought in the protocols and the agreed-upon economic principles:

(a) An agreed satisfactory reparations programme. This is fully provided for in the documents, but some at any rate of the Americans, particularly Mr. Pauley, think that it is inevitable that Russia will do what she likes in her own zone and has no business to interfere with what we do in ours. This may lead to trouble hereafter.

(b) Acceptance of the prior charge on exports.

We secured this at the last moment—see paragraph 19 of the Economic Principles. The Americans, who had so passionately advocated this principle swung round to the opposite extreme. They thought that, in fact, exports and imports would have to be arranged on a zonal basis and that the formula would tie their hands. *However, they dropped their objections at the last moment.*

---

[67] Ibid., 520–21.

[68] FO 934/1/2, "Economic Principles," in *DBPO*, series 1, vol. 1, calendar 495ii. It is worth noting that when Bevin raised this argument, Byrnes did not protest that the interpretation was wrong but simply "asked why they did not handle this in their own way since they were in control in their zone." See *FRUS*, 1945, *Potsdam Conference*, vol. 2, 521.

(c) Full acceptance of Germany as one economic unit for the purposes of the Control Commission.

Here again the documents entirely endorse this view, but we know that Mr. Pauley believes it to be quite unrealistic.[69]

American officials were not immune to the temptation to interpret Potsdam in ways that went directly against the spirit of the deal Byrnes had negotiated with Molotov. For example, less than three days after Potsdam, Pauley informed Clay that the reparations question was "inseparably interwoven" with the development of common export-import programs for all of Germany.[70] In contrast to Byrnes, who had explicitly assured the Soviets that they would have a totally free hand to remove whatever they wished from their zone, Pauley now "interpreted" a paragraph in the Potsdam Protocol in the following manner: "As I view it this means that the Allied Control Council should make every attempt to arrange for reparations removals throughout Germany on a uniform basis both as to type, kind, and extent of such removals."[71] Clayton, who had urged Byrnes to accept Soviet participation in determining the character of reparations removals in the west without suggesting any kind of reciprocity in the east, also attempted to reclaim rights that Byrnes had explicitly renounced.[72]

Not surprisingly, the Soviets protested the idea that the Western powers had the right to codetermine what they could remove from the eastern zone.[73] An interpretation of Potsdam along these lines would have denied them precisely what Byrnes had promised at the conference: a totally free hand within their zone. Significantly, Byrnes himself was well aware that these reinterpretations of Potsdam had no justification. In a cable sent to Undersecretary of State Dean Acheson and Clayton from the London Conference, Byrnes stated that "There is [a] serious question in my mind as to whether the approach to the German reparations problem taken by the Department in its recent communication to the Soviet, British, and French Governments correctly reflects the spirit of the Potsdam Protocol

---

[69] Memorandum by Sir D. Waley, August 2, 1945, in *DBPO*, series 1, vol. 1, 1260. Emphasis added. These were the three conditions that the British had established for accepting the zonal framework.

[70] Pauley to Clay, August 4, 1945, *FRUS*, 1945, vol. 3, 1242.

[71] Pauley to Clay, August 11, 1945, *FRUS*, 1945, vol. 3, 1251–52. Paragraph 14 (f) of the protocol did support this interpretation, but Pauley surely knew that Byrnes had sold the zonal plan on the basis that the Soviets had a free hand in their zone.

[72] See Clayton to Harriman, September 6, 1945, *FRUS*, 1945, vol. 3, 1284; and Clayton to Byrnes, September 10, 1945, RG 84, Records of the U.S. Political Advisor for Germany 1944–49, Classified Cables From the State Department, box 2, National Archives, College Park, Md. (hereafter NA).

[73] For Soviet protests regarding the American interpretation of the agreement, see *FRUS*, 1945, vol. 3, 1257, 1295.

or is likely to produce any tangible results."[74] Byrnes indicated he wanted to discuss the entire matter when he returned to Washington, but there are no records of any further meetings on the subject. Since Clay continued to interpret the Potsdam reparations settlement along the lines set out by Clayton and Pauley, it would appear that Byrnes either came to accept this interpretation of the reparations settlement or found it politically expedient to do so. In either case, the virtues of establishing a clear line between the western and eastern zones were lost even on the reparations question.

FRANCE AND THE GERMAN QUESTION

The reparations settlement clearly pointed in the direction of a divided Germany. The rest of the Potsdam Protocol suggested that Germany was to be run as a single unit with central administrations. Which conception of postwar Germany ultimately was to prevail was greatly complicated by the fact that French officials wasted little time in announcing their own concerns about the implications of the Potsdam settlement. Officially, the French argued that the decision to establish central administrative agencies was premature because it seemed to imply that at some point a centralized government with authority over all of Germany would evolve out of the occupation process. In diplomatic language, the French government "reserved" its position on this aspect of the Potsdam Protocol because of its belief that "it is impossible to foresee at the present time whether such an evolution corresponds to the interests of European peace and to the wishes of the population involved."[75] Unofficially, French diplomats were much more direct about their reasons for opposing the Potsdam settlement. Jefferson Caffery, the American ambassador to France, reported to Washington that "the French are convinced that despite the Potsdam declaration the Soviet government intends without delay to lay a solid foundation for the establishment of a central German Communist government to eventually take over power in Germany."[76]

French concerns about the Soviet Union reinforced their determination to prevent the reestablishment of a united Germany with sovereignty over the Ruhr and the Rhineland. The French thesis on postwar security

[74] Byrnes to Acheson and Clayton, September 28, 1945, *FRUS*, 1945, vol. 3, 1319.

[75] *FRUS*, 1945, *Potsdam Conference*, vol. 2, 1555.

[76] RG 59, 851.001/8–1345, August 13, 1945, NA. A week earlier, French Foreign Minister Georges Bidault had told Caffery that the French were opposed to central administrations because "it is the intention of the Soviet government to Sovietize all Germany as rapidly as they can do so." See *FRUS*, 1945, *Potsdam Conference*, vol. 2, 1549. Caffery was very sympathetic to French concerns about central administrations and the Soviet Union. See Steven P. Sapp, "The United States, France, and the Cold War: Jefferson Caffery and American-French Relations, 1944–49" (Ph.D diss., Kent State University, 1978), 78–148.

against Germany, which they had outlined to the British as early as August 1944, was based on two fundamental assumptions rooted in the lessons of the interwar period. The first assumption, as John Young points out, was that the reestablishment of a united Germany in control of both the Ruhr and the Rhineland would eventually be powerful enough to "break free of obligations placed on it from outside in a peace treaty in the style of Versailles."[77] The French thesis was based on the belief that collective security and disarmament treaties could not serve as viable substitutes for reducing the structural basis of German power. It is for this reason that France insisted on an immediate and permanent decision to remove the Ruhr from German authority. The second assumption of French policy was that neither Great Britain nor the United States could be counted on to maintain occupation forces in Germany for very long after the war. As early as November 1944, Bidault attempted to justify a "privileged position" for France in the postwar control of Germany because the "British and Americans will one day want to go home. We will remain."[78]

French views on security were obviously strongly influenced by the lessons of the previous peace settlement, but de Gaulle and other officials were not oblivious to the vastly different distribution of power that had emerged as a result of the war. Like Churchill, de Gaulle was very quick to recognize the collapse of the classical European balance-of-power system and Western Europe's total dependence on the United States. During a meeting with Caffery on May 5, 1945, de Gaulle noted that "after the war there would be only two real forces in the world: The USA and the Soviets. . . . The British Empire will not be strong enough to count for much. If I cannot work with you I must work with the Soviets in order to survive even if it is only for a while and even if in the long run they gobble us up too."[79] In the view of Colonel Dewarin, the head of French intelligence and a close associate of de Gaulle's, Russia's predominant position on the continent meant that France had no alternative but to seek close relations with the United States. According to Dewarin, Franco-American disagreements over Germany were of strictly minor importance because of the more compelling threat posed by the Soviet Union.[80] However, in the immediate aftermath of Potsdam, America's long-term presence and objectives in Europe were still far too uncertain for de Gaulle to simply

---

[77] John W. Young, *France, the Cold War and the Western Alliance, 1944–49* (Leicester, England: Leicester University Press, 1990), 26. See also William I. Hitchcock, *France Restored: Cold War Diplomacy and the Quest for Leadership in France, 1944–54* (Chapel Hill: University of North Carolina Press, 1998).

[78] Bidault interview of November 11, 1944, cited in A. W. DePorte, *De Gaulle's Foreign Policy, 1944–46* (Cambridge, Mass.: Harvard University Press, 1968), 161.

[79] Caffery to Acting Secretary of State, May 5, 1945, *FRUS*, 1945, vol. 4, 686.

[80] RG 59, 711.51/11–2045, November 20, 1945, Caffery to Byrnes, Transmitting Memorandum of Conversation with Colonel Dewarin (Passy), NA.

abandon the French thesis on Germany in order to get along with the United States. For example, as he explained to Caffery in November 1945, he could not abandon his opposition to U.S. policy on central administrations because the price of pursuing a mistaken course in Germany was much greater for France than it was for the United States: "You are far away and your soldiers will not stay long in Europe. It is hard for you to understand the difference: it is a matter of life and death for us; for you, one interesting question among others."[81]

De Gaulle and Bidault had outlined their views at length to Byrnes and Truman during a visit to Washington in late August 1945, but neither the president nor the secretary of state was very receptive to the French thesis on Germany. When de Gaulle suggested that the Potsdam framework potentially left the door open to either a rebirth of independent German power or to Soviet domination, both Truman and Byrnes replied that "the German danger should not be exaggerated." In their view, France should concentrate on her own economic reconstruction and not worry about the "somewhat remote" prospects of a new German menace.[82] As for the centerpiece of the French thesis, the detachment of the Ruhr from Germany, Byrnes confessed that he "did not see how an amputation of the kind demanded by Mr. Bidault could be more effective than the force of the whole world organized in the United Nations."[83] Byrnes also suggested that French plans for the Ruhr were unnecessary because America would be willing to sponsor a twenty-five-year disarmament treaty against Germany when the occupation came to an end.[84]

The American-French meetings of August 1945 marked the start of a long postwar tradition in which differing strategies and tactical disagreements over Germany would make it hard to achieve common objectives. Both Bidault and Byrnes were interested in preventing the extension of Soviet influence into the western zones, but they spoke right past each other during these meetings. On the one hand, Byrnes clearly did not appreciate the French fear that central administrations operating out of Berlin might facilitate the extension of Soviet influence into Western

---

[81] Caffery to Secretary of State, November 3, 1945, *FRUS*, 1945, vol. 3, 890.

[82] Memorandum of Conversation between President Truman and General de Gaulle, August 22, 1945, *FRUS*, 1945, vol. 4, 707–8.

[83] Memorandum of Conversation between Bidault and Byrnes, August 23, 1945, *FRUS*, 1945, vol. 4, 720. See also Irwin M. Wall, "Harry S. Truman and Charles de Gaulle," and the comments by Melvyn Leffler in *De Gaulle and the United States: A Centennial Reappraisal*, ed. Robert O. Paxton and Nicholas Wahl (Oxford: Berg Publishers, 1994), 117–29, 134–38.

[84] Memorandum of Conversation between Byrnes and Bidault, August 24, 1945, *FRUS*, 1945, vol. 4, 724. Bidault was not at all impressed with either Byrnes's or Truman's views during these meetings. He later told the British ambassador to the United States that he had "found the President and Mr. Byrnes very ignorant of the background of international affairs." See Mr. Balfour to Mr. Bevin, August 26, 1945, in *DBPO*, series 1, vol. 5, *Germany and Western Europe: 11 August–31 December 1945* (London: Her Majesty's Stationery Office, 1990), 75.

Europe. In his view, France had little reason to be concerned about the fact that there would be "a man in Berlin who would administer all the railroads of the shrunken country."[85] On the other hand, neither Bidault nor de Gaulle made any serious effort to reconcile the apparent contradiction between their position on central administrations and their support for international control of the Ruhr. Byrnes was highly conscious of the fact that the Soviets would not be receptive to a purely nominal role in the administration and control of the Ruhr.

Byrnes suggested to Bidault that the future of the Ruhr could be discussed at greater length after the French elections scheduled for November, but de Gaulle was determined to force the German question to the top of the diplomatic agenda. The French thought that since Germany was the key issue of the peace settlement, the Council of Foreign Ministers (CFM) should settle this question before resolving questions of lesser importance. Molotov was more than willing to engage in discussions about the future of the Ruhr, but Bevin declared that he was unwilling to discuss the issue at the present time. After a brief discussion, it was agreed that the future of the Ruhr should be addressed through normal diplomatic channels before it was considered by the CFM. However, in order to ensure that French concerns would be taken seriously, Bidault also submitted a memorandum which warned that the French representatives on the Allied Control Council would not be empowered to make any decisions related to the Ruhr and the Rhineland until after the CFM had resolved the issue. The French were not engaging in idle threats, as they proved over the course of the next few weeks by vetoing the establishment of a central transport administration and refusing to permit the amalgamation of trade unions on a national level.[86]

None of the diplomats at the CFM seems to have been very concerned about Bidault's threat, but Eisenhower and Clay viewed the French decision as a fundamental challenge to the implementation of the Potsdam Protocol and the preservation of the wartime alliance in Germany. Determined to get a quick answer to the question of whether the Soviets would cooperate with the Western powers in running Germany as a single economic unit, Clay and Eisenhower were unwilling to accept the idea that French concerns about the future of the Ruhr constituted a legitimate reason for delaying the establishment of central administrations. Even before the French officially vetoed the creation of a central transport administration on September 22, Eisenhower openly criticized their position in the ACC and, according to William Strang, "went so far as to say that if it was not possible to get early agreement in Berlin to run Germany as an

---

[85] Memorandum of Conversation between Byrnes and Bidault, *FRUS*, 1945, vol. 4, 720.
[86] See CFM (45) 17, "Control and Administration of Germany," *FRUS*, 1945, vol. 3, 869–71.

economic whole and to set up central administrations, he would recommend to his government that he should be recalled to the United States and that the U.S. forces of occupation should be withdrawn."[87]

Clay was so determined to get around the French veto in the ACC that he immediately approached Great Britain and the Soviet Union with proposals to establish central administrations within their own zones. Impressed by Clay and Eisenhower's repeated statements to the effect that the French position on central administrations would lead to a rapid American withdrawal from Europe, Strang and Field Marshall Montgomery were also in favor of having their government put diplomatic pressure on the French.[88] Acknowledging that the French position was based on fear of the Russians exploiting central administrations for their own purposes, Montgomery nevertheless argued that they should be brought into line with the Anglo-American position:

> But the French attitude towards a dismembered Germany with no central administration will merely result in the Americans leaving Europe, and the Russians will then appear on the Rhine thus tending to make the French position more difficult still. . . . The French are cutting their own throats by standing out against the agreed conclusions of the American, British and Russian delegations. Their future safety and security lies in being firmly in the quadripartite set-up and not a dissenting member. The Americans are getting restive and if they were to pull out the French would be worse off.[89]

The efforts of the British and American occupation authorities to pressure the French were doomed from the start because both Bevin and Byrnes had already decided not to pursue such a course. As early as September 30, Bevin cabled Montgomery and told him that he "had spoken to United States Secretary of State on this whole question of French attitude in Berlin and asked him that General Eisenhower may be instructed not to press the French too hard on matter for the time being."[90] More important, Bevin essentially told Bidault during the London CFM that he and Byrnes were in agreement that France would not be subjected

---

[87] Sir W. Strang to Mr. Harvey, September 21, 1945, in *DBPO*, series 1, vol. 5, 142. For Eisenhower's frustration with the French veto in the ACC, see also Murphy to Secretary of State, October 20, 1945, *FRUS*, vol. 3, 846–47.

[88] See Control Commission to War Office, October 5; Strang to Bevin, October 27; and B. Montgomery to A. Street (Control Office), October 30, all in *DBPO*, series 1, vol. 5, 178–82, 289–93, and 306–7. For an excellent review of the British position on central administrations, see John Young, "The Foreign Office, the French, and the Post-War Division of Germany, 1945–46," *Review of International Studies* 12 (1986): 223–34.

[89] B. Montgomery to A. Street (Control Office), October 30, 1945, in *DBPO*, series 1, vol. 5, 307.

[90] See October 5, 1945, in *DBPO*, series 1, vol. 5, 179.

to heavy pressure to change their position in the Allied Control Council on central administrations.[91] France's ability to flaunt the will of the Big Three on the question of central administrations, which has impressed so many historians, becomes far less impressive when viewed in the context of Bevin's assurances to Bidault.

Clay and Murphy returned to Washington in early November to argue the case for putting diplomatic pressure on France. Their efforts were bolstered by the submission of the Byron Price Report to President Truman on November 9, 1945. Price, sent by Truman to Germany in order to provide an independent analysis of the problems confronting the American occupation authorities, concluded that the deadlock in Berlin was "due almost entirely to the rigid opposition of the French" and that breaking the impasse in the ACC was so important to the objectives of American foreign policy that "use of the full force and prestige of American diplomatic power to that end is fully warranted."[92] In effect, both Price and Clay were calling for a reversal of American policy toward France because, as H. Freeman Matthews, director of European Affairs, frankly acknowledged to Clay on November 3, "the State Department had taken no steps to bring pressure to bear upon the French to cooperate with the other members of the Control Council in carrying out the Berlin Protocol with respect to the treatment of Germany as an economic unit."[93]

In the first of many such clashes with State Department officials, Clay rejected the implicit suggestion put forward by James Riddleberger, chief of the Division of Central European Affairs that he should focus on Soviet rather than French violations of Potsdam. Indeed, the Soviets could not have asked for a better defense of their behavior in Germany than the one Clay provided for them during his meeting with the State Department. In the absence of central administrations, Clay argued that the Soviets were partially justified in preventing free interzonal movement within Germany. If the four occupying powers were to be ranked by their willingness to adhere to the Potsdam agreement, Clay suggested that the Soviet Union would place second: "The entire record of the Control Council showed that the USSR was willing to cooperate with the other powers in operating Germany as a single political and economic unit. The USSR had blocked no more than one or two papers in the Control Council which is more than can be said for the other members."[94]

---

[91] For Bevin's reassurance to Bidault, see Cooper to Mr. Dixon, October 4, 1945, in *DBPO*, series 1, vol. 2, *Conferences and Conversations 1945: London, Washington, and Moscow* (London: Her Majesty's Stationery Office, 1985), 485.

[92] Byron Price Report, November 9, 1945, RG 59, Records of the Office of the Assistant Secretary of State for Occupied Areas, 1946–49, box 3, NA.

[93] Resume of Meeting at State Department, November 3, 1945, in *Clay Papers*, 1:112.

[94] Resume of Meeting at State Department, *Clay Papers*, 1:113.

Clay's perspective toward the Soviet Union and France in the months after Potsdam was heavily influenced by his continuing support for the broad goals and tactics of Roosevelt's wartime diplomacy. As John McCloy pointed out to British officials who were disturbed about Clay's behavior in the ACC, "Clay was a firm believer in Four-Power collaboration. . . . he was nervous that any appearance of ganging up against the Russians by the Americans and the British might make Four-Power collaboration difficult or impossible, and as a matter of tactics was therefore perhaps much too inclined from time to time to go through the motions of aligning himself with the Russians."[95] The fact that the Soviets professed their support for the establishment of central administrations was sufficient evidence for Clay to conclude that cooperation in Germany remained possible. Prior to the establishment of central administrations, Clay was essentially willing to give the Soviets a free pass on adhering to the Potsdam agreements. In his view, "the acid test of our ability to work effectively with the USSR would come when German central administrations were established, when the zonal barriers were lifted and when it becomes necessary to work out policies for all of Germany on matters such as the public debt and the currency issue."[96]

Clay's efforts to have the Truman administration put diplomatic pressure on France undoubtedly raised a series of personal and political dilemmas for Byrnes. First, since Truman was still willing to completely delegate the handling of foreign affairs to his secretary of state, Byrnes was clearly the key figure who could determine whether or not the "full force and prestige of American diplomatic pressure" would be put toward ending French obstructionism in the ACC. With the War Department already on record in support of Clay's position, Byrnes would undoubtedly become the main target of criticism if the army's explanation for the impasse in Germany became a subject of domestic controversy.[97] Second, and often overlooked in historical accounts of the bureaucratic rivalry over American policy toward Germany in 1945–46, Byrnes's personal loyalty was to Clay rather than to the lower officials of the State Department, whom he gener-

[95] Strang was concerned about Clay's tendency to direct his fire at the British and the French despite the fact that he "knows very well that, were the French difficulty about central administrations removed, the Russian difficulty about freedom of access to their zone would remain, he pretends that the Russians are playing the game while we are not, and makes a point of lining himself up with them against us when an opportunity occurs." See Strang to Harvey, October 29, 1945, in *DBPO,* series 1, vol. 5, calendar 61ii; and for McCloy's assessment of Clay, see Halifax to Cadogan, November 29, 1945, in *DBPO,* series 1, vol. 5, calendar 61ii.

[96] Resume of Meeting at State Department, *Clay Papers,* 1:112.

[97] After Clay's visit, Secretary of War Robert Patterson repeatedly sought to push the State Department on the issue of France's compliance with Potsdam. See *FRUS,* 1945, vol. 3, 893, 908–9, 922–23.

ally held in contempt.[98] Finally, Clay was not exactly demanding support for a radical or controversial policy in Germany: all he was asking for was diplomatic support in order to implement an agreement that Byrnes himself had negotiated at Potsdam.

Despite all of these factors in favor of supporting Clay's position toward France, Byrnes clearly decided against making any real diplomatic effort to end the impasse in the ACC. Byrnes was unwilling to openly approve of the French position on central administrations, yet his efforts to alter their stance can hardly be characterized as serious diplomatic pressure. Shortly after Clay's visit to Washington, Byrnes told Couve de Murville, political director of the French foreign office (Quai d'Orsay), that the United States remained committed to the establishment of central administrations and that he was soon going to express to the British and the Soviets his willingness to establish arrangements for the three zones.[99] On December 6, 1945, he instructed Caffery to inform Bidault that "if the [Potsdam] agreement can be implemented in no other way we will, with great reluctance, agree to having the agencies in question operate in the Russian, British and American zones."[100] However, since both the British and the Russians had already indicated that they would not support the establishment of either bizonal or trizonal arrangements in Germany, it is very difficult to view Byrnes's statements as a serious attempt to pressure the French into changing their position in the ACC. Although the combined pressure of the Big Three would surely have made it exceedingly difficult for the French to maintain their position, Byrnes did not even raise the matter of central administrations during the Moscow Conference.[101]

[98] For extensive examples of the closeness of the Clay-Byrnes friendship, see Jean Edward Smith, *Lucius D. Clay: An American Life* (New York: Holt, 1990), 188–214, 384–89. Although both Smith and John Gimbel emphasize bureaucratic rivalries between the State and War Departments, they also argue that Byrnes supported the OMGUS position on Germany. However, if Byrnes truly shared Clay's perspective then it is very hard to account for the fact that he effectively sided with anti-Soviet and pro-French officials in the State Department. For a more sympathetic assessment of the role of lower-level officials in the State Department, see Heike Bungert, "A New Perspective on French-American Relations during the Occupation of Germany, 1945–48: Behind-the-Scenes Diplomatic Bargaining and the Zonal Merger," *Diplomatic History* 18 (summer 1994): 333–52.

[99] Memorandum of Conversation by the Secretary of State, November 20, 1945, *FRUS*, 1945, vol. 3, 907–8.

[100] *FRUS*, 1945, vol. 3, 916.

[101] Byrnes's unwillingness to raise the issue in Moscow provides more evidence that he was not in agreement with Clay's position. According to a document in the French archives, Clay told one of his French colleagues shortly before Moscow that "if the USSR agrees, as Great Britain already does in principle, you will be excluded from the government within a few days." Cited in Jean Lacouture, *De Gaulle: The Ruler* (London: Harper Collins, 1991), 65. France's understandable concerns about Clay's statement can be found in Caffery to Secretary of State, December 18, 1945, *FRUS*, 1945, vol. 3, 922. Some insight into why Clay may have thought Byrnes was going to solve the question of central administrations in

De Gaulle's decision to resign from the government in January 1946, combined with some moderate public statements by the French socialists, raised Clay's and Murphy's hopes that renewed diplomatic pressure by Byrnes might now be able to break the impasse in the ACC. After discussing the issue with the two of them on January 24, Byrnes did take some modest steps to persuade France to abandon its opposition to central administrations. On February 1, 1946, Byrnes had Caffery deliver a letter to Bidault asking him to reassess his position on the issue. Byrnes told Caffery that he should "discreetly" point out that such a review would create a more favorable atmosphere for the forthcoming negotiations over an American loan to France.[102] A few days later Byrnes told Henri Bonnet, the French ambassador to the United States, that he had never approved of France's use of the veto and requested that they abandon it because it created "an utterly impossible situation" in Germany.[103]

The efforts by the new French government to increase the chances of success in the loan negotiations did spark an internal debate over German policy, but in the end Bidault and the Quai d'Orsay were able to successfully maintain their opposition to central administrations. Once again, despite the obvious leverage he possessed due to the upcoming negotiations, Byrnes was unwilling to apply the degree of pressure that might have altered the French stance on central administrations. When Caffery reported to Washington that Bidault was threatening to resign if the socialists pushed him too far on the issue of Germany, the State Department quickly responded that the issue "should not be pressed to a point where there is a real danger of Bidault's resignation and of a split in the coalition government which could rightly or wrongly be attributed to our intervention and which would have wide political ramifications in France."[104]

Bidault's formal rejection of Byrnes's request for a change in French policy demonstrated how little the basic situation had changed since he and de Gaulle had first presented their position to the United States in

---

Moscow can be found in the diary of James Pollock, Clay's advisor on German governmental affairs. See Pollock Diary, box 58, Bentley Historical Library, University of Michigan. Regardless of what Clay thought, Byrnes did not try to resolve the ACC impasse in Moscow.

[102] Secretary of State to Caffery, February 1, 1946, *FRUS*, 1946, vol. 5, 496–98. For a record of the Clay, Murphy, and Byrnes meeting in London, see Murphy to Matthews, January 29, 1946, U.S. Polad, Classified General Correspondence, RG 84, box 2, NA. Bidault complained to Bevin that he was "being pressed very much" by the United States on central administrations, specifically referring to Byrnes's "unpleasant note." See "Conversation between Bevin and Bidault in the Foreign Office," February 18, 1946, in *Die Ruhrfrage, 1945/46*, ed. Steininger, 522–23.

[103] Memorandum of Conversation between Byrnes and Henri Bonnet, February 6, 1946, Records of the Office of European Affairs (Matthews-Hickerson File), 1934–1947 (Washington, D.C.: National Archives and Records Service, 1982), reel 10.

[104] *FRUS*, 1946, vol. 5, 511.

August 1945. Bidault agreed with Byrnes that a prolonged period of occupation provided the best security guarantee against Germany, but he continued to maintain that France "nonetheless cannot ignore the fact that this occupation will eventually end." Since the occupation of Germany was bound to come to an end, Bidault reiterated that France could not compromise the "guarantees of the future," including the separation of the Ruhr and the Rhineland, which would prevent Germany from once again becoming a menace. Whatever else Bidault may have thought about American policy in the aftermath of Potsdam, he was evidently still not convinced that France could rely on a lengthy or permanent U.S. commitment to the occupation of Germany. As he told Caffery shortly after the restatement of his stand on central administrations, "The factor that worries him constantly is that we might withdraw our occupation forces from Germany at an early date."[105]

ONE GERMAN PROBLEM OR TWO?

For the American and British occupational authorities, political events in the Soviet zone in early 1946 mandated a speedier resolution of the impasse over central administrations caused by French obstructionism. The specific cause of American and British concern was the growing movement toward a fusion in the eastern zone of the Socialist (SPD) and Communist (KPD) parties. Well aware of the lack of popular support for the KPD, the Soviet military administration in Germany had been pressuring the SPD to agree to a merger of the two parties into one single workers party. Given the bitter history of relations with the KPD, in addition to all of the liabilities of being associated with the party favored by occupational authorities engaged in mass rapes and the widespread dismantling of German factories, it is not surprising that many SPD leaders were very reluctant to agree.[106] Indeed, as late as December 1945, the SPD leader Otto Grotewohl was willing to openly voice doubts about the wisdom of combining the parties. But by February 1946, having been subjected to pressure and harassment by the Soviets, Grotewohl decided that the "iron curtain" had come to stay and that the best course for the SPD

---

[105] RG 59, 751.00/3–2346, Caffery to Secretary of State, March 23, 1946, NA.

[106] The fusion process between the SPD and KPD in the eastern zone is, of course, much more complicated than summarized here. There was certainly some genuine support among both the leadership and the rank and file of the SPD for the creation of a unified party. For a full discussion of these issues, see Henry Krisch, *German Politics under Soviet Occupation* (New York: Columbia University Press, 1974), 101–214; Naimark, *The Russians in Germany*, 276–84; Loth, *Stalin's Unwanted Child*, 26–34; and Charles Pennachio, "The East German Communists and the Origins of the Berlin Blockade Crisis," *East European Quarterly* 24 (September 1995): 293–314.

was to merge with the KPD.[107] The fact that influential figures in the eastern zone SPD were no longer willing to resist Soviet pressure for the establishment of a unified party, partly because of their belief that the Western powers had already written them off, came as a great shock to many British officials in Berlin. As one Foreign Office official noted, "This decision in fact means that we can kiss good-bye to democracy on the Western pattern for what is practically half of pre-war Germany which politically is now being reduced to a Balkan level."[108]

The fusion of the SPD and KPD had tremendous political implications that extended beyond the eastern zone. If Stalin's only concern was with political control in the eastern zone, he could simply have forced the SPD to dissolve itself into the KPD and spared himself all of the complications involved in the creation of the Socialist Unity Party (SED). A more plausible interpretation of the fusion decision is that Stalin was hoping to create a political party that could have appeal in both the western and eastern zones. The fear in the West that Stalin was aiming for German hearts and minds by creating a unified and potentially more attractive party led the British to view any identification with French proposals for Germany as a clear liability. Bevin had been somewhat sympathetic to French plans for detaching the Ruhr, but the forced merger of the SPD and KPD now put him into opposition to these plans.[109] If the Western powers were shortly going to have to combat a Soviet-sponsored party waving the banner of German unity from a secure base in the east, British support for the detachment of the Ruhr and the Rhineland would be a formidable liability in gaining the allegiance of the German populace. Close relations with France were still considered crucial for the British, but they could not be achieved or pursued without considering the effect of these policies on the Germans. As one British official noted, the most depressing fact about the events in the Soviet zone was that less than nine months after the end of the war it was now imperative to actively consider "Germany as a potential factor in 'power politics.'"[110]

---

[107] In conversations with the British, Grotewohl argued that it was futile to resist any longer because the French position on central administrations ensured that the SPD would not receive any help from the West. Of course, the fact that he himself was "being tickled by Russian bayonets" was the more proximate cause. See Steel to Foreign Office, February 7, 1946, in *Die Ruhrfrage, 1945/46,* ed. Steininger, 486. For the British reaction to events in the Soviet zone, see also Noel Annan, *Changing Enemies: The Defeat and Regeneration of Germany* (New York: W. W. Norton, 1995), 187–202.

[108] Minute by A. A. E. Franklin, February 7, 1946, in *Die Ruhrfrage, 1945/46,* ed. Steininger, 487.

[109] For an overview of the lengthy Anglo-French discussions concerning the Ruhr, see Sean Greenwood, "Bevin, the Ruhr, and the Division of Germany: August 1945–December 1946," *Historical Journal* 29 (1986): 203–12.

[110] C. O'Neill, "German Communists and Social Democrats in Berlin and the Russian Zone," February 13, 1946, in *Die Ruhrfrage, 1945/46,* ed. Steininger, 514.

Murphy and Clay were also very concerned about the implications of events in the Soviet zone. Murphy warned that the recent propaganda campaign in favor of a united Germany had grave implications for American foreign policy because it suggested that the Soviet Union was establishing "a foundation on which to build a favored position for itself vis-à-vis the German population, to gain eventual German confidence, and to work for a close affiliation between a new German Reich and the USSR."[111] As always, Murphy believed that the first step in combating the consolidation of Soviet control in the east was stopping French obstructionism in the Allied Control Council. His recommendation to Washington was that support for the French in other areas should be withheld until they developed "a more favorable attitude" on central administrations.[112] Events in the Soviet zone in 1946 did not yet convince Murphy, as it did some members of his staff, that America should abandon its efforts to establish four-power cooperation in Germany and write off the eastern zone. The heavy-handed tactics employed by the Soviets in their zone were not a great surprise to Murphy, and he did not believe that the adoption of official policy positions favored by average Germans would lead them to forget the actual activities of the Red Army in Germany.[113] Murphy was also optimistic that in the future "Western ideas will more successfully penetrate the Soviet Zone than has been the case during the past."[114]

Appointed to his position by Roosevelt in September 1944, Murphy recalled in his memoirs that the president had urged him to "bear in mind that our primary postwar objective was Soviet-American cooperation—without which world peace would be impossible—and that Germany would be the proving ground for such cooperation."[115] Murphy was still not convinced in early 1946 that the Soviets had conclusively failed this test in Germany. In a letter to Dewitt C. Poole, who had recommended that the Western powers accept the permanent division of Germany at the

---

[111] Murphy to Secretary of State, February 24, 1946, *FRUS*, 1946, vol. 5, 506. Clay sent a similar cable to the War Department, arguing that the emergence of a German communist party advocating the retention of the Ruhr and the Rhineland "has more political significance than any to date." See Clay to Hilldring, February 22, 1946, in *Clay Papers*, 1:164.

[112] Murphy to Secretary of State, February 24, 1946, 506–7. Like Strang, Murphy also partially blamed the French for the turn of events in the eastern zone because of his belief that the establishment of central administrations would have led to "the gradual relaxation of zonal barriers." See Murphy to Secretary of State, March 19, 1946, U.S. Polad Germany Post Files, 1945–49, Office of Political Advisor, RG 84, box 4, Classified Cables (Sent), NA.

[113] See Murphy to Matthews, March 28, 1946, U.S. Polad Germany Post Files, 1945–49, Office of Political Advisor, RG 84, box 1, Top-Secret Correspondence, NA; and Murphy to Matthews, May 3, 1946, box 58, Robert Murphy Papers, Hoover Institution, Stanford University. In both of these letters, Murphy pointed out why he disagreed with the more pessimistic conclusions drawn by his staff members, Louis Weisner and Perry Laukhuff.

[114] Murphy to Matthews, May 17, 1946, RG 59, Records of the Central European Division, 1944–53, box 3, NA.

[115] Murphy, *Diplomat among Warriors*, 227.

Elbe, Murphy wrote that he could not disagree more because "such a solution would be the surest guarantee of another European war."[116] Until it
was absolutely proven that the Soviet Union had hostile intentions toward the United States and that it would not be possible to cooperate with
them in Germany, Murphy believed that it was still better to try to cooperate with them on "one German problem, not two."[117]

The Rooseveltian approach to the Soviet Union lived on in the minds of
Murphy and Clay, but the warm reception accorded to George Kennan's
"Long Telegram" in 1946 was just one of many indications that the
Truman administration was increasingly receptive to new approaches.[118]
Kennan had long maintained that the Clay/Murphy approach to the
Soviet Union and the German question was fundamentally wrong and
that it was foolish to think that the country could be run as a single unit
with the Soviet Union.[119] Less than a week after receiving Kennan's famous
dispatch, the State Department requested his comments on Murphy's recent cable about the implications of Soviet policies in Germany. Although
never directly addressing Murphy's specific recommendation—exerting
more pressure on France over the issue of central administrations—
Kennan proceeded to launch a devastating attack on the entire OMGUS
approach to the German question. Cautioning against "undue optimism"
about the potential for central administrations to break down exclusive
Soviet control in the east, Kennan argued that a united Germany would
emerge only if it was completely under Soviet control. In his view,
American and British acceptance of the Oder-Neisse line at Potsdam had
essentially eliminated the possibility of establishing a united Germany on
any terms the Western powers could accept. Rather than pursuing a unified Germany that would be vulnerable to Soviet penetration, Kennan
recommended that the West should "carry to its logical conclusion the
process of partition which was begun in the east and to endeavor to rescue western zones of Germany by walling them off against eastern penetration and integrating them into the international pattern of western
Europe rather than into a united Germany."[120]

Kennan's perspective on Germany was rejected by OMGUS, but even
the State Department bureaucracy was by no means monolithically lined
up behind his approach to the German question in early 1946. Lower-level

[116] Murphy to Dewitt Poole, February 6, 1946, box 59, Murphy Papers, Hoover Institution.
[117] Murphy to Dewitt C. Poole, February 6, 1946, and Murphy to Poole, April 11, 1946, box
59, Murphy Papers, Hoover Institution.
[118] For the circumstances and reception accorded the Long Telegram of February 1946, see
George F. Kennan, *Memoirs, 1925–50* (New York: Atlantic, Little, Brown, 1967), 271–91.
According to Murphy, Clay's reaction to the telegram was "pretty violent." See Murphy to
Matthews, April 3, 1946, box 58, Murphy Papers, Hoover Institution.
[119] Kennan, *Memoirs, 1925–50*, 258.
[120] See Kennan to Secretary of State, March 6, 1946, *FRUS*, 1946, vol. 5, 516–20 (quotation
on 519); and also Kennan to Offie, May 10, 1946, *FRUS*, vol. 5, 555–56.

officials in the Division of German and Austrian Economic Affairs, such as Walt Rostow and Charles Kindleberger, shared Clay's and Murphy's aversion to simply accepting the division of Germany as an unavoidable fact of life. After assessing the respective merits of the Kennan and Murphy positions on Germany, David Harris concluded that America should continue to champion the cause of a unified Germany because "the most certain way of making Western Germany Communist is to try to bar the road to Communism by partitioning Germany."[121] As Rostow notes, although he and other officials in the State Department recognized that a unified Germany would provide the Soviets with room for maneuver in the West, they "rejected the notion that the United States—and the West as a whole—was incapable of coping with such Soviet efforts."[122] Commenting on a War Department paper that supported Kennan's argument that a unified Germany was likely to be a communist Germany, Charles Kindleberger still maintained that accepting the division of Germany remained an unattractive and potentially disastrous course for the United States.[123]

Whether America's German policy would follow the path proposed by Kennan or the path preferred by Clay and Murphy was still Byrnes's call to make in 1946. At Potsdam, Byrnes had crafted a reparations settlement based firmly on Kennanesque assumptions about the impossibility of running Germany as a unit, but he had also encouraged Clay and Murphy in their efforts to run Germany as a single unit in cooperation with the Soviet Union. But his ability to avoid making a clear and unambiguous choice between the Kennan and OMGUS positions on Germany was coming to an end by the spring of 1946. Ironically, it was the reparations settlement itself which forced the larger questions of the future of Germany to the surface. The Potsdam settlement had provided that within six months after the conference the Allied Control Council should determine the overall level of industry to be retained in the postwar German economy, with the excess machinery to be distributed among the various reparations claimants. Because the Soviet share was to be based on a four-power assessment of the level of postwar German industry necessary to enable the country to survive without outside assistance, the entire process raised many of the same problems that Byrnes had sought to avoid in

---

[121] Harris to Riddleberger and Matthews, "Future Policy toward Germany," March 26, 1946, reprinted in *The Division of Europe after World War II*, ed. Walt W. Rostow (Austin: University of Texas Press, 1982), 165–79 (quotation on 176). For Riddleberger's comments, which were generally positive, see Riddleberger to Matthews, March 28, 1946, RG 59, Records of the Central European Affairs Division, box 1, NA.

[122] Rostow, *The Division of Europe*, 59.

[123] Charles Kindleberger, Comment on "Ultimate Disposition of Ruhr and Rhineland," May 3, 1946, Records of Central European Affairs Division, box 2, NA. Kindleberger was commenting on a War Department paper written by Colonel C. H. Bonesteel. The paper itself is reprinted, without Kindleberger's critique, in *Die Ruhrfrage, 1945/46*, ed. Steininger, 666–80.

putting forward a zonal reparations plan. If the Soviet Union and the Western powers could not agree on an overall reparations plan, there was no good reason to expect that they could agree on the levels of industry sufficient to maintain the German standard of living. To make matters even worse, the Soviet Union had every interest in advocating very low levels of industrial capacity in order to increase their reparations share, while the British and the Americans had every interest in maintaining higher levels in order to eventually reduce the burden of support for the German population. For both of these reasons, as John Gillingham notes, the Level of Industry (LOI) negotiations were inherently "an exercise in futility and madness because fundamental disagreement between the USSR and the United States/United Kingdom about what constituted an acceptable minimum standard of living undercut any satisfactory basis for compromise."[124]

Gillingham is correct to emphasize the elements of futility and madness involved in the LOI negotiations, but on March 28, 1946, the four occupying powers did eventually sign an agreement establishing target figures for many of the key industries in Germany. The main force behind the agreement was undoubtedly Clay, who generally took a middle ground between the vastly different levels of industry proposed by the British and the Russians. As John Backer argues, Clay probably saw little reason "to fight too long about figures which soon might become meaningless."[125] Behind Clay's reasoning was the fact that the LOI plan was based on the assumption that Germany was to be treated as a single economic unit with a common export-import plan. For all of his frustrations with the French, and despite all of his hopes of maintaining postwar cooperation in Germany, Clay had always entertained doubts about the Soviet Union's willingness to adhere to this aspect of the Potsdam agreement. In the month after the LOI plan was signed, Clay's principal concern was to determine whether or not the Soviets would accept a common export-import plan. After hearing that a Soviet official had stated in the ACC that his country would continue to organize foreign trade on a zonal basis, Clay warned the Soviets on April 8 that the reparations plan would not be carried out if they maintained this position. His purpose in raising the issue was "to smoke out now the Soviet position."[126] On April 20, Clay protested the Soviet dismantlement of an agricultural processing plant and warned that "if this is to be the practice, I feel that reparations deliv-

---

[124] John Gillingham, *Coal, Steel, and the Rebirth of Europe, 1945–55* (New York: Cambridge University Press, 1991), 108. For an archivally based account by a British participant in the LOI negotiations, see Cairncross, *The Price of War,* 100–58. For an early but still useful account by two American participants, see B. U. Ratchford and W. D. Ross, *Berlin Reparations Assignment* (Chapel Hill: University of North Carolina Press, 1947).

[125] John Backer, *Priming the German Economy* (Durham, N.C.: Duke University Press, 1971), 78.

[126] Clay to Echols, April 8, 1946, *Clay Papers,* 1:187.

eries must be stopped until our program as a whole can be reviewed."[127] Clay was not bluffing, and on May 3 he announced that all further work on dismantling plants for purposes of reparations in the American zone would be suspended until the Potsdam agreement was adhered to in its entirety.[128]

The purpose of the reparations stop has been the subject of much scholarly debate. In his memoirs, Clay explicitly argued that the reparations stop was directed against the Soviet Union. However, for understandable reasons, scholars have treated Clay's explanation with considerable skepticism since his memoirs, written at the height of the Cold War, clearly sought to downplay the extent of his frustrations with France and the State Department in the 1945–46 period. Since the publication of John Gimbel's *The American Occupation of Germany* in 1968, historians have increasingly accepted the argument that the reparations stop was directed equally, if not more so, against France.[129] Indeed, by the time Gimbel published *The Origins of the Marshall Plan* in 1976, he had essentially reached the position that the reparations stop was exclusively directed against France: "Clay's action was clearly an attempt to break the impasse that France had caused in Berlin. It was an attempt to force government-level decisions on Germany by jolting the State Department and forcing it to respond to his, Patterson's and Murphy's requests, pleas and recommendations for pressure on France."[130]

There is certainly some evidence to support the Gimbel thesis. First, the reparations stop held up all shipments from the American zone, and Clay later emphasized in a press conference that his action was not directed specifically against the Soviet Union.[131] Second, as Walt Rostow noted during his visit to Berlin a month after the reparations stop, some OMGUS officials thought that Clay's reparations stop was intended to put pressure on France rather than on the Soviet Union: "Whether correct or not it is the Berlin view that Clay's hold-up of reparations is designed rather more to get the French obstruction cleared up than to show up Soviet intentions."[132] Finally, there is also a great deal of evidence to show that Clay continued to maintain the same basic perspective on the German question after the reparations stop that he had held before May

[127] Clay to Sokolovsky, April 20, 1946, cited in John Gimbel, *The American Occupation of Germany: Politics and the Military, 1945–49* (Stanford, Calif.: Stanford University Press, 1968), 59.

[128] Backer, *Priming the German Economy*, 110.

[129] For examples of how the Gimbel thesis on the halt to reparations has become a commonly accepted interpretation, see Melvyn Leffler, *A Preponderance of Power: National Security, the Truman Administration, and the Cold War* (Stanford, Calif.: Stanford University Press, 1992), 118; and Eisenberg, *Drawing the Line*, 212.

[130] Gimbel, *Origins of the Marshall Plan*, 98.

[131] See transcript of May 27 press conference in *Clay Papers*, 1:218–23.

[132] Rostow to Kindleberger, July 10, 1946, in *The Division of Europe*, 143.

3.[133] Clay did not view the move as the final end of attempts to work out an acceptable German settlement with the Russians, and the French continued to be a frequent target of his anger.

However, the Gimbel interpretation of the reparations stop is flawed because it is based on the premise that Clay was operating on his own authority and had not cleared his actions with the State Department. The key figure in deciphering the real purpose of the reparations stop, however, is Byrnes rather than Clay. As we now know from a memorandum of conversation prepared by Bevin in early May 1946, Byrnes authorized the reparations stop in advance and it was explicitly part of a planned "showdown" with the Russians. According to Bevin, Byrnes told him that he had "authorized Clay to take the line that there was to be no more delivery of reparations until the problem of Germany as a whole was settled and a system arrived at which provided for exports to pay for imports."[134] Clay may well have thought that the reparations stop would also help resolve the problems the French were causing in the ACC, but the reason why Byrnes permitted him to take such a step had very little to do with France.[135]

The real significance of the reparations stop, of course, is not that Clay was upholding the letter of the Potsdam agreement, but that Byrnes was now repudiating the spirit of the deal he had made with the Soviets. Byrnes knew full well that he had explicitly promised the Soviets that if they agreed to a zonal reparations plan they could take what they wished from their own zone and that they would get their share of reparations from the western zones, regardless of whether the British and American zones were operating at a deficit. Clay's position in the ACC effectively negated both of these concessions because a common export-import plan meant that the Soviets would no longer have a free hand in their zone— either to remove plants or to take reparations from current production— and that their own share of reparations from the western zones would

---

[133] See, for example, Stuart Symington's memoranda of his conversations with Clay in July 1946. Referring to the "diplomatic genius of FDR," Clay told Symington that the situation in Germany with the Soviets was "far from hopeless, and could be worked out." See Interview with General Clay, July 25, 29, 30, box 1, Stuart Symington Papers, HSTL.

[134] FO 800/513, "Anglo-American Discussions, Minute by the Secretary of State for Foreign Affairs," May 5, 1946. I thank Mike Spirtas for providing me with this document. For additional evidence on Byrnes's role in the reparations stop, see Charles Kindleberger's oral history at the Truman library. Unsure about how Clay could have taken such an important step without State Department authorization, Kindleberger discussed the issue with James Riddleberger, who basically gave away the game: "Have you ever contemplated the possibility that Mr. Byrnes at the Council of Foreign Ministers in Paris telephoned him and authorized it?" See Charles Kindleberger Oral History, 1973, HSTL, 30–31.

[135] That Byrnes was unconcerned about French obstructionism in the ACC can also be seen in Bevin's memoranda. See FO 800/513.

now be held hostage until they agreed to a set of economic principles that would end their ability to take what they wished from their zone.[136]

Molotov waited until the second session of the Paris CFM in July 1946 before responding to both the reparations stop and Byrnes's offer of a disarmament treaty directed against Germany. His two major statements at the Paris meeting suggest that, like the Western powers, the Soviet Union was preparing for the open collapse of the Grand Alliance in Germany. In his first statement, Molotov brutally rejected the disarmament treaty as an inadequate safeguard against Germany, denounced Clay's "unlawful statement" in the ACC halting reparations deliveries to the Soviet Union, and revived the Soviet claim that it was entitled to the ten billion dollars in reparations that had allegedly been promised at Yalta.[137] Molotov's second speech was directed at the German populace rather than to Byrnes, Bidault, or Bevin. Arguing that the Soviet Union never had any intention of treating the German people harshly, Molotov sought to identify the Western powers with a program of Morgenthauism, partition, and the separation of the Ruhr from Germany. According to Molotov, the Soviet Union would oppose all of these policies because it was "incorrect to adopt the course of Germany's annihilation as a state or that of its agrarianization, including the annihilation of its main industrial centers."[138] By directly identifying the Western powers with all of the policies feared by the Germans, Molotov substantially raised the stakes in his response to the reparations stop.

Byrnes's response to Molotov was to offer to merge the American zone with any other zone willing to treat Germany as an economic unit on the basis of the Potsdam agreement. Whether Byrnes would have made the offer if Molotov had not delivered his provocative speech or if Bevin had not threatened to organize the British zone on a unilateral basis is not clear, but the general idea of proceeding with the organization of the western zones was not a spur of the moment reaction on his part.[139] As

---

[136] This interpretation of the reparations stop largely follows Kuklick's *American Policy and the Division of Germany,* 205–15. As Geoffrey Warner correctly points out, "A reading of the Potsdam protocol shows that the Russians were right in maintaining that the delivery of reparations from the western zones did not depend on settlement of other matters." See Geoffrey Warner, "The Division of Germany, 1946–48," *International Affairs* 51 (January 1975): 63.

[137] *FRUS,* 1946, vol. 2, 842–47.

[138] Ibid., 869.

[139] For different reasons, both John Gimbel and Anne Deighton have emphasized that Byrnes was acting defensively in order to prevent Bevin from carrying out this threat. See Gimbel, *The Origins of the Marshall Plan,* 107–11; and Anne Deighton, *The Impossible Peace: Britain, the Division of Germany, and the Origins of the Cold War* (New York: Oxford University Press, 1990), 93–108. Bevin's own description of the Paris CFM suggests that Byrnes was far more determined than Bevin to proceed with a western strategy: "Mr. Byrnes had expressed his willingness for full co-operation between the American and other Zones and had sug-*gested to him privately that arrangements should at once be made for co-operation between the British*

early as June 4, Byrnes had confidentially told a Washington columnist that "he has almost given up hope for a united Germany. He does not believe that the Russians have any intention of opening that country up. . . . He said he thought that the present British, American and French zones, lumped together, could be made self-supporting."[140] Only Great Britain accepted Byrnes's offer, but the French had made it known privately before the second session of the Paris CFM that they would cooperate informally with the United States and Great Britain as long as they were not pressured into doing so.[141] The decision to proceed with the negotiations that ultimately resulted in the establishment of "Bizonia" shortly after the end of the Paris CFM represented another major step in the consolidation of the zonal division of Germany.

CONCLUSION

The worst nightmare of American postwar planners was well on its way to becoming a reality by the summer of 1946. Both the Americans and the Soviets were now openly competing for the allegiance of the German people and blaming each other for the breakdown of cooperation in Germany. How far the process of blame and recrimination would go from here, or whether the breakdown of relations could somehow be reversed, was probably less than clear to both sides in 1946. Although both the reparations stop and Byrnes's decision to fuse zones with the British can be seen as harbingers of things to come, they can also be seen as efforts to get the Soviets to adhere to the Potsdam Protocol in its entirety rather than a clear and definitive break with Potsdam. Most American policymakers in 1946 were not yet thinking ahead to the creation of a West German state, let alone to the rearmament of the German population within Western-controlled zones. We still know much less concerning Soviet thinking about the future of Germany in this period, but it is probably safe to assume that the Soviets in 1946 did not envision the inevitability of protracted crises and all-out war over Western actions designed to restore the power of Western Germany. Nevertheless, by 1946 both sides were already much closer to dangerous confrontation than to the time when Roosevelt and Stalin could pleasantly discuss whether

---

and American zones to the exclusion of the Russian Zone. The Foreign Secretary had thought that it would be a mistake at this stage to commit ourselves irrevocably to a measure which implied a clear division between Eastern and Western Germany" (emphasis added). See CAB 128/6, C.M. 46, July 15, 1946, *Cabinet Papers: Complete Classes from the CAB and PREM Series in the Public Record Office,* series 3 (Wiltshire: Adam Matthew Publications, 1996).

[140] See Edgar Mowrer to James Pollock, June 4, 1946, box 61, Pollock Papers, Bentley Library, University of Michigan.

[141] Caffery to Secretary of State, June 11, 1946, *FRUS,* 1946, vol. 5, 566–67.

Germany should be partitioned into five or six states and toast the future execution of thousands of German officers.

Political scientists still tend to think that the division of Germany flowed naturally from the emergence of a bipolar structure dominated by American and Soviet power. Historians correctly view the division of Germany in a much less deterministic fashion. Explaining the division of Germany in terms of structure would be much more compelling if policymakers of that period overwhelmingly had thought that Germany would and should be divided after the war. But we simply do not find such a consensus. The emergence of America and the Soviet Union as superpowers did not point to a clear, mutually acceptable solution of the German problem in terms of either division or unity. Even the British, often mistakenly viewed as far more willing to accept the division of Germany than the Americans, were unsure about the proper course for the West to pursue in Germany. As Ernest Bevin argued in May 1946, the division of Germany should not be easily accepted by the West because "we should have lost the one factor which might hold us and the Russians together, viz., the existence of a single Germany which it would be in the interest of us both to hold down."[142] Neither intellectual theory nor the lessons of history provided postwar policymakers with a clear answer to the question of whether Germany should be unified or divided. It is for this reason that George Kennan could argue vigorously for accepting the reality of a divided Germany in 1945–46 and argue just as vigorously for trying to preserve a united Germany in 1948–49. To argue that Kennan was clearly right or wrong in either one of these periods assumes that there was an obvious right or wrong solution to the German Problem. Even with the benefit of hindsight, definitive conclusions about what American policy should have been in 1946 remain little more than informed speculation.

Stalin's postwar plans also cannot be given as a satisfactory answer to the question of why Germany was divided after the Second World War. In *Drawing the Line,* Carolyn Eisenberg provides a confusing but thought-provoking analogy for thinking about the breakdown of great power cooperation in Germany: "As in a divorce where the party filing papers is not necessarily the one who caused the rupture, formal situations are not always illuminating."[143] Actually, in the case of Germany, Eisenberg's argument suggests that the party formally filing for divorce is the same one who bears "primary" responsibility for the rupture. It is true that throughout the early postwar period the Soviet Union most often appears to be the party trying the hardest to head off the division of Germany, as well as the party most willing to make concessions necessary to preserve

---

[142] Cited in Alan Bullock, *Ernest Bevin: Foreign Secretary, 1945–51* (New York: W. W. Norton, 1983), 268.

[143] Eisenberg, *Drawing the Line,* 485–86.

the allied "marriage" in Germany. The newest Cold War history based on Soviet and East German documents generally does not support the idea that Stalin was content with a divided Germany, or that he had written off the possibility of maintaining good relations with the West in order to limit German power and obtain reparations. This revelation should not be surprising because Stalin had every reason to hold the door open to good relations with the allies in Germany. At the most basic level, Stalin needed good relations with the Western powers if he hoped to get any reparations from the wealthiest portions of Germany. In addition, a divided Germany would also provide Stalin with little leverage in influencing what the Western powers would ultimately decide to do with their zones. In short, it was much harder for Stalin to write off the western zones than it was for the Western powers to write off the eastern zones. If one party was going to file divorce papers over Germany, it was inevitable that the Western powers would do it because for Stalin a bad marriage and an impoverished Germany was better than a good marriage and a powerful West Germany that he could neither control nor influence.

Although there may indeed have been a "missed opportunity" for preserving a united Germany in 1945–46, both the guilty verdict and the charge of American responsibility for the fate of East Germany and Eastern Europe needs to be put into context. The idea that Stalin would have ultimately accepted a parliamentary, democratic regime for Germany in the Western sense of the term, even if he could have been satisfied on the reparations question, is not compelling. Stalin's willingness to allow the formation of noncommunist political parties in the eastern zone and the holding of "formal" elections in 1946 is of much less significance than his clear intent to dominate and control the political forces in the east. The forced merger of the KPD and the SPD, as well as his constant harassment and coercion of liberal forces throughout the eastern zone, does not suggest that Stalin was willing to eventually let the Germans of this region make their own political choices. Any illusions Stalin may have had that the Soviets would be freely accepted by the Germans were surely undercut by the dismal results in Berlin of the October 1946 elections, the last free elections held within the eastern zone.[144] Sooner or later, the fact that Soviet sponsored or associated forces could not maintain popular support in the east would have brought Stalin into conflict even with those Americans, such as Clay and Murphy, who most wanted to avoid it. Clay's unwillingness to meekly accept the division of Germany was based on the belief that the West should aim for "the right to contest for its philosophy throughout Germany and to extend its fron-

[144] For the belief that the Soviets were willing to accept a parliamentary, democratic regime in Germany, see Loth, *Stalin's Unwanted Child*, 1–58. For a recent account skeptical of Loth's perspective, see Stefan Creuzberger, "The Soviet Military Administration and East German Elections, Autumn 1946," *Australian Journal of Politics and History* 45 (1999): 89–98.

tier to the borders of Poland and Czechoslovakia, thus encouraging any will for democracy in these peoples."[145] To say the least, it is doubtful that Stalin would have accepted the political conditions that Clay and other Americans would inevitably have demanded in exchange for significant reparations from the West.

America's German policy after Potsdam is often seen as an abandonment of Roosevelt's grand design of postwar cooperation with the Soviets. In this view, Clay, Murphy, and other heirs of the Rooseveltian legacy were ultimately defeated by the children of darkness, represented in this period by Kennan and other State Department officials. Although there certainly is a basis for viewing Clay and Murphy in this fashion, we should not overlook the fact that their approach to Germany differed from Roosevelt's in several crucial respects. First, FDR overwhelmingly thought of Germany in terms of division rather than unity. The reflexive identification historians make between the division of Germany and hostile relations with the Soviet Union may be valid, but it is not one that Roosevelt shared. Second, FDR did not think that America could or should attempt to run Germany as a single unit in intimate cooperation with the Soviets on every possible matter of concern. As he stated as early as September 1944, "We have to remember that in their territory they will do more or less what they wish. We cannot afford to get into a situation of merely recording protests on our part unless there is some chance of the protests being heeded."[146] Roosevelt's sober recognition of the limits of American influence in the Soviet zone in Germany, deplorable as it may have been from a Wilsonian perspective, represented a far more realistic approach to postwar cooperation in Germany than Clay's hope of using the Potsdam agreement to create a unified, democratic, and pro-Western state.

Viewed from this perspective, James F. Byrnes was the true and legitimate heir of the FDR legacy at Potsdam. The reparations settlement he proposed was based on the recognition that the Soviets would do more or less what they wished in their zone and that such a deal did not have to mean the abandonment of amicable relations. Recognition of the new Polish border with Germany, the freedom and blessing to take whatever they wanted from their zone, and a percentage of the surplus industry of the Ruhr was not necessarily a bad deal from the Soviet perspective even if it did not meet Stalin's maximum objectives. Revisionist historians often argue that Potsdam was a much worse settlement than the one envisioned at Yalta, but under the Yalta framework there was no promise of the Western Neisse as the final border, and the Yalta agreement certainly

---

[145] Clay to Byrnes, November 1946, *Clay Papers*, 1:281.
[146] FDR to Stettinius, September 29, 1944, *FRUS, 1945, Conferences at Malta and Yalta*, 155.

would not have given the Soviets the freedom and blessing to take whatever they wanted from their zone. Rather than faulting Byrnes for abandoning the Potsdam framework in 1946, his real fault lies in his inability and unwillingness to extend and reinforce the logic of the zonal reparations plan. The great tragedy of the postwar world was not the division of Germany, but the fact that this division led to a prolonged and very dangerous confrontation between America and the Soviet Union—that neither country wanted or desired in 1945.

[4]

Years of Danger and Opportunity: The Restoration of a European Balance of Power

No final solution of the German problem is possible until ERP [European Recovery Program] has invigorated western Europe so that it may develop a military strength which makes Soviet domination of Europe impossible. I doubt if such a military strength would be developed with Germany under quadripartite control. We have gone too far with western Europe to have any hope of establishing a quadripartite control of Germany which would not retard the development of western Europe and a unified Germany can come now with safety only when the balance of power in Europe is restored.

Lucius Clay, July 1947

American thinking about the long-term conditions of stability in Europe was thoroughly transformed over the course of 1947–49. Lasting European stability was no longer held to rest on maintaining cooperation with the Soviet Union or on the destruction of German power. The new theory of European stability espoused by Lucius Clay, formerly one of the most ardent advocates of maintaining great power cooperation, came to reflect the overall grand strategy of the Truman administration in this period.[1] Neither a settlement with the Soviet Union over Germany nor the internal buildup of American military power were seen as viable long-term solutions to the destruction of the balance of power wrought by the Second World War. American strategy was based on the idea that the key to lasting European stability lay in the creation of a powerful Western Europe able to defend its security against both the Soviet Union and Germany without an absolute and total reliance on American power.

The goal of restoring a European balance of power was far removed from FDR's goal of great power cooperation, but the basis of both strategies was a recognition of the skewed nature of the bipolar distribution of power that emerged as a result of the war. Roosevelt's grand design had

---

[1] Clay to Draper, July 15, 1948, in *The Papers of Lucius Clay*, ed. Jean E. Smith, 2 vols. (Bloomington: Indiana University Press, 1974), 2:744.

been based on the assumption that America's preponderance of power vis-à-vis the Soviet Union provided an indefinite window of opportunity to establish a cooperative pattern of relations in postwar Europe. Virtually all of the components of FDR's vision had been abandoned by 1947, but what remained constant was the underlying assumption that a very favorable distribution of power still offered a window of opportunity to fundamentally recast the nature of the European state system. The Soviets could and undoubtedly would probe for opportunities to expand their power and influence in this period, but American military officials did not believe that they would seriously risk actions that might lead to war because "at least for the next ten or fifteen years, the gains to be derived internally during peace outweigh the advantages of any external objective that might be attained at the risk of war."[2] As late as December 1947, even fervent cold warriors such as James Forrestal maintained that the Truman administration had "years of opportunity" in which to restore the European balance of power: "As long as we can outproduce the world, can control the sea and can strike inland with the atomic bomb, we can assume certain risks otherwise unacceptable in an effort to restore world trade, to restore the balance of power—military power—and to eliminate some of the conditions which breed war."[3]

But America's years of opportunity were also years of danger. As Forrestal pointed out, the calculated risk assumed by the United States and its Western European allies was that the Soviet Union would not initiate military action during the period in which an indigenous European balance of power was being restored. Although U.S. decision-makers may have based their strategy on the premise that the Soviets would not intentionally embark on global war, they did not rule out the possibility of a war arising from miscalculation or an action-reaction process during a period of crisis. And if such a war did occur, U.S. military planners were the first to acknowledge, little could be done to prevent the Soviets from overrunning continental Europe in a matter of weeks or months. What made the situation even more precarious for both America and its allies was that restoring the European balance of power necessitated the revival of German power, a measure which more than any other had the potential of provoking the Soviets into launching a general war.

This chapter examines the interconnection between the restoration of a European balance of power, the revival of West Germany and Western

---

[2] Joint Planning Staff (JPS) 789, "Concept of Operations for Pincher," March 2, 1946, in *Design for Global War: The Pincher Plans*, vol. 2 of *America's Plans for War against the Soviet Union, 1945–50*, ed. Steven T. Ross and David Rosenberg (New York: Garland Publishing, 1989), 4.

[3] Walter Millis, ed., *The Forrestal Diaries* (New York: Viking Press, 1951), 350–51.

Europe, and the division of Europe into two competing blocs. These were not in any sense separate issues. The restoration of a European balance of power, of course, meant the organization of Western Europe as a power complex able to stand up against the Soviet Union. Correctly recognizing that this was not an objective that the Soviet Union was likely to support to, and one which it would logically oppose as incompatible with its own interests, the Truman administration increasingly based its policies after 1947 on the premise that the Soviets must be excluded from the affairs of Western Europe and the western zones of Germany. Although some American officials still advocated the pursuit of a unitary solution to Germany in early 1947, there was virtual unanimity against pursuing such solutions by the end of 1947.

The announcement of the Marshall Plan in June 1947 marks the beginning of America's long and ultimately elusive quest to establish a united Western Europe. The economics of the Marshall Plan may have been very complex, but the theory of European unity that lay behind it was very simple: Integrated within a framework of supranational or federal institutions, Germany's power and sovereignty could be progressively increased without simultaneously threatening the security of France and the rest of Western Europe. If liberated from the German problem and the inefficiencies of organizing its affairs on a nationalist basis, Western Europe could eventually be transformed into a third center of power fully equal to the United States and the Soviet Union. Strategists such as George Kennan and John Foster Dulles did not believe that European unification was one of several possible futures for Germany and Western Europe. In their view, European unification was the *only* viable long-term solution to both the German problem and the decline of Western Europe as a center of power. It is not at all an accident that Kennan and Dulles viewed a permanent American military presence in Europe as an unnatural and undesirable solution for both of these problems. While European unification certainly had an idealistic component, the urgent need for a united Western Europe was directly connected to the belief that neither the German problem nor the collapse of the European balance of power could forever be resolved by the permanent presence of American forces on the continent.

Although American officials believed that European unification offered the only safe solution to the German problem in the long term, the Truman administration could not defer the revival of the western zones of Germany until a united Europe came into existence. Few choices made by the Western powers in the postwar era were as consequential as the ones made to proceed in the direction of creating a West German state over the course of 1948. The division of Germany had been widening since Potsdam, but the decision to create a separate West German state posed a fundamental challenge to the Soviet Union. Stalin's imposition of the Berlin Blockade in June 1948 dramatically revealed the risks and consequences involved in restoring the European balance, but by this point the Western powers were in agreement that the establishment of West Germany was not a subject that was open for negotiations with the Soviet Union. Not even George Kennan could disrupt the new consensus. Way ahead of his time in advocating a frank recognition of the division of Germany and Europe in early 1945, Kennan reversed course at exactly the moment when his earlier views had become common currency within the Truman administration. Despite the eloquence of his arguments for pursuing a general settlement based on the unification of Germany and the withdrawal of occupation forces to seaport garrisons, Kennan's "Program A" was never viewed by the vast majority of administration officials or the Western European allies as a viable alternative. Even though many analysts within the American government believed that the Soviets might be quite willing to negotiate a general settlement along the lines advocated by Kennan, the heart of the matter was that by the time the Paris CFM met in May 1949 to discuss the German question, the Western powers had already decided that they preferred the dangers posed by division rather than the ones posed by the unification of Germany.

THE ORIGINS OF THE MARSHALL PLAN: GERMANY AND THE MOSCOW CFM

Clay's reluctance to accept the division of Germany was still strong at the beginning of 1947. Despite the suspension of reparations and the decision to form Bizonia out of the British and American zones, Clay was still hopeful that a German settlement could be reached with the Soviet Union. Based on conversations with his Soviet counterparts in Berlin, Clay and other OMGUS officials believed that the Soviets would be willing to treat Germany in accordance with the Potsdam agreements if they were provided with reparations from current production in the western zones in exchange. The Soviet desire for current reparations had long been apparent to American officials. American policy since Potsdam had been to reject current reparations as inconsistent with the terms of the protocol and simply impossible to provide under the agreed Level of Industry plan. However, Byrnes had left himself room for maneuver by implying in his Stuttgart speech that current reparations might be possible if the level of permitted German industry was raised. Not convinced that Potsdam definitively ruled them out, Clay was more than willing to consider a deal based on current reparations because of his unwillingness to divide Germany on the basis of a rigid stance on this question. If the levels of industry were raised to accommodate the payment of current reparations

and the Soviets were willing to agree to political as well as economic unification, Clay clearly thought the advantages of providing current reparations more than outweighed the disadvantages.[4]

Clay's optimism about a deal based on current reparations was not
widely shared within the American government. The official State
Department position papers for the Moscow CFM, March to April 1947,
which largely consisted of restatements of Byrnes's Stuttgart speech, reflected the prevalent fatalism within the department over the prospects
for a settlement.[5] For officials such as Walter Bedell Smith, U.S. ambassador to the Soviet Union, it was very important for the U.S. delegation at
Moscow to be prepared for an "indefinite prolongation of negotiations"
and to accept the further separation of the eastern and western zones
rather than settle for a "hollow unification" of Germany.[6] Like most
American officials, Smith justified the continued partition of Germany as
a regrettable but unavoidable necessity brought about by Soviet policies.
In contrast, John Foster Dulles openly rejected the desirability of a united
Germany even if an agreement with the Soviet Union was attainable.
Dulles, who had lobbied for a place in the American delegation by send-
ing General Marshall a copy of a recent speech he had delivered on
Europe and the German question, was quite frank about his lack of en-
thusiasm for a unified Germany. In the speech, entitled "Europe Must
Federate or Perish," Dulles implicitly criticized the official basis of
American policy since Potsdam by arguing that the occupying powers in
Germany should "think more in terms of the economic unity of Europe
and less in terms of the Potsdam dictum that Germany shall be a single
economic unit."[7] In his view, any German settlement with the Soviet
Union should be deferred until the Ruhr was integrated into Western
Europe and the region itself was greatly strengthened.[8]

---

[4] See John Backer, *Winds of History: The German Years of Lucius Dubignon Clay* (New York:
Van Nostrand, 1983), 149–80; Carolyn Eisenberg, *Drawing the Line: The American Decision to
Divide Germany, 1944–49* (Cambridge: Cambridge University Press, 1996), 248–61; and Clay
to Byrnes, *Clay Papers*, 1:279–84.

[5] See Cohen to Secretary of State, February 12, 1947, and the official position papers in
Foreign Relations of the United States, 1947, vol. 2 (Washington, D.C.: Government Printing
Office, 1972), 158–63, 201–23. For the general feeling of pessimism within the State
Department prior to the CFM, see Daniel Yergin, *Shattered Peace: The Origins of the Cold War
and the National Security State* (Boston, Mass.: Houghton Mifflin, 1977), 297.

[6] Smith to Secretary of State, January 7, 1947, *FRUS*, 1947, vol. 2, 139–42.

[7] John Foster Dulles, "Europe Must Federate or Perish," speech delivered before the
National Publishers Association, January 17, 1947, printed in *Vital Speeches of the Day* 13:
234–36 (quotation on 235). As Armin Rappaport notes, the Dulles speech was given a great
deal of attention because it was reported that both Senator Vandenberg and Thomas Dewey
had approved it in advance. See Armin Rappaport, "The United States and European
Integration: The First Phase," *Diplomatic History* 5 (spring 1981): 121–49.

[8] See Dulles's comments on the OMGUS and State Department position papers, March 7,
1947, box 533, vol. 1, John Foster Dulles Papers, Seeley G. Mudd Library, Princeton
University, Princeton, N.J. (hereafter JFD Princeton).

Dulles was opposed to the establishment of a united Germany for several reasons. First, drawing on the theories of world politics he had developed during the interwar period, Dulles argued that a "dynamic" state such as Germany, left to its own devices, would probably bandwagon with the Soviet Union rather than balance with the West in order to regain its prewar position on the continent. Second, Western efforts to prevent a united Germany from aligning with the Soviet Union by according it favorable treatment would ultimately be counterproductive because the indirect effect of such a policy would be the triumph of communism in France. Finally, Dulles argued that even if a united Germany were able to maintain its independence from the Soviet Union, its resulting bargaining power would be incompatible with the stability and peace of Europe.[9] If Dulles envisioned any scenarios in which the establishment of a united Germany would serve the interests of the United States and Western Europe, he clearly chose not to divulge them to Marshall or anyone else in the State Department.

Why did Dulles openly lobby to attend a conference in which his preferred outcome was a continuation of the stalemate between the United States and the Soviet Union? Based on the available evidence, it is hard to avoid the conclusion that one of his major reasons for attending the Moscow CFM was to make sure that the U.S. delegation would *not* reach any agreement with the Soviet Union on the German question.[10] Indeed, Dulles made it clear both before and during the conference that he was quite content to leave Moscow without a settlement and, more important, warned Counselor of the State Department Benjamin Cohen and other officials that he would openly oppose American policy if it reflected what he termed the "anti-French views of Murphy and Clay."[11] Although Clay hoped to end the stalemate in Germany, Dulles was content to see it continue indefinitely. As he wrote to Senator Arthur Vandenberg even before the CFM was over, " . . . the current zonal basis will continue, which, I

[9] Dulles memo of March 7, 1947. Much like Randall Schweller in his recent theoretical work, Dulles believed that "dynamic" or revisionist states tended to bandwagon rather than balance. See Randall Schweller, "Bandwagoning for Profit: Bringing the Revisionist State Back In," *International Security* 19 (summer 1994): 72–107. For a further discussion of Dulles's theories of international politics in the 1930s, see Ronald W. Pruessen, *The Road to Power* (New York: Free Press, 1982), 153–79.

[10] For a critical account of Dulles's role at the Moscow CFM, see Jean E. Smith, "The Decision to Divide Germany," in *Shepherd of Democracy? America and Germany in the Twentieth Century*, ed. Carl C. Hodge and Cathal J. Nolan (Westport, Conn.: Greenwood Press, 1992), 73–85.

[11] Dulles, Council of Foreign Ministers Meeting in Moscow, February 27, 1947, box 533, vol. 1, JFD Princeton. For further evidence of Dulles's efforts to prevent any deals being made at the Moscow CFM, see Charles P. Kindleberger, *The German Economy, 1945–47: Charles P. Kindleberger's Letters from the Field* (Westport, Conn.: Meckler Corporation, 1989), 143, 157, 160.

think, is good. It is useful to have more time to consolidate the Western zones and not expose them yet to Communist penetration."[12]

Since the Soviets had made it clear that their overall cooperation on the German question was dependent on the prior resolution of the reparations issue, the fate of the Moscow CFM would essentially turn on whether Marshall backed Clay's position on current reparations. Despite the belief that the Soviets might be willing to trade their adherence to the treatment of Germany as a single economic unit for an unspecified amount of current reparations, the State Department recommended to Marshall before the conference that he should continue to oppose any change in official policy except as a last resort.[13] Marshall essentially followed this advice at the Moscow CFM, although he was clearly more willing to contemplate the possibility of a deal involving current reparations than many other American officials.[14] Early in the conference, after Bevin told Marshall that he was not at all sure what Potsdam said about current reparations, the general stated that the U.S. delegation was opposed to any concessions to the Soviet Union. However, after the deadlock over Germany had become readily apparent, he asked Truman to approve instructions which would have allowed studies on the feasibility of a limited program of current reparations.[15] Marshall's reasons for wavering were noted by Dulles in a letter he sent to Vandenberg during the conference:

> But I do not think that the Secretary is as convinced as I am that to give the Soviets rights to large reparations from current production of the Western zones will, in effect, make the Soviets master of all Germany—including the Ruhr—and with that all Europe will go under. He feels, more than I do, that because our military establishment is disintegrating and because Congress may soon cut off appropriations for a considerable army in Europe, and the reserves to back it up, we cannot have a "strong" policy in Europe.[16]

Marshall ultimately chose not to pursue serious negotiations on the issue.[17] Since the Soviets had made reparations from current production

---

[12] Dulles to Vandenberg, March 29, 1947, box 533, vol. 1, JFD Princeton.

[13] *FRUS*, 1947, vol. 2, 217–18. Kindleberger thought that the Soviets made it "very clear that they are prepared to agree to economic unity on something much like our terms" provided that they were satisfied on current reparations. See Kindleberger, *The German Economy*, 157.

[14] See Philip Zelikow, "George C. Marshall and the Moscow CFM Meeting of 1947," *Diplomacy and Statecraft* 8 (July 1997): 97–124.

[15] *FRUS*, 1947, vol. 2, 273–75, 298–307, 422–23.

[16] See Dulles to Vandenberg, April 4, 1947, box 533, vol. 1, JFD Princeton. Clay had similar views about the need to reach a settlement before Congress cut off military appropriations to American troops in Germany. See Kindleberger, *German Economy*, 157.

[17] Marshall was willing to consider limited current reparations as a substitute for plants already allocated to the Soviet Union. For an insider's account of the State Department position

an "absolute condition" of their acceptance of the principle of German economic unity, the rest of the Moscow CFM was largely an exercise in futility. Whether the Soviets would actually have made serious political and economic concessions in exchange for current reparations, or whether an acceptable economic arrangement was feasible and worth pursuing, were eminently debatable questions at the time and continue to be a subject of historical debate. For these reasons alone, claims about a "missed opportunity" at Moscow for preserving the wartime alliance and establishing a united Germany should be treated with considerable skepticism.[18] However, what does seem beyond question is that none of the Western delegations, including the U.S. delegation, were very interested in exploring how much it might have cost to purchase an objective—German economic unity—that Marshall was publicly proclaiming to be "vital to the success of the occupation and the future peace of the world."[19]

Even though American policymakers had generally not held out great hopes for the Moscow CFM, its failure was viewed as the end of the road in terms of solving the German problem through great power cooperation. Even Clay and Murphy abandoned their hopes for a unified Germany after the Moscow CFM. Soviet perspectives were much less fatalistic. For his part, Stalin does not seem to have placed a great deal of significance on the failure of the Moscow CFM. In a meeting with Marshall and Smith on April 15, 1947, he stated that no one should be very pessimistic about the lack of progress because the negotiations represented only "the first skirmishes and brushes of reconnaissance forces" on the German question.[20] Less than a month after the end of the conference, Stalin reiterated this assessment in the Soviet journal *New Times*: "The value of the Moscow conference is that the position of the powers on the disputed issues has become clarified. And this clears the way—given goodwill on both sides—for the necessary, if exacting work of reconciling the different points of view and arriving at agreed decisions."[21] As Scott Parrish argues, it is quite possible that Stalin had no long-range objectives at this time but was simply holding out for a better deal on Germany.[22]

---

on current reparations at Moscow, see Edward Mason, "Reflections on the Moscow Conference," *International Organization* 1 (June 1947): 475–87. For a further discussion of Marshall's perspective at Moscow, see Forrest Pogue, *George C. Marshall: Statesman, 1945–49* (New York: Viking, 1987), 168–96.

[18] For the missed opportunity thesis, see Smith, "The Decision to Divide Germany," 77–85. Eisenberg contrasts American intransigence and Soviet willingness to make concessions in *Drawing the Line,* 289–317.

[19] The quotation is from Marshall's statement of March 17, 1947, *FRUS,* 1947, vol. 2, 256.

[20] Memorandum of Conversation between Marshall and Stalin, April 15, 1947, *FRUS,* 1947, vol. 2, 344.

[21] Cited in William Taubman, *Stalin's American Policy: From Entente to Detente to Cold War* (New York: Norton, 1982), 172.

[22] Scott Parrish, "The Turn toward Confrontation: The Soviet Reaction to the Marshall Plan, 1947," Working Paper no. 9, Cold War International History Project (May 1994), 9; and

However, if Stalin thought that he was reassuring Marshall and the State Department with these relatively optimistic assessments of the Moscow CFM, he badly miscalculated. By all accounts, Marshall was deeply affected by Stalin's assessment because he deduced from it that the Soviets were willing to countenance—and hoped to benefit from—an extended stalemate over Germany and the continuation of economic stagnation in Europe. The theme that Marshall emphasized in his radio address after his return to the United States was directly the opposite of Stalin's: "The patient is sinking while the doctors deliberate."[23] Of course, even before Marshall returned from the CFM, State Department planners were already working on the problem of European economic recovery. Within days after returning to Washington, Marshall greatly accelerated this process by appointing George Kennan as director of the Policy Planning Staff (PPS).[24]

Kennan was an obvious choice to devise an American strategy based on strengthening Western Europe. He had been among the first to advocate that postwar American foreign policy should be based squarely on the assumption of a divided Europe and the impossibility of any real collaboration with the Soviet Union. Although the Marshall Plan was surely not the product of a single individual, Kennan's contributions to the origins of what eventually became the European Recovery Program were second to none. For example, Marshall's emphasis on the need for European responsibility and initiative in his famous speech at Harvard University on June 5 was taken directly from the recommendations put forward by Kennan's Policy Planning Staff in the weeks preceding the speech.[25]

It cannot be emphasized enough that the Marshall Plan was conceived from the start by Kennan and other officials as a program for the economic rehabilitation of Western Europe. The participation of the Soviet

---

Geoffrey Roberts, "Moscow and the Marshall Plan: Politics, Ideology, and the Onset of the Cold War, 1947," *Europe-Asia Studies* 46 (1994): 1371–86.

[23] See Forrest Pogue, "George C. Marshall and the Marshall Plan," in *The Marshall Plan and Germany*, ed. Charles S. Maier (New York: Berg Publishers, 1991), 46–70 (quotation on 49).

[24] For a good discussion of the planning process prior to Marshall's return from the Moscow CFM, see Scott Jackson, "Prologue to the Marshall Plan: The Origins of the American Commitment for a European Recovery Program," *Journal of American History* 65 (March 1979): 1043–68.

[25] For Kennan's role in the formulation of the Marshall Plan, see Wilson D. Miscamble, "George F. Kennan, the Policy Planning Staff, and the Origins of the Marshall Plan," *Mid-America* 62 (April–July 1980): 75–89; Miscamble, *George F. Kennan and the Making of American Foreign Policy, 1947–50* (Princeton: Princeton University Press, 1992), 43–74; and George F. Kennan, *Memoirs, 1925–50* (New York: Atlantic, Little, Brown, 1967), 325–53. The emphasis on European initiative and responsibility runs throughout the PPS paper, "Policy With Respect to American Aid to Western Europe," May 23, 1947, in *The State Department Policy Planning Staff Papers*, ed. Anna Kasten Nelson (New York: Garland Press, 1980), 1:3–11 (hereafter *SDPPSP*).

Union was neither sought nor desired. Indeed, Kennan's first memo on the subject explicitly referred to the fact that the Policy Planning Staff was working on "a set of principles which it feels should be observed in framing a master plan for US assistance to western Europe."[26] Although Kennan had indicated in this original memo that the possibility of participation should be left open for the Soviet satellites in Eastern Europe, a week later he essentially admitted that the purpose of such an offer would be solely for tactical and propaganda reasons. If it proved necessary to advance a program for general European economic recovery, as he thought it might, Kennan argued that "it would be essential that this be done in such a form that the Russian satellite countries would either exclude themselves by unwillingness to accept the proposed conditions or agree to abandon the exclusive orientation of their economies."[27]

Contrary to what he suggests in his memoirs, neither Kennan nor any other top officials in the administration were really willing to "play it straight" on the issue of Soviet participation in any program of economic aid for Europe.[28] U.S. officials were well aware that they would be in a strong position to place highly unappealing conditions on Soviet participation, and they were quite prepared to do so in the event that the Soviets showed any interest in the European Recovery Program. For example, as Clayton explained to Bevin shortly after Marshall's speech, the United States would expect the Soviets to contribute raw materials to any short-term program for European economic recovery and that during this phase of the program the Soviets would have little basis for claiming American aid. Clayton acknowledged that the Soviets might have a reasonable claim for credits and loans in the long-term phase of the program, but as one of the British representatives quickly pointed out, they would

---

[26] Memorandum by the Director of the Policy Planning Staff, May 16, 1947, *FRUS, 1947*, vol. 3, 221.

[27] See "Policy With Respect to Western Europe," in *SDPPSP*, 9. In a February 1948 draft of a speech on the Marshall Plan, Kennan explained why the Eastern Europeans could not explicitly be excluded from participation: "We could not say to one country: 'You belong to it'—and to another one: 'You are already lost to the cause of human freedom; we've written you off.' This would have been political folly. It would have been ruinous to the program. Some way or other, the Europeans had to be forced to make this determination." See "Background to the Marshall Plan," February 28, 1948, box 17, Kennan Papers, Seeley G. Mudd Library, Princeton University, Princeton, N.J. Kennan and some other officials also hoped that the Marshall Plan might help drive a wedge between the Soviet Union and the satellite states. See Melvyn Leffler, "The United States and the Strategic Dimensions of the Marshall Plan," *Diplomatic History* 12 (spring 1988): 277–306.

[28] The phrase is used by Kennan in *Memoirs, 1925–50*, 342. In a much earlier oral history interview with Harry Price, Kennan properly described the "lose-lose" nature of the options presented to the Soviets by Marshall's offer: " . . . in a sense, we put Russia over the barrel. . . . When the full horror of [their] alternatives dawned on them, they left suddenly in the middle of the night." Cited in Charles L. Mee, *The Marshall Plan: The Launching of Pax Americana* (New York: Simon and Schuster, 1984), 136.

then have to apply for membership in the World Bank and reveal information about their gold reserves.[29] In short, after the Soviet Union had contributed raw materials to the reconstruction of Western Europe and allowed its satellites to orient their economies to the West, there was a slight possibility that American policymakers might consider it eligible for loans at some unspecified point in the future.

As American officials suspected from the start, the Soviets did indeed exclude themselves and the satellites from any open participation in the Marshall Plan. Molotov's stance at the Paris Conference arranged by Bevin and Bidault in late June 1947 was so contrary to the basic spirit of Marshall's call for a joint European program that there was no need to invoke any of the additional conditions that American officials had previously discussed.[30] The Soviet hope that the Marshall Plan could be turned into a postwar lend-lease form of American aid with no strings attached was dashed very quickly. Molotov made it clear that the Soviet Union would not go along with an all-European plan for reconstruction that required them to provide information about their national resources. Secure in the knowledge that the American offer of aid was not at all dependent on Soviet participation, Bevin and Bidault made little effort to broker a compromise.[31] Worried that the Soviets might attempt to place a Trojan horse in any program for European reconstruction, Bevin told the British Cabinet that "from a practical point of view it is far better to have them definitely out than half-heartedly in."[32] American policymakers did not disagree with Bevin's assessment.

[29] Memorandum of Conversation between Clayton and British Cabinet Members, June 26, 1947, *FRUS,* 1947, vol. 3, 291. Soviet intelligence sources informed Moscow of the substance of Clayton's discussions with the British before Molotov met with Bevin and Bidault to discuss the American offer. See Vladislav Zubok and Constantine Pleshakov, *Inside the Kremlin's Cold War: From Stalin to Khruschev* (Cambridge, Mass.: Harvard University Press, 1996), 105. For the Soviet reaction to the Marshall Plan based on new documentation, see Mikhail M. Narinsky, "The Soviet Union and the Marshall Plan," Working Paper no. 9, Cold War International History Project (May 1994), 41–51.

[30] The negotiations with Molotov can be followed in *FRUS,* 1947, vol. 3, 297–307.

[31] Both Bevin and Bidault told American officials of their hope that they would not reach an agreement with Molotov. For domestic reasons, Bidault made a greater effort to at least appear accommodating. See John W. Young, *France, The Cold War, and the Western Alliance, 1944–49* (Leicester, England: Leicester University Press, 1990), 152–54; and William C. Cromwell, "The Marshall Plan, Britain, and the Cold War," *Review of International Studies* 8 (October 1982): 233–49.

[32] Public Records Office, C.P. (47) 197, Memorandum by the Secretary of State For Foreign Affairs, July 5, 1947. While critical of Molotov's tactics and negotiating style, factors which have been so emphasized in the historical literature, Bevin himself suggested that the Soviet refusal to participate in the Marshall Plan could be explained in very simple terms: "The Soviet Government itself can never have hoped to be able to get much for itself out of the Marshall invitation; and its refusal to undertake a heavy job of work which offered little return is not, on the face of it, unexpected."

Excluding the Soviet Union from any program involving American financial aid was a necessary precondition for tackling the immediate problem confronting the Truman administration: the revival of Western Europe and the western zones of Germany. For very understandable reasons, Marshall had not said a word in his Harvard speech about the role Germany would play in the process of European recovery. But silence did not imply ignorance because Marshall was well aware that it was foolish to talk about European economic recovery, or about reducing the burden on the American taxpayer, without also improving the chaotic situation that prevailed in Bizonia.[33] Indeed, Marshall had already taken a fundamental step in this direction during the Moscow CFM by directing Clay to begin negotiations with the British over administrative reforms and an increase in the permitted level of production of the German steel industry. As the delegates from sixteen European nations arrived in Paris to prepare their response to the American offer, Clay and Brian Robertson, deputy British military governor for Germany, were all set to announce that Germany's permitted level of steel production would be increased from 7.5 to 11.2 million tons.[34]

The Marshall Plan, of course, did not end French concerns about the restoration of German power. Bidault made it clear that France would not accept silently the bizonal decisions simply because of the promise of American financial aid. From Bidault's perspective, regardless of the merits of the bizonal agreement itself, Anglo-American decisions were utterly incomprehensible. First, announcement of bizonal reforms played directly into the hands of the Soviet propaganda line that the real purpose of the Marshall Plan was to restore German power. Having just taken a considerable political risk in siding with the United States and Great Britain against the Soviet Union, Bidault was understandably furious at the precarious position he would be placed in domestically after the announcement of a revised German level of industry appeared to validate the communist line. Second, since German steel production was presently less than half of the permitted level of 7.5 million tons, Bidault could see no reason why the United States was in such a hurry to announce a new level of industry, particularly since the general European conference called to discuss Marshall's offer was just about to begin. Although freely acknowledging that France must ultimately coordinate its policies with

---

[33] See Memorandum of Conversation between Marshall and Lord Inverchapel, June 30, 1947, in *Memoranda of Conversation of the Secretary of State, 1947–52*, microfiche publication (Washington, D.C.: Department of State, 1988), fiche 60. The connection between German recovery and the ERP is the main thesis of John Gimbel's *The Origins of the Marshall Plan* (Stanford, Calif.: Stanford University Press, 1976), esp. chaps. 11–15.

[34] The process leading up to the Clay-Robertson agreement can be followed in *FRUS*, 1947, vol. 2, 472–91, 909–31.

those of Washington and London, Bidault threatened to resign if the decision to raise the level of German industry was not postponed until a later date.[35]

To say the least, Bidault's protests about Anglo-American policies in the bizone marked a less than auspicious beginning for the new course in postwar American diplomacy. Although Marshall and Caffery defended the need for an agreement on new levels of industry to Bidault and other French officials, they were willing to concede that any announcement of the decision should be postponed until after the French had an opportunity to state their concerns. However, at the same time that Marshall was providing reassurances to Bidault, he was also reassuring the War Department that the Clay-Robertson agreement would not be modified unless its maintenance threatened the overall success of the ERP or the survival of democracy in France.[36] Marshall was prepared to help save Bidault's political standing, but he was not yet prepared to accept the force of any arguments that the French might present against the substance of the Anglo-American agreement on the bizone.[37]

Not surprisingly, the tenuous nature of the State Department-War Department agreement was quickly exposed when Secretary of War Kenneth C. Royall announced in Berlin that he had no knowledge of any agreement to consult with the French before raising the level of German industry. Royall's purpose in making the statement was to pacify Clay, who had once again threatened to resign after hearing of the decision to postpone the announcement of the level of industry agreement.[38] Furious at how Royall's statement threatened to undo all of the progress the State Department had made with the French in resolving the crisis over the previous few weeks, Undersecretary of State Robert Lovett actually told Marshall that the incident "serves to demonstrate the unworkable and, indeed, dangerous nature of any such type of understanding with the War Department on matters affecting US foreign policy."[39] The United States

[35] See Caffery to Secretary of State, July 11, 1947, 983–86; Bidault to Marshall, July 17, 1947, *FRUS,* 1947, vol. 2, 983–86, 991–92; and Memorandum of Conversation between Lovett and Henri Bonnet, July 18, 1947, in *Memoranda of Conversation of the Secretary of State,* fiche 5.

[36] For the decision to postpone the announcement, see Marshall to Bidault, July 21, 1947, *FRUS,* 1947, vol. 2, 1003–4. For the agreement with the War Department that the bizonal level of industry would be vigorously defended, see *FRUS,* 1947, vol. 2, 1004–5, 1009–11.

[37] Lower-level State Department officials such as Henri Labouisse recommended that Marshall defend the principle of real consultation with the French over the LOI in his negotiations with the War Department and take the issue to Truman if it proved necessary. It is clear that Marshall chose not to take such a confrontational position with the War Department. See H. R. Labouisse, "Certain Aspects of our Policies and Operations with Respect to Germany," July 23, 1947, RG 59, Records of the French Desk, box 2, NA.

[38] See Clay-Royall Teleconference, August 8, 1947, in *Clay Papers,* 394–97.

[39] Lovett to Marshall, August 3, 1947, *FRUS,* 1947, vol. 2, 1016.

subsequently agreed to discuss the agreement with the French but not before making it clear that the substance of the agreement would not be altered. After six weeks of conflict over the issue, the bottom line to the entire affair was that the final Clay-Robertson agreement of August 29
remained exactly as it was before Bidault had lodged his protests.

If the early returns of Marshall's initiative to moderate French concerns
about German recovery were mixed, the same assessment applied to the
progress made by the Europeans in their efforts to draft a joint report at the
Paris Conference. U.S. officials placed a great deal of importance on the ability of the Europeans to devise an indigenous and collective program for
economic recovery. Before Marshall delivered his speech at Harvard,
Kennan had argued that if the Europeans were unwilling to take the initiative in drafting an overall program for recovery, the only conclusion that
could be drawn by the United States was that "rigor mortis has already set
in on the body politic of Europe as we have known it and that it may be already too late for us to change decisively the course of events."[40] The fact
that the Western Europeans responded enthusiastically to Marshall's
speech, and were willing to openly defy the Soviet Union in the process,
suggested that the situation was not as dire as Kennan thought it might
have been in May 1947. Nevertheless, after witnessing the Europeans
struggle to draft a viable recovery program, Kennan was impressed by the
"pathetic weakness" of their efforts. Indeed, the situation in Paris was so
bad that Kennan was now amenable to the need for the United States to
take a much larger role than he had originally thought desirable in drafting a recovery program: "This would mean that we would listen to all that
the Europeans had to say, but in the end we would not *ask* them, we would
just *tell* them what they would get."[41]

Kennan often drew more pessimistic conclusions than his colleagues,
but this time his assessment was well within the general State Department
consensus. After reading reports from Paris by Clayton and Caffery,
Lovett complained to both of them that the Europeans did not appear to
be paying enough attention to the principles of self-help and mutual aid
in drafting a recovery program.[42] Less than a week before the participants
were supposed to produce their report, Lovett cabled Marshall that the
results of the conference were a disappointment and "all that has come
out so far is sixteen shopping lists which may be dressed up by some large
scale but very long-term projects such as Alpine power, etc."[43] When the

[40] "Policy With Respect to American Aid to Western Europe," 8.
[41] Memorandum by the Director of the Policy Planning Staff, September 4, 1947, *FRUS,
1947*, vol. 3, 397–405 (quotations on 402).
[42] Lovett to the Embassy in France, August 14, 1947, *FRUS*, 1947, vol. 3, 356.
[43] Lovett to Secretary of State, August 24, 1947, *FRUS*, 1947, vol. 3, 372–73; and
Memorandum of Conversation between Lovett and Bonnet, August 21, 1947, in *Memoranda
of Conversation of the Secretary of State*, fiche 160.

European states eventually came up with a preliminary aid estimate of $29.2 billion over four years, American officials decided that the level of "friendly assistance" in the drafting of a European program would have to be much greater than initially envisioned.[44]

A large part of the explanation for American dissatisfaction with the Paris Conference can be attributed to the strictly pragmatic concern that the Europeans were drawing up a recovery program that Congress might find very difficult to support. However, an additional source of concern was the fact that the representatives from the various countries were acting as if they were representing traditional and viable nation-states. This should not have been such a cause for alarm since, after all, the participants were representing nation-states but, as Kennan later noted in his memoirs, one of the underlying purposes behind the Marshall Plan was "to force the Europeans to begin to think like Europeans, and not like nationalists, in their approach to the economic problems of the continent."[45]

THE MARSHALL PLAN AND THE LOGIC OF WESTERN EUROPEAN UNITY

Would the states of Western Europe have been better off if the Truman administration had never proposed or funded the European Recovery Program? Few political scientists or historians have ever seriously considered such a heretical proposition, but several of the leading architects of postwar American foreign policy did periodically speculate about whether the provision of financial aid and security guarantees would have a detrimental impact on Western Europe in the long-run.[46] "It is

---

[44] See Caffery to Secretary of State, August 31, 1947, *FRUS, 1947*, vol. 3, 391–96. For an excellent discussion of the Paris Conference from the perspective of U.S. officials, see Michael Hogan, "Paths to Plenty: Marshall Planners and the Debate over European Integration, 1947–48," *Pacific Historical Review* 35 (August 1984): 337–66. For accounts that devote more attention to Western European and British perspectives, see Alan Milward, *The Reconstruction of Western Europe* (Berkeley: University of California Press, 1984), 69–89; and the chapter on the Marshall Plan in Alex Danchev, *Oliver Franks: Founding Father* (Oxford: Clarendon Press, 1993), 57–83.

[45] Kennan, *Memoirs, 1925–50*, 337.

[46] This question should not be confused with the question of whether the Marshall Plan was necessary for Europe's economic recovery, which has certainly sparked a great deal of debate in recent years. For the argument that the Marshall Plan was not necessary for European recovery, see Milward, *The Reconstruction of Western Europe*; and Alan Milward, "Was the Marshall Plan Necessary?" *Diplomatic History* 13 (spring 1989): 231–53. For criticisms of the Milward thesis, see Melvyn Leffler, *A Preponderance of Power: National Security, the Truman Administration, and the Cold War* (Stanford, Calif.: Stanford University Press, 1992), 159–61; Michael J. Hogan, *The Marshall Plan: America, Britain, and the Reconstruction of Western Europe, 1947–1952* (New York: Cambridge University Press, 1987), 430–34; and Lawrence Kaplan, "The Cold War and European Revisionism," *Diplomatic History* 11 (spring 1987): 143–56.

quite possible," John Foster Dulles suggested during Senate hearings on the North Atlantic Pact in 1949, "that the historian may judge the European Recovery Act and the Atlantic Pact were the two things which prevented a unity in Europe which in the long run may be more valuable than either of them."[47] Less than two months after Marshall's speech at Harvard, Lovett was already urging American officials to make the Western Europeans understand that their overriding objective must be to adjust themselves to "certain basic changes which have occurred and are continuing to occur in their international position. . . . the Europeans might make more progress if they were to assume that there was no one to help them, to imagine that they had no choice but to try to work out an acceptable economic future without any outside support."[48] Both Dulles and Lovett assumed that without American intervention, Western Europeans would realize that their only possible hope for a prosperous future would lie in an amalgamation of their collective power and the abolition of national sovereignties. If American aid and protection led the Western Europeans to think otherwise, then such aid would be a grave mistake.

To a greater or lesser degree, most American officials after 1947 shared the premise that the revolutionary transformation in the global distribution of power wrought by the Second World War required an equally revolutionary transformation of the way in which the states of Western Europe conducted their affairs. America's support for Western European integration after 1947 may well have been the first time in history that a great power encouraged unity rather than disunity in the region, as Armin Rappaport points out, but from the perspective of the Truman administration there could not have been a more obvious policy choice.[49] One will search in vain for any great debates within the American foreign policy establishment in the late 1940s and the early 1950s over whether a more unified Europe was in the national interest. What debates there were over European unity in the late 1940s largely revolved around tactical considerations, such as whether the Truman administration was doing enough to forward the integration process or whether Great Britain should be encouraged to take a greater role in Europe.[50]

---

[47] Dulles testimony of May 4, 1949, Senate Committee on Foreign Relations, hearing on the North Atlantic Treaty, 81st Cong., 1st sess., part 2, 369.

[48] Lovett to the Embassy in France, August 14, 1947, *FRUS, 1947*, vol. 3, 356–57.

[49] Rappaport, "United States and European Integration," 121.

[50] Hogan emphasizes the debate between "planners" and "traders" within the administration, but these debates were relatively narrow in scope. See Hogan, *Marshall Plan*, 54–87. For the arguments over whether to rely on Britain or France in furthering the integration process, see Klaus Schwabe, "Efforts towards Cooperation and Integration in Europe, 1948–50," in *The Western Security Community, 1948–50*, ed. Norbert Wiggershaus and Roland G. Foerster (Providence, R.I.: Berg Publishers, 1993), 29–42.

No American statesmen in the late 1940s laid out the case for Western European unity more effectively than did John Foster Dulles in his various speeches and frequent appearances before Congressional committees. For Dulles, the fundamental point of departure for any analysis of postwar Europe had to be based on a recognition that the classical European state system was now obsolete. Although Europe may have previously been able to absorb the costs of a system based on the unrestrained sovereignty of the nation-state, the Second World War had clearly brought this period of history to a close.[51] In a statement before the Senate Foreign Relations Committee in November 1947, Dulles emphasized the danger that America would inadvertently salvage the sovereignty system and the inherent limits to European recovery if the underlying pattern of relations among the states of Western Europe remained unaltered:

> Europe has always been plagued by the multiplicity of its states. Today, more than ever, Europe cannot afford the luxury of excessive nationalism. Western Europe has suffered grave blows. Some of these can be offset by rebuilding and modernizing the old structure. But some of these blows cannot be overcome in this way. The position of western Europe is changed not only superficially but fundamentally.[52]

In Dulles's view, the United States had to be very careful that in its efforts to restore Western Europe's economic position it did not help to rescue an obsolete system. Specifically, America needed to make it clear to the states of the region that economic aid or security guarantees could not be seen as a substitute for fundamental steps toward the establishment of supranational and federal institutions. As he told the Council on Foreign Relations in February 1948, the Marshall Plan would be a complete failure if it allowed the Europeans to avoid making the hard choices that they would undoubtedly make if there was no prospect of American aid and protection:

> To recreate the conditions that existed before the war would not only be a waste of money but a positive misuse of money. It would be wrong to use our resources to rebuild separate sovereignties in Europe, if without our help they might be forced to come together

---

[51] Dulles, "The Unification of Western Europe," April 7, 1948, box 35, JFD Princeton; and Address by the Honorable John Foster Dulles before the American Club of Paris, November 18, 1948, box 36, JFD Princeton. For an overview of Dulles's views on European unity, see Pruessen, *Road to Power*, 298–354.

[52] Statement by the Honorable John Foster Dulles before the Senate Foreign Relations Committee, November 14, 1947, box 32, JFD Princeton.

through necessity. But it would be proper to use our resources if they will help to induce them toward unity.[53]

How the United States could encourage the Western Europeans toward greater unity without simultaneously diminishing the pressures for unity was, as Dulles readily admitted, a "matter of great delicacy."[54] Dulles's belief that the root cause of Europe's troubles could be traced to an obsolete system led him to adopt a rather schizophrenic view toward all of the major initiatives put forward by the Truman administration between 1947 and 1948. Despite his eloquent defense of the Marshall Plan before various congressional committees, Dulles was privately quite critical of the fact that the State Department watered down the concept of European unity in drawing up the ERP. In his view, furthering the idea of unity inherent in Marshall's speech was far more important than the aid levels or the administration of the ERP. Nevertheless, despite his belief that Europe must ultimately federate or perish, Dulles did not support congressional efforts aimed at linking American aid to tangible measures toward greater integration on the part of the states of Western Europe.[55] Dulles's concern that American efforts might be counterproductive to European unity also influenced his opinion about the efficacy of security guarantees. When Marshall and Lovett first broached to him the idea of concluding a treaty with the Brussels Pact nations in April 1948, Dulles immediately voiced his concern that "any permanent arrangement might seem to guaranty the status quo and make it less likely, rather than more likely, that the western European democracies would unite as to create strength between themselves."[56]

However, despite his fear that American guarantees might act as an impediment to European unity, Dulles eloquently defended the case for short-term measures designed to restore indigenous European power in his testimony before the Senate. Dulles drew a clear, negative causal rela-

[53] Discussion Meeting Group: Marshall Plan Group, February 2, 1948, box 37, JFD Princeton.

[54] Dulles Testimony, January 8, 1948, U.S. Congress, Senate Committee on Foreign Relations, *European Recovery Program*, 80th Cong., 2d sess., 605.

[55] See "Discussion Meeting Group"; and Dulles to Fulbright, March 15, 1948, box 36, JFD Princeton. Dulles's views on the efficacy of pressuring Western Europe would later change. See John Foster Dulles, *War or Peace* (New York: Macmillan Company, 1950), 211–23.

[56] See Memo of Blair House Meeting, April 27, 1947, box 37, JFD Princeton. It is also worth noting that Dulles wanted a short time period on any American commitment because "we were dealing with a temporary and transitional situation and that permanent long-term commitments would be out of place." In Lovett's memorandum of the same conversation, Dulles is reported to have said that "the agreement should also be designed to further the basic concept of ERP to the end of ultimate union or fusion among the Western European countries. He emphasized that any attempt to freeze the Western European countries in their old habits of thought, association and economics would be futile and, in his opinion, against our national interests." See Memorandum of Conversation by Lovett, April 27, 1948, *FRUS*, 1947, vol. 3, 106.

tionship between the level of American support for Europe and the efforts the states of Western Europe would make toward achieving greater unity. It is worth pointing out why Dulles did not draw the opposite conclusion: namely, that the more secure the Europeans were with America's commitment to the continent, the more likely that they would be willing to experiment with unprecedented steps in the direction of federalism and supranationalism. The major reason Dulles's thinking did not run in this direction was that he did not believe any American statesmen could or should guarantee such a long-term commitment to Europe. For this reason it would be a fatal mistake for the Western Europeans to believe that they could proceed at a very slow pace toward unity:

> I think our policy also should discourage Europe from believing that they can proceed indefinitely without taking the step which their security demands, in the illusion that we can be relied upon indefinitely to rescue them from their own errors. In the first place, I do not believe that the American people want that responsibility. In the second place, I do not believe it will be possible for us again to prepare and effect the rescue in time, over such a distance. We will subtract from the likelihood of Europe effecting her own cure if we nurture the illusion that she can count on us; and we will add to that likelihood to any extent that we help Europe to see the awful danger she faces and the emptiness of reliance upon us.[57]

The final point to note about Dulles's analysis of the long-term prospects of Western Europe after the Second World War is that his thinking was characterized by equal degrees of pessimism and optimism. If Western Europe had a bleak future as a collection of highly independent and competitive sovereignties, its prospects as a united federation were considered to be virtually limitless. In his view, a federated Western Europe would be "an area of political and economic unity which would have the population, the institutions, the ideals and the resources necessary to make it one of the great units of power in the world. Such a unit could be fully comparable to the United States or to the Soviet Union."[58] Dulles meant the term "fully comparable" literally. In the long-term, he did not see a united Western Europe as merely a junior partner of the United States, or as an entity that could not ultimately provide for its own defense against the Soviet Union. When asked by a member of the Senate Foreign Relations Committee whether the United States would extend security guarantees to Western Europe in conjunction with the ERP, Dulles

---

[57] Dulles, "Long-Term Aims," n.d. (probably circa 1948), box 32, JFD Princeton.
[58] Dulles, "The Unification of Western Europe," 6.

responded: "I would not know that we would have to come to their defense under those conditions. I do not think we would. They are plenty strong themselves. They have over 200,000,000 people—educated able people. If they stand together those 200,000,000 do not have to depend upon our 140,000,000 people. They are stronger than we are. It is only because they are divided that they are weak."[59]

To the dismay of congressional enthusiasts for European unity such as J. William Fulbright, the Truman administration was never willing to state the case for European unity as strongly as Dulles.[60] But the restraint of administration officials in advocating European unity was quite understandable because they did not want to be open to the charge that they were interfering in the sovereign affairs of independent states. More important, the Truman administration did not want to be placed in the position of having to cut off aid to states in the region if they failed to satisfy the conditions some members of Congress wished to attach to the ERP. Indeed, since Great Britain had made it perfectly clear that it would vigorously oppose any movement designed to further the process of supranationalism or federalism on the continent, the Truman administration would have been placed in the uncomfortable position of alienating its most valuable ally if it accepted the conditions on aid that Fulbright and others wanted to attach. For all of these reasons, despite the importance placed on obtaining congressional support, the administration refused to go any further in public than to state that it welcomed and supported any and all efforts that led in the direction of greater European integration or unity.[61]

Privately, the differences between the Truman administration and congressional enthusiasts for European unity were much less pronounced. Like Dulles, many State Department officials believed that Europe's ills were rooted in too many sovereignties and that the long-term cure for the region was to be found in federalism and supranationalism. As early as May 1947, in his famous report on conditions in Europe that Marshall subsequently incorporated into his Harvard speech, Clayton argued that "Europe cannot recover from this war and again become independent if her economy continues to be divided into many small watertight com-

---

[59] Dulles testimony, January 8, 1948, Senate Committee on Foreign Relations, 613. See also Dulles, *War or Peace*, 212–13, 220–21.

[60] For Fulbright's efforts to promote European unity, see the biography by Randall Bennett Woods, *Fulbright: A Biography* (New York: Cambridge University Press, 1995), 137–44.

[61] The sensitivity of the administration to all of these issues can be seen in the debate in late 1949 over whether Paul Hoffman, the head of the Economic Cooperation Administration, should use the word "integration" or "unity" in a speech he was scheduled to deliver. The State Department officials recommended that Hoffman use integration because its lack of specificity provided them with more flexibility with both the allies and Congress. See Hogan, *Marshall Plan*, 272–74.

partments as it is today."[62] Similarly, before the Paris Conference revealed that the Europeans would resist the imposition of such conditions, Charles Bohlen suggested that the United States make it clear that "the only politically feasible basis on which the U.S. would be willing to make the aid available is substantial evidence of a developing overall plan for economic cooperation by the Europeans themselves, perhaps an economic federation to be worked out over 3 or 4 years."[63] For Kennan, the establishment of some sort of a federal structure in Europe was the only "reasonable hopeful" way in which the region could conceivably avoid Russian or German domination in the future.[64] But regardless of how much they thought that the future of Europe depended on unification, members of the Truman administration were well aware of the fact that advances in this direction could not be dictated by Americans. Evaluating their commitment to European unity by comparing it to the proposals of those who did not share their responsibilities, such as those of Congress or private advocacy groups, is a test in which they will always come up short. The real test of how seriously the Truman administration took the concept of European unification can be seen in how they responded to later French initiatives in this direction, such as the Schuman Plan and the European Defense Community.

THE VICIOUS CIRCLE: THE LONDON PROGRAM AND THE ORIGINS OF NATO

American officials thought about the restoration of a European balance of power in terms of separate components that could be pursued sequentially, with the military component postponed until after the attainment of economic reconstruction and political stability. Consequently, State Department thinking about the future of Western Europe throughout

[62] May 27, 1947, *FRUS*, 1947, vol. 3, 232.

[63] "Summary of Discussion on Problems of Relief, Rehabilitation, and Reconstruction of Europe," May 29, 1947, *FRUS*, 1947, vol. 3, 235.

[64] PPS/23, "Review of Current Trends U.S. Foreign Policy," February 23, 1948, in *SDPPSP*, 110. In a lecture at the Naval War College in October 1948, Kennan repeated his view that a European federation was the only positive alternative to German leadership: "A far more preferable alternative from our standpoint would be a federation of some sort in Western Europe in which the cumulative initiative and strength and hopes of the European peoples could be assembled to govern the whole place in one great federated state. That is, in fact, the only alternative that we can seek, because there is no single European power today who has either the will or the ability to take leadership in the sense of providing the political push to animate the life and the military power of the entire continent." Kennan address at the Naval War College, October 11, 1948, box 17, Kennan Papers, Princeton University.

1947 was devoid of any serious consideration of how and when the military element of the balance of power would be addressed. More than anyone else, Bevin was responsible for bringing the military question into the overall equation much sooner than anticipated. In the aftermath of the London CFM, Bevin suggested that he, Marshall, and Bidault should begin working toward the creation of a spiritual federation backed by "power, money and resolute action."[65] What Bevin meant by these phrases was by no means obvious to anyone at the time. French officials were impressed by the "remarkable imprecision" of his words, and Marshall, unsure of what had been proposed to him, actually sent one of his advisors to find out from Foreign Office officials exactly what their boss had in mind.[66] Nevertheless, despite the lack of clarity in Bevin's initial proposal—or quite possibly because of it—the idea of creating a military alliance between the United States and Western Europe soon became an essential component of Western strategy.

Bevin put forward his initiative immediately after the failure of the London CFM in December 1947. The proceedings of the conference are not worth examining in detail because by this point in time the CFM was no longer a forum for serious diplomacy. A telling indication of how American officials approached the German question on the eve of the CFM can be seen in their reactions to widespread rumors that the Soviets might propose a general troop withdrawal from Germany. Rather than viewing the Soviet proposal as a possible defensive reaction to the Marshall Plan or as an indication that Moscow might be willing to cut a deal over Germany, American officials such as U.S. Ambassador to the Soviet Union Walter Bedell Smith argued that the United States must "clarify impossibility of US even considering such [a] proposal until power factor now represented by allied troops replaced by native elements of stability."[67] Even Kennan, who in less than a year would put for-

---

[65] British Memorandum of Conversation of December 17, 1947, meeting, *FRUS, 1947,* vol. 2, 815.

[66] For Marshall's confusion about the meaning of Bevin's proposal, see John Hickerson Oral History, Columbia Oral History Project, 1974, 26. As John Baylis points out, the Foreign Office was similarly unsure about what Bevin had in mind. See Baylis, "Britain, the Brussels Pact, and the Continental Commitment," *International Affairs* 60 (autumn 1984): 615–29. For the French reaction, see Young, *France, the Cold War, and the Western Alliance,* 173.

[67] For American concerns about the possibility of the Soviets proposing a troop withdrawal, see *FRUS, 1947,* vol. 2, 690–91, 896–98. The possibility was taken seriously enough that the JSSC was directed to examine its military implications. In addition to opposing a troop withdrawal, the JSSC also took the opportunity to point out that the Germans were potentially the nation most capable of resisting forceful Soviet expansionism. For this reason they suggested that the United States establish a German government based on the principle of self-determination and assist it "until Germany is able effectively to defend this principle." See JCS 1811/1, "Military Implications in an Early Withdrawal of Occupation Forces From Germany," November 14, 1947, in Records of the Joint Chiefs of Staff, Part 2, 1946–53: Europe and NATO (Frederick, Md.: University Publications of America, 1980), reel 1 (hereafter RJCS: Europe and NATO with appropriate reel number).

ward his own proposal for a general troop withdrawal, recommended an outright rejection at London of any "ruses" designed to get American forces out of Germany: "For us to yield to such tactics would plainly undermine the ability of western Europe as a whole to withstand communist pressure and would of course be inconsistent with the aims of our program of aid to Europe."[68] Despite the benefits that the United States thought the Soviets would reap from putting forward such a proposal, Molotov ended the suspense shortly before the CFM when he told the French that he had no intention of proposing a mutual withdrawal of troops from Germany.[69]

As always, the formal discussions over Germany at the London CFM were dominated by the reparations question. Along with Molotov's vitriolic attacks on both the Marshall Plan and the fusion of the American and British zones in Germany, the Soviet foreign minister actually retreated from his previous position by dropping the condition that reparations had to be settled prior to any agreement on economic unity.[70] Despite the heavy-handed way that Molotov presented his case, Marshall remained worried that the Soviets might actually make it difficult to move forward with the ERP in Germany. As he cabled to Lovett during the conference: "It is plainly evident that Molotov is not only playing for time but is consistently, almost desperately, endeavoring to reach agreements which really would be an embarrassment to us in the next four to six months rather than true evidence of getting together."[71] Marshall's fears turned out to be exaggerated, however, because Molotov was unwilling to moderate the Soviet position on reparations to the extent that would have been necessary to put the Western powers in a potentially embarrassing situation. More important, it is quite unlikely that there was any proposal the Soviets could have made regarding Germany that would have been treated seriously by the Western powers. In a letter sent to Eisenhower during the CFM, Smith expressed the reality of the situation quite well. The real problem facing the United States, according to Smith, was the need to avoid appearing hypocritical since "we really do not want nor intend to accept German unification in any terms that the Russians might agree to, even though they seemed to meet most of our requirements, since, as they have declared war on European recovery, we know very

---

[68] PPS/13, "Resume of World Situation," November 6, 1947, in *SDPPSP*, 133.

[69] *FRUS*, 1947, vol. 2, 712–13. The common assumption that the Soviets would have welcomed the withdrawal of American troops from Germany may not be accurate. As Caroline Kennedy-Pipe shows, Stalin and Soviet planners always assumed and were generally favorably disposed to an American troop presence in Germany. See *Stalin's Cold War: Soviet Strategies in Europe, 1943–56* (Manchester: Manchester University Press, 1995), 44, 67, 100–1.

[70] For the Soviet position on reparations at the London CFM, see *FRUS*, 1947, vol. 2, 756–60, 790–93.

[71] Ibid., 765.

well from past experience that they would operate to prevent the resources of Germany from contributing."[72]

If the meetings at the CFM level were devoid of any real significance,
the same certainly cannot be said of the postconference discussions held
between the three Western powers. In addition to setting in motion the
process that eventually culminated in the North Atlantic Treaty, the post-
London meetings also began the process that led to the formation of a
West German state.[73] The precise linkage between the two was probably
less than clear at the time, but over the first few months of 1948 the inex-
orable connection between the creation of a West German state and the
formation of a Western military alliance quickly became obvious to all
concerned. Indeed, the simple reality that neither subject could be discussed in isolation from the other was brought home immediately after
the London meetings when the French protested the announcement of another round of bizonal reforms in early January 1948.

The French protests were an understandable reaction to a comedy of
diplomatic errors committed by the United States and Great Britain.
During his conversations with Bidault in London, Marshall had attempted to reach an understanding about the need for the Western powers to coordinate their future policies in Germany. Bidault readily agreed
and indicated his willingness to begin discussions over Germany as soon
as possible. Unfortunately, although Marshall may have said all the right
things about the need for greater tripartite consultation, he failed to inform Bidault that Clay and Robertson were already close to reaching an
agreement on a series of measures designed to reorganize the political
structure of Bizonia.[74] In Marshall's defense, he may have thought that
consultations with the French were unnecessary because of a belief that
the reforms were a strictly bizonal affair. However, particularly after the
events of the preceding summer, Marshall should have been aware of the
fact that no French government could afford to look the other way when
important decisions were taken in the bizone. Failing to tell Clay that he
should at least solicit French views prior to his discussions with the
Germans in Frankfurt was clearly not the proper way to start moving toward greater tripartite cooperation.

Bidault and other French officials, of course, were angered by what
they felt was a clear betrayal of Marshall's promise to include them in future discussions of German affairs. However, they were more upset about
the fact that the Anglo-American agreement implied that their participation in the affairs of western Germany would be on a "take-it-or-leave-it"

---

[72] Smith to Eisenhower, December 2, 1947, in *The Papers of Dwight David Eisenhower: The
Chief of Staff*, ed. Louis Galambos (Baltimore: Johns Hopkins University Press, 1978), 9:2130.
[73] The records of these conversations can be found in *FRUS*, 1947, vol. 2, 811–30.
[74] Ibid., 813–15, 827–29.

basis.[75] In stark contrast to the position they had taken in the level-of-industry dispute the previous summer, the State Department now had little sympathy for French protests about bizonal reorganization. Adopting a perspective toward France that Clay had assumed much earlier, one official at the State Department's French Desk blamed the French government itself for not educating the public to the reality that the Germany of 1948 was vastly different from the Germany of 1919. According to Woodruff Wallner, an official in the Division of Western European Affairs, the French people "must be told not to tremble at the Frankfurt mouse as if it were a Berlin lion."[76] Even Marshall, on the eve of the London Conference on Germany, instructed Caffery to inform French officials that it was time for them to drop their focus on an "outmoded and unrealistic" potential German threat.[77]

Sentiments such as these reveal a fundamental misunderstanding on the part of many American officials about what was really worrying the French in early 1948. To be sure, concern about issues such as the future government structure in the western zones and control arrangements for the Ruhr reflected an underlying belief that Germany could, particularly if allied with the Soviet Union, emerge as a future threat to the security of France and the other Western democracies. However, the major concern of the French in early 1948 was not the emergence of an eventual German threat, but the possibility that the Soviet Union might view the consolidation of the western zones as a provocation and that its response might spark a sequence of events ultimately leading to a war that would be utterly catastrophic to both France and the rest of Western Europe.[78] The reasons why French officials were more sensitive than their American and British counterparts to the risks involved in establishing a West German state and to the possibility of provoking a Soviet military reaction are not at all difficult to discern. Whatever community of interest existed among the three Western powers in peacetime would simply vanish the moment a war broke out on the continent. Although Western Europe was considered an important power center prior to the outbreak of war, its value to American and British military planners was sharply reduced in the event

[75] See Memorandum of Conversation between W. Wallner and Mr. Wapler, January 10, 1948, in *Memoranda of Conversation of the Secretary of State*, fiche 333. See also *FRUS, 1948*, vol. 2, 20–21, 34–35.

[76] Wallner to Bonbright, January 15, 1948, *FRUS*, 1948, vol. 2, 28.

[77] Secretary of State to Embassy in France, February 19, 1948, *FRUS*, 1948, vol. 2, 70–71. In later cables which are neither printed nor referred to in *FRUS*, Caffery reported that both Robert Schuman and Bidault agreed with these views. See RG 59, 751.00/2–2248, February 22, 1948, NA.

[78] For French threat perceptions at this time, see Irwin M. Wall, "France and the North Atlantic Alliance," in *NATO: The Founding of the Alliance and the Integration of Europe*, ed. John Gillingham and Francis Heller (New York: St. Martin's Press, 1992), 45–46; and Young, *France, The Cold War, and the Western Alliance*, 190.

of a general war. Because Western Europe was considered to be indefensible for the foreseeable future, strategic planning was centered around the waging of an air offensive against the heart of Soviet industrial and war-making power. For this purpose, defending air bases in Great Britain and the Cairo-Suez region was deemed a far more important objective than preventing Western Europe from being occupied by the Soviets. According to prevailing military estimates in 1948, the Soviets would be able to occupy all of Western Europe in less than six months and it would be up to two years before the United States could even begin attempting to eject them from the continent.[79]

The fact that the Soviets could quickly overrun Western Europe, of course, was not very alarming to American military planners or top political officials because the overall military situation made it difficult for them to see how the Soviets could rationally decide to initiate a global war. The West was well aware of Soviet weaknesses, and American planners certainly did not believe that the overall military balance could in any way be construed to favor the Soviet Union in the late 1940s.[80] The fact that the Soviet Union could overrun Western Europe was obvious to all concerned, but equally obvious was the fact that the Soviets would be running tremendous risks if they initiated general war. The military balance in Europe did not ensure that a war might not erupt out of a process of miscalculation, but it did suggest to American planners that the Soviets would not consciously embark on the path of global war:

> We believe that the USSR does not at the present time desire to become involved in a global war, but that it will continue to pursue an aggressive expansionist policy by economic, political, and subversive means, and by threat of war by reason of its large forces in

[79] For war planning in 1948, see especially JSPG 496/4, February 11, 1948 (codename *Broiler*), in *Plan Frolic and American Resources*, vol. 6 of *America's Plans for War against the Soviet Union, 1945–50*, 1–207; and JCS 1725/52, "Joint Outline War Plans for Determination of Mobilization Requirements for War Beginning 1 July 1949," August 26, 1948 (codename *Cogwheel*), in *Assessing the Threat*, vol. 10 of *America's Plans for War against the Soviet Union, 1945–50*, 168–210. For British military planning, which was also based on an immediate withdrawal from Western Europe, see COS (47) 102 (0), May 1947, reprinted in Julian Lewis, *Changing Direction: British Military Planning for Post-War Strategic Defense, 1942–47* (London: Sherwood Press, 1988), 370–87; Paul Cornish, *British Military Planning for the Defense of Germany, 1945–50* (New York: St. Martin's Press, 1996), 104–29; and John Kent and John W. Young, "The 'Western Union' Concept and British Defence Policy, 1947–48," in *British Intelligence, Strategy, and the Cold War*, ed. Richard J. Aldrich (London: Routledge, 1992), 166–92.

[80] See Leffler, *A Preponderance of Power*, 133–35, 218–19; Mark Trachtenberg, *A Constructed Peace: The Making of the European Settlement, 1945–63* (Princeton: Princeton University Press, 1999), 84–91; and Phillip A. Karber and Jerald Combs, "The United States, NATO, and the Soviet Threat to Western Europe: Military Estimates and Policy Options, 1945–63," *Diplomatic History* 22 (summer 1998): 399–430.

being. If the Soviets cannot achieve world domination by these means, they may resort to war when they estimate they can gain a decisive victory. In the meantime, being realists, they are preparing for the unsought war which could come about during periods of aggravated international tension.[81]

How privy the French were to American and British war planning in early 1948 is not clear, but there is no doubt that Bidault and other top officials grasped the basic point that their counterparts were not intending to do very much about preventing the occupation of France by Soviet forces.[82] In a meeting with General Harold Bull in late January 1948, Bidault spoke about the widespread belief in France that in the event of war "the United States does not plan to defend Western Europe but will abandon this area to the Soviets and base its defense lines possibly on the Pyrenees, but chiefly on North Africa." Even though Bidault had not the "slightest doubt" that the United States would eventually emerge victorious, he also made it clear that this would be of little comfort to the people of France, since in the period before victory "the Russian hordes will occupy the area, raping women and deporting the male population for slave labor in the Soviet Union; that France and Western Europe will be occupied and devastated by the Soviet hordes and atomized by the United States."[83] The belief that a U.S. victory would be of little value to France because it would come too late was a constant concern for Bidault throughout 1948. As he told Caffery in June: "If we were sure you would drop atomic bombs fast enough and often enough, we would not be so worried but we doubt that you will. It would be easy for the Russian

[81] Joint Intelligence Committee, "Estimate of Soviet Intentions and Capabilities, 1948–55," January 2, 1948, in Records of the Joint Chiefs of Staff, Part 2, 1946–53: The Soviet Union, reel 2. For a similar analysis, see "Report on Soviet Intentions Prepared by Joint Intelligence Committee," April 1, 1948, *FRUS*, 1948, vol. 1, 550–57.

[82] As early as October 1947, Caffery reported to Washington that the French General Staff wanted to conduct secret conversations with U.S. military officials. While both Lovett and army officials were agreeable to talks, Caffery was told that it was not considered "that they should be regarded as a matter of urgency." For Caffery's letter and Lovett's response, see RG 59, 851.20/10–2347, NA; and for the Army's response, RG 59, 851.20/11–1447, NA. An excellent account of the origins of Franco-American military talks can be found in Bruna Bagnato, "France and the Origins of the Atlantic Pact," in *The Atlantic Pact Forty Years Later: An Historical Reappraisal*, ed. Ennio Di Nolfo (Berlin: Walter de Gruyter, 1991), 79–110. The British military was also opposed to talks with the French in early 1948 because "if staff talks were held now we would have little to reveal to the French which was not utterly discouraging." See Michael Dockrill, "British Attitudes towards France as a Military Ally," *Diplomacy and Statecraft* 1 (March 1990): 49–70 (quotation on 59–60).

[83] Memorandum of Conversation by Macarthur, January 29, 1948, *FRUS*, 1948, vol. 3, 617–22 (quotations on 617, 620). According to Arnold Wolfers, General Revers, chief of the French General Staff, expressed the belief that "it is demoralizing to believe that we have been given up." See Conversations with Leading Frenchmen and Italians, May 6, 1948, in RJCS: Europe and NATO, reel 4.

armies to overrun France and we shudder to think of what would happen to our beautiful country. We are defenseless, as you well know."[84]

Bidault and other French officials did not necessarily believe that war with the Soviet Union was a certainty in the immediate future, but they definitely accorded it a greater likelihood than officials in the United States and Great Britain. The crisis atmosphere brought about by the Czech coup in February 1948, Western moves toward the creation of a West German state, and Soviet pressures on Berlin all contributed to the belief that events might ultimately climax in the outbreak of war. According to Robert Murphy, Couve de Murville told Clay and him in early April that "war with the Soviet Union within the next two or three years is inevitable—and that may mean this year."[85] Bidault was not as pessimistic as de Murville, but he too did not rule out the possibility of a Soviet attack. As he told the Canadian ambassador to the Netherlands in July 1948, "I am almost convinced that the Soviet Union will not attack us. But that's not the same thing as saying 'I believe it's going to be a fine day and I'm not taking my umbrella.' . . . Our information does not permit us to conclude in the absolute impossibility of a Soviet invasion."[86]

French perceptions about the immediacy of the Soviet threat to Europe led them to adopt a much different perspective than the United States on what needed to be done to redress the balance of power in Europe. Throughout the first nine months of 1948, the French were far more interested in the immediate and concrete measures that could bolster their security than haggling over the precise and formal terms of a security treaty. American officials, far less concerned about the immediate possibility of war with the Soviet Union and with much less to lose if their assessments were wrong, adopted a much more relaxed and long-term approach to the entire question of military arrangements with Western Europe. Rather than taking measures designed to alleviate French security concerns, American negotiators focused on preserving the principles of European unity and self-help in the military sphere, moving forward on the establishment of a West German state, and leaving the door open for the eventual participation of Germany in any future security system.

State Department officials established the connection between Germany, European unity, and the creation of a Western security system right at the start of discussions with the British in January 1948. Following his conversations with Marshall in London, Bevin sent a lengthy summary of his ideas to Washington in early January. Despite the fact that Bevin explicitly acknowledged that at some point Germany would have

---

[84] Caffery to Secretary of State, June 2, 1948, *FRUS*, 1948, vol. 2, 317.

[85] Murphy to Hickerson, April 8, 1948, *FRUS*, 1948, vol. 2, 169.

[86] Cited in Escott Reid, *Time of Fear and Hope: The Making of the North Atlantic Treaty* (Toronto: McClelland and Stewart, 1977), 17.

to be brought into the framework of the Western system, American officials were worried because Bevin wished to proceed by concluding treaties similar to the Anglo-French Treaty of Dunkirk in 1947, which was exclusively directed against Germany. Although Kennan and John Hickerson, director of the Office of European Affairs, had vastly different ideas about the wisdom of concluding a military alliance, both men emphasized to Marshall that the Dunkirk model was not the proper way for the British to proceed because it would make it harder to bring Germany into the system in the future.[87]

Not surprisingly, Kennan and other officials were determined to steer British thinking onto a path more compatible with their own views about the need for Western European unity. Kennan had a great deal of praise for Bevin's emphasis on European unity, but he argued that the political and economic aspects of union should precede any consideration of the military component. Indeed, Kennan thought that Bevin should be encouraged to drop the military aspect. Although one of Bevin's central purposes was to gain U.S. support and participation in a Western security system, Kennan wanted the Europeans to work out arrangements among themselves and "not bother their heads too much in the initial stage about our relationship to this concept" because "if they develop it and make it work, there will be no real question as to our long-term relationship to it, even with respect to the military guarantee."[88] In the British view, there were two major problems with Kennan's logic. First, it perpetuated the "vicious circle" that they were desperately trying to break out of in early 1948. As Lord Inverchapel explained the problem to Lovett, "Without assurance of security, which can only be given with some degree of American participation, the British government are unlikely to be successful in making the Western Union a going concern. But it appears from your letter that, until this is done, the United States government for their part does not feel able to discuss participation."[89] The second problem with Kennan's line of thinking was that the British were worried that the conclusion of a purely European pact might inadvertently "encourage the American school of thought which believes that Western security can be sufficiently assured by a Western regional pact without American participation."[90]

---

[87] See Kennan to Secretary of State, January 20, 1948, *FRUS*, 1948, vol. 3, 8. For an excellent discussion of the conflict between Kennan and Hickerson over the value of a military alliance, see Miscamble, *George F. Kennan and the Making of American Foreign Policy*, 116–23.

[88] *FRUS*, 1948, vol. 3, 8.

[89] See ibid., 19. For a general discussion of British efforts to gain a solid commitment from the United States in early 1948, see Martin H. Folly, "Britain, the United States, and the Genesis of the North Atlantic Treaty," *Diplomatic History* 12 (winter 1988): 59–77.

[90] The quotation is from a Foreign Office document of late January 1948, cited in John Baylis, *The Diplomacy of Pragmatism* (London: Macmillan, 1993), 70.

Explaining the vicious circle to American officials was of little help to the British because the Truman administration took seriously the objective of encouraging European self-help. Despite the vast differences between economic and military cooperation, American officials believed that the Marshall plan model applied equally as well to Bevin's embryonic efforts to form a military alliance. Rejecting a British request for immediate Anglo-American talks on security, Lovett explained to Inverchapel that Marshall thought it was very important that "the initiative in this matter remain in Europe, as in the case of the initiative in connection with the European Recovery Program."[91] Another reason for encouraging the British to take the lead on the security question was the simple fact that officials within the Truman administration were themselves far from clear about America's role in a European security organization. Even Hickerson, the most "Atlanticist" official within the State Department, acknowledged that there were valid arguments on both sides about the merits of U.S. participation. Although Hickerson played a key role in the planning that resulted in the creation of NATO, he noted that he had "envisaged the creation of a third force which was not merely the extension of US influence but a real European organization strong enough to say 'no' both to the Soviet Union and the United States, if our actions should seem to so require."[92]

American officials might have been able to ignore the fact that uncertainty about their long-term presence in Europe was impeding the creation of a military alliance, but they could not so easily overlook the fact that the same uncertainty also was impeding progress on the German question at the London Conference. Prior to the conference, anticipating that the Western Europeans would raise the question of security against Germany, the State Department had reached the very important decision that it would no longer consider Byrnes's disarmament treaty as a viable solution for the prevention of future German aggression.[93] The State Department hoped that the entire question of security against Germany could be deferred until after Bevin had concluded his negotiations, but the American negotiators at London quickly realized that France and the Benelux countries needed to be reassured on the security question before considering lesser issues. Lewis Douglas, American ambassador to Great Britain and head of the American delegation, concluded that reassuring

[91] *FRUS*, 1948, vol. 3, 23.

[92] Memorandum of Conversation by Hickerson, January 21, 1948, *FRUS*, 1948, vol. 3, 11. John Kent and J. W. Young have convincingly shown that for much of 1948 the British were also very receptive to the idea of creating a "third force" in Western Europe. See John Kent and J. W. Young, "British Policy Overseas: The 'Third Force' and the Origins of NATO," in *Securing Peace in Europe, 1945–62*, ed. Beatrice Heuser and Robert O'Neill (London: Macmillan, 1992), 41–64.

[93] See "Security against Germany," February 11, 1948, *FRUS*, 1948, vol. 2, 60–63; and Memorandum of Conversation by Achilles, February 13, 1948, *FRUS*, 1948, vol. 2, 63–65.

the French on the general security question was the key to making further progress on Germany: "There is little doubt that if the French were assured of long-term United States defensive cooperation against German aggression, in other words, that we would fight on the Rhine in such an eventuality, the French would relax in their attitude regarding German industry and reconstruction."[94]

Marshall was willing to go along with Douglas's strategy as long as the French understood that in return they were expected to go along with the restoration of power and self-governance to the West Germans.[95] Douglas was given permission to informally tell French and Benelux officials that the United States would support the creation of a military security board and consult with the Europeans in the event of any future threat of German aggression. More important, Douglas told them that it was "very unlikely that American forces would be withdrawn from Germany for a long time—until the threat from the East had disappeared."[96] None of these implicit promises, of course, represented a very significant advance on either Byrnes's disarmament treaty or the pledge contained in the Stuttgart speech to keep American forces in Europe. However, in the aftermath of the Czech coup in late February and Soviet pressures on Berlin, they clearly took on a far greater significance for French officials than they might have under other circumstances.

French concern over the possibility of war with the Soviet Union in early 1948 pulled their German policy in two different directions. On the one hand, they were eager to finally align their Germany policy with the United States and Great Britain as rapidly as possible. For example, after the Military Governors in Berlin were unable to resolve their differences about whether a German provisional government should be formed prior to the establishment of a constituent assembly, Couve de Murville flew to Berlin in order to break up the impasse rather than wait for the reconvening of the London conference. In exchange for abandoning plans to establish a provisional German government, de Murville agreed to support the convening of a constituent assembly no later than September 1, 1948. Clay and Murphy were thrilled with the proposal because it resolved the most controversial point in the negotiations and allowed the establishment of a West German government "far in advance of anything heretofore suggested."[97] When one considers that de Murville himself regarded the creation of a Western German government as the "most provocative act one could possibly think of against the Soviet Union," it is apparent that the French were very conscious of the risks they were taking by going along

[94] Douglas to Secretary of State, March 2, 1948, *FRUS*, 1948, vol. 2, 110–11.

[95] Secretary of State to Douglas, March 4, 1948, *FRUS*, 1948, vol. 2, 123.

[96] Douglas to Secretary of State, March 6, 1948, *FRUS*, 1948, vol. 2, 138.

[97] *FRUS*, 1948, vol. 2, 170. The dispute over whether to establish a provisional West German government can be followed on 151–60.

with the United States and the Great Britain on the rapid formation of a West German government.[98]

Not surprisingly, as the London Conference drew to a close in May 1948, the French began to have last minute doubts about the course they had chosen. The Quai d'Orsay warned President Vincent Auriol on May 17 of the dangers involved and suggested that he request a reconsideration of the London decisions. Three days later, the French government formally proposed that the Western powers consider suspending announcement of the convocation of a German constituent assembly primarily because of its fear that the Soviets might interpret this decision as a threat and a "prelude to the constitution of a German military force."[99] As Caffery reported to Washington, Bidault was very concerned that "the Soviet Union might retaliate against the establishment of a government in West Germany by driving the Western powers out of Berlin."[100] However, neither Great Britain nor the United States was willing to consider postponing the implementation of the London decisions. Not only would there be no high-level consideration of French concerns about the possibility of Soviet retaliation, both the United States and Great Britain made it very clear that they would proceed with the London decisions regardless of whether France went along.[101]

Western solidarity over Germany hung in the balance for the first two weeks of June 1948 as the French National Assembly deliberated over the London decisions. Parliamentary approval was by no means assured since Bidault faced a hostile coalition composed of both communists and Gaullists. Getting the London program past the National Assembly would largely depend on his powers of persuasion because, as Caffery noted, "Bidault is the only man in the French government who would have approved the recommendations of the London conference. . . . There is no one else in sight who will openly and publicly defend the recommendations."[102] Although his efforts ultimately cost him the post of foreign minister, Bidault was able to gain approval of the London program on June 16 in a very narrow decision (300 to 286). Within the space of a week, as the French had feared from the start, the Soviets began implementing the Berlin Blockade.

---

[98] Note of May 10, 1948, cited in Rene Girault, "The French Decision-Makers and Their Perception of French Power in 1948," in *Power in Europe? Great Britain, France, Italy, and Germany in a Postwar World*, ed. Josef Becker and Franz Knipping (Berlin: Walter de Gruyter, 1986), 59.

[99] The French memorandum is printed in an annex to CAB 129/27, C.P. (48) 134, Talks on Germany: Memorandum by the Secretary of State for Foreign Affairs, May 29, 1948, *Cabinet Papers: Complete Classes from the CAB and PREM Series in the Public Record Office*, series 3 (Wiltshire: Adam Matthew Publications, 1996).

[100] *FRUS*, 1948, vol. 2, 266.

[101] Ibid., 269, 301, 334.

[102] Caffery to Secretary of State, June 7, 1948, *FRUS*, 1948, vol. 2, 321.

The event immediately preceding the blockade was the announcement of currency reform in the western zones on June 18. American officials debated what larger purposes the Soviets might be entertaining, but they were well aware of the purely defensive and technical reasons behind the Soviet decision to start the blockade.[103] Having already faced intermittent Soviet harassment of traffic into Berlin throughout 1948, Clay's first impulse was to refrain from making any vigorous protests to the Soviet Union until he could better gauge the situation. As he told some OMGUS officials on June 19, "If they had put in a currency reform and we didn't, it would have been the first move we would have had to take."[104] The threat of currency reform, of course, was far from the only reason behind the Berlin Blockade. On July 4, Sokolovsky finally made it clear to the Western powers that the larger goal of the blockade was to force a reconsideration of the London decisions on Germany. Adopting a stance that would be maintained throughout the crisis, Marshall immediately rejected any deals that would have involved suspending the London decisions in exchange for a Soviet lifting of the blockade.[105]

The Truman administration was determined to stand firm concerning Berlin, but the vast majority of both military and political officials were determined to do so without provoking a war with the Soviet Union. In mid-July the administration announced that it was sending sixty B-29 bombers to Britain on a training mission, but the planes were not modified to carry atomic weapons and the bombs themselves remained in the hands of the Atomic Energy Commission.[106] More important, the administration emphatically rejected Clay's and Murphy's belief that the blockade should be directly challenged by sending an armed convoy to Berlin. Clay thought that the Soviets would back down because they did not want a war at that time, but he was also operating from considerably more optimistic assumptions about the military than the rest of the administration. According to Forrestal, Clay believed that the United States did not have to act on the prevailing assumption that the Soviets would

---

[103] See Daniel F. Harrington, "The Berlin Blockade Revisited," *International History Review* 6 (February 1984): 88–112. As Harrington notes, Western currency reform "threatened the Soviet zone with economic disaster. The old Reichmarks, soon to be worthless in the west, would flow east; speculators, not knowing the details of the western conversion, would try to dump them in the Russian zone, where they remained legal tender" (96).

[104] Cited in ibid., 96. As Murphy recognized, certain of the Soviet actions were "not unreasonable in view natural defensive action to protect Soviet Zone from influx of old currency." See Murphy to Secretary of State, June 19, 1948, *FRUS*, 1948, vol. 2, 910.

[105] See *FRUS*, 1948, vol. 2, 946–50.

[106] For discussions of the military aspects of the Berlin crisis, see Kenneth W. Condit, *The Joint Chiefs of Staff and National Policy, 1947–49* (Wilmington, Del.: Michael Glazier, 1979), 128–44; Richard Betts, *Nuclear Blackmail and Nuclear Balance* (Washington, D.C.: Brookings Institution, 1987), 24–31; Yergin, *Shattered Peace*, 378–80; Herken, *The Winning Weapon*, 257–60; and Avi Shlaim, *The United States and the Berlin Blockade, 1948–49* (Berkeley: University of California Press, 1983).

immediately overrun France in the event of war and also suggested that "twenty good divisions could hold up the Russians on the Rhine."[107] Unfortunately, even if Clay's estimate of what it would take to hold the Russians on the Rhine were correct, the Western powers did not have twenty good divisions on the continent at the time of the Berlin crisis.[108]

Instead of sending an armed convoy to Berlin with all of the risks that such a course would have entailed, the administration attempted to resolve the crisis through a direct approach to Stalin. Rather than engaging in mutual recriminations, Ambassador Smith and Stalin both expressed their appreciation of the situation faced by the other side and a desire to work out acceptable arrangements for Berlin. For example, although Stalin started off the meeting by insisting that the London program had to be officially suspended in exchange for the termination of the blockade, he was willing to drop this condition because it would put the Western powers in a "difficult situation."[109] Even Smith, a hardliner of long-standing, was quite impressed with the performance put on by both Stalin and Molotov. As he cabled Washington after the meeting, "Doubt if I have ever seen Molotov so cordial and if one did not know real Soviet objectives in Germany would have been completely deceived by their attitude as both literally dripping with sweet reasonableness and desire not to embarrass."[110]

Significantly, Stalin told Smith during their meeting, as he had told Marshall after the Moscow CFM, that he had "always been confident that after much skirmishing they could return in the end to a basis for agreement." Without engaging in too much speculation about the nature of Soviet objectives in Germany, it is very plausible to conclude that Stalin was tacitly admitting to Smith that he had overplayed what had always been a very weak hand.[111] The point at which skirmishing would be

[107] See Millis, ed., *Forrestal Diaries*, 460. For more general discussions of why Clay and Murphy advocated sending an armed convoy to Berlin, see Robert D. Murphy, *Diplomat among Warriors* (Garden City, N.Y.: Doubleday & Co, 1964), 314–17; and Jean Edward Smith, *Lucius D. Clay: An American Life* (New York: Henry Holt, 1990), 494–513.

[108] On Western force levels and Clay's optimism, see Wolfgang Krieger, "American Security Policy in Europe before NATO," in *NATO: The Founding of the Atlantic Alliance*, ed. Gillingham and Heller, 107–8. Relying on the discussion in *The Forrestal Diaries*, Krieger states that Marshall "assured the President that a Russian advance westward could probably be stopped at the Rhine." What Marshall actually said to Truman was far more modest and ambiguous: "He felt there was some chance of containing the Russians in Western Europe. . . . " See *Forrestal Diaries*, 459.

[109] Smith to Secretary of State, August 3, 1948, *FRUS*, 1948, vol. 2, 999–1006 (quotation on 1005).

[110] Smith to Secretary of State, August 3, 1948, *FRUS*, 1948, vol. 2, 1006. See also Walter Bedell Smith, *My Three Years in Moscow* (Philadelphia: J.B. Lippincott Company, 1950), 230–60.

[111] *FRUS*, 1948, vol. 2, 1004. For Soviet motives during the Berlin crisis based on new documents, see Michail M. Narinskii, "The Soviet Union and the Berlin Crisis," in *The Soviet Union and Europe in the Cold War, 1943–53*, ed. Francesca Gori and Silvio Pines (New York: St. Martin's Press, 1996), 57–75.

transformed into something far more serious for Stalin was clearly September 1, 1948, the date on which the German constituent assembly was scheduled to convene. Indeed, he told Smith that the only element of the London conference to which he objected was the provision establishing a West German government. If the Western powers went ahead with this step, Stalin argued, there would be simply nothing left to discuss. Rather than going ahead with their plans for West Germany, Stalin held out the possibility that the four powers could still reach an agreement on a single government for all of Germany, a solution which he claimed "would automatically solve the Berlin question."[112]

Although we may never know exactly what Stalin was aiming at in the blockade of Berlin, it can be stated with a fair degree of confidence that there was virtually nothing the Soviets could have done in August 1948 that would have deflected the Western powers from the course they had pursued since the London CFM. It is hard to think of what Stalin might have proposed that could have stopped the escalation process, but it is clear that he was unwilling to propose terms that might have made the Western powers stop and reconsider their commitment to the London program. Even at this late date Stalin was still reiterating to Smith that in the event of a four-power meeting devoted to Germany, he would insist on current reparations and a voice in the control of the Ruhr.[113] But the Western powers had resisted these conditions since Potsdam and their willingness to make any concessions on reparations and the Ruhr had vanished by the time of the Berlin crisis. More important, few Western officials still shared the premise that Stalin was seeking to take advantage of; namely, the belief that quadripartite control in Germany was preferable to separate spheres of control. No one had proclaimed the importance of this principle more than Clay, but even he now viewed the restoration of a balance of power in Europe as a goal of much greater importance than maintaining the fiction of quadripartite control. Where Clay previously had been willing to make concessions to keep alive the possibility of German unity and U.S.–Soviet cooperation, he was now unwilling to deviate at all from the policy of building up German and Western European strength:

[112] Ibid., 1003.
[113] Ibid., 1003–4. The CIA believed that Stalin would actually settle for much less on Germany. Although he might start out by asking for current reparations, the agency thought he would settle for a resumption of the already scheduled deliveries that Clay suspended in May 1946. Furthermore, while the Soviets might start by asking for four-power control of the Ruhr, they thought that Stalin would eventually accept "some voice in the economic administration of the Ruhr." Interestingly, the CIA concluded that it would be worthwhile to gamble on negotiations because of the dangers of the Berlin crisis. See Memorandum for the President from R. H. Hillenkoetter, August 6, 1948, *Declassified Documents Reference System* (Washington, D.C.: Carrollton Press, 1987), 1987/2176.

I think that any expectation that a stable, peaceful world can result from a general peace settlement is over-simplification of the problem. We are at peace now or, at least, we are not engaged in active war. We do not need to be plunged into war. The conditions of stability, both economic and political, which make for a long peace are returning to Europe. When the freedom-loving, democratic countries of Western Europe are on their feet economically and able to protect their freedom, then we may expect a long peace.

Was it impossible by August 1948 for America to reverse course and contemplate a cooperative and negotiated solution to the German question? How would one know when it was "safe" to pursue German unification and when a European balance of power had been restored? Why would Stalin respond to the restoration of a European balance of power by agreeing to reunify Germany, an action which would decisively accelerate the deterioration of the Soviet Union's position in Europe? Having answered the first question negatively, Clay probably did not spend too much time thinking about the problems involved in the later stages of negotiation after the Western powers had attained overwhelming strength. Strangely, it was Clay's main antagonist, George Kennan, who was now seriously thinking about how to devise a comprehensive and negotiated solution to the German problem.

RETHINKING THE DIVISION OF GERMANY AND EUROPE

Historians continue to debate whether Kennan's advocacy of serious negotiations with the Soviet Union over the German question after August 1948 represented a fundamental change in his thinking about the future of Europe.[114] A case can certainly be made that Kennan's views on Germany after the blockade were consistent with his long-term vision of the future of Europe, but it is hard to overlook the fact that these same views had led him to consistently support the division of Germany and Europe since at least the Yalta Conference. In all likelihood, it is not until the start of the Berlin crisis that Kennan came to appreciate that the conflict between pursuing the short-term policy of containment and the long-term objective of ending the division of Europe could no longer be ignored.

Kennan's task in August 1948 was to develop ideas about what position the United States should take if and when Stalin lifted the blockade and the four powers began negotiations over the future of Germany. His

[114] John Lamberton Harper minimizes the importance of the shift in Kennan's thinking on Germany and Europe in *American Visions of Europe* (Cambridge: Cambridge University Press, 1994), 206–9. For a contrasting assessment, see Anders Stephanson, *Kennan and the Art of Foreign Policy* (Cambridge: Harvard University Press, 1989), 117–56.

first paper on the subject, PPS/37, consisted of a very even-handed listing of the advantages and disadvantages of proceeding with the London program or changing course and seeking a general settlement with the Soviets for the unification of Germany, the end of military government, and the withdrawal of occupation forces to garrisons located on the periphery of Germany.[115] Indeed, an opponent of German unification would have had a very difficult time developing stronger arguments against pursuing a general settlement than the ones put forward by Kennan in PPS/37. First, a general settlement would restore substantial sovereign powers to a nation composed of people that Kennan himself believed were "confused, embittered, self-pitying, and unregenerate."[116] Second, Kennan rated it as a "very good prospect" that a united Germany would be strongly nationalistic, authoritarian, and susceptible to offers from the Soviet Union. Finally, without some form of real union in Europe, Kennan believed that a settlement making Germany the sole great power in Central Europe would "reestablish, in essence, the status quo of 1920, and invite the same ensuing disasters."[117]

Nevertheless, despite the serious risks involved in the unification of Germany, Kennan still believed that this course was preferable to carrying out the London program. In his view, the creation of a united Germany also offered some very attractive elements for both the United States and Western Europe: it would eliminate the problem of Western access and rights in Berlin, avoid the solidifying of the division of Europe into two hostile blocs, and move Soviet military forces further back to the East. What seems to have tipped the balance for Kennan in favor of a general settlement in 1948 was his belief that the risks and dangers associated with the unification of Germany—which he viewed as inevitable—would not necessarily be reduced in the future. Rather than debating whether a general settlement was preferable to a purely Western settlement, Kennan believed that the real question for the Truman administration to decide was whether the unification of Germany would be easier to achieve now or at some unspecified point in the future.

It did not take very long for Kennan to find out that his answers diverged considerably from those provided by the rest of the Truman administration. Although Kennan thought that the Western powers would

---

[115] PPS/37, "Policy Questions concerning a Possible German Settlement," August 12, 1948, in *SDPPSP*, 322–34.

[116] Ibid., 329. Although often portrayed as a strong Germanophile, Kennan's views about Germany were much more ambivalent than the label suggests. Later in the debate over Program A, Kennan suggested that "the Germans are by and large a sick people from whom no political impulses emerge in any clear and healthy form." *FRUS*, 1949, vol. 3, 97. For a study of Kennan which emphasizes the importance of his emotional attachment to Germany, see Walter Hixson, *George Kennan: Cold War Iconoclast* (New York: Columbia University Press, 1989), 15, 53, 88.

[117] PPS/37, 329–30.

be negotiating from strength in 1948, the overwhelming consensus among both political and military officials was that Western Europe needed to be greatly strengthened before the administration even attempted to reach a general settlement with the Soviet Union over Germany. The Office of European Affairs rejected PPS/37 because "it would be highly dangerous to unite Germany along the lines you propose until Western Europe is stronger, both economically and militarily."[118] Charles Saltzman, assistant secretary of state for occupied areas, believed that "we would do better to wait before proposing the withdrawal of all occupying forces until the present relative power position of the Western Allies, vis-à-vis the Soviet Union improves."[119] At a time when the United States was in the process of negotiating the terms of an alliance with the Western Europeans, officials in the War Department were also very concerned that Kennan's proposal might derail the building up of both American and Western European military strength. In their view, it would be hard to reconcile the seeming inconsistency between the North Atlantic Treaty and a proposal to "withdraw, at a relatively early date, its military forces from the very area of the world where the US desires to provide the greatest deterrent to the expansion of Soviet Communism."[120]

Arguments along these lines presented a fundamental obstacle to the consideration of PPS/37 because they challenged one of Kennan's key premises: the belief that the Western powers could move forward with the London program and NATO while also pursuing serious negotiations with the Soviet Union over the future of Germany. Saltzman agreed with Kennan that some day the United States would have to get its occupation forces out of Germany, but he pointed out that "if we talk seriously about agreeing to a unified free Germany and the withdrawal of all occupation forces, the responsible German leaders will certainly refuse to cooperate in pushing forward any plans for a Western Germany."[121] One highly in-

---

[118] *FRUS*, 1948, vol. 2, 1287.

[119] Saltzman to Kennan, "Policy Questions concerning a Possible German Settlement," September 20, 1948, RG 59, Records of the Central European Affairs Division, box 1, NA.

[120] Informal Working Paper Prepared by Plans and Operations at the War Department, "Military Implications Deriving from the Establishment of a Free and Sovereign German Government," September 3, 1948, PPS Records, box 15, NA. An official in Occupational Affairs made similar arguments: "To offer the present plan would confuse our own public, our Allies and the Germans as to the constancy and strength of existing policies in Western Germany under the London Agreement." See Walter Wilds to Jacob Beam, October 21, 1948, RG 59, Records of Western European Affairs: Miscellaneous German Files, box 8, NA.

[121] Saltzman to Kennan, "Policy Questions concerning a Possible German Settlement." The West Germans would certainly have been furious with the United States if Program A had been adopted because OMGUS officials had told them in July to stop worrying about how to adapt their constitution to an all-German solution and "frankly recognize split of Germany as fact." See Murphy to Secretary of State, July 9, 1948, *FRUS*, 1948, vol. 2, 384. Toward the very end of the process of establishing a West German state, Adenauer would make exactly the threat that Saltzman pointed to in his comments on PPS/37. See Memorandum of Conversation by Hillenbrand, RG 59, 862.00/5–249, NA.

fluential West German, Konrad Adenauer, had already expressed to American officials his fear that negotiations with Moscow might result in the abandonment of the London program and the subsequent discrediting of those who had chosen to support the Western powers.[122] More important, in contrast to Kennan's assumption that unification was the primary goal for German politicians, Adenauer did not seem to have a great deal of hope or interest in a unified Germany under prevailing circumstances.[123] After speaking with the future leader of West Germany for the first time in November 1948, Murphy reported that "While Adenauer did not say so in so many words, he left me with the clear impression that he does not look for nor hope for the inclusion of parts of East Germany in the government now under consideration at Bonn."[124]

Another deterrent to the adoption of PPS/37 was the anticipated reaction of the French. Although Kennan did not appreciate at the time the extent to which the West Germans would be willing to support the London program, he was acutely conscious from the start of how difficult it would be to sell PPS/37 to the French. In a meeting with a group of outside consultants in mid-September, he acknowledged that the chances of the French accepting his proposal were "roughly about 50–50—perhaps a little better. . . . Let's say that the French would put up an awful howl and not like it, and if they accepted it they would do so only very reluctantly because they were dragooned in."[125] Kennan had specifically put in the provisions for the withdrawal of troops to peripheral garrisons in order to reassure the French, but officials who were closer to Paris correctly pointed out that his ideas would not meet with a favorable reception. After reading an early draft of a fall 1948 policy paper authored by Kennan, PPS/42, Bohlen readily confirmed Kennan's suspicion that the French would not support a German settlement based on this type of withdrawal:

---

[122] See Memorandum of Conversation by Maurice Altaffer, RG 59, 862.00/8–1748, NA.

[123] According to Ernst Lemmer, a high official in the Soviet zone CDU between 1945–47, Adenauer had told him as early as 1946 that "we are now rid of the colonial territories in the East, and I welcome this fact." See RG 59, 862.00/9–748, NA. There is evidence to suggest that Adenauer had written off the possibility of a united Germany even earlier. See Manfred Overesch, "Senior West German Politicians and Their Perception of the German Situation in Europe, 1945–49," in *Power in Europe*, ed. Becker and Knipping, 117–34.

[124] Memorandum of Conversation by Murphy, November 24, 1948, *FRUS*, 1948, vol. 2, 445.

[125] Special Consultative Group on German Policy Questions, September 23, 1948, PPS Records, box 15, NA. The group assembled by Kennan included people such as Dean Acheson, James Conant, and Hamilton Armstrong. Given the lack of institutional support for Program A, Kennan would frequently refer to the support provided to his ideas by this group over the coming months. A reading of the transcripts contained in the PPS files supports Miscamble's assessment that the outside consultants were not without their own misgivings about Kennan's plans. See Miscamble, *George Kennan and the Making of American Foreign Policy*, 148–49.

The effect of the physical withdrawal of American and British troops from their present positions in Germany to the northern seaports would, I think, be very serious in France and Western Europe generally. The French neurosis on security is even stronger than I had anticipated before coming here and the one faint element which they cling to is the fact that American troops, however strong in number, stand between them and the Red Army. If you add to that the strong fears to be generated with the prospect of returning power to Germans at the present juncture, I am sure that the general line of approach suggested in your letter would have a most unfavorable reaction in France and probably in Holland and Belgium as well.[126]

There is no need to speculate about how Great Britain would have reacted to Program A because the Foreign Office conducted a parallel debate in the summer of 1948 over the merits of a general settlement which far surpassed in quality the one held on the American side.[127] Pessimistic about the prospects of ever resolving the Berlin situation on either a short- or long-term basis, General Robertson initiated the debate in July by proposing the formation of a single German government and the withdrawal of occupation forces to areas on the periphery of Germany.[128] Robertson's guiding premise was that the Soviets had badly damaged themselves in the fight for the soul of Germany and that the Western powers should "take a chance on the Germans" and "take advantage of this wave of anti-

---

[126] Bohlen to Kennan, October 25, 1948, RG 59, Records of Charles E. Bohlen, box 4, NA. Bohlen was commenting on PPS/42, "Position of the United States with respect to Germany Following the Breakdown of Moscow Discussions," November 2, 1948, *FRUS*, 1948, vol. 2, 1240–46. Were it not for the need to provide psychological reassurance to the French, Kennan indicated that he would be willing to totally withdraw all American forces from Germany. See his comments in Special Consultative Group on German Policy Questions, 6–8. Kennan was always schizophrenic in regard to French concerns about Germany. His attitude is best captured by his comment that French fears about Germany were "understandable and at the same time it is really a mistake." See "Contemporary Problems of Foreign Policy," September 28, 1948, box 17, Kennan Papers, Princeton University. Kennan's lectures throughout this period are full of references to the "irrationalism" of the French position on Germany. For examples, see "Estimate of the International Situation," November 8, 1948; and "Where Are We Today?" December 21, 1948, also in box 17, Kennan Papers, Princeton University. For an excellent discussion of the differences between the State Department's two leading experts on the Soviet Union, see John L. Harper, "Friends, Not Allies: George F. Kennan and Charles E. Bohlen," *World Policy Journal* 12 (summer 1995): 77–88.

[127] See Rolf Steininger, "Germany after 1945: Divided and Integrated or United and Neutral?" *German History* 7 (April 1989): 5–18; and Steininger, "Wie die Teilung Deutschlands verhindert werden sollte: Der Robertson Plan aus dem Jahre 1948," *Militargeschichtliche Mitteilungen* 18 (1983): 44–89. All of the subsequent Foreign Office (FO) records cited in this section are reprinted in full in the latter Steininger article.

[128] FO 371/70501/C5540, "Appreciation of the Present Situation in Berlin and the Effect on Our Policy for Germany as a Whole," July 12, 1948, 60–63.

Communism which is sweeping Germany from the Oder to the Rhine."[129] Robertson received a far more respectful hearing from the Foreign Office than Kennan did from the State Department, but the general response to his plan was also negative. The risks involved in counting on the Germans to cast their lot with the West rather than the East were deemed to be too great to be left to chance. The head of the German Department in the Foreign Office agreed with Robertson that the chances of Germany turning to communism were small, but at the same time argued against his plan because the chances of a united Germany turning to aggressive nationalism and a policy of playing off East versus West were too high to ignore.[130] Some analysts in the Foreign Office thought that the risks associated with a united Germany might be more manageable at some point in the distant future, but other analysts had argued even before the presentation of the Robertson Plan that neither the West nor the East could or should tolerate a united Germany under any circumstances.[131]

The complications that Kennan's proposal would have raised within the alliance might not have loomed so large if the prospects of reaching a quick agreement with the Soviet Union over Germany were considered favorable. However, as Kennan readily acknowledged throughout the development of Program A, the chances of the Soviets accepting even his outline of a settlement were far from promising since it essentially offered them little more than a chance to peacefully withdraw from Germany if and when they felt such a course might be in their interest. Although Kennan seems to have been amenable to at least considering the possibility of concessions on both reparations and the Ruhr in order to increase the prospects of Soviet acceptance, he was dissuaded from doing so by those who recognized that such provisions would lessen the chances of Program A surviving the domestic political process. Having dealt with Congress extensively throughout the postwar period, Dean Acheson reminded Kennan that any proposal containing concessions on reparations was doomed from the start because Congress would not subsidize reparations payments to the Soviet Union.[132] As for the Ruhr, Kennan indicated to Marshall as late as October 18 that he was willing to offer the Soviets three out of eighteen votes in the Ruhr Control

[129] FO 371/70504/C6057/3/18, Robertson to Strang, July 20, 1948, 70–72 (quotation on 71). Earlier, Robertson had argued that "there was little chance of this becoming a Communist Government since the Germans were very opposed to Communism and the Russians after all they had suffered at their hands." See FO 371/7051/27973, "Note of an Informal Meeting Held on July 12." I thank Michael Spirtas for providing me with this document.

[130] FO 371/70628/C6868/154/18, Note by Patrick Dean about the Robertson Plan, September 2, 1948, 81.

[131] See FO 371/70587/C3653/71/18, Statement by R. M. A. Hankey, May 14, 1948, 59.

[132] For Acheson's comments on reparations, see "Special Consultative Group on German Policy Questions," 9, 51–52.

Authority in return for the establishment of a similar control authority in Silesia. Although there is no evidence that Marshall ever responded to the letter, it is obvious that someone indicated to Kennan that this provision would also not be acceptable: the final draft of Program A explicitly ruled out any mention of Soviet participation in control arrangements for the Ruhr.[133]

Leaving aside all of the criticisms lodged against the substance of Program A, the biggest obstacle that Kennan faced in the fall of 1948 was the firm reluctance of Marshall and others to discuss larger questions related to Germany under the duress of the Berlin Blockade. Kennan accepted the fact that the United States could not negotiate under duress, but he clearly hoped to move Marshall away from the rigid position that the Berlin crisis could be ended simply by working out arrangements limited to currency and Western access to the city. In effect, Kennan accepted the logic of Stalin's position that a viable solution to the Berlin crisis had to be directly related to the larger question of the future of Germany.[134] Nevertheless, Kennan was willing to accept a makeshift solution to the Berlin crisis in order to begin negotiations over the future of Germany, but Marshall was not. In discussions with the British and the French in late October, Marshall stated his belief that "it was important that there should be no indication of any weakness or excessive desire to find a way out which would be regarded by the Russians as an act of appeasement."[135] Regardless of what Marshall may have thought about the substance of Program A, he clearly rejected Kennan's advice that the United States should be open to the idea of solving the crisis within the wider framework of the German question. With no CFM in sight, Program A was relegated to the "back burner" for the remainder of 1948.[136]

Kennan's ideas about Germany had received very little support since he had first put them forward in August 1948, but a combination of circumstances revived some interest in Program A at the start of 1949. First, the army leadership in Washington grew more concerned about the continuing stalemate in Berlin and what was perceived as French and British intransigence in moving forward with the London program. Surprisingly, given his close relationship with Forrestal and Clay, Royall outlined a plan in early January which called for the withdrawal of occupation forces to numbers even lower than those suggested by Kennan.[137] Second,

---

[133] Kennan to Marshall, October 18, 1948, PPS Records, box 15, NA. For the final draft of Program A (November 12), in which control of the Ruhr is exclusively limited to France, Britain, Germany, and the Benelux nations, see *SDPPSP*, 340–71.

[134] See PPS/42, in *SDPPSP*, 471–89.

[135] The quotation from Marshall is in RG 59, 862.00/10–2748, "Meeting of the Three Foreign Ministers at the Quai d' Orsay: The Berlin Situation," October 27, 1948.

[136] Kennan, *Memoirs, 1925–50*, 428.

[137] See Royall to Forrestal, January 19, 1949, *FRUS*, 1949, vol. 3, 82–84. Only three months before, Clay had told Forrestal and Royall, in reference to the garrison proposal, that "any of

although Dean Acheson, who replaced Marshall as secretary of state in January 1949, was totally unsympathetic to Royall's suggestion that the United States should consider getting out of Germany, he accepted the idea of setting up an interdepartmental committee whose purpose would be to develop a long-range statement of America's German policy. Significantly, given the almost total lack of support that the bureaucracy had heretofore extended to Program A, Acheson decided to appoint Kennan as the head of the NSC Sub-Committee on Germany.[138]

Since he had spent much of the last six months thinking intensively about the German question, it is not surprising that Kennan's contributions to the work of the subcommittee were in line with his earlier views. The new wrinkle that he added was a recommendation that the United States should defer the establishment of a West German government and instead establish a provisional West German administration. Partly influenced by Stalin's answers to questions submitted to him by Kingsbury Smith in late January, in which the Soviet leader omitted mentioning the currency issue as a condition for ending the blockade, Kennan suggested to Murphy that the Western powers might now want to approach the West Germans with the idea of postponing the establishment of a government pending a four-power meeting with the Soviets. Undoubtedly reflecting his conversations with Adenauer, Murphy told Kennan that he should not be influenced by Stalin's newspaper interviews and that he should abandon the idea of a provisional administration because "it would be most unwise to create in West Germany further doubt over the firmness of our intentions regarding Western Germany."[139] Having supported the idea of keeping the door open to an all-German solution in 1945–46 when Kennan wanted to slam it shut, Murphy was now totally unsympathetic to his concern that the establishment of a West German government would "crystallize a split Germany and freeze a dividing line from Lubeck to Trieste."[140]

Kennan was obviously unconvinced by these arguments because he submitted a paper on March 8 that incorporated virtually all of the ideas

---

the suggestions that had been current about getting out of Germany would be the beginning of our losing it." Forrestal certainly agreed with Clay: "I said to Royall it was most important that we try to convince the President he should not attribute undue significance to this proposal and that . . . withdrawal from Germany means withdrawal from Europe and in the long run the beginning of the third world war." See *Forrestal Diaries*, 507.

[138] See Digest of Meeting of NSC Sub-Committee on Germany, January 28, 1949, box 219, PSF, HSTL. For an excellent discussion of the relationship between Kennan and Acheson, see Wilson Miscamble, "Rejected Architect and Master Builder: George Kennan, Dean Acheson, and Postwar Europe," *Review of Politics* 58 (summer 1996): 437–68.

[139] Memorandum for the Files, February 19, 1949, box 77, Robert Murphy Papers, Hoover Institution, Stanford University.

[140] Ibid.

that he had outlined to Murphy a month earlier.[141] Murphy, who had just been appointed acting director of German and Austrian Affairs, was clearly furious with Kennan for persisting along these lines. We do not know what Murphy said to Kennan after reading this paper, but it was obviously forceful and effective. Although Kennan still maintained that his recommendation was valid, he told Acheson the very next day that "he deferred to the opinions expressed by those directly concerned with operations in Germany to the effect that it was too late for the U.S. to change its position regarding the establishment of a West German government." Whatever relief Murphy may have felt about Kennan's change of position was mitigated, however, upon hearing Acheson's own views about Germany. Declaring that he had almost been persuaded by Kennan's logic about the merits of a provisional administration, Acheson indicated that "he did not understand either how we ever arrived at the decision to see established a Western German government or state. He wondered whether this had not rather been the brainchild of General Clay and not a governmental decision."[142] With good reason, Murphy was bewildered that Acheson and Kennan could still entertain these thoughts after all that had been done over the course of 1948. As he wrote to Clay on March 10, 1949:

> At this late hour such performance would seem incredible to me, and yet I have found evidence of it here. Part of it arises, I am sure, from a lack of knowledge of the true situation. In the case of one important person, I found he did not understand the nature of our commitments under the London Agreement and was going along on the assumption that this was an *ad hoc* thought and not a decision arrived at by governments after deliberate negotiations after a period of months.[143]

Ironically, Kennan's ideas about abandoning the London program in favor of a provisional German administration may have had exactly the opposite effect than the one he intended. Referring to Acheson and

[141] Paper Prepared by the Director of the Policy Planning Staff, March 8, 1949, *FRUS, 1949*, vol. 3, 96–102.

[142] Memorandum of Conversation by Murphy, March 9, 1949, *FRUS, 1949*, vol. 3, 102–5 (quotations on 102). Acheson's receptiveness to Kennan's ideas was not as ringing as scholars occasionally suggest since he qualified it by saying that "he did not quite follow the conclusion arrived at or understand how the proposed solution would work."

[143] Murphy to Clay, March 10, 1948, box 57, Murphy Papers, Hoover Institution. Enclosing a copy of this letter to Riddleberger, Murphy asked his replacement in Germany to "spend some overtime" in an effort to change Kennan's views. Murphy warned Riddleberger that "there is an element of apprehension in his thinking, which if allowed to prevail would in the end, I am sure, destroy our position in Western Germany." See Murphy to Riddleberger, March 10, 1949, box 59, Murphy Papers, Hoover Institution.

Kennan's "tendency to back slide" on the establishment of a West German state, Murphy urged Clay to meet with French Foreign Minister Robert Schuman in order to resolve as quickly as possible the intractable problems over the occupation statute and the principles of trizonal fusion.[144] Although the connection with the policy debates in Washington should not be drawn too tightly, Clay and Schuman did meet shortly afterwards and the impasse over the occupation statute was broken.[145] Rather than continuing with the overly complex and detailed occupation statute that was in place, Clay and Schuman agreed that what was needed was a much simpler document. During the first week of April, after meetings in Washington between Acheson, Schuman, and Bevin, the three Western powers had reached total agreement on all of the questions that had been deadlocked for months. Kennan could not have been displeased with the adoption of a simpler occupation statute, but it is undeniable that yet another step had been taken toward the creation of a West German state.[146]

With the signing of the North Atlantic Treaty on April 14, 1949, the Western powers were on the verge of a sweeping victory over the Soviet Union in the decisive theater of the Cold War. The Soviets were fairly quick to acknowledge the victory. Within weeks after the signing of the North Atlantic Treaty and as a result of secret discussions between Philip Jessup and Jacob Malik, Soviet representative to the United Nations, the Soviets agreed to lift the blockade of Berlin in exchange for a meeting of the CFM. The extent of the capitulation on the part of the Soviets cannot be underestimated because the Western powers made it explicitly clear that there would be no postponement of their efforts in West Germany before or during the CFM.[147] Nevertheless, despite the vindication of the strategy pursued by the Western powers since the London CFM, the lifting of the blockade was viewed as something of a mixed blessing. Bevin was very concerned about where the whole process of negotiations might lead. He wanted to have the West Germans "'in his pocket' before talking with the Russians."[148] Clay interpreted the lifting of the blockade as a complete change in Soviet tactics and thought that it was quite possible that they might now "accept a solution of the German problem very largely on our terms, to include acceptance of the occupation statute and

---

[144] Murphy to Clay, March 10, 1949.

[145] For a record of the meeting, see Caffery to Secretary of State, March 22, 1949, *FRUS*, 1949, vol. 3, 115–18.

[146] The meetings in Washington and the final agreements can be found in *FRUS*, 1949, vol. 3, 156–86.

[147] See Philip Jessup, "Park Avenue Diplomacy: Ending the Berlin Blockade," *Political Science Quarterly* 87 (September 1972): 377–400; and *FRUS*, 1949, vol. 3, 694–751.

[148] For Bevin's concerns about even negotiating with the Soviets, see Douglas to Secretary of State, April 25, 1949, 730–31 (quotation on 730), and Bevin to Secretary of State, undated (circa May 1, 1949), 749–50, both in *FRUS*, 1949, vol. 3.

perhaps even the Bonn constitution."[149] But even on these terms, Clay was far from convinced that a German settlement at this time was in the Western interest:

> Their purpose will be, however, to prevent the new Germany from being oriented toward the West and integrated into an association of Western European nations. Thus, they would create a buffer state which if we tended to lessen our present efforts they could exploit by promises and other means. The creation of the new German government under these conditions could be to our advantage if, after its creation, we continue with the type and kind of effort which has been so disastrous to communism in Europe during the past two years. The inherent danger is the well-known tendency of democracies to rest on their laurels and their probable loss of enthusiasm in proceeding with re-armament and similar measures vital to a restoration of balance in Europe.[150]

The views of Clay and Bevin, of course, were of considerable importance in influencing the Western approach to the upcoming CFM, but the decisive position was still held by Acheson. And unlike Bevin and Clay, Acheson was not present at the creation of the London program and did not have the same emotional commitment to it. For this reason, he was more than willing to at least give a sympathetic hearing to Kennan's opposing views on the German question in the weeks leading up to the CFM. Acheson's willingness to consider both a general settlement on Germany and a regrouping of troops was undoubtedly increased by the fact that Jessup, a very close friend, openly endorsed the approach recommended in Program A.[151] Although he ruled out the idea of a general troop withdrawal from Germany, up until May 11 Acheson seems to have been willing to consider a regrouping: "A possible regrouping of troops which would have the effect of removing Russian troops eastward and possibly ending their presence in and passage through the Eastern

---

[149] Clay to Voorhees, May 1, 1949, in *Clay Papers*, 1137–38. See also Kellerman to Murphy, "Expectation of Soviet Move re Berlin," April 21, 1949, RG 59, 862.00/4–2149, NA. The belief that the Soviets were going to make major concessions on Germany at the CFM meeting was fairly widespread within the administration. See Kohler to Secretary of State, May 6, 1949, *FRUS*, 1949, vol. 3, 864–67. The CIA also felt that the Soviets were likely to pursue a policy aimed at establishing a detente in Central Europe. See CIA 5–49, May 17, 1949, box 206, PSF, HSTL; and ORE-48–49, "The Soviet Position in Approaching the CFM," May 18, 1949, box 257, PSF, HSTL.

[150] *Clay Papers*, 2:1138.

[151] See Jessup to Ware Adams, March 19, 1949, PPS Records, box 15, NA; and Jessup to Secretary of State, April 19, 1949, *FRUS*, 1949, vol. 3, 859–62. Of course, it is also true that Acheson was equally willing to provide support to opponents of Program A during this period.

European countries may have important advantages. It deserves the most careful study. It is essential to any further unification of Germany and of Germany with the West."[152]

Over the course of the next few days, however, any enthusiasm that Acheson might have had for Program A and the regrouping of forces to seaport garrisons simply vanished. In order to account for this seemingly sudden reversal, many scholars have emphasized the importance of a front page article in the *New York Times* by James Reston on May 12 which revealed the garrison provisions of Program A in fairly accurate detail. For example, Wilson Miscamble argues that British and French concerns about the implications of the Reston article provided the "major provocation and impetus" for Acheson to back away from Program A.[153] Rather than emphasizing the importance of the military's criticism of the withdrawal to seaport garrisons in accounting for the demise of Program A— the main factor that Acheson pointed to in his memoirs—Miscamble argues that the British and French reaction "acted as a brake on, indeed a fatal barrier to, any American initiative."[154]

Unfortunately, the evidence provided by Acheson's meetings with his principal advisors on May 12 does not provide much support to the thesis that the furor over the Reston article was all that crucial in defeating Program A. During two meetings held on the day that Reston's article appeared, and before the negative European reaction could have become a crucial factor in the process, Acheson was already rejecting Kennan's program. At a meeting held at 10:00 A.M., Acheson accepted the JCS argument against a withdrawal of forces to seaport garrisons: "It was decided that it

---

[152] Acheson, "An Approach to the CFM," May 11, 1949, *FRUS*, 1949, vol. 3, 873; and Jessup summary of meetings with Acheson, May 7, 1949, PPS Records, box 15, NA. Earlier Acheson had indicated to Bevin that he was considering the "possibility of a sort of peripheral withdrawal from Germany which would ease the Berlin situation." See Memorandum of Conversation by Secretary of State, March 31, 1949, *FRUS*, 1949, vol. 3, 157.

[153] Miscamble, *George F. Kennan and the Making of American Foreign Policy*, 170. The importance of the Reston article in the demise of Program A is also emphasized in John Lewis Gaddis, "The United States and the Question of a Sphere of Influence in Europe, 1945–49," in *Western Security: The Formative Years*, ed. Olav Riste (New York: Columbia University Press, 1985), 78; and Thomas Schwartz, *America's Germany: John J. McCloy and the Federal Republic of Germany* (Cambridge, Mass.: Harvard University Press), 39–40.

[154] Miscamble, *George F. Kennan and the Making of American Foreign Policy*, 171. For Acheson's emphasis on the military's objections to any regrouping of Western troops in the northern seaports, see *Present at the Creation: My Years in the State Department* (New York: W. W. Norton and Company, 1969), 291–92. With a total lack of enthusiasm, the JCS were willing to consider a possible regrouping of forces along the Rhine. See Voorhees to Johnson, May 11, 1949, enclosing the views of the JCS on "Military Considerations in the Conclusion of any Agreement with Respect to Germany," in *RJCS: Europe and NATO*, reel 2; and Johnson to Secretary of State, May 14, 1949, *FRUS*, 1949, vol. 3, 875–76. Clay's reaction was more vehement: "We cannot lose Germany now except by throwing it away and this proposal would do just that." See Clay Teleconference with Voorhees and Dorr, May 5, 1949, *Clay Papers*, 2:1149.

would be unrealistic to think that we could obtain sufficiently great compensation from the Soviets to justify putting forward the Bremen proposal. It was agreed that if regrouping of troops was discussed at Paris, we could try to get rid of the Soviet line of communication through Poland on the ground that it was not required and that Poland was not an occupying power."[155] Later in the day Acheson essentially brought an end to the debate by adopting the position that opponents of a negotiated settlement had always put forward in defense of the London program: "The Secretary stated that he had come to the conclusion that the western German government must inevitably be established and that unification of Germany should take place by the eastern zone Laender joining it."[156] In short, by the time the British and the French voiced their concerns about the Reston article to Bohlen and Jessup, the fundamental decision against pursuing a German settlement that reflected the assumptions or objectives of Program A had already been made.

Acheson's rapid adoption of the Murphy/Clay approach to Germany after May 12 suggests that either his intellectual attraction to Kennan's views was never very strong or that he simply reached the honest conclusion that the tripartite arrangements in West Germany should not be jeopardized by an uncertain and risky pursuit of a united Germany. Whatever the reasons behind his shift in thinking, Acheson's intellectual transformation to the Murphy/Clay position was completed well before the start of the Paris CFM. The U.S. stance on Germany during the Paris CFM stands as an example of how to craft a diplomatic position in order to guarantee that a settlement will not be reached. No further consideration of reparations. No Soviet participation in the Ruhr. No four-power treaty on German disarmament until the final peace treaty. The relinquishing by the Soviets of ownership of any plants in the eastern zone. Garrisons for the Western powers in the vicinity of the Rhine with the Soviets all the way back in Stettin. As if all of this somehow might still be acceptable to the Soviets, Acheson added one additional feature: "It might be stated that although the U.S. recognizes its commitment at Potsdam to support incorporation of the Northern part of East Prussia into the Soviet Union, it would welcome a proposal of the Soviet Union to yield its claim to this area in Poland's favor as compensation for an adjustment along Poland's western frontier."[157] Although Acheson would later suggest in his mem-

---

[155] See RG 59, 862.0146/5-1249, "Preparations for CFM on Germany-meeting in the Secretary's Office May 12, 10:00 A.M." One of the reasons why the JCS rejected any withdrawal to Bremen was that it "would not appear to fit in with the spirit of the North Atlantic Pact, nor with present informal arrangements with the Western Union."

[156] Preparations for CFM on Germany—meeting in the Secretary's Office May 12, 2:00 P.M. in *Memoranda of the Secretary of State, 1949–51* and *Meetings and Visits of Foreign Dignitaries, 1949–52*, microfiche publication (Washington, D.C.: Department of State, 1988), fiche 938.

[157] See "U.S. Position at the Council of Foreign Ministers," May 15, 1949, *FRUS, 1949*, vol. 3, 895–903 (quotation on 902).

oirs that these terms were "severe but not impossible," he was well aware at the time that they were severe *and* impossible. As Senator Vandenberg correctly noted after hearing Acheson explain the positions he would take in Paris, "it looks to me as though you are going to put up a program to the Russians at this conference to which the answer is 'No' unless there is total and complete repentance on their part with respect to their entire Eastern European policy."[158]

Safe in the knowledge that he was speaking in executive session, Acheson was not afraid to acknowledge that Vandenberg had perfectly understood his program for the CFM. Vandenberg was not afraid to acknowledge that he agreed with Acheson's adoption of this position. The representatives of Britain, France, and the leaders of the West German Christian Democratic Union (CDU) had already made it clear that they also supported both the assumptions and the goals of Acheson's policy. One rarely finds such a strong degree of agreement in international affairs on important issues, but with the notable exception of George Kennan, by May 1949 there was a rather strong consensus within the American government and its Western European allies on the merits of a divided Germany.

CONCLUSION

It is not at all obvious how the Soviets might have responded if the Truman administration had approached them with a German settlement along the lines of Program A. Even though it may be true that the Soviets would have rejected a settlement along Kennan's lines as too risky, it is also quite possible that these risks might have been perceived as better for them than the continuation of America's approach to Germany and Western Europe since the failure of the Moscow CFM. More than fifty years after the start of the Berlin crisis, George Kennan still believed that the Soviets "would have paid a higher price than most people think to get the American forces out of Germany."[159] Stalin may well have accepted

---

[158] Acheson, *Present at the Creation*, 292. For Acheson's testimony of May 19, 1949 in Executive Session before the Senate Committee on Foreign Relations, see the Historical Series, *Reviews of the World Situation, 1949–50* (Washington, D.C.: Government Printing Office, 1974), 1–22 (quotation on 16). At a meeting of the NSC on May 18, Acheson stated that "the basic concept of this CFM meeting was that we should go ahead with the Western German government, and that any unification of Germany as a whole should grow out of that.... He felt there would be fewer and less painful difficulties by going ahead with the West German government than by attempting to unite Germany first." Keeping in mind Acheson's "concept" of the CFM, it is hard to place a great deal of importance on the rigidity of the Soviet position at the CFM. It is clear that neither side was prepared to negotiate. See Memorandum for the President, May 18, 1949, box 220, PSF, HSTL.

[159] George Kennan, "A Letter on Germany," *New York Review of Books*, December 3, 1998, 20.

Kennan's proposal as a basis for a settlement in 1949, but he was probably not motivated by a desire to get American forces out of Germany. The removal of American forces from Germany was never a major objective of Soviet policy in the 1940s. The element of American policy that did bother Stalin was the restoration of German power in the West and the elimination of any Soviet voice in the future of West Germany. Kennan's plan offered the Soviets a mutual reduction of forces, but it did not offer them very much in terms of controlling German power.

Ironically, Kennan's defeat in 1949 was partially a result of the success of his earlier analyses of the future of Europe. In a PPS paper of February 1948, Kennan had argued that "a federated Europe, into which the parts of Germany are absorbed but in which the influence of the other countries is sufficient to hold Germany in her place" would be necessary in order to avoid either Russian or German domination of Western and Central Europe.[160] American strategy was squarely based on these premises in 1949, partly due to Kennan's advocacy. Rightly or wrongly, the vast majority of Western officials now believed that Kennan's Program A and an American troop withdrawal would risk all of the progress in this direction achieved by the Marshall Plan and the North Atlantic Treaty.

---

[160] PPS/23, "Review of Current Trends U.S. Foreign Policy," February 23, 1948, in *SDPPSP*, 110.

[5]

Temporary and Permanent Solutions: German Rearmament and the European Defense Community

It was true that the French would not be unduly frightened of a large German army (10–15 divisions) provided it was masked by a powerful American and United Kingdom force permanently stationed on the continent. But they could not trust the Americans to remain faithful to their present ideas; what was wanted was a 100-year or forty-year treaty binding the Americans to Europe. This was obviously unrealistic, so the French must stand on their former position.

M. Lebel, Quai d' Orsay official, 1950

Often reduced to little more than a footnote by historians and political scientists, the establishment of the European Defense Community (EDC) was by far the single most important objective of American foreign policy in the early 1950s. A supranational security regime designed to make West German rearmament more acceptable to the French, the EDC became the cornerstone of American efforts to transform Western Europe from a collection of independent states to a more collective and unified region. Although Winston Churchill once described the EDC as a "sludgy amalgam," many American policymakers saw it as the key element in the rebirth of Europe and in winning the Cold War. Indeed, American policymakers sometimes spoke as if the success or failure of the EDC would determine the overall fate of Western civilization. For David Bruce, the EDC was "the most significant thing which has happened in western civilization, not in my time, not in our time, but for a period of hundreds of years."[1] For Dean Acheson, the signing of the EDC treaty in May 1952 was an event that "may well prove to be one of the most important and most far reaching events of our lifetime. . . . We have seen the beginning of the realization of an ancient dream—the unity of the free peoples of Western

---

[1] David Bruce testimony of June 11, 1952, Hearings before the Senate Committee on Foreign Relations, Executive Q and R, *Convention on Relations with the Federal Republic of Germany and Protocol to the North Atlantic Treaty*, 82d Congress, 2d session, 64.

Europe."[2] If France and Germany did not seize this last chance to resolve their problems within the framework of the EDC, John Foster Dulles feared that Europe would "return to the dark ages."[3]

The hopes and fears that American policymakers expressed for the European Defense Community were not merely examples of rhetorical excess and overselling. The actions of U.S. government officials throughout this period were consistent with their words. For example, it is now clear beyond any doubt that the Truman administration's unenthusiastic reaction to Stalin's note of March 10, 1952, proposing the reunification of Germany was largely a function of its unwillingness to allow anything to interfere with the signing of the EDC treaty and the contractual agreements with West Germany.[4] It is also clear that the Eisenhower administration's decision not to explore seriously the possibilities of a general Cold War settlement in the aftermath of Stalin's death in 1953 was largely the result of U.S. unwillingness to take any diplomatic initiatives which might interfere with the ratification of the EDC treaty.[5] If there is any validity to the belief that there were still "missed opportunities" for ending the Cold War peacefully in the early 1950s, there is no more significant reason for why they were missed than the importance placed by American policymakers on the creation of the EDC.

The American obsession with the European Defense Community is often seen as merely a pragmatic reaction to the French rejection of arming West Germany within the framework of NATO. Although there were certainly pragmatic reasons behind American support for the EDC, both the Truman and Eisenhower administrations supported it primarily because they sincerely believed it represented the best long-term solution to the German problem. For both administrations, but particularly for the Eisenhower administration, the EDC was an essential element in transforming the basic power structure of the international system. The EDC, it was thought, would free Europe from worrying about the restoration of West German power and sovereignty and therefore would further considerably the integration and unity of Western Europe. Since from the U.S. perspective political unity was all that Western Europe needed to become a fully capable third power in the international system, the EDC

[2] Dean Acheson, *Present at the Creation: My Years in the State Department* (New York: W. W. Norton and Company, 1969), 647.

[3] MacBride Minutes, July 11, 1953, *Foreign Relations of the United States, 1952–54*, vol. 5 (Washington, D.C.: Government Printing Office, 1983), 1622.

[4] For an excellent collection of documents from American and British archives showing the relationship between the EDC, the contractual agreements, and the Stalin Note of March 10, 1952, see Rolf Steininger, ed., *Eine Chance Zur Wiedervereinigung?* (Bonn: Verlag Neue Gesellschaft, 1985); and Steininger, *The German Question: The Stalin Note of 1952 and the Problem of German Reunification* (New York: Columbia University Press, 1990).

[5] See W. W. Rostow, *Europe after Stalin: Eisenhower's Three Decisions of March 11, 1953* (Austin: University of Texas Press, 1982).

was a crucial element in transforming the structure of the system from a latent tripolar system to a fully tripolar system. With the German problem solved and a united Western Europe in place, it would be possible for Eisenhower to accomplish one of his most important objectives: the complete withdrawal of all American forces from Europe.

THE GERMAN REARMAMENT
QUESTION BEFORE THE KOREAN WAR

Rumors and speculation about American plans for the rearmament of West Germany were frequent during the period between the signing of the North Atlantic Treaty and the Korean War. For the most part, the vehement disavowals of any plans to rearm Germany put forward by Acheson and Truman on these occasions were an accurate statement of official policy. Although the American military establishment became increasingly convinced that Germany should be rearmed as quickly as possible, Acheson and the State Department bureaucracy continued to believe that the political costs and potential risks outweighed the military benefits which might be gained from the addition of German divisions to NATO.[6] Without the crisis atmosphere brought about by the Korean War in June 1950, it is very likely that the strong political reasons for postponing the question of German rearmament would have prevailed for the immediate future.

The lack of any sense of urgency about German rearmament before the Korean War reflected a more general lack of urgency about the conventional rearmament of Western Europe. The Truman administration resisted the thesis that the formation of the North Atlantic Pact was by itself a sufficient deterrent to a Soviet invasion of Western Europe. Acheson and other officials viewed the rearmament of the NATO allies as an objective that had to remain subordinate to the goals of political stability and economic reconstruction. Since the NATO allies could not afford to rearm themselves, and the administration did not want them devoting scarce resources toward rearmament, the alliance generally held a fairly relaxed attitude toward the imbalance of ground forces on the continent. Acheson went out of his way to reassure Congress that neither the administration nor its allies were going to attempt to match Soviet ground forces in Europe. In his view, all that Western Europe needed in terms of conventional forces was enough to prevent a rapid conquest of the continent until American airpower could take a devastating toll on Soviet military

---

[6] See Lawrence Martin, "The American Decision to Rearm Germany," in *American Civil Military Decisions*, ed. Harold Stein (Birmingham: University of Alabama Press, 1963), 645–63.

forces.[7] How much was enough and how long it would take for the NATO allies to achieve this level of forces was left unspecified, but Acheson, Chairman of the Joint Chiefs of Staff Omar Bradley, and Secretary of Defense Louis Johnson were all careful to make it clear to Congress that there were no ambitious plans to achieve quickly a satisfactory military balance.[8]

The addition of German military forces to NATO would obviously have shortened the period in which Western Europe could be made defensible, but before the Korean War Acheson was determined to keep German rearmament out of any discussions related to military affairs. This decision was more than a tactical move because Acheson appears to have been sincerely opposed to German rearmament throughout 1949. Although less widely noted than his dismissal of the stationing of American troops in Europe permanently, Acheson offered a similar uncategorical rejection of German rearmament during an appearance before the Senate Foreign Relations Committee in May 1949:

> If you permit any army at all of any kind, you get into a difficulty that you spoke of, because what they do is to create a general staff for the Army. That is the first great error. Then they have those quick enlistments. If you have 100,000 men you keep turning that over and you train a vast number. But I think everybody is clear that it would be quite insane to make any sort of army of any kind whatever.[9]

Due to the conventional force imbalance, few military officials on either side of the Atlantic would have agreed with Acheson's idea that rearming Germany was insane, but hardly any influential political officials in either the United States or Western Europe were contemplating a change in policy during 1949.[10] Interestingly, the most important political

---

[7] See Acheson testimony of August 8, 1949, U.S. Senate, Hearings before the Committee on Foreign Relations, *Military Assistance Program*, 81st Congress, 1st session (Washington, D.C.: Government Printing Office, 1949), 13, 27; and Acheson testimony of April 27, 1949, U.S. Senate, Hearings before the Committee on Foreign Relations, *North Atlantic Treaty*, 33–37.

[8] See Omar Bradley testimony of July 29, 1949, U.S. House of Representatives, Committee on Foreign Affairs, *Military Assistance Program*, pt. 1., vol. 5: *Historical Series* (Washington, D.C.: Government Printing Office, 1976), 26; and Louis Johnson testimony of August 9, 1949, U.S. Senate, Hearings before the Committee on Foreign Relations, 81st Congress, 1st session, *Military Assistance Program*, 67–70.

[9] Acheson testimony of May 19, 1949, in Executive Session before the Senate Foreign Relations Committee, Historical Series, *Reviews of the World Situation, 1949–50* (Washington, D.C.: Government Printing Office, 1974), 14–18 (quotation on 14).

[10] As Georges-Henri Soutou points out, even French military officials were advocating German rearmament by 1948–49. See his chapter, "France and the German Rearmament Problem, 1945–55," in *The Quest for Stability: Problems of West European Security 1918–57*, ed. R. Ahmann, A. M. Birke, and M. Howard (London: Oxford University Press, 1993), 487–512. For the views of the British military at this time, see Spencer Mawby, *Containing Germany: Britain and the Arming of the Federal Republic* (New York: St. Martin's Press, 2000), 20–40.

figure in the West who was seriously thinking about the need for German rearmament was Konrad Adenauer. Despite that fact that Germans were ostensibly prohibited from even discussing military issues, Adenauer let American officials know on several occasions throughout 1949 that he was in favor of a German defense contribution. Even after being reassured by American officials that they were confident in the deterrent currently provided by American airpower and that the likelihood of a Soviet tank attack proceeding undetected through the fog of North Germany was extremely low, Adenauer continued to raise the rearmament issue throughout the summer of 1949.[11] In July 1949, he told OMGUS officials that he "favored admitting Germany to the Atlantic Pact" and the inclusion of German soldiers in a European army.[12] Sounding a theme to which he would often return in the future, Adenauer argued in August that German rearmament within the framework of a European army was essential because "the American taxpayer will not agree to have part of the United States Army, or at least a unit strong enough to defend Western Germany and Western Europe, permanently stationed in Germany."[13]

Regardless of how logical it might have seemed to Adenauer and some Western military officials to begin making plans for rearming Germany, the leading policymakers on the American side were all in agreement that it was counterproductive to even speculate about the issue in the prevailing atmosphere of 1949. The immediate task facing the Truman administration was furthering the political and economic integration of the Federal Republic of Germany into Western Europe, not the strengthening of NATO's ground forces. Making progress in this area was difficult enough without the specter of German rearmament hovering ominously in the background. Speculation about German rearmament, particularly by such well-known figures as Lucius Clay or Adenauer, only raised suspicions that hindered progress in political and economic areas.[14] Acheson

[11] Memorandum of Conversation between Hillenbrand and Adenauer, RG 59, 862.00/ 4–1149, NA. It is interesting that Adenauer continued to reveal his conversations with German military figures because OMGUS officials reportedly had been very distressed in January 1949 to read a report concerning Adenauer's discussions about rearmament with General Hans Speidel. See Hans-Peter Schwarz, *Konrad Adenauer: A German Politician and Statesman in a Period of War, Revolution and Reconstruction* (Providence, R.I.: Berghahn Books, 1995), 405–6.

[12] See Department of Army cable CC 9192 of July 18, 1949, attached to RG 59, 862.00 (W)/7–1849, NA.

[13] Memorandum of Conversation by Altaffer, RG 59, 862.00/8–849, NA.

[14] For the troubles caused by the persistent rumors about German rearmament, see Memorandum by Perkins to Secretary of State, October 11; Memorandum of Conversation by Perkins, November 16; and Secretary of State to McCloy, November 21, all in *FRUS, 1949,* vol. 3, 285–86, 317–18, 340–42. According to the editors of *FRUS,* the attached memorandum for the October 11 memo by Perkins could not be found in the Department of State files. The memorandum, which actually can be found in RG 59, 862.20/10–1049, NA, consisted of a warning to Perkins that one of Truman's friends was about to present him with a lurid report about covert military plans and activities in Germany.

could not help but agree when the French ambassador complained to him in December 1949 that something had to be done to stop the persistent rumors about German rearmament. In his view, these rumors were "interfering with the main task before all of us which was the integration of Germany into the European scene."[15]

Unlike rearmament, the question of how to integrate Germany into Western Europe was a topic of serious debate within the Truman administration throughout 1949. The British had sparked the debate in April 1949 by asking Kennan whether it would be possible for them to have extensive discussions with American planners about the future of Europe.[16] The British were directly concerned with policies toward Western Europe, but Kennan and a distinguished group of outside consultants broadened the discussion to include the future of Europe as a whole.[17] In PPS/55, "Study of U.S. Stance toward Question of European Union," submitted to Acheson in July 1949, Kennan essentially argued that the United States should continue to pursue the establishment of a continental European union because of the need to absorb Germany into a larger unit and to provide an institutional framework which could eventually attract the Soviet satellites toward the West. More important, since neither a unified Germany nor the absorption of the Eastern European satellites were of much relevance after the Paris CFM, Kennan argued that the administration should not attempt to force Great Britain to assume the leadership of a European unification movement or be expected to merge its sovereignty into any continental arrangements.[18]

If the future leader of the European unity movement was not going to be Great Britain, the obvious question that followed from Kennan's policy

[15] Memorandum of Conversation between Acheson and Henri Bonnet, December 1, 1949, in *Memoranda of Conversation of the Secretary of State, 1947–52*, microfiche publication (Washington D.C.: Department of State, 1988), fiche no. 1118. Unfortunately, Acheson did not have the ability to prevent the Germans from raising the issue. In January 1950, after the publication of an article in the *Herald Tribune* reporting on Adenauer's contacts with German military figures, McCloy was forced to officially deny reports that American officials had been discussing the rearmament issue with the Germans. See RG 59, 762A.5/1–1950 and 762A.5/1–2050, NA.

[16] Jebb to Kennan, April 7, 1949, *FRUS, 1949*, vol. 4, 289–91. The British specifically wanted to know whether the State Department envisioned a united Western Europe developing into a third global power. As a result of internal discussions, Bevin and the Foreign Office definitively rejected the concept as a possible or desirable policy goal. See CAB 129/37, C.P. (49) 208, "European Policy," October 18, 1949, *Cabinet Papers: Complete Classes from the CAB and PREM Series in the Public Record Office*, series 3 (Wiltshire: Adam Matthew Publications, 1996).

[17] The outside consultants included academics such as Hans Morgenthau and Arnold Wolfers. See Michael J. Hogan, *The Marshall Plan: America, Britain, and the Reconstruction of Western Europe, 1947–1952* (New York: Cambridge University Press, 1987), 258–61.

[18] PPS/55 in *The State Department Policy Planning Staff Papers*, ed. Anna Kasten Nelson (New York: Garland Press, 1980), 1:82–100 (hereafter *SDPPSP*); and Minutes of the Meeting of the American Members of the Combined Policy Committee, September 13, 1949, *FRUS, 1949*, vol. 1, 520–22.

paper was who the alternative candidate for European leadership would be. In his memoirs, Kennan suggested that his guiding assumption at the time, albeit one not "specifically expressed in the paper," was that France would "naturally and unquestionably" be the dominant force within any federal union that emerged on the continent.[19] However, a more plausible explanation for the lack of any reference in PPS/55 to France's leadership role is that Kennan's commitment to this objective was tenuous. His real candidate for European leadership was Germany rather than France. As he suggested at a Policy Planning Staff meeting in May 1949, "I am afraid while we cannot say so, what we have to do is to persuade the Europeans to find a way to permit *Germany's* leadership to become manifest without involving military and political controls of a nationalist Germany over the other countries of Europe."[20] The evidence clearly suggests that Kennan was growing increasingly frustrated at what he perceived as France's clear failure to seize the leadership role in Western Europe, its "neurotic" worries about being abandoned in Europe by America and Great Britain, and its continuing concerns about the restoration of German power. In a bitter response to Charles Bohlen, who had vigorously defended the legitimacy of French concerns about the direction of American policy toward Western Europe, Kennan essentially offered a negative answer to the question he had posed: "Can we really expect that the French will show greater capacity for leadership at some future date, when Germany has emerged from many of the present controls and handicaps?"[21]

No blueprint for the future direction of American policy toward Western European unity emerged from the debate over PPS/55, primarily because Acheson took a middle ground between Kennan and his critics. Acheson was not unsympathetic to the basic argument advanced in PPS/55. For example, he shared Kennan's belief that Great Britain could

---

[19] For Kennan's account of these discussions over the future of Europe, see George F. Kennan, *Memoirs, 1925–50* (New York: Atlantic, Little, Brown, 1967), 449–68 (quotation on 455).

[20] See 81st Meeting of the Policy Planning Staff, May 20, 1949, PPS Records, box 32, NA.

[21] See Bohlen to Kennan, October 6, 1949; Kennan to Bohlen, October 12, 1949; and Bohlen to Kennan, October 29, 1949, in RG 59, Records of Charles E. Bohlen, box 1, NA. Kennan's letter suggests that he was not as opposed to the rearmament of Germany as he implied in his memoirs: "Now the brutal fact is that a program for the defense of the continent which attempts to leave out of account the military experience and skills and energies of the Germans is not a sound one. In promoting the idea of union in Europe we have tried to give the French an opportunity to create arrangements by which this German strength could be employed for European purposes without permitting it to assume again the position of the protagonist of German national power. . . . If we are unable to make any progress along these lines there can be only two alternatives: (a) a western Europe in which the capacity for resistance to Russian military attack is a pretense rather than a reality, or (b) a revival of German military strength on a straight national basis."

not and should not be expected to merge its sovereignty into supranational institutions to the same extent as the continental nations. Although Kennan's critics were convinced that progress in European integration required full British participation in order to provide a counterbalance to German power, Acheson was far more optimistic about France's ability to assume leadership in this area.[22] Indeed, he sought to encourage the French to move forward without Great Britain by letting Foreign Minister Schuman know that the United States would fully support any and all efforts toward European integration. French officials were probably thrilled to hear Acheson state that a Franco-German understanding in Europe "could only be brought about by the French, and only as fast as the French were prepared to go; and that, therefore, the role of the US and UK in this matter was to advise and assist the French and not put them in the position of being forced reluctantly to accept American or UK ideas."[23]

Acheson's desire to support the French in late 1949, however, was tempered by his assessment that Germany's integration into Western Europe could not proceed at a slow pace. Despite all that had been accomplished in West Germany throughout 1948 and 1949, Acheson did not believe that the allies had the luxury of proceeding slowly in taking other steps aimed at cementing Germany's ties with the West. As Thomas Schwartz and other scholars have argued, American policies toward the Federal Republic were greatly influenced by policymakers' particular reading of the lessons of the interwar period and the failure of the Weimar Republic.[24] Regardless of the accuracy of their historical interpretation, American officials were convinced that the failure of the Weimar Republic was partially caused by the fact that German democrats were discredited in the eyes of the populace by their inability to moderate the harsh terms of the Versailles settlement. By not making early concessions after Versailles to moderate democrats which might have helped them combat the appeal of the extreme nationalists, the Western powers subsequently found themselves locked

[22] See Acheson to the Embassy in France, October 19, 1949, *FRUS, 1949*, vol. 4, 469–72. At an October meeting of U.S. ambassadors in Paris, the consensus reached by Bohlen, McCloy, Douglas, and David Bruce was that European integration could not make progress if Britain did not fully participate. See Summary Record of a Meeting, October 21–22, *FRUS, 1949*, vol. 4, 472–94. As John Harper notes, Acheson wanted the British to participate in Western European integration but he was unwilling to push them into it against their will and was willing to support efforts at integration which did not include the British. See John Lamberton Harper, *American Visions of Europe* (Cambridge: Cambridge University Press, 1994), 219–20.

[23] See *FRUS, 1950*, vol. 4, 339.

[24] See Thomas Schwartz, *America's Germany: John J. McCloy and the Federal Republic of Germany* (Cambridge: Cambridge University Press, 1991), 57–83; and Mary N. Hampton, "NATO at the Creation: U.S. Foreign Policy, West Germany, and the Wilsonian Impulse," *Security Studies* 4 (spring 1995): 610–56.

in a vicious circle because later concessions only seemed to vindicate the tactics of the extremists and further discredit the democratic parties. For American policymakers, the only way out of the vicious circle after the Second World War was to make concessions to moderate democrats as early as possible but somehow to do so in a manner that did not lead German officials into thinking that even larger concessions could be coerced from the Western powers through explicit or implicit threats.

The Weimar-type struggle between moderate democrats and extreme nationalists was personified in the conflict between Adenauer and Kurt Schumacher, the respective leaders of the two dominant political parties in the Federal Republic. At first glance, Schumacher would appear to be an unlikely object of concern for the Western powers because he was unquestionably democratic—an opponent of Nazism who had spent over a decade in a concentration camp. Furthermore, Schumacher was an uncompromising anticommunist with absolutely no illusions about the nature of the Soviet Union or the possibility of a neutral Germany. Even Acheson, who considered Schumacher to be a dangerous fanatic, paid him a backhanded compliment when he acknowledged before the U.S. Senate that the leader of the Social Democratic Party (SPD) "would be adorning the first lamp post" if the communists ever gained control over Germany.[25] Nevertheless, Schumacher's overall political stance created a difficult situation for the Western powers because of his conviction that the road to power for the SPD lay in exploiting nationalist sentiments. Well aware of how badly the SPD had been damaged in the interwar period by the perception that it was insufficiently nationalist, Schumacher was intent on making sure that the his party would not be vulnerable to this charge after the Second World War. "Never again," Schumacher told an American diplomat, "will the Social Democrats be less nationalist than the parties of the right."[26] Indeed, as V. Stanley Vardy argues, Schumacher's postwar SPD essentially turned Marxist orthodoxy on its head in an effort to portray itself as the party most committed to the defense of German national interests.[27]

Schumacher's determination to exploit nationalist sentiments led him to pursue a strategy based on vitriolic attacks against the policies of all of

[25] See Acheson testimony of January 10, 1950, in *Reviews of the World Situation, 1949–50*, 118; and the transcript of the Princeton Seminars, October 10–11, 1953, 766, box 89, Dean Acheson Papers, HSTL. For the classic study of Schumacher's personality and its impact on the SPD, see Lewis J. Edinger, *Kurt Schumacher: A Study in Personality and Political Behavior* (Stanford: Stanford University Press, 1965).

[26] See Charles Thayer, *The Unquiet Germans* (New York: Harper & Brothers, 1958), 137.

[27] See V. Stanley Vardy, "Germany's Postwar Socialism: Nationalism and Kurt Schumacher," *Review of Politics* 27 (April 1965): 220–44; Gordon D. Drummond, *The German Social Democrats in Opposition, 1945–62* (Norman: University of Oklahoma Press, 1982), 12–33; and Dietrich Orlow, "Delayed Reaction: Democracy, Nationalism, and the SPD, 1945–1966," *German Studies Review* 16 (1993): 77–102.

the occupying powers, with the harshest attacks directed against France. In contrast to Adenauer, who believed that the quickest way to end the occupation regime was by increasing the level of trust the Western powers had in Germany, Schumacher thought that the occupying powers would only make concessions in response to concerted pressure. Narrowly defeated by Adenauer and the Christian Democratic Union (CDU) in the initial German elections of September 1949, Schumacher's strategy for a later SPD victory was to convince the populace that their interests would be better defended by him—and by a party committed to German national interests—rather than by Adenauer, whom he sought to tarnish with the label "Chancellor of the Allies."

In a perfect world, the Western powers might have been able to combat Schumacher's efforts by making it clear that they would not be swayed an inch by efforts to play the nationalism card. Unfortunately, this perfect world did not at all correspond to how American officials viewed the nature of the German situation in late 1949. It was very easy to say, as John McCloy did in October 1949, that the Western powers should not worry about offending German nationalism and "crack down immediately on the Germans if they get out of line."[28] However, as McCloy himself would frequently argue in the years to come, the East-West struggle for the soul of Germany was a game that the Western powers could easily lose if they did not play their cards carefully. In words that both Adenauer and Schumacher would have endorsed, McCloy later argued that two of the principal ways to lose the struggle for Germany were to ignore her legitimate demands to be treated as an equal partner and to retain unnecessary restrictions on her sovereignty:

> Greatest danger to West—that Germany might be tempted to throw in her fortunes with those of the East—is to be met not by imposing upon Germany restrictions which will make Germans resent Western interference and mistrust any German government which cooperates with West, but by ensuring that legitimate aspirations of the Germans are realized within Western concert. . . . We know that World War II came not only because Germany rearmed nor even because Allies failed to intervene to prevent rearming. It came because German democracy bore the taint of defeat and because it lacked vigor and prestige to ride out bad times—people turned against it when the going got hard. What German democracy needs and has never had is success in eyes of German people.[29]

---

[28] *FRUS*, 1950, vol. 3, 287–90. For McCloy's concerns about a resurgence of German nationalism, see Frank M. Buscher, "The U.S. High Commission and German Nationalism, 1949–52," *Central European History* 23 (March 1990): 57–75.

[29] McCloy to Secretary of State, April 25, 1950, *FRUS*, 1950, vol. 4, 633–37.

It did not take too long for Acheson and McCloy to conclude that the United States had a very great stake in making sure that Adenauer rather than Schumacher emerged victorious in the battle for support of the German people. After meeting the two of them for the first time in November 1949, Acheson concluded that Schumacher was "a fanatic of a pure and dangerous type" and that "therefore our hope in Germany lay with the Christian Democrats and the Chancellor."[30] The problem, of course, was that Adenauer could not expect to remain in power if the German people came to believe that the SPD offered a more viable strategy for overcoming the restrictions imposed by the occupation powers. Adenauer wanted to sell himself to the allies as a moderate German committed to the same goals and values as the Western powers, yet he was well aware of the fact that he could not sell himself or the CDU to the German people in this fashion. Indeed, Adenauer's primary strategy for remaining in power was to convince the population that Schumacher's aims could be accomplished only through his policies of cooperation with the Western powers. If the Western powers wanted to help maintain in Germany a leader who would combat what he called the "cheap nationalist demands" of the SPD, Adenauer persuasively argued to them that it was in their self-interest to make every possible concession to his legitimate demands.

All of the Western powers recognized the force of Adenauer's logic and the dangers involved in Schumacher coming to power based on a program of German nationalism. Unfortunately, no matter how sincere Adenauer was about his desire for cooperation with the West, French officials were understandably reluctant about altering the occupation regime in ways that might ultimately serve to benefit Schumacher or somebody even worse. The demagoguery engaged in by many German politicians during the opening session of the Bundestag over the issue of dismantling factories left a distinctly negative impression about the future prospects of democracy and moderation in the Federal Republic. In addition, just as Adenauer's domestic situation forced him to demand concessions from the Western powers, French domestic politics made it very difficult to grant concessions. Even Jean Monnet, who was very sympathetic to the arguments Adenauer was putting forward about the need for France to treat the Germans with greater equality, recognized that French domestic politics made it very difficult to move forward. "So long as we remained locked into the postwar situation, in fact, a kind of crazy logic would make us repeat all the errors of the past."[31]

[30] For Acheson's comments, see the transcripts of the Princeton Seminars, October 10–11, 1953, 766, box 89, Acheson Papers, HSTL. See also the minutes of his meeting with Adenauer and Schumacher, *FRUS*, 1950, vol. 3, 308–14.

[31] Jean Monnet, *Memoirs* (Garden City: Doubleday & Company, 1978), 284. On Monnet's crucial role in postwar French politics, see John Gillingham, "Jean Monnet and the European

Like many American policymakers, Monnet believed that the sovereign state system was the structural cause of the "crazy logic" that made it so difficult for France and Germany to establish cooperative and mutually beneficial relations. Unlike American policymakers, however, Monnet had a specific proposal for permanently altering the dynamic of national rivalry that was both practical and revolutionary. In May 1950, when Franco-German relations were at a very low point, Monnet persuaded Schuman to put forward a plan calling for the pooling of Franco-German coal and steel production under the joint supervision of a European High Authority. Without at all slighting the idealistic and progressive elements that lay behind the Schuman Plan, the immediate aim of Monnet's proposal was to protect French economic interests and to create a more viable framework for controlling Germany.[32] Indeed, as Oliver Harvey, the British ambassador in France, insightfully noted at the time, the central purpose of the Schuman Plan was to replace the control of Germany by "repressive institutions" such as the International Ruhr Authority with cooperative institutions which the Germans might be persuaded to freely accept because they contained the promise of equal treatment.[33]

Adenauer was far too politically sophisticated not to realize the mixed motivations behind the Schuman Plan, but he warmly embraced it because he shared Monnet's conviction that the only permanent solution to legitimate concerns about German power were to be found in the integration of the Federal Republic into Western Europe on the basis of complete equality. He himself had previously put forward proposals along the same lines as the Schuman Plan, but it was far better for him politically that the proposal was of French origin. In the short term, the offer of an equal partnership provided him with a badly needed foreign policy triumph against Schumacher and validated the course he had pursued since the establishment of the Federal Republic. In the long run, Adenauer also thought that the Schuman Plan represented a decisive first step toward the creation of a European federation that could ultimately emerge as a "third force" in world affairs.[34] Although he might have increased his bargaining leverage by adopting a cautious attitude toward the French

Coal and Steel Community: A Preliminary Appraisal," in *Jean Monnet: The Path to European Unity*, ed. Douglas Brinkley and Clifford Hackett (London: Macmillan, 1991), 129–62.

[32] For the national interest calculations that lay underneath the Schuman Plan, see John Gillingham, *Coal, Steel, and the Rebirth of Europe, 1945–55* (New York: Cambridge University Press, 1991), 228–35; and A. W. Lovett, "The United States and the Schuman Plan: A Study in French Diplomacy, 1950–1952," *Historical Journal* 39 (1996): 425–55.

[33] Harvey to Younger, June 16, 1950, in *DBPO*, series 2, vol. 1, *The Schuman Plan, the Council of Europe and Western European Integration, May 1950–December 1952*, (London: Her Majesty's Stationery Office, 1986), 182–86 (quotation on 183).

[34] Konrad Adenauer, *Memoirs, 1945–53* (Chicago: Henry Regnery Company, 1966), 258–59; and Hans-Peter Schwarz, *Konrad Adenauer*, 505–6.

plan from the outset, Adenauer quickly informed Schuman and Monnet that Germany would enthusiastically support their initiative.

American officials were equally impressed by the possibilities opened up by the Schuman Plan. Averell Harriman thought that the plan might turn out to be "the most important step towards economic progress and peace of Europe since [the] original Marshall speech on ERP."[35] Dulles, who had long enjoyed a close relationship with Monnet, told Acheson that the Schuman Plan was exactly the type of arrangement for the Ruhr that he and Marshall had envisioned putting forward at the Moscow Conference of 1947. In Dulles's view, the Schuman Plan was "brilliantly creative and could go far to solve the most dangerous problem of our time, namely the relationship of Germany's industrial power to France and the West."[36] Acheson had even more reason to be impressed with the French proposal because he and his advisors had been searching in vain for some dramatic initiative that could reestablish Western momentum in the Cold War. Troubled by the current focus on dreary topics like the European Payments Union, Acheson wanted the State Department to come up with ideas for Europe that had more popular appeal since "there would be no holidays or torch-light parades in celebration of a payments union."[37] With its promise of permanently ending Franco-German conflict over the Ruhr, the Schuman Plan was far more than Acheson could have possibly hoped for from the French in 1950. Having taken the position during the debate over PPS/55 that American policy should be based on the assumption that the French could and would eventually seize the mantle of leadership in Western Europe, Acheson had every reason to feel personally vindicated by the Schuman Plan.[38]

THE KOREAN WAR AND NSC 68

The euphoria that prevailed within the Truman administration after the announcement of the Schuman Plan was brought to an abrupt halt with the outbreak of the Korean War on June 25, 1950. The conflict in Korea definitively ended the period of the Cold War in which considerations

[35] Harriman to Secretary of State, May 20, 1950, *FRUS*, 1950, vol. 3, 702.

[36] Dulles to Acheson, May 10, 1950, *FRUS*, 1950, vol. 3, 695–96 (quotation on 695). See also Dulles to Monnet, May 23, 1950, box 49, John Foster Dulles Papers, Seeley G. Mudd Library, Princeton University (hereafter JFD Princeton).

[37] Memorandum of Conversation of March 7, 1950, *FRUS*, 1950, vol. 3, 638–42 (quotation on 639).

[38] For Acheson's reaction to the Schuman Plan, see *Present at the Creation*, 382–89; Michael Hogan, "Dean Acheson and the Marshall Plan," in *Dean Acheson and the Making of U.S. Foreign Policy*, ed. Douglas Brinkley (New York: St. Martin's Press, 1993), 16; and Cabinet Meeting, May 19, 1950, box 1, Matthew J. Connelly Papers, HSTL.

about the military balance in Europe could be automatically assigned a much lower priority than the achievement of political objectives such as the improvement of Franco-German relations and Western European integration. Of course, the impact of the Korean War had the effect that it did because it reinforced the common perception that current policies were inadequate in the aftermath of the successful Soviet testing of an atomic bomb and the shattering of the atomic monopoly. Acheson and Paul Nitze, who had succeeded Kennan at Policy Planning, had already anticipated the need for major adjustments in policy before the Korean War, as seen by the wide-ranging review of policy that eventually culminated in the drafting of the National Security Council document NSC 68 in April 1950.[39] The concerns about Soviet intentions addressed by NSC 68 would have been quite compelling with or without the war, but, as many scholars have pointed out, it is quite likely that Truman would have resisted the massive expansion of the military budget envisioned by the authors of NSC 68 if it were not for the Korean War.[40]

Whether or not the Truman administration would have proposed the rearmament of Germany in the summer of 1950 if there had been no Korean War is perhaps the easiest of the many counterfactuals to address with confidence. The authors of NSC 68 did not propose the rearmament of Germany and there is a great deal of evidence to suggest that the Korean War led the Truman administration down a path that it would have otherwise postponed. To be sure, the American military establishment had been stepping up pressure on the State Department to alter its policy on German rearmament in the months before Korea. When asked to comment in late April on a proposed State Department protest against the militarization of the East German police by the Soviets, the JCS suggested that the administration should consider taking advantage of the opportunity presented to abandon its own restrictions on West German

[39] For the origins of NSC 68, see Samuel Wells, "Sounding the Tocsin: NSC-68 and the Soviet Threat," *International Security* 4 (fall 1979): 116–58; Joseph M. Siracusa, "NSC 68: A Reappraisal," *Naval War College Review* 33 (November–December 1980): 4–14; and Michael Hogan, *A Cross of Iron: Harry S. Truman and the Origins of the National Security State, 1945–54* (Cambridge: Cambridge University Press, 1998), 265–314. The document itself is published in *FRUS*, 1950, vol. 1, 234–92.

[40] For arguments that suggest Truman probably would have maintained the status quo in defense spending if not for Korea, see Ernest R. May, "The American Commitment to Germany, 1949–55," *Diplomatic History* 13 (fall 1989): 431–60; and Pollard, "Economic Security and the Origins of the Cold War: Bretton Woods, the Marshall Plan, and American Rearmament, 1944–50," *Diplomatic History* 9 (summer 1985): 286–89. While not at all denying the impact of the Korean War on the subsequent course of the Cold War, the following studies suggest that the administration would have pursued the course of NSC 68 with or without the conflict in Asia: Walter Lafeber, "NATO and the Korean War: A Context," *Diplomatic History* 13 (fall 1989): 461–78; and Melvyn P. Leffler, *A Preponderance of Power* (Stanford: Stanford University Press, 1992), 355–60.

rearmament.[41] In what was clearly an effort to force Truman and the State Department to reverse their position on Germany, Secretary of Defense Johnson forwarded the pro-rearmament views of the JCS to the National Security Council in early June 1950. Correctly recognizing that the primary arguments against German rearmament would be related to concerns about its effect on the French, the JCS bluntly recommended in NSC 71 that the State Department should consider applying political pressure in order to overcome French opposition.[42]

If it had not been for the outbreak of the Korean War, there is little evidence to suggest that Truman, Acheson, or the State Department bureaucracy would have suddenly found these arguments compelling. Truman was not at all pleased with the views contained in NSC 71, particularly when they were coupled with a cable from McCloy reporting that the British were stirring up the Germans on the rearmament question. Since Potsdam, Truman had rarely felt a need to directly intervene in German affairs, but open advocacy of rearmament by the British and the American military obviously touched a nerve. He denounced NSC 71 as "decidedly militaristic" and speculated that the British motivation for raising the issue was to destroy Western European unity by frightening the French.[43] Truman's sentiments were shared by Henry Byroade, Acheson's leading advisor on German affairs. As late as June 8, 1950, Byroade restated the State Department's standard position against German rearmament to John Ohly, an official in the Defense Department:

> There is nothing to hide in our policy concerning rearmament of Germany. We have no hidden motives such as the establishment of a police force as the beginning of an army in disguise. . . . Whether Germany could have such forces and be trusted not to become a menace depends on many things that are not yet worked out. . . . It is therefore premature in the opinion of the State Department for the question of German rearmament to be raised. We face in the next

[41] See Draft JCS Memorandum to the Secretary of Defense, April 30, 1950, Enclosure A in JCS 2124, in Records of the Joint Chiefs of Staff: Europe and NATO, reel 2 (hereafter RJCS: Europe and NATO with appropriate reel number). For a thorough examination of the archival evidence showing the military's growing determination to alter administration policy on German rearmament before Korea, see Joseph B. Egan, "The Struggle for the Soul of Faust: The American Drive for German Rearmament, 1950–55" (Ph.D. diss, University of Connecticut, 1985), 130–37.

[42] NSC 71, "Extracts of Views of the Joint Chiefs of Staff with Respect to Western Policy Toward Germany," June 8, 1950, *FRUS*, 1950, vol. 4, 686–87.

[43] See Truman's memos on these two issues in *FRUS*, 1950, vol. 4, 688–89 and McCloy's cable reporting on British activities, RG 59, 762A.5/6–1350, NA. Acheson was also alarmed at the reports of British activities and instructed McCloy and Douglas to inform the British that they were "seriously misinformed" if they thought the United States would support any arrangements they worked out with the Germans. See Acheson to McCloy, June 21, 1950, *FRUS*, 1950, vol. 4, 689–90; and RG 59, 762A.5/7–650, and 762A.5/7–850, NA.

year or 18 months a very critical period in Germany which we hope to guide in the right direction by our influence. Only under the most obvious and imminent threat would we desire to see the German uniform re-enter the picture during this period."[44]

Did Korea qualify as such an obvious and imminent threat? The initial reaction of the State Department to the outbreak of war in Korea suggests that neither Byroade nor Acheson immediately believed that the fighting in Asia made it essential to reverse course on Germany. In NSC 71/1, a paper drafted by Byroade shortly before the war and approved by Acheson in early July, the State Department reasserted its opposition to German rearmament. In addition to arguing that rearmament would impede the development of democracy in Germany, the State Department again emphasized the harmful effects that rearmament would have on the French. Although France had been moving rapidly forward in adopting progressive policies toward Germany, as shown by the Schuman Plan, the State Department believed that "this trend could be entirely reversed by an attempt on our part at this time to bring about the rearming of Germany."[45] However, for reasons that are still not very clear, Acheson reversed his course on the question of German rearmament over the next couple of weeks. By the end of July, he had convinced Truman that the question henceforth to be addressed by the administration was no longer whether to rearm Germany, but rather how to do so "without disrupting anything else we were doing and without putting Germany into a position to act as the balance of power in Europe."[46]

Acutely conscious of how difficult it would be to rearm Germany without alienating France, the State Department formulated a two-step strategy to accomplish Acheson's objectives. The first step was to bolster the American and British presence in Europe before directly raising the question of Germany's role in Western defense arrangements. German rearmament was inevitable, but the State Department wanted to avoid a tight

[44] Byroade to John Ohly, June 8, 1950, RG 59, Records of Western European Affairs: Miscellaneous German Files, box 8, NA. For Byroade's reluctance about rearming the Germans, see his superb oral history interview at the Truman library (1988). Byroade's timetable reflected the influence of McCloy's popular thesis that Western control over Germany was becoming a "wasting asset" that would not last for more than the next 18 months. See Minutes of Meetings of the NSC, reel 1. The wasting asset argument, of course, cut both ways. As one member of the Policy Planning Staff pointed out, since Germany was inevitably going to have some sort of police force and armed forces, it made sense to make a start while the Western powers could exert influence over the process. See Cannon to Nitze, June 14, 1950, PPS Records, box 16, NA.

[45] NSC 71/1, "Views of the State Department on the Rearmament of Western Germany," July 3, 1950, *FRUS*, 1950, vol. 4, 691–95.

[46] Memorandum of Conversation by Acheson, July 31, 1950, *FRUS*, 1950, vol. 3, 167–68. Schwartz is surely correct in arguing that McCloy's cables from Germany during this period played a large role in the reversal of policy. See Schwartz, *America's Germany*, 124–30.

and formal linkage between increasing the American presence and German rearmament. According to Lewis Douglas, U.S. ambassador to Great Britain, the prospect of German armed forces would become much more palatable to the rest of the alliance after the United States assumed overall command for Europe's defense, dispatched additional troops to the continent, and helped France rectify all of the deficiencies in its armed forces. When all of these measures had been completed—and not a moment before—Douglas thought the United States would then be in a position to consider proposing the rearmament of Germany to its allies. The sequence and the timing of the steps were of crucial importance for Douglas because "to plunge Germany into this matter too soon, before we have made our commitments and the French will to fight has been substantially encouraged, is hazardous business."[47]

Another way in which the State Department sought to overcome opposition to German rearmament was by placing its defense contribution firmly within the framework of a unified Western Europe. Starting from the premise that Germany could not and should not be allowed to rearm on a traditional nationalist basis, McCloy and David Bruce developed a complicated plan for including German contingents in what they called a "European Defense Force." Although understandably vague about the details of the proposed force, the State Department was convinced that a European institutional framework was the only way in which Germany could be safely rearmed. If the United States was willing to exert the leadership that would be necessary to gain support for the EDF, the State Department thought the Western Europeans would willingly make a partial surrender of sovereignty and the EDF could become "a driving force toward further unification in Western Europe."[48] In McCloy's view: "We should make certain that the European army is genuine and not merely a hollow shell or facade and that there are adequate safeguards against its later transformation into national forces. We should visualize this European Defense Force as a step on the road to European federation or integration."[49]

The American military establishment was vehemently opposed to the State Department's thinking about how to rearm Germany. In a fatally flawed application of logic, the JCS did not think that the rearmament of Germany would lead to political conflict within the alliance because "practically all of the military leaders of the Western European nations

[47] Douglas to Secretary of State, August 2, 1950, *FRUS*, 1950, vol. 3, 177–79 (quotation on 178–79).
[48] See Establishment of a European Defense Force, August 16, 1950, *FRUS*, 1950, vol. 3, 212–20 (quotation on 213); and McCloy to Secretary of State, August 3, 1950, 180–82. It is interesting to note that Nitze endorsed the idea of a European army but emphasized to Acheson that it would be better for the proposal to be made by the French rather than the United States. See Nitze to Acheson, August 8, 1950, PPS Records, box 28, NA.
[49] McCloy to Truman, September 10, 1950, box 178, PSF, HSTL.

[187]

have expressed themselves privately in favor of controlled rearmament of Western Germany."[50] Since the military did not believe that rearming Germany on an essentially national basis posed any serious problems, it is not surprising that they did not see any need for a European Defense Force. The JCS felt that the United States should not ask the rest of the European nations to surrender sovereignty in order to prevent Germany from rearming on a national basis. Rather, the JCS proposed, Germany's sovereign status should be raised within the alliance, albeit in a controlled fashion and under the auspices of NATO.[51] In addition, the military was unwilling to provide Acheson with any flexibility concerning the principle of German rearmament. With the full support of Louis Johnson, the JCS rejected the dispatch of additional American forces to Europe or the appointment of a Supreme Commander for NATO until the other members of the alliance had given their unambiguous consent to the principle of German rearmament. If the French could not be persuaded on the merits of the case, Omar Bradley told his British counterparts that they would simply have to be pressured into going along.[52]

The military had lost the vast majority of battles over German policy with the State Department since 1945, but this time its leverage was too much for even Acheson to overcome. Acheson thought the "one package" approach was a serious tactical mistake, but since he did not have the freedom to abandon it he pulled out all the stops to get the allies on board at the New York meeting of the North Atlantic Council (NAC) in September 1950. A master in the art of negotiating with allies, Acheson probably believed that he could sell the one package even with the rigid conditions on German rearmament imposed by the Pentagon. After all, Acheson was offering the NATO allies what he rightly described as a revolutionary departure in the history of American foreign policy. In exchange for the stationing of additional American forces in Europe and the appointment of a Supreme Commander, all that Acheson needed from the alliance was a commitment in principle that Germany would be allowed to contribute military units to the defense of Europe. Furthermore, he made it clear that he was very flexible on the timing and the conditions under which the process of rearming Germany would proceed. Having become convinced that German rearmament was an integral element in the defense of Europe, Acheson was willing to gamble that France and the rest of the NATO allies could be persuaded to reach the same conclusion.

---

[50] JCS 2124/9, Rearmament of Western Germany, July 20, 1950, RJCS: Europe and NATO, reel 2.

[51] See JSSC Draft Memorandum for the Secretary of Defense, September 1, 1950, in RJCS: Europe and NATO, reel 2.

[52] Lord Tedder to Chiefs of Staff, September 6, 1950, in *DBPO*, series 2, vol. 3, *German Rearmament: September–December 1950* (London: Her Majesty's Stationery Office, 1989), calendar 2i.

Acheson's gamble was only partially successful. He was able to sell the British on the merits of the one package proposal, which was not an inconsiderable achievement since even Bevin was far from convinced that the time was right to begin establishing German military units. Bevin was not opposed to the principle of rearmament, but he was concerned about alienating the French, putting the Germans into a strong bargaining position, and possibly provoking the Soviet Union into action before Western military strength had been restored.[53] As an intermediate step between doing nothing and rearming Germany, Bevin wanted the allies to create an effective Federal Gendarmerie composed of 100,000 volunteers that would replicate and be able to counter the East German *Bereitschaften*.[54] Explicitly given instructions that ruled out accepting the principle of German rearmament before he left for New York, Bevin was only able to convince the British cabinet to go along with the one package proposal after he assured cabinet members that Acheson would not bolster the American commitment to Europe without acceptance of rearmament.[55] Despite their doubts, Bevin and the vast majority of British officials concluded that the benefits of the American offer outweighed the misgivings they had about German rearmament. Long accustomed to hearing American military plans for liberating the continent after a Soviet invasion, the British military were ecstatic about the implicit shift in the American proposal from liberation to defense. According to Air Marshall William Elliot, the appointment of a supreme allied commander in Europe (SACEUR) and the stationing of additional forces represented a level of American commitment "far more than we could have ever hoped for."[56]

Selling German rearmament to the British, of course, was a much easier task than selling it to the French. Informed about the American proposal shortly before he left Paris for the New York meetings, Schuman had already warned Acheson that he should not put the rearmament question

[53] For Bevin's opposition to German rearmament, see "Record of a Meeting Held in the Secretary of State's Room, August 21, 1950," calendar 3i; and D.O. (50) 66, "German Association With the Defence of the West," August 29, 1950, calendar 3i, both in *DBPO*, series 2, vol. 3; and Bevin to Acheson, September 4, 1950, *FRUS*, 1950, vol. 3, 264–66.

[54] For the rationale behind creating a counterpart to the Bereitschaften rather than an army, see Minute by Mr. Mallett, September 12, 1950, *DBPO*, series 2, vol. 3, 32–34. Opinions within the American government to the British proposal were mixed. McCloy disliked the idea but some officials in the PPS thought the British proposal was superior to the EDF concept. See McCloy memo of September 7, 1950, RG 59, Records of Western European Affairs: Miscellaneous German Files, box 8, NA; and Cannon and Marshall to Nitze, September 6, 1950, RG 59, Records of the Bureau of European Affairs, Lot File 55 D 258, box 1, NA.

[55] See Attlee to Bevin, September 14, 1950, 44–45, and "Extracts From a Cabinet Meeting of September 15, 1950," both in *DBPO*, series 2, vol. 3, 58–61.

[56] Memorandum by Air Marshall Sir W. Elliot, October 19, 1950, *DBPO*, series 2, vol. 3, 174–79 (quotation on 178).

on the NAC agenda because to do so would only publicize allied differences over Germany.[57] Schuman was not lacking in substantive reasons for opposing a decision in principle to rearm Germany, but unlike Acheson he did not approach the issue as an exercise in logic in which the benefits of the American package were coolly weighed against the disadvantages. The fact that Acheson could offer counterarguments or safeguards against Germany were of little importance because Schuman maintained that no French government could remain in power if it sanctioned the principle of rearmament. Since it was not possible to alter the realities of French domestic politics, and since it would take a considerable period of time before Germany could be rearmed in any event, Schuman suggested that the question be postponed until French public opinion could be swayed.[58] If France were forced to make an immediate decision on the principle of German rearmament, Schuman prophetically warned Acheson and Bevin, "everything might go wrong."[59]

Schuman was actually far more sympathetic to Acheson's arguments than many of his fellow cabinet members, including Defense Minister Jules Moch. Brought to New York by Schuman in order to explore possible ways out of the impasse, Moch made it clear that he and the French cabinet were unwilling to accept the principle of German rearmament. Moch also emphasized the parliamentary difficulties that would be involved in accepting the American proposal, yet he did so in a manner that led Bevin and others to conclude that domestic politics was simply a "pretext" invoked to justify his own opposition to rearming Germany.[60] Declaring that the Germans could not be trusted to remain a loyal member of the alliance, Moch let it be known to British officials that he would not be susceptible to either threats or inducements on the question of rearmament. According to a British military official, Moch told him "if the Americans insisted on making German re-armament a condition of the help they were offering, he would prefer to forego both, and content himself with five instead of ten French divisions, and place these on the French Frontier instead of in Germany."[61]

The professional diplomats of the Quai d' Orsay were also opposed to German rearmament. Underlying all of their specific criticisms of the American proposal was a general skepticism that the Western powers would be able to control Germany after it was rearmed. Arguing that the Germans would always be primarily guided by their interest in unifica-

[57] Bruce to Secretary of State, September 5, 1950, *FRUS*, 1950, vol. 3, 267–68.
[58] For Schuman's arguments against German rearmament, see *FRUS*, 1950, vol. 3, 296, 299–300, 312, 342; and *DBPO*, series 2, vol. 3, 69.
[59] See British record of conversation in *DBPO*, series 2, vol. 3, 35–36 (quotation on 36).
[60] Bevin to Attlee, September 26, 1950, in ibid., 104.
[61] Moch conversation with Air Marshall Elliot, cited in ibid., 104. For a good synopsis of Moch's position, see *FRUS*, 1950, vol. 3, 384, 1412–16.

tion, Rene Massigli feared that the Germans would eventually drag the rest of the alliance into a preventive war against the Soviet Union.[62] Another French official claimed that France simply could not trust the Germans to adhere to any restrictions placed on them or the United States to continue to enforce any restrictions in the future.

> Whatever was said now as to the number of German divisions, he was sure that in two years Germany would have the largest army in Europe and would be in a position to dictate to us once more. He said it was inevitable that they would have a General Staff whatever was said now. In four years time Western Germany, having recovered her strength and freedom, would naturally concentrate on the restoration of German unity. That might involve us in either of two ways. The Germans might seek to detach themselves and threaten to go over to the East if we did not support them, or alternatively, they would push us into an aggressive war for the restitution of the lost provinces.[63]

It is not at all surprising that Acheson was unable to overcome such fundamental objections to the principle of German rearmament in the space of two weeks. What is surprising is the fact that he suspended his better judgment and attempted to do so in the first place. As remarkable as it may seem, given the fact that a French rejection of the principle of German rearmament was very predictable, neither Acheson nor the State Department bureaucracy seems to have given any prior thought to the serious consequences involved if the French continued to hold out. First, after all of the publicity surrounding the meetings in New York, it was no longer possible to put the German rearmament question back into a box until the United States and France resolved their differences in private. Second, Adenauer, who would probably have been content with the establishment of a Federal Gendarmerie, as the British proposed, was now left in a very vulnerable position vis-à-vis the Social Democrats and other opponents of German rearmament. Third, despite the fact that an increased American presence in Germany and the appointment of a supreme commander would have made it easier for both Adenauer and Schuman to win over their opponents, Acheson was now unable to do anything until the French had given their consent in some form. Much of the alliance diplomacy of the next four years can be seen as an attempt to

---

[62] See Minute from Mr. Schuckburgh to Sir R. Makins, September 21, 1950; and Memorandum of Conversation by Ernest Davies, September 29, 1950, both in *DBPO*, series 2, vol. 3, 84–85 and calendar 54i.

[63] Harvey to Foreign Office, October 1, 1950, *DBPO*, series 2, vol. 3, calendar 54i.

recover from the damage caused by the premature effort to sell the one package proposal in September 1950.[64]

THE PLEVEN PLAN FOR A EUROPEAN ARMY

Mutually acceptable compromises to the impasse over German rearmament were not immediately obvious to any of the participants after the failure in New York. Both U.S. and French officials believed that the only way out was for the other side to accept some face-saving compromise that conceded the substance of the dispute. Overlooking the fact that his country was in a minority of one, Moch told British officials that their government should do all it could "to save the face of the United States" since he would break apart the coalition government rather than accept the principle of German rearmament.[65] Although some British officials agreed that the inability of any French government to gain the approval of the National Assembly made it more logical to work on modifying the American position, the dominant line of thought within the Foreign Office was that Britain should do nothing which might lead Acheson to withdraw his offer. Since the French were operating from such a weak bargaining position, the British cabinet did not believe that they would be able to maintain their stance against the rest of the NATO alliance for very long.[66]

Acheson himself was also fairly confident that the French would withdraw their opposition to German rearmament before the next meeting of the NATO Defense Committee, which was postponed until the end of October in order to give Schuman more time to come up with a solution. However, Acheson also seems to have been preparing the groundwork for the abandonment of the one package proposal in the event that the French were still unable to agree. After the firing of Defense Secretary Johnson, Acheson possessed more flexibility to maneuver around the conditions of the one package. As early as October 10, Acheson told Robert Lovett that it was "probable" that a final solution to German rearmament would not be found by the deadline but that "steps should be taken so that we are on the road toward finding the solution."[67] Six days later, Acheson suggested to George Marshall, who had replaced Johnson as Secretary of Defense, that the United States might not want to delay the establishment of the integrated force in the event that the French were still

[64] Acheson himself frankly acknowledges his mistake in going along with the one package proposal in *Present at the Creation*, 437–40.

[65] See Harvey to Bevin, October 7, 1950, *DBPO*, series 2, vol. 3, 155.

[66] See Minute by Mr. Young; and Notes of an Informal Meeting at No. 10 Downing Street, October 20, 1950, both in *DBPO*, series 2, vol. 3, 186–89.

[67] Memorandum by Acheson, October 10, 1950, *FRUS*, 1950, vol. 3, 1950, 368.

holding out, particularly if it seemed likely that they would be able to agree within a short period of time.[68] Rather than specify exactly what the French had to do to in order to comply with the one package proposal, Acheson wanted the French themselves to come up with an alternative proposal for rearming the Germans.

The French did come up with their own proposal for rearming Germany. But instead of accepting the framework of the American proposal with a few minor alterations and a few more safeguards, which is what Acheson was undoubtedly hoping for, the French vastly complicated matters by presenting an entirely new framework for rearming Germany. On October 24, 1950, shortly before the NATO meetings were scheduled to resume, Premier René Pleven delivered a speech to the National Assembly calling for the creation of a European army based on the same supranational principles as the Schuman Plan. According to Pleven, France and each of the other participants would allocate part of their forces to a European army, which would be supervised by an overarching political superstructure composed of a Defense Minister, a larger Council of Ministers, and a European Parliament. In order to ensure the European character of the force, the French proposed that integration of the participating national forces would take place at the "smallest possible unit," which the French somewhat comically suggested should be at the level of a battalion.[69] Pleven and other French officials promised that their proposal offered the most rapid way of obtaining a German defense contribution, but also made it clear that any negotiations to establish a European army would have to wait until after the conclusion of negotiations over the Schuman Plan.[70]

Stripped of the appeals to collective security and the unity of Europe, the explicit purpose of the Pleven Plan was to prevent the creation of a national German army and a supporting defense establishment, both of which Pleven argued would inevitably lead to a revival of militarism. Although the authors of the plan, such as Monnet and Schuman, did believe that Germany could make a defense contribution if it were under the control of a supranational authority, the common denominator behind support for the plan among French officials was that it would delay any decision on German rearmament for the immediate future. Because the Pleven Plan offered the promise of infinite delay in rearming Germany, it was acceptable to Moch and other French officials who wanted to prevent

---

[68] Acheson to Marshall, October 16, 1950, *FRUS*, 1950, vol. 3, 381–82.

[69] The text of the Pleven Plan is printed in Margaret Carlyle, ed., *Documents on International Affairs 1949–50* (London: Oxford University Press, 1953), 339–44.

[70] For Pleven's conditions, see RG 59, 762A.5/10–2650, NA. The importance placed on the prior conclusion of the Schuman Plan negotiations undoubtedly came from Monnet, who told McCloy as early as September 14, 1950, that national rearmament would wreck the negotiations over the ECSC and lead to the return of Germany's "traditional temptations." See RG 59, 762A.5/9–1450, NA.

any form of German rearmament. It was also acceptable to the National Assembly, which approved the Pleven Plan by a vote of 348 to 224. However, the real significance of the vote was in the concurrent resolution passed by the Assembly noting its approval of the government's "determination not to permit the creation of a German army and General Staff."[71] As G. H. Soutou argues, in approving the Pleven Plan the National Assembly was casting "a vote *against* the rearmament of Germany rather than *for* the European Army."[72]

The Pleven Plan had many different purposes, but none of them were designed to facilitate the process of German rearmament. Privately, some French officials let their British counterparts know that the proposal should not be taken too seriously. According to one official in the French embassy, the Pleven Plan "if carried out on the basis which the French Assembly had been led to understand, would be military and political nonsense."[73] Another described the plan as a "canard" which the French "had been forced to let loose in the face of American impetuosity. . . . In fact it was so obviously full of difficulties that his government might be quite glad to find some alternative which would satisfy their fears about German rearmament."[74] Massigli admitted that France believed Germany could only be rearmed safely within the framework of Europe, but acknowledged that the more immediate purpose of the plan was to devise "a measure of self-protection against American pressure."[75]

French diplomats do not seem to have spoken to their American counterparts with the same degree of candor they exhibited in their conversations with the British. Nevertheless, the Pleven Plan was so transparently designed to postpone any form of German rearmament that Acheson immediately understood why the French had proposed it and what it was meant to accomplish. Informed of the rough contours of the French pro-

---

[71] *New York Times,* October 26, 1950, 3.

[72] Soutou, "France and the German Rearmament Problem," 499. See also Pierre Guillen, "France and the Defense of Western Europe: From the Brussels Pact (March 1948) to the Pleven Plan (October 1950)," in *The Western Security Community, 1948–50,* ed. Norbert Wiggershaus and Roland G. Foerster (Providence, R.I.: Berg Publishers, 1993), 125–48.

[73] Memorandum of Conversation between M. Lebel and A. Gilchrist, October 25, 1950, *DBPO,* series 2, vol. 3, calendar 84i.

[74] Memorandum of Conversation between M. de Crouy Chanel and Pierson Dixon, October 26, 1950, *DBPO,* series 2, vol. 3, calendar 84i.

[75] Memorandum of Conversation between Massigli and Dixon, October 30, 1950, *DBPO,* series 2, vol. 3, calendar 84i. After a meeting with Monnet, Pleven, and Schuman on October 27, McCloy cabled Acheson that he felt the French were sincerely attempting to find a way to rearm Germany. See RG 59, 762A.5 10–2650 and 762A.5/10–2850, NA. Concerned that the French might have "pulled a certain amount of wool over Mr. McCloy's eyes as regards the purity of their motives in advancing the Pleven proposals," the British Foreign Office let American officials know exactly what Massigli and Lebel had told them about the purpose of the plan. See Trimble to Laukhuff, enclosing "French Embassy Views on East-West Relations," November 2, 1950, RG 59, 762A.5/11–250, NA.

posal by Bohlen on October 15, Acheson instructed him to tell Schuman that their proposed solution would not be acceptable to the United States because it envisioned postponing any action on German rearmament for much too long.[76] In stark contrast to the enthusiastic reception that had been given to the Schuman Plan, Acheson and other officials did not express any great optimism about the Pleven Plan. Leaving aside the question of timing, Acheson was very critical of the substance of the French plan because of its obvious military defects and its discrimination against Germany. Although the Germans might be willing to join a European army based on equality among the participating states, Acheson argued, there was no chance they would accept an organization "where they are openly, in fact blatantly, labeled as inferiors."[77]

Acheson's opposition to the Pleven Plan only increased when Moch made it clear on a trip to Washington that France was only prepared to discuss the question of German rearmament within the framework approved by the National Assembly. Sending Moch to sell the Pleven Plan to the alliance was foolish because his presentation certainly did not convey an impression that the proposal was serious or feasible.[78] If nothing else, his intransigent defense of the Pleven Plan solidified support within the rest of NATO for the one-package proposal. Rather than leading the charge against the French proposal, Acheson and Marshall decided to let the other members of the alliance raise their own objections. With the exception of Belgium and Luxembourg, every other member explicitly rejected the French plan, viewing it as a nonviable basis for rearming Germany. The British, who might have been able to moderate some of the criticism directed at the French, were particularly brutal in rejecting the Pleven Plan. Arguing that no military expert could find the French plan satisfactory, British Defense Minister Emanuel Shinwell claimed that the Pleven Plan "would only excite laughter and ridicule in USSR." In Acheson's view, even if it were to have the full diplomatic support of the United States, the concept of a European army would be impossible to sell to the rest of the alliance after Moch's dismal presentation.[79]

[76] See Bohlen to Secretary of State, October 15, 1950; and Acheson to Embassy in France, October 17, 1950, *FRUS*, 1950, vol. 3, 377–80, 384–85.

[77] Acheson to the Embassy in France, October 27, 1950, *FRUS*, 1950, vol. 3, 410–12 (quotation on 412).

[78] Sincere advocates of a European army warned Bruce in advance that Moch might alienate the rest of the alliance in defending the Pleven Plan because he did not really believe in the concept. See Bruce Memorandum of Conversation with Paul Devinat, RG 59, 762A.5/10–2750, NA. Devinat was later sent to the United States by Schuman in order to "counteract the miserable impressions created by Jules Moch." See RG 59, 751/11–1750, and Memorandum of Conversation between Devinat and Jessup, December 2, 1950, RG 59, Lot 53 D 211, Office Files of Philip Jessup, box 2, NA.

[79] See *FRUS*, 1950, vol. 3, 415–32 (quotation on 420); and Memorandum of Conversation between Acheson and Marshall, October 27, 1950, box 67, Acheson Papers, HSTL.

The most important candidate for membership in any European army was also unenthusiastic about the Pleven Plan. As Acheson had predicted, the Germans were not willing to accept the inferior position assigned to them in the French proposal. Despite his enthusiasm for European unity, Adenauer immediately instructed one of his advisors to inform Schuman that he was very disappointed with the discrimination against the Germans contained in the French plan.[80] According to General Hays, Adenauer was also worried about the lack of any provision for U.S. participation and leadership in the proposed European army because he was "quite sure" that the Europeans could never resolve the difficulties involved in the project by themselves.[81] Regardless of the substance of the plan, which conceivably could have been improved through negotiations, Adenauer simply did not believe that German rearmament could have been postponed until the institutional framework of a united Europe was in place. Like Acheson and the authors of NSC 68, Adenauer thought that Western Europe had a very limited period of time in which to build up its defenses. In his view, the "period of grace" provided by American superiority in atomic weapons "should be exploited to utmost in building Western defense. . . . Germany should make just contribution to Western defense in order to make Russian land attack as risky as possible."[82] In a speech to the Bundestag on November 8, Adenauer welcomed the Pleven Plan as a contribution to European integration, but he also suggested that discussions about the plan should not be allowed to stand in the way of more immediate measures aimed at improving Western defenses against the Soviets.[83]

The importance Adenauer placed on the speedy resolution of the rearmament question had as much to do with internal German politics as it did with the overall strategic situation. Adenauer had hoped that Schumacher and the SPD would put aside partisan politics in the debate over rearmament, but this proved to be an illusory hope. Schumacher's position on rearmament reflected both sincerely held views about Western military strategy and an opportunistic desire to exploit the situation in order to weaken Adenauer and the CDU. At the strategic level, Schumacher argued that Germany could not even begin to safely rearm until the Western powers had vastly increased their military forces and

[80] Herbert Blankenhorn diary entry of October 25, 1950, published in Herbert Blankenhorn, *Verständnis und Verständigung: Blätter eines Politischen Tagebuchs 1949 bis 1979* (Frankfurt/Main: Propyläen Verlag, 1980), 115–16.

[81] Hays to McCloy, RG 59, 762A.5/10–2850, NA.

[82] Adenauer's views were reported by McCloy in RG 59, 762A.00/10–1150, NA. The timing was crucial for Adenauer. See RG 59, 762A.00/10–1350, NA.

[83] The text of Adenauer's speech to the Bundestag on November 8, 1950, is contained in RG 59, 762A.00/11–1350, NA. Adenauer actually asked McCloy if he should endorse the French proposal before making the speech. McCloy told him not to because it was impractical in its present form. See RG 59, 762A.5/11–850, NA.

adopted a strategic concept based on an offensive war of movement in the East. At the domestic level, Schumacher stated that the SPD would not go along with rearmament until the Bundestag had sanctioned its legality and new elections had been held.[84] Schumacher's guiding premise was that Germany was in a favorable position to extract concessions from the Western powers and that Adenauer would have to make concessions to him in order to gain the necessary support from the SPD. Already faced with opposition to rearmament from pacifists within his own party, Adenauer recognized from the start that the opposition of Schumacher and the SPD was going to make it very difficult to gain popular and legislative support for rearmament.[85]

Indications that the German people were receptive to the SPD line on rearmament made Schumacher's position particularly ominous for both Adenauer and the Western powers. Local elections in Germany held shortly after the Bundestag debate had registered gains for the SPD and U.S. officials attributed the result at least partially to the fact that the SPD was able to win over both pacifists and those who demanded greater equality and other concessions as a precondition of rearmament. Although the results were by no means a clear repudiation of either Adenauer or the CDU, they did make it clear that the German people could not be counted on to enthusiastically support rearmament. Even worse, some U.S. officials feared that Schumacher had successfully sold the idea that Adenauer was more concerned with pleasing the allies on the rearmament question than with defending German interests. "The recent elections have suggested that a large segment of the German public view Adenauer as a Manipulator more identified with Allied pressures upon German participation than the interests of the German people."[86]

---

[84] See Memorandum of Conversation between Carlson and Waldemar Von Kneeringen, RG 59, 762A.5/10–450, NA; Schumacher's speech to the Bundestag of November 8, 1950, RG 59, 762A.00/11–1350, NA; the U.S. High Commissioner for Germany (HICOG) report entitled "The Developing Coalition against German Rearmament," RG 59, 762A.5/11–15550, NA; and Schumacher's memorandum on rearmament sent to Adenauer in February 1951, RG 59, 762A.5/4–2051, NA. For an excellent secondary analysis of Schumacher's and SPD views, see Drummond, *German Social Democrats in Opposition,* 44–50.

[85] Adenauer was also very worried throughout this period about the possibility that Schumacher's negative stance might encourage isolationist sentiment and lead the United States to abandon its plans for strengthening NATO. For his concerns about American public opinion, see Memorandum of Conversation between Byroade and Krekeler, RG 59, 762A.00/11–1550, NA. In contrast, Schumacher felt free to adopt uncompromising positions because he did not take the threat of renewed isolationism seriously: "The retreat of the United States from Europe is a dangerous propaganda formula which fails as an instrument to exert pressure on the German people. . . . There is no American policy which would be in a position to abandon Europe. America's world leadership and her position with respect to communism would not allow such a course." See RG 59, 762A.5/4–2051, NA.

[86] See Sims to Byroade, "Presentation to the Germans," RG 59, 762A.00/12–150, NA; and McCloy's analysis of the elections in RG 59, 762A.00/11–2950 and 762A.00/12–550, NA.

Not surprisingly, Adenauer sought to eliminate the effectiveness of the SPD's appeal to nationalist sentiments by putting forward his own "preconditions" for German rearmament. In an Aide-Memoire presented to the High Commissioners on November 16, Adenauer spelled out the numerous concessions that the allies would have to make in order for him to gain popular support for rearmament. Among other things, Adenauer wanted the occupation statute replaced by a system of contractual arrangements, a reduction in occupation costs, an immediate halt to dismantling, and an end to war crimes trials.[87] The Western powers themselves wanted to move progressively in this direction, although they certainly did not want to do so under conditions and a timetable set by either Adenauer or Schumacher. However, as much as they would have appreciated it if Adenauer had refrained from placing political conditions on German rearmament, both the Americans and the British realized that he had little choice since the SPD was determined to attack him because he was selling out Germany's national interests and accepting an inferior status within the alliance. As one British official correctly noted, the dynamic of the internal debate over rearmament would inevitably force the Western powers to make even more rapid and sweeping concessions to Germany: "Yesterday's elections in South Germany, while they strengthen Schumacher's hand against Adenauer, also strengthen Adenauer's hand against us—he can now say to us 'You see what I mean. Unless I have big concessions to bribe them with, how can I win such people over to the need for German rearmament.' "[88]

Acheson was distressed by the developments in Germany, but it took the military disaster at the Yalu River on the North Korean border with China in late November 1950 before he moved decisively to end the conflict with the French over rearmament. The reversal of fortunes in Asia and the prospect of a delay in sending American forces to the continent made it imperative to work out an acceptable compromise with the French that would allow him to appoint Eisenhower supreme commander before the situation in Europe deteriorated even further. Referring directly to the tragic events in Korea, Acheson urged Schuman to accept as quickly as possible a proposal that had been put forward by Charles Spofford, the American representative on the NAC. The essence of the Spofford Plan consisted of an agreement that the French would permit the immediate raising of German troops up to the level of a regimental combat team (RCT). No one believed that RCTs were a viable military unit, but Acheson did not want to hold up a solution because of France's unwillingness to accept full German army divisions. In exchange for France accepting the principle of German rearmament, Acheson agreed to

[87] See *FRUS*, 1950, vol. 4, 780–84.
[88] See Minute by A. G. Gilchrist, November 21, 1950, *DBPO*, series 2, vol. 3, calendar 103i.

appoint a supreme commander and to support French efforts to organize a European army conference in Paris.[89] Despite the fact that Bevin was furious at the United States for agreeing to back the French on the European army, which he thought was a potential "cancer on the Atlantic body," the Spofford Plan was formally accepted by the NAC in late December.[90]

The Spofford Plan represented Acheson's final retreat from the one package proposal. In return for the revolutionary commitment to station additional troops in Europe and to appoint an American SACEUR, Acheson had received in exchange little more than the right to directly negotiate the terms of rearmament with the Germans. Although the Spofford Plan allowed for the immediate raising of troops up to the level of RCTs, the provisions were irrelevant because Adenauer had already publicly announced before the plan was even adopted that he would not rearm under the discriminatory conditions agreed to by the alliance.[91] As much as Adenauer wanted to move ahead with rearmament, internal German politics made it impossible for him to comply with the Spofford Plan. Indeed, in the aftermath of the German elections and the reversal suffered by U.S. forces at the Yalu, virtually every intelligence assessment concluded that if Adenauer wanted to remain in power he would have no choice but to ask for concessions far more extensive than the Western powers were willing to grant at the time.[92]

Acheson and his State Department advisors were well aware of the reality that Adenauer would not leap at the chance to rearm in accordance with the Spofford Plan, but this objective had become far less important after the unexpected turn of events in Korea. Actually, the prospect of deferring German rearmament for a period of time was now viewed positively by many American and British officials. One of the main reasons behind this change in perspective can be attributed to the fact that the Yalu disaster led American and British officials to take more seriously the

---

[89] For the provisions of the Spofford Plan, see *FRUS, 1950,* vol. 3, 457–64; and Doris M. Condit, *The Test of War, 1950–53* (Washington, D.C.: Government Printing Office, 1988), 327–35. A regimental combat team consisted of 6,000 men, which was generally considered to be one-third of a division.

[90] While everyone reassured him that he should not worry about American support for the European Army because it remained highly unlikely that the French would be successful in their efforts, Bevin was worried that the French might succeed. See Memorandum by Bevin, November 24, 1950, *DBPO,* series 2, vol. 3, 291–96 (quotation on 293).

[91] Kirkpatrick to Bevin, December 12, 1950, *DBPO,* series 2, vol. 3, 354–55; and CAB 129/43, C.P. (50) 311, "German Participation in the Defence of Western Europe," December 12, 1950, *Cabinet Papers.*

[92] This assessment of Adenauer's domestic predicament was shared by the CIA, HICOG, and military sources. See CIA/RR 37–50, "The Political Implications of West German Military Contributions to Western European Defense," December 11, 1950, box 251, PSF, HSTL; McCloy to Secretary of State, RG 59, 762A.00/12–850, NA; and CINCAFE to COF, RG 59, 762A.00 (W) 12–1550 and 762A.00 (W) 12–2950, NA.

Soviet Union's warning that they would not tolerate West German rearmament.[93] By promising to postpone German rearmament until after NATO forces had been strengthened, the Spofford Plan lessened the danger that the Soviets might launch a preventive attack in Europe. Of equal importance, Acheson hoped that a more relaxed approach to German rearmament would reduce West Germany's bargaining leverage in the upcoming political and military negotiations. As he told policymakers at a Cabinet meeting in early December, "Germans now feel they are the key to Western Europe and have gotten to feel that we will have to make concessions to them. It is important now to let them stew for a time."[94]

THE ORIGINS OF THE EUROPEAN DEFENSE COMMUNITY

The institutional form of German rearmament was one of the more important conflicts which had been papered over with NATO's acceptance of the Spofford Plan. The fundamental question to be decided was whether Germany would be armed on an essentially nationalist basis within NATO or whether it would be rearmed within a supranational, European framework. In order to reach an acceptable compromise with France, Acheson agreed to support verbally the convening of a European army conference in Paris, while the French agreed to accept direct negotiations over the terms of rearmament between the High Commissioners and the Federal Republic at Petersberg. Although the rest of the alliance went along with the idea of a European army conference, very few policymakers believed the French would have very much success in the Paris negotiations. Even before the publication of Acheson's letter to Schuman expressing support for the European army conference, the State Department was establishing the outer limits of American support. First,

---

[93] The heightened awareness of the dangers of rearming Germany before NATO had been strengthened can be seen in a memo prepared by Perry Laukhuff, director of the Office of German Political Affairs, in early December. Laukhuff asked a question that had been remarkably absent from American thinking before the Chinese attack at the Yalu River: "What right, when you come down to it, have we to think that the Russians will sit by while we rearm Western Germany? . . . Certainly, in our present state of weakness in Europe we have no forces with which to protect the process of rearmament in Germany. Perhaps it does make more sense to conduct German rearmament only after we have built up a strong army in Europe." See Laukhuff to Byroade, RG 59, 762A.5/12–550, NA.

[94] Cabinet Meeting, December 6, 1950, box 1, Matthew J. Connelly Papers, HSTL. As Acheson explained to the Senate Foreign Relations Committee, "Once you get a German thinking that he is the most important person in the world, then the whole progress of rearmament and the whole progress of defense and rearmament in Europe depends on him, you have done yourself a great disservice. You have to make him think it doesn't make a bit of difference what he does. Then he will make more sense." See Acheson testimony before the Senate Foreign Relations Committee, December 9, 1950, in *Reviews of the World Situation*, 417. For Eisenhower's and Lovett's views, see *FRUS*, 1950, vol. 3, 578–80.

Acheson informed American officials stationed abroad that they should not put any pressure on the other members of the alliance to go along with the French plan. Second, Acheson reiterated his determination to raise German troops up to the level of RCTs as soon as agreement was reached at Petersberg, regardless of how the European army conference was proceeding.[95] In short, American support for the French basically ended with the publication of Acheson's letter to Schuman: the French would have to win over Germany and the rest of the alliance on their own. As Robert Hooker, an official on the Policy Planning Staff correctly noted, all of the qualifications and conditions being erected by the State Department did not reflect very much enthusiasm for the lofty objectives sought by the French: "Thus, although the Secretary's letter implies some sort of political union, we apparently propose either not to say what we meant, or to say that we meant much less than our words seemed to mean."[96]

Acheson's lukewarm support for the European army concept might have led to renewed conflict with France if the Germans had shown any willingness to accept the interim program for rearmament provided for in the Spofford Plan. However, the negotiations at Petersberg quickly confirmed that Adenauer was not bluffing when he declared that Germany would not accept the Spofford Plan as an interim or permanent basis for rearmament. As Theodore Blank, Adenauer's chief representative at Petersberg, told the High Commissioners, in order for Germany to begin the process of rearmament, certain "preconditions" would have to be met by the Western powers. The most important precondition, of course, was that the occupation regime would have to be transformed into a set of contractual agreements that substantially restored Germany's sovereignty in both domestic and foreign affairs. Once this condition was satisfied and the Bundestag had approved the terms of any agreement reached with the Western powers, Germany would be willing to rearm as long as its armed forces were treated on the basis of full equality with the

---

[95] For the efforts within the State Department to qualify American support for the European army concept in early 1951, see *FRUS, 1950*, vol. 3, 755–59, 760–62, 764. The French had made publication of an official letter of American support for the European army conference a condition of their acceptance of the Spofford Plan.

[96] Robert Hooker to Paul Nitze, January 23, 1951, PPS Records, box 28, NA. Interestingly, given the widespread association of the PPS throughout this period with hardline policies, Hooker and other PPS officials such as John Ferguson were advocating a very cautious approach to German rearmament because of the possibility of a Soviet response. See NIE-17, "Probable Soviet Reactions to a Remilitarization of Germany," December 27, 1950, and NIE-4, "Soviet Courses of Action with Respect to Germany," February 1, 1951, both in box 253, PSF, HSTL; Robert Hooker, "A Proposed Policy towards Western Germany and Western Europe Assuming Failure of the Council of Foreign Ministers," January 12, 1951, PPS Records, box 28, NA; and John Ferguson, "Some Proposals for Our Policy Re: Germany," January 5, 1951, PPS Records, box 16, NA.

other members of the alliance in "organization, armament, and command structures."[97]

The emphasis placed by the Germans during the Petersberg negotiations on political and military equality ruled out any interim solution based on the formation of small regimental combat teams—either as a transitional or permanent arrangement. When asked by the High Commissioners if the Germans would be willing to form RCTs if they were treated on the basis of equality in every other respect, Blank responded that he would reconsider the merits of the smaller units only when the rest of the members of NATO demonstrated a similar willingness to restructure their own divisions into RCTs.[98] In rejecting RCTs as both politically unacceptable and militarily ineffective, the Germans were well aware of the fact that they had an unassailable case, since the military establishments of all of the Western powers considered the division the smallest viable unit for organizing combat forces. Indeed, General Hans Speidel effectively made the case for the creation of German divisions by quoting extensively from the American military's own field manual.[99] The emphasis on equality and military efficiency also ruled out the entire concept of a European army as the French understood it because Speidel explicitly rejected the view that divisions could be created by combining forces from several nations. According to Speidel, simply supplying mixed divisions would present a logistical nightmare because "Bavarians would want sauerkraut and beer, French troops white bread and red wine, and Italians spaghetti and chianti."[100]

Given his interest in solidifying Germany's integration into the West as quickly as possible in early 1951, Adenauer might have instructed his negotiators at Petersberg to moderate their stance if the Western powers demonstrated any real interest in reaching a compromise. However, for quite different reasons, none of the Western powers had any burning desire to speed up the pace of the negotiations with the Federal Republic in early 1951. This was obviously the case with the French, but it was also true for both Great Britain and the United States.[101] Having already secured the appointment of Eisenhower as supreme commander, and still very concerned about the possibility of provoking the Soviets before ad-

[97] Hays to Secretary of State, January 17, 1951, *FRUS,* 1950, vol. 3, 993–96 (quotation on 994).
[98] Hays to Secretary of State, February 17, 1951, *FRUS,* 1951, vol. 3, 1016–20 (quotation on 1019).
[99] Hays to Secretary of State, January 27, 1951, *FRUS,* 1951, vol. 3, 999. For an American criticism of both RCTs and mixed divisions that parallels Speidel's views in virtually every respect, see JCS 2073/95, "Military Aspects of German Participation in the Defense of Western Europe," November 29, 1950, RJCS: Europe and NATO, reel 5.
[100] See Hays to Secretary of State, March 2, 1951, *FRUS,* 1951, vol. 3, 1024.
[101] Adenauer and other German officials tended to blame only the British and the French for the slow pace of negotiations. See the bitter comments made by Adenauer to Joseph Alsop, *FRUS,* 1951, vol. 3, 1026–27.

ditional American forces had been sent to Europe, the British were now quite content to drag out negotiations with the Germans for as long as possible.[102] Acheson and Eisenhower would undoubtedly have welcomed more progress in the Petersberg negotiations than either the French or the British, but neither of them were willing to make serious concessions to the Germans. By conveying the impression that rearmament was no longer a matter of great urgency to the United States, both Acheson and Eisenhower were hoping that Adenauer and the SPD would reduce the scope of the concessions they were demanding from the Western powers.[103] It is precisely for this reason that Acheson decided to simply accept the fact that an interim solution which would permit the Germans to start the process of rearmament was not in the cards.[104]

The European army negotiations in Paris were as fruitless as the meetings on German rearmament in Petersberg. The lack of progress was to be expected since the Germans put forward the same conditions for rearmament during both sets of negotiations and made no concessions to the European principles contained in the Pleven Plan. Upon hearing the German proposals, Hervé Alphand, the French official in charge of the Paris meetings, immediately denounced them as unacceptable because of their inconsistency with the concept of a truly integrated European army. Without integration of forces at the RCT level and the creation of mixed divisions, Alphand argued, the German proposals would result in the formation of a traditional coalition of independent national forces rather than anything resembling a supranational European army.[105] Since the Germans were firmly committed to their own proposals, and the French made it clear that they could offer no new proposals until after their June 1951 elections, the European army conference proceeded to meet without resolving the fundamental differences between the two sides. Even enthusiastic supporters of the concept of the European army, such as Bruce and his staff at the U.S. embassy in Paris, found it very difficult to make the case that the French were having much success in winning anyone over to

---

[102] For the British position on German rearmament, see CAB 129/44, C.P. (51) 43, Memorandum on German Rearmament Prepared by Minister of State Kenneth Younger, February 7, 1951, *Cabinet Papers;* and CAB 128/19, C. M. (51), 12th Conclusions, February 8, 1951, *Cabinet Papers;* and Saki Dockrill, *Britain's Policy for West German Rearmament, 1950–55* (Cambridge: Cambridge University Press, 1991), 56–58. To the dismay of some American officials, the British were quite open about the merits of proceeding very slowly in negotiating the terms of rearmament with the Germans. See *FRUS,* 1951, vol. 3, 428–29, 1020–22.

[103] *FRUS,* 1951, vol. 3, 399, 1412. Both Adenauer and Schumacher enthusiastically welcomed Eisenhower's position because of his emphasis on treating all of the NATO allies on the basis of equality, which is ironic since one of the main purposes of having Eisenhower de-emphasize the need for an immediate German contribution was to reduce the bargaining leverage of both German leaders. See RG 59, 762A.00 (W)/2–251, NA.

[104] Secretary of State to McCloy, February 1, 1951, *FRUS,* 1951, vol. 3, 1002–3.

[105] Bruce to Secretary of State, March 9, 1951, *FRUS,* 1951, vol. 3, 774–78.

their position in the negotiations.[106] Those who were cynical about the prospects of a European army, such as American military officials, saw little in the Paris negotiations to alter their views. As U.S. Major J. G. K. Miller concluded as early as April 1951, "While the European Army Conference has been intermittently in session for little over a month it is not too early to predict its failure to achieve the objective sought by the French. . . . For the foreseeable future, it must be considered that the participating countries will not give up sovereignty as proposed by the French in the most vital of all fields—security."[107]

Nearly nine months after the United States had first raised the question, the possibility of a German defense contribution seemed as remote as ever at the beginning of June 1951. Acheson's patience with the lack of progress in resolving the German rearmament question was clearly running out. With the end of the French electoral campaign and the collapse of the preliminary talks with the Soviets concerning a possible meeting of the CFM, Acheson believed that two of the primary obstacles to resolving the German rearmament question had finally been removed. Acheson thought that the way out of the impasse continued to be French acceptance of the short-term necessity for national German rearmament while those nations interested in joining a European army worked out the complex details and political problems involved in creating a supranational defense institution. Even though the German conditions at Petersberg had made it impossible to work out an interim solution, Acheson believed that their proposals were "reasonable" and provided a solid basis for agreement. Acknowledging that the French were unlikely to agree with either his assessment or his proposed solution, Acheson made it clear to Bruce that he was not going to be restrained by this consideration for very much longer:

> It would seem that logic would be on our side if we firmly pressed the French to agree to many of the German suggestions as acceptable and desirable modifications of Brussels Agreement, and that the Three Powers should join in recommending such alterations to NATO as a whole. On the military side this would presumably remove German opposition to proceeding under Brussels Agreement and allow rapid decision on their part in joining defense effort.[108]

[106] See the paper prepared by the U.S. embassy in Paris, "Analysis of the European Army Conference through June 22, 1951," *FRUS*, 1951, vol. 3, 789–98. For the British view, see CAB 129/45, C.P. (51), 128, "The European Army," May 8, 1951, *Cabinet Papers*.

[107] Major J. G. K. Miller, G3/Plans Division, "German Contribution to the Defense of Western Europe," April 24, 1951, RG 330, Assistant Secretary of Defense (International Security Affairs), Subject File 1951–53, box 170, NA.

[108] Acheson to the U.S. Embassy in France, June 28, 1951, *FRUS*, 1951, vol. 3, 803.

It is difficult to fault the logic of Acheson's position on German rearmament. The final report of the High Commissioners supported his belief that the Petersberg proposals did not contain any insuperable barriers to an agreement. Of the six basic objections the Germans raised against the provisions of the Spofford Plan, five were variations on the theme that the basic unit of their armed forces had to be a national division rather than an RCT.[109] Since no one but French political officials advocated the military advantages of RCTs, the Germans were not advancing a position that the rest of the alliance was going to have any difficulty conceding. Both the State Department and the military establishment also accepted the validity of the final German objection noted in the report of the High Commissioners, which asserted their right to form a single national Defense Ministry.[110] The Germans had been uncompromising at Petersberg, but the High Commissioners believed that German leaders would be willing to make compromises in order to achieve a final agreement. If they were satisfied on the basic issue of equality, the Germans indicated that they would probably be able to achieve a large majority in the Bundestag for passing the legislation necessary to begin raising armed forces.[111]

In contrast to their optimism regarding the Petersberg report, Adenauer and other German officials continued to be highly skeptical about the prospects of a European army. At the start of the Paris Conference, Adenauer had told McCloy that the French proposals were "so deficient that he had taken steps to avoid any leaks about it for fear of adverse German reaction."[112] Although McCloy urged Adenauer to keep an open mind on the issue until the negotiations were completed, it does not appear that the German leader's views became any more positive over the next few months. According to Walter Hallstein, one of Adenauer's closest foreign policy advisors, the Chancellor's views were in a "state of flux" because he supported the general concept of a European army but rejected the specific plan being discussed in Paris. The specific plan, Adenauer felt, was "not a European plan at all but a French plan." Hallstein indicated that Adenauer and other officials still had their doubts about whether the French were sincere about wanting to create a true European army or whether it was "just a dodge to make sure that any

---

[109] The Allied High Commissioners for Germany to the Governments of the United States, the United Kingdom, and France, June 8, 1951, *FRUS*, 1951, vol. 3, 1044–47. Even McCloy, who was sympathetic to French concerns about a German national army, was fairly optimistic about the Petersberg report. See McCloy to Eisenhower (n.d. but circa June 8, 1951), box 75, Pre-Presidential Correspondence, Dwight D. Eisenhower Presidential Library, Abilene, Kans. (hereafter DDEL).

[110] See Secretary of State to HICOG, May 1, 1951, *FRUS*, 1951, vol. 3, 1035–36.

[111] Report of the High Commissioners, June 8, 1951, *FRUS*, 1951, vol. 3, 1044–47.

[112] *FRUS*, 1951, vol. 3, 771.

German troops which may be raised are placed under French command."[113] Finally, Hallstein suggested that the need to win over the German people to rearmament simply made it politically impossible for the Chancellor to accept the discriminatory elements contained in the French proposals.[114] Like Acheson, Adenauer wanted NATO to accept the Petersberg report as the immediate basis for German rearmament.[115]

The only real obstacle to adopting the Petersberg report as the basis for German rearmament, of course, was the expected opposition of the French. Acheson's efforts to create a situation of strength in Europe would certainly have been dealt a serious setback if the French maintained a firm position toward any form of rearmament outside the framework of the Pleven Plan. However, in suggesting to Bruce that the time had come to bring France into line with the rest of the alliance, Acheson probably did not think that his course would lead to an all-out conflict. After all, he had acquiesced to the European army conference and provided France the opportunity to win over the Germans and the other members of the alliance. In addition, since Acheson was not at all recommending the termination of efforts to establish a European army, he probably thought that the French government would be able to save face vis-à-vis the National Assembly without a great deal of difficulty. Finally, Acheson also had to be aware of the fact that the French government had a great deal to lose if it was unwilling to compromise on the German question. Among other things, France would be opposing a course of action preferred by the rest of the alliance, jeopardizing the success of the European Coal and Steel Community, and throwing away any chance of a long-term Franco-German rapprochement. If the French were to attempt to play a game of diplomatic chicken with the United States by remaining intransigent over the question of German rearmament, Acheson had to feel very confident that they would be forced to swerve first in order to avoid a collision. Indeed, one of the more intriguing puzzles of the postwar era is explaining why Acheson ultimately chose to ignore the logic

---

[113] S. M. Cleveland, Conversation with Hallstein on European Army, June 21, 1951, RG 84, Paris Embassy Files, "Records Pertaining to the Paris Conference for the Organization of a European Defense Community," box 14, NA (hereafter referred to as Paris Embassy Files, Paris Conference with appropriate box number). Ivonne Kirkpatrick accurately noted Adenauer's mixed feelings about the French proposal when he reported that the Chancellor shared the views of German expert opinion that the Pleven Plan was "military nonsense" but also continued to voice support for the general concept. See Kirkpatrick to Mr. Morrison, May 28, 1951, *DBPO*, series 2, vol. 1, 571.

[114] Cleveland, Conversation with Hallstein on European Army, 2. Adenauer could not help but be influenced by these considerations since Schumacher's major criticism of the European army rested on its discrimination against the Germans. See RG 59, 762A.00/3–2851, NA.

[115] See McCloy to Secretary of State, July 6, 1951; and Bruce to Secretary of State, July 11, 1951, both in *FRUS*, 1951, vol. 3, 1487–89, 824–26.

behind pressuring France to go along with the Petersberg report in favor of the far riskier European army solution.

David Bruce's "Long Telegram" of July 3, 1951, undoubtedly played a major role in leading Acheson to reconsider the utility of pressuring the French. In a *tour de force* of diplomatic advocacy, Bruce made a compelling case that attempting to rearm Germany on the basis of the Petersberg report would threaten America's long-term interests in Europe.[116] Arguing the merits of the French position came easy to Bruce because he sincerely believed that the Petersberg report would lead to the creation of a national German army that might once again become an instrument for the pursuit of militarist objectives. Bruce argued that national German rearmament might be tolerable for the period when the United States maintained substantial troops on the continent, but that it could not be considered a viable solution for the future: "After US commander and US troops are withdrawn, national components in NATO will surely revert to separate national armies unless there is a permanent European political structure. Revival of German national force would make permanent Franco-German rapprochement most unlikely because of its effects on both French and German attitudes."[117] For Bruce, Acheson was operating under a dangerous illusion if he really believed that it was possible to rearm Germany on a national basis and then hope that a European army would eventually come into existence.[118]

Bruce's telegram was not effective because it pointed out the long-term benefits of a European army. Acheson had always accepted the validity of this argument. Where Acheson parted company with Bruce and other advocates of a European army was on the question of timing: he tended to think that working out all of the complicated political and financial institutions associated with such a project would take far too long and prevent the rapid creation of countervailing power to the Soviets on the continent. What Bruce managed to do in his telegram was to make an effective case that American support for a European army would bring German units into being faster than any other solution. If the French were forced to reluctantly accept the Petersberg report, Bruce argued that they would find other ways to delay German rearmament, such as dragging their feet in the contractual negotiations. Conversely, if Acheson endorsed the principle that Germany could only be rearmed within the context of a European

---

[116] See Bruce to Secretary of State, July 3, 1951, *FRUS*, 1951, vol. 3, 805–12. For a full appreciation of how Bruce crafted his argument in a manner designed to appeal to Acheson, see Martin F. Herz, *David Bruce's "Long Telegram" of July 3, 1951* (Lanham, Md.: University Press of America, 1978).

[117] Bruce to Secretary of State, 806.

[118] For a similar criticism of Acheson's proposed course of action, see Hooker to Nitze, July 11, 1951, Comments on the Secretary's July 6 Paper, PPS Records, box 28, NA. The paper Hooker is referring to, which reiterated Acheson's earlier arguments, can be found in *FRUS*, 1951, vol. 3, 813–19.

army, Bruce suggested that the French would be less troublesome in the contractual negotiations and more willing to modify the untenable elements of their proposals, such as the insistence on RCTs. Once the French knew that they had the wholehearted support of the United States and the Germans were made to realize that they did not really have a national rearmament option, Bruce believed that the European army negotiations would make rapid progress.

Although Bruce did not place his argument in historical context, he was essentially arguing for a modification of the stance the Truman administration had adopted toward European integration since 1947. If American officials really believed that the future of Western Europe ultimately depended on the creation of federal or supranational institutions, as Acheson and so many others had stated since the introduction of the Marshall Plan, Bruce implied that it would be a great mistake for the United States to adopt a posture of cautious support or indifference toward a project which had the potential to permanently end the system of unrestrained sovereignty and purely national armies in Western Europe. A project as ambitious as the creation of a European army could not possibly get off the ground if the United States did not assume an active leadership role in bringing it into existence. The French obviously did not have the power or the influence to convert the Germans or anyone else to their ideas, particularly when the rest of the alliance rightly perceived an attitude of ambivalence or opposition on the part of the United States. But if American power and influence were to be decisively and unambiguously placed behind the creation of a European army, Bruce thought that Acheson had a golden opportunity to permanently shape the future of Western Europe away from nationalism and toward unification. As he wrote to Assistant Secretary of State for European Affairs George Perkins shortly after sending his telegram to Acheson, "My judgment is that if we throw our influence decisively on the side of the European Army we will be able to bring quick and positive results from this present Conference with all the permanent advantages for the North Atlantic Community and Europe that such a move promises."[119]

EISENHOWER AND THE
EUROPEAN DEFENSE COMMUNITY

Bruce's opinions carried a great deal of weight with Acheson, but his telegram did not end the debate within the Truman administration over the European army. Some officials thought that it was highly im-

---

[119] Bruce to Perkins, July 5, 1951, RG 59, Records of the Office of European Regional Affairs: Files of J. Graham Parsons, box 2, NA.

plausible for Bruce to argue that working out all of the arrangements for a European army would not lead to additional delays in rearming Germany.[120] Other officials, such as Charles Spofford, struck at the heart of Bruce's argument by questioning whether the administration should even be making plans based on the premise of the eventual withdrawal of American forces from Europe. According to Spofford, "In view of physical power relationships it is difficult to conceive of the development at any time in the foreseeable future of individual or collective strength of European members sufficient to stand up diplomatically or militarily to USSR except as part of larger effort in which US is a full partner."[121] Finally, the Defense Department warned Acheson that he should not be "trapped into a position where we would have accepted the European army as a step which must precede any other action, thereby depriving ourselves of any freedom of action and putting ourselves entirely in the hands of the French."[122]

Acheson was intellectually sympathetic to all of these arguments. Although he himself had originally raised the point that a European army would be desirable for the time when American troops were no longer stationed in Europe, Acheson now accepted Spofford's view of the situation rather than Bruce's:

> There appears to be an increasing tendency to disregard the long-range problem of development of cooperation both in military and other fields in the Atlantic Community, and to treat European integration and a European Army as final solutions for all problems including that of security against Germany. This is a dangerous tendency and we think it ought to be checked both in our own long-range interests and in the interest of bringing about more widespread European support for the idea of European integration, including European Defense forces.[123]

---

[120] See Ridgeway Knight's criticisms of the long telegram in RG 59, 762A.5/7–1351, NA.

[121] Spofford to Secretary of State, July 8, 1951, *FRUS*, 1951, vol. 3, 821–23 (quotation on 822).

[122] Memorandum by the Secretary of State, July 16, 1951, *FRUS*, 1951, vol. 3, 837.

[123] See Secretary of State to the Embassy in France, July 16, 1951, *FRUS*, 1951, vol. 3, 835. Acheson's line of argument is misunderstood by Dockrill. In her view, Acheson emphasized the Atlantic Community because of his concern that the European army was "a French device to attain the leadership of Western Europe which, if successful, might threaten America's interests in the future." See Dockrill, *Britain's Policy for West German Rearmament*, 69. What the telegram actually states is that the Netherlands opposed a European army because they did not want to be exposed to French or German leadership. In addition, Acheson's fear was not that the French would be successful in establishing a European army, but rather that they would be unsuccessful: "We cannot be sure that western Europeans are sufficiently strong by themselves to outweigh German influence in future European Defense Forces."

Bruce and McCloy were able to overcome these solid arguments against the European army solution for one and only one reason: they had won Eisenhower over to their position by June 1951. Eisenhower had not previously adopted a public position on the European army, but like every other military official in NATO he was privately skeptical about its viability under prevailing circumstances. As he later told Marshall, he originally refused to lend any support to those advocating a European army because he felt the entire concept seemed to "include every kind of obstacle, difficulty, and fantastic notion that misguided humans could put together in one package."[124] Establishing a European army would be "putting the cart before the horse," he told journalist C. L. Sulzberger in March 1951, because the political basis for unity had not yet been created on the continent.[125] Western Europe was no closer to political unity in June 1951, but by that time Eisenhower was willing to fully support the European army. In a rousing speech delivered to the English Speaking Union on July 3, Eisenhower extolled the benefits that would accrue to all of the members of the Atlantic Community from the establishment of a "workable European federation."[126] More important, Eisenhower threw all of his support behind Bruce and McCloy's position that German rearmament had to be placed within the institutional framework of a European army.

To understand Eisenhower's rapid conversion on the subject of the European army, it is necessary to grasp the basic elements of his views about the nature of the threat posed by the Soviet Union, the actual and potential distribution of power in Europe, and the purposes of American intervention in continental affairs. Eisenhower had long abandoned his wartime faith in the possibility of cooperation with the Soviets, but he still did not consider them to be a formidable opponent when matched against the combined strength of the Western powers. In contrast to the authors of NSC 68, Eisenhower did not believe that the Soviet acquisition of the atomic bomb in 1949 had altered the generally favorable balance of power that had existed since the end of the Second World War. He did not fear an imminent Soviet invasion of Western Europe, nor did he believe that war would result from the strengthening of NATO's military power or the rearmament of Germany. As he told Sulzberger in December 1951, "The Russians were fully aware that a long war would be a question of

---

[124] Eisenhower to Marshall, August 3, 1951, in *The Papers of Dwight David Eisenhower: NATO and the Campaign of 1952*, ed. Louis Galambos (Baltimore: Johns Hopkins University Press, 1989), 12:458 (hereafter *TPDDE*). He later told Truman that he originally considered the European army as "cockeyed an idea as a dope fiend could have figured out." See Meeting of the President with General of the Army Dwight D. Eisenhower in the Cabinet Room of the White House, November 5, 1951, box 118, PSF, HSTL.

[125] See C. L. Sulzberger, *A Long Row of Candles* (New York: Macmillan, 1969), 651.

[126] Dwight D. Eisenhower, "The Challenge of Our Time," July 3, 1951, reprinted in *Vital Speeches of the Day* 17 (July 1951): 614.

relative productive capability, and we alone had three times their economic capacities. For that reason they would certainly not start a war."[127] Even during his congressional testimony at the time of the "Great Debate" on stationing U.S. troops in Europe, when he had every incentive to emphasize the immediacy and awesomeness of the military threat posed by the Soviets, Eisenhower saw it as extremely unlikely that the Soviets would risk a war in Europe: "If they declare war now, they are fools. They cannot win on the global picture instantly and quickly by a complete knockout."[128]

Eisenhower's confidence in 1951 that the Soviets would not launch a war in Europe during the period that Acheson and Nitze saw as the period of maximum danger seems curious and somewhat contradictory since he was simultaneously advocating a much larger initial commitment of ground forces to Europe than the administration thought necessary. The contradiction between a relaxed view of the immediate military threat and the emphasis on a rapid and large buildup of American power in Europe did not exist in Eisenhower's own calculations, however, because the utility of sending as large an American force as possible had very little to do with purely military considerations. His rationale for sending a larger force rested on the belief that the greater the American commitment to Europe, the more likely the other members of NATO would feel confident enough to make the sacrifices necessary to construct a viable defense force.[129] Making the Western Europeans believe that they did not have to remain forever defenseless in the face of Soviet military power was what Eisenhower considered to be his most important goal as

[127] See "Notes of a Meeting at the White House," January 31, 1951, *FRUS, 1951*, vol. 3, 449–58; and Sulzberger, *A Long Row of Candles*, 708.

[128] Eisenhower testimony of February 1, 1951, U.S. Senate, Committee on Foreign Relations and the Committee on Armed Forces, *Assignment of Ground Forces to Duty in the North Atlantic Area*, 82d Congress, 1st session, 25. To gain a better understanding of Eisenhower's views on the Soviet Union at this time it is worth reading a paper written by Rear Admiral L. C. Stevens and delivered at the National War College in January 1951. Much like George Kennan, Stevens argued that the Western powers tended to vastly overrate Soviet capabilities, that the Kremlin leadership was highly conscious of their inferiority in relative power vis-a-vis the West, and that the Soviets were unlikely to initiate a global war. Eisenhower wrote in his diary that, with a few minor exceptions, Stevens's paper "represents my beliefs exactly." See Eisenhower diary entry, March 3, 1951, in *TPDDE*, 12:90; and Rear Admiral L. C. Stevens, "A National Strategy For the Soviet Union," January 25, 1951, Records of the NSC, box 19, HSTL. For an excellent analysis which notes some of the similarities between Kennan and Eisenhower's strategic conceptions, see Richard H. Immerman, "Confessions of an Eisenhower Revisionist: An Agonizing Reappraisal," *Diplomatic History* 14 (summer 1990): 319–42.

[129] As he wrote to Harriman during the Great Debate, after learning that the administration had declared that it had no intention of sending more than four additional divisions to Europe, "I do not see how we can find, in fearful limitations of this character, any real inspiration for the European populations." Yet Eisenhower also indicated that he favored limitations on the time of the American commitment. That the Europeans might be equally discouraged by the knowledge of the temporary nature of the American commitment did not seem to occur to Eisenhower. See Eisenhower to Harriman, March 8, 1951, *TPDDE*, 12:104.

SACEUR. This was a sincere belief on his part because he thought that with a collective approach to defense the Western Europeans were ultimately quite capable of holding their own against the Soviets.

Eisenhower was quite open throughout 1951 that he viewed the presence of American ground forces in Europe as a temporary commitment designed to tide Western Europe over until it had developed its own latent strength. Unlike other administration officials, who were very reluctant to directly answer questions about the future level of American forces in Europe during the Great Debate, Eisenhower frankly acknowledged: "I do not know if you could get to zero, but that would be the objective in any planning in which I took part."[130] Alfred Gruenther, Eisenhower's Chief of Staff and closest confidant, told a group of visiting Congressmen during the summer of 1951 that the general's "philosophy is that these troops are there temporarily. He is referring particularly to the ground troops. In the long run it will not be feasible to have, in time of peace, large American ground forces stationed in Europe; they will be withdrawn eventually."[131] In the short term, Eisenhower agreed that there was no alternative to placing American forces in Europe, which is why he was adamantly opposed to the traditional isolationism of Taft and Hoover, but he was also convinced that American power was not and could not become a permanent substitute for the development of indigenous European power. Although Eisenhower did not officially place a date on the withdrawal of American forces, he did offer a projected timetable to one of his associates from Columbia University:

In any event, the present question is how to inspire Europe *to produce for itself those armed forces that, in the long run, must provide the*

---

[130] Eisenhower testimony of February 1, 1951, U.S. Senate, Committee on Foreign Relations and the Committee on Armed Forces, in *Assignment of Ground Forces*, 19. In contrast, Marshall stated that the United States might be able to withdraw a division in later years, and Bradley frankly admitted that he would rather keep the six divisions in Europe for another twenty years if it would prevent a war. See their testimony in ibid., 38–75, 126–52. For an overview of the Great Debate in Congress, see Ted Galen Carpenter, "United States's NATO Policy at the Crossroads: The Great Debate of 1950–51," *International History Review* 8 (August 1986): 389–415; and Phil Williams, *The Senate and US Troops in Europe* (London: Macmillan, 1985), 43–108.

[131] See Gruenther's testimony of August 10, 1951, Hearings before the Committee on Foreign Relations and the Committee on Armed Services, *Mutual Security Act of 1951*, 82d Congress, 1st session, 210. It should be noted that Gruenther did make a distinction between ground forces and airpower, which he and Eisenhower thought would take the Europeans a longer time to create on an indigenous basis. Incidentally, it should be pointed out that the qualifications about the phase-out of the American commitment were often given after reporters published stories based on Eisenhower's off-the-record comments about when American forces could be withdrawn from Europe. For two examples of such backtracking, see ALO 369, General Persons to General Reber, October 4, 1951; and ALO 407, Gruenther to General Lanham, October 16, 1951, both in RG 349, Records of Joint Commands, US European Command, Outgoing Messages (1951–53), box 32, NA.

only means by which Europe can be defended. Over the years, I agree that there is no defense for Western Europe that depends exclusively or even materially upon the existence, in Europe, of strong American units. . . . While I do not know the length of time that some occupational troops may necessarily be in Germany, I would say this: If in ten years, all American troops stationed in Europe for national defense purposes have not been returned to the United States, then this whole project will have failed.[132]

Surprisingly, since advocates of European unity had often emphasized the themes of independence from American aid and the potential power of a united Western Europe, Eisenhower does not seem to have drawn the connection between the two until June 1951. His conversion to the cause of European unity as an immediate objective was undoubtedly facilitated by the buck-passing and unwillingness to subordinate national objectives that he encountered during his first few months as SACEUR. When these difficulties were added to the continuing impasse over a German defense contribution, Eisenhower began to believe that European unity was an essential element in the solution to the short- and long-term problems facing NATO. In a diary entry of June 11, he wrote that he was "coming to believe that Europe's security problem is never going to be solved satisfactorily until there exists a U.S. of Europe. . . . It seems scarcely necessary to enumerate the problems that arise out of or are exaggerated by the division of Western Europe into so many sovereign nations."[133] Although worried that the current crop of political leaders might be too fearful, cautious, and lazy to establish a United States of Europe, Eisenhower believed that "inspired" leaders could and should make the effort: "American help—which could radically be reduced both in scope and duration—would quickly render such an organization immune to attack! With this one problem solved—all lesser ones could soon disappear. I could write a *volume* on the subject."[134] Like Bruce and McCloy, Eisenhower believed that the time had come for American leadership to take an active interest in bringing about a Western European federation as rapidly as possible. A gradual and slow evolution toward unity held no appeal. As he wrote to Averell Harriman in late June:

Of course—as so many others think—I believe there is no real answer for the European problem until there is definitely established a United States of Europe. As a consequence of the present tensions and emergencies, I believe that such a step should be taken by

---

[132] Eisenhower to Edward John Bermingham, February 28, 1951, *TPDDE*, 12:76–77.
[133] Eisenhower diary entry, June 11, 1951, *TPDDE*, 12:214.
[134] Ibid., 215.

Europe's political leaders in a single plunge. The sooner the better! I get exceedingly weary of this talk about a step-by-step gradual, cautious approach. The United States and Britain could afford to do almost anything to support and make successful such a venture, because by this act, our entire objectives in this region could be instantaneously achieved.[135]

Having become convinced that a United States of Europe was the way to achieve America's entire objectives on the continent, Eisenhower was now ready to be sold on the idea that the European army was the essential step toward his larger goals. Jean Monnet, after being coached by American officials Robert Bowie and William Tomlinson, successfully convinced Eisenhower and Gruenther of the merits of the European army in a June 21 meeting.[136] Despite his concerns about the dangers of viewing European unity as the "final solution" for all problems, a view which Eisenhower certainly held, Acheson was no longer willing to hold out against the coalition in favor of the European army. By the end of July, Acheson decided to stop fighting for an immediate German contribution to NATO; and support for the European army, soon to be rechristened as the European Defense Community, became official American policy.[137]

The underlying tension between the Acheson and Eisenhower conceptions of the European army was left unresolved by this debate. It might well have been very clear in Acheson's mind that the EDC would be a complement to NATO and that its creation would not eliminate the need for American forces to be stationed in Europe on a permanent basis. But this conception was certainly not shared by Eisenhower, who viewed the EDC as a crucial step in ultimately making it possible for American forces to be withdrawn from Europe. However, if one were to assume that American forces were to be in Europe on a permanent basis and that NATO provided a permanent institutional framework, it is not at all clear why an exclusively European institution such as the EDC was also necessary. To say the least, European observers were equally uncertain about what the American switch to support for the EDC implied about the future. The Benelux nations were distressed by the shift in American policy precisely because they were concerned that the formation of the EDC might lead to a diminution of NATO and the withdrawal of American

[135] Eisenhower to Averell Harriman, June 30, 1951, *TPDDE*, 12:398. See also Sulzberger, *Long Row of Candles*, 647–48.

[136] Memorandum of Conference, June 21, 1951, RG 84, Paris Embassy Files, Paris Conference, box 14, NA. For Monnet's account of the meeting with Eisenhower, see his *Memoirs*, 358–59.

[137] For the final agreement, see Acheson and Lovett to the President, July 30, 1951, *FRUS*, 1951, vol. 3, 849–52.

forces.[138] On the other hand, Konrad Adenauer eventually supported the EDC decision for reasons quite similar to Eisenhower's:

> The United States would not for ever keep troops in Europe and Europe itself must therefore take lasting and effective measures against Soviet expansionism (with such assistance as the United States might offer). This was only possible if Europe was genuinely united. The Pleven Plan was, to his mind, the only possible method of protecting Europe permanently. The North Atlantic Treaty Organization aimed rather at the present threat and at maintaining peace in the coming years; it would not meet the long-term need.[139]

THE EDC TREATY AND THE FUTURE OF EUROPE

The American decision to support the European Defense Community over the NATO solution did not resolve the underlying issues and problems involved in the rearmament of Germany. Acheson hoped that the EDC process would lead to a speedier resolution of the issues and a greater willingness to accept interim solutions, but the French were quite insistent that the restoration of German sovereignty and rearmament could not be separated. Until the EDC treaty was negotiated and ratified by all parties involved, Germany would not regain its sovereignty or be permitted to begin rearming. Negotiating the treaty would not be easy because unlike the original Pleven Plan the EDC would have to be a viable institution that the Germans would willingly accept. The fundamental purpose of the EDC was to develop rules, procedures, and institutions that would control the process of German rearmament, but the EDC treaty itself could not explicitly codify this objective. The German mantra throughout the EDC negotiations was "equality and nondiscrimination" within the European community, which essentially meant that no clause of the treaty could be applicable only to Germany. Although some restrictions on Germany could be weakly justified because it constituted a strategically exposed area, in general restrictions on Germany would apply equally to France, Italy, and the Benelux countries. Not surprisingly, since Germany and France entered these negotiations from vastly different positions, principles of equality and nondiscrimination would help Germany gain freedoms and force France to surrender them. As one State Department official noted, "The Germans are having some success

---

[138] Bruce to Secretary of State, *FRUS*, 1952–54, vol. 5, 572–74; and Dirk Stikker, *Men of Responsibility* (New York: Harper & Row Publishers, 1965), 304.

[139] CAB 129/47, C.P. (51) 236, Annex II, Statement by the German Federal Chancellor at Mr. Stikker's Dinner Party on 3rd August, August 16, 1951, *Cabinet Papers*.

in using the chosen instrument of the French—the EDC—as a means of crushing the French design for dual controls through the EDC and through contractual arrangements."[140]

French concerns about the EDC framework were brought to the surface at the beginning of 1952. Under growing pressure from both the cabinet and the National Assembly, Schuman sent Acheson a letter that made it clear how far Germany and France were from a final agreement. Calling for greater solidarity between the United States, Great Britain, and France in imposing conditions on Germany outside the EDC framework, Schuman reminded Acheson that the EDC was "a concept which cannot alone solve the problem of security in relation to Germany."[141] Pointing to Germany's inherent demographic and economic superiority over France, Schuman basically suggested that a purely European framework could never balance or contain Germany. In addition to the long-term fears about German power, French policymakers were also increasingly concerned about their short-term ability to maintain superiority over Germany within the EDC because of their commitments in Indochina. With their ability to balance German power uncertain in both the short and long term, it is not surprising that the French were having second thoughts about the EDC.

The Schuman letter, which represented the official views of the French cabinet, could not have come at a worse time for the Truman administration because it threatened the timetable for completing the negotiations before the Lisbon meeting of NATO scheduled for February. The fact that Schuman, a sincere advocate of European unity and reconciliation with Germany, was voicing concerns about the ability of the EDC to control Germany was ominous because of the tremendous respect he enjoyed throughout the administration. Acheson had just gone before Congress and praised Schuman for the leading role he had taken in healing the historic breach between France and Germany that dated back to the breakup of Charlemagne's empire. If Schuman and Adenauer could reach agreement on the EDC treaty and the contractuals, Acheson was willing to proclaim a final victory in the most important conflict of the Cold War: "If we can just get over this next eight weeks, I think we have such power, forward power in Europe that there, at least, our problems are over."[142] Conversely, Acheson warned Congress that a failure at this point in the

---

[140] Sims to Byroade, Subject: Schuman Letter, January 31, 1952, RG 59, 762.00/1–3152, NA.

[141] Schuman to Secretary of State, January 29, 1952, *FRUS*, 1952–54, vol. 5, 7. Some American policymakers accepted the French argument that restrictions on Germany should be ensured through the contractual agreements rather than within the EDC. See Laukhuff to Lewis, "Security Safeguards," RG 59, 762A.5/1–1652, NA.

[142] Acheson testimony of January 15, 1952, House Committee on Foreign Affairs, Selected Executive Session Hearings, *European Problems* (Washington, D.C.: Government Printing Office, 1980), 170.

negotiations would be much more than a temporary setback because it would lead to the victory of the domestic forces within Germany and France unalterably opposed to European unification. In his view, "The moment to act is now. If it passes, and if the Schumacher tendency in Germany and the de Gaulle tendency in France get going, I am afraid it is passed in our lifetime."[143]

What specifically made the Schuman letter so unsettling to Acheson and other American officials was its focus on issues related to Germany's potential dominance of the European community and its possible secession from the EDC. The EDC provided an institutional framework within which German power could be restrained and monitored, but it could not change the fact that Germany would inevitably become the most powerful actor within the community. As McCloy correctly noted, the greatest worry for France was that Germany would obtain a position of dominance through the EDC and then secede from it at a later date.[144] The French insistence on stronger outside commitments from the United States and Great Britain was essentially a recognition of the fact that there was no purely continental solution to the German problem. The logical consequence of the French position was that Germany should also become a member of NATO in addition to the EDC, as several American officials pointed out, but Schuman wanted the United States to explicitly reiterate the fact that NATO membership was not open to Germany.[145]

Regardless of the merits of the concerns raised by the Schuman letter, the fact that Schuman was compelled to send the letter reflected the basic fact that marshaling a clear majority in France for the EDC treaty could not be taken for granted. How difficult it would be for any French government to pass the EDC through the National Assembly became clear after a vote on the treaty was held on February 19, 1952. A resolution in favor of the EDC was ultimately passed by a majority of 387 to 287, but the "recommendations" attached to the resolution by the National Assembly severely restricted the meaning of the favorable vote. As the Socialist leader Guy Mollet pointed out, the recommendations were actually "conditions" that the socialists would require in order to ratify the treaty.[146] One condition required that the United States and Great Britain

---

[143] Ibid., 165.

[144] McCloy to Secretary of State, February 1, 1952, *FRUS*, 1952–54, vol. 5, 15–16.

[145] The American position on German membership in NATO was that it was logical and inevitable at some point, but that there was no need for either the French or the Germans to raise the issue at the present time. See Memorandum of Conversation between Mr. Dejuniac and Lewis, RG 59, 862.19/1–2852, NA; and Acheson to Schuman, February 4, 1952, *FRUS*, 1952–54, vol. 5, 19–21.

[146] See "Interview of Philip Bonsal with Guy Mollet, Secretary General of the French Socialist Party," February 21, 1952, in U.S. Polad Germany Post Files, 1945–49, Office of the Political Advisor, RG 84, Records Pertaining to the European Defense Community, box 9, NA.

would guarantee the EDC against any breach or violation by a member state, with the guarantee to take the form of "the maintenance of sufficient U.S. and British troops on the European Continent as long as appears necessary." A second condition directed the government to renew efforts to obtain British participation in the EDC, even if it meant watering down the supranational character of the body. The assembly also recommended that French troops in Europe should at all times be at least equal to those of any other member. Finally, the Assembly reiterated its position that German membership in the EDC did not imply membership in NATO and that no state with territorial claims should be considered for membership in the alliance.[147]

All of these conditions raised considerable difficulties because they did not allow for simple solutions. The EDC treaty already provided that French forces would be superior in number to German forces, but the Assembly resolution reflected the realization that the conflict in Indochina would probably make it impossible for France to build forces up to the permitted level. The French fear was that Germany, which obviously had no overseas commitments, would be able to maintain superior forces in Europe. The logical consequence of the French position on the relationship between the EDC and Vietnam, one that would become explicit over time, was that they could not be expected to ratify the EDC treaty until the situation in Vietnam was resolved and French forces could return home.[148] The French desire for greater British participation in, or association with, the EDC was also not amenable to a quick solution. The British government was far less hostile to the EDC than Bevin had been in late 1950, but they were not contemplating any major participation in the EDC. Although Foreign Secretary Anthony Eden was eventually willing to consider some form of British participation in order to salvage the EDC, the Truman administration was well aware from Prime Minister Churchill's recent visit to the United States that the maximum level of British involvement was unlikely to satisfy the French.[149]

The "guarantee" question also posed difficulties for Acheson. What the French seemed to want was a clear statement that America would maintain a sufficient number of troops in Europe for as long as necessary, and "sufficient" and "as long as necessary" were not simply to be decisions made in America. Acheson had a great deal of sympathy for the French request, yet a precise commitment along these lines was deemed to be politically impossible and potentially counterproductive. No presidential declaration could legally bind future administrations to a promise that

---

[147] The National Assembly resolution can be found in Denise Folliot, ed., *Documents on International Affairs, 1952* (London: Oxford University Press, 1955), 81–83.

[148] See Jasmine Aimaq, *For Europe or Empire? French Colonial Ambitions and the European Army Plan* (Lund, Sweden: Lund University Press, 1996).

[149] See Lovett to Eisenhower, January 24, 1952, *FRUS, 1952–54*, vol. 6, 859–61.

would keep a specified number of troops in Europe for any specific length of time. Acheson was also unwilling to reopen old debates with Congress over new commitments. In addition, as Acheson pointed out to Truman, the French request was bound to raise uncomfortable questions about the overall purpose of American troops in Europe. The idea that American troops were in Europe to make sure that Germany lived up to its EDC commitments was not one that Acheson wanted to encourage by stating it directly: "It must be made clear that our troops are not in Europe to police the obligations of friends but to prevent aggression from without. Any suggestion to the contrary would be most disadvantageous."[150] Despite the fact that Acheson made it clear that America's guarantee could not go beyond a declaration that it would view any threat to the integrity of the EDC with the utmost seriousness, the French would continue to push for a stronger commitment all the way up to the signing of the EDC treaty in May 1952.[151] Like the other recommendations approved by the National Assembly, the French demand for a more solid troop commitment would continually return to plague the ratification process over the next two years.

Hammering out the final details of the contractual agreements and the EDC treaty would have been difficult under the best of circumstances, but Acheson's task was made even more complicated with the publication of Stalin's March 10 note on Germany. The interest of the Soviet Union in unified solutions for Germany was not new, but the approach taken by Stalin in March 1952 was different than previous efforts. Rather than appealing to popular desires among the Western occupying powers for a settlement, Stalin's note was primarily directed at the people of West Germany. Realizing that the popular West German response to the note would be the most crucial factor in determining the success or failure of his initiative, Stalin added elements that he thought would appeal to all German nationalists, such as an end to denazification, the creation of a national army, and the removal of all occupying forces. As a condition for unification and the withdrawal of all occupation forces from Germany within a year, the new German government would have to agree not to join any alliance directed against any state that had participated in the coalition that defeated Hitler.[152] Acceptance of such a proposal, of course, would have prevented any form of German participation in the EDC or NATO.

---

[150] Acheson to Truman, February 16, 1952, *FRUS*, 1952–54, vol. 5, 79.

[151] For last-minute attempts by the French to strengthen the American guarantee, see *FRUS*, 1952–54, vol. 5, 631–34, 677–78.

[152] The Stalin note is published in *FRUS*, 1952–54, vol. 7, 169–72. While his own conclusions on the Stalin Note are debatable, the documents compiled by Rolf Steininger remain the best starting point for any examination of Western policy in 1952. See Steininger, *Eine Chance zur Wiedervereinigung?*, 93–308.

Western statesmen were sure that Stalin's minimum purpose was to disrupt the process of signing the EDC treaty and the contractuals, but they were uncertain about whether he also had larger purposes in mind. As Eden told the cabinet on March 12, the Stalin note was certainly an "astute manoeuvre," but it might also "reflect a sincere desire on their part to make a further effort to the achievement of a united Germany."[153] Even though the sacrifice of East Germany might lead to great difficulties for the Soviet Union, Eden thought the note might be sincere because a settlement along the lines of the note would probably be in Stalin's best interest.[154] Even the Quai d'Orsay, which was originally inclined to view the Stalin note as a clumsy and counterproductive propaganda move, quickly changed its assessment. Within a matter of days after their initially dismissive assessment of its importance, the French informed the British that they now viewed the Soviet proposals for unification as "much more than a tactical move" and as "a serious but very dangerous attempt to settle the German question."[155] Some lower-level officials within the American government were also open to the possibility that Stalin might be willing to make concessions leading to a united Germany, but Acheson did not because he thought it would be too risky for the Soviets to give up control of East Germany. Convinced that Stalin would not agree to Western terms on unification, the American approach to the note was designed to avoid a general four-power conference, expose the Soviet unwillingness to accept truly free elections in Germany, and exploit the opportunities presented to gain more popular support for the EDC.[156]

Given the great success of Western policy and the total failure of Soviet policy in Germany, it is not surprising that some scholars have concluded that Stalin was seriously willing to sacrifice East Germany in exchange for keeping West Germany out of NATO.[157] However, recent scholarship based on Soviet and East German archives strongly suggests that Stalin and the officials involved in the preparation of the note did not really believe that it was anything more than a move to disrupt the final stage of

---

[153] CAB 128/24, March 12, 1952, *Cabinet Papers*.

[154] Eden's comments can be found in the margins of the March 14 report on French attitudes filed by Frank Roberts in Steininger, *Eine Chance zur Wiedervereinigung?*, 136.

[155] Attitude of the Quai d'Orsay, Report from Frank Roberts, Foreign Office, March 14, 1952, and Eden to Harvey, March 26, 1952, both published in Steininger, *Eine Chance zur Wiedervereinigung?*, 136. See also the report of French attitudes toward the Stalin Note contained in Bonsal to Acheson, March 15, 1952, in Steininger, *German Question*, 139–40.

[156] *FRUS*, 1952–54, vol. 6, 172–327; Steininger, *German Question*, 128–38; and Steininger, *Eine Chance zur Wiedervereinigung?*, 157–59, 170–72. For Acheson's views, see also RG 59, 762.00/3–2652 and 762.00/4–1152, NA.

[157] See Steininger, *German Question*, 94–99; and Wilfried Loth, *Stalin's Unwanted Child: The Soviet Union, the German Question, and the Founding of the GDR* (New York: St. Martin's Press, 1998), 132–40.

the EDC negotiations.[158] If Stalin did entertain any hopes of entering into negotiations with the Western powers over Germany, he appears to have abandoned them fairly early in the process. Less than a month after the issuance of the first note on Germany, Stalin told the East German communists that the Western powers would not agree to any proposals that they might make on the German question and that it was now time for them to "organize their own state."[159] Although the "battle of the notes" between the two sides would go on for several months, the Soviet initiative did not sidetrack the Western powers from completing the contractual agreements and the EDC treaty.

The new documentary evidence on Stalin's intentions in March 1952 helps clarify an important episode in Cold War history, but the Soviet side of the story should not obscure a rather obvious point. No matter how serious Stalin might or might not have been about negotiating a united Germany in March 1952, it is hard to see how even a "reasonable" Soviet proposal would have been acceptable to the Western powers. According to one journalist, Dean Acheson admitted that "neither the United States nor the USSR wanted a settlement on the present terms. . . . The soundest course to take now, he said, was to continue as we now are in trying to build up a strong Western Europe until the Russians felt that the cost would be too high for them and they would agree on a settlement."[160] From Acheson's perspective, the Federal Republic's integration into the EDC and other Western institutions was not a bargaining chip to be traded away for Soviet concessions over Germany. A national German army had been rejected as dangerous even within the confines of the Western alliance, and it was no more palatable in the context of unification. According to Acheson, the Soviet proposal represented "a step backwards" which would "jeopardize the emergence in Europe of a new era in which international relations would be based on cooperation and not on rivalry and distrust."[161] Exchanging West Germany's integration into the EDC and other European institutions for a united Germany with a national army—combined with mutual troop withdrawals—did not seem to represent an opportunity at all to the Western powers. It is primarily for this reason—not doubts about the sincerity or seriousness of the Stalin

[158] Gerhard Wettig, "Stalin and German Reunification: Archival Evidence on Soviet Foreign Policy in Spring 1952," *The Historical Journal* 37 (1994): 411–19; Vojtech Mastny, *The Cold War and Soviet Insecurity: The Stalin Years* (New York: Oxford University Press, 1996), 134–39; and Ruud Van Dijk, "The 1952 Stalin Note Debate: Myth or Missed Opportunity for German Unification?" Working Paper no. 14, Cold War International History Project (May 1996).

[159] Stalin's views can be found in the *Cold War International History Project Bulletin*, no. 4 (fall 1994): 34, 48.

[160] See RG 59, 762.00/4–1152, NA.

[161] *FRUS*, 1952–54, vol. 7, 190.

note—that the Western powers forged ahead with the signing of the EDC treaty and the contractuals on May 26, 1952.

NO ALTERNATIVES: EISENHOWER, DULLES, AND THE EDC

The signing of the EDC treaty and the contractual agreements with Germany in May 1952 was undeniably a tremendous victory for both Acheson and Truman. German rearmament and the restoration of sovereignty to the Federal Republic had a great potential for fatally disrupting the Western alliance, but Acheson had managed to gain both of these goals with the consent of the allies. As Acheson wrote to Truman, "We now have successfully completed another phase in our postwar policy: containment of the new threat with the cooperation of our former enemy."[162] Speaking before the Senate Foreign Relations Committee after his return from Europe, Acheson suggested that the agreements might lead "toward the unification of Western Europe into a federal organization which will be large enough to be strong, vigorous and, we hope in time, to take over its own defense on the basis of a strong economic foundation."[163] Nevertheless, although Acheson had solid grounds for optimism about the future, both he and the vast majority of American policymakers could only maintain this position by underestimating the obstacles in the way of EDC ratification in France. Until all six members of the EDC ratified the treaty, West Germany would be prohibited from rearming and the substantial restoration of her sovereignty provided for by the contractual agreements would also remain in abeyance. In short, Acheson's victory in May 1952 was dependent on French ratification of the treaty, which was by no means certain.

What would be done in the event that France failed to ratify the treaty, or if delays in France jeopardized Adenauer's electoral prospects, were questions that Acheson and the State Department understandably preferred to avoid in 1952. When the State Department and Policy Planning Staff in late 1952 finally attempted to answer the question of U.S. alternatives in the event of a French failure to ratify the treaty, they essentially concluded that there were no viable alternatives. It is for this reason that one analyst suggested that nonratification of the treaty by either France or Germany "would present us with the most serious diplomatic and strategic crisis of the post-war world."[164] Such a conclusion about nonratification obviously seems far too alarmist in retrospect, but it accurately reflects how most American officials would continue to view the situation

[162] Acheson to Truman, May 26, 1952, *FRUS, 1952–54*, vol. 5, 681.

[163] Acheson testimony of June 2, 1952, U.S. Senate, Committee on Foreign Relations, Executive Session, 82d Congress, 2d session, 481.

[164] Moore to Williamson, October 17, 1952, Miriam Camps Files, box 1, NA.

for the next two years. All alternatives to the EDC were and would continue to be seen as either decidedly inferior, illusory, or both. Bringing Germany directly into NATO—perhaps the best of all possible options— was seen as both inferior and illusory because the French were unlikely to accept Germany in NATO if they were unwilling to vote them into the EDC. Arming Germany outside of the NATO framework was for obvious reasons not greeted enthusiastically by anyone, although military officials were willing to consider it if better options were not possible. Adopting a strategy of peripheral defense was seen as an abandonment of the entire NATO strategy and as a serious defeat for U.S. objectives. Abandoning any form of German rearmament was seen as an option that would lead the American public to reject NATO and the principle of collective defense. Indeed, American strategists generally remained cautiously optimistic about the prospects of EDC ratification primarily because they believed everyone, including the French, could see that the alternatives to it were much worse.[165]

Supporters of the European Defense Community in France certainly would not have disagreed with the bleak American assessment of the alternatives, but the nature of domestic politics in the Fourth Republic made it extremely difficult to develop a winning coalition for the EDC.[166] The conflation of German rearmament with the EDC hurt both causes because the political actors most willing to accept rearmament, the Gaullists, were the most vehement opponents of the supranational EDC. Conversely, supporters of the EDC and European integration were often those who were most reluctant to see Germany rearmed. The Center-Left coalitions in the National Assembly that had originally sponsored the Schuman and Pleven Plans were replaced by Center-Right coalitions after March 1952. After the election, supporters of the EDC warned Acheson that a majority for ratification of the treaty did not exist in the National Assembly.[167] Elected with the help of dissident Gaullists, Pinay obviously did not want to openly associate himself with the EDC cause. The U.S. embassy in Paris was unsure if he even supported the treaty.[168] Although the balance of EDC supporters and opponents within France was a close one, the intensity with which the two sides waged the battle was vastly different. Reasoned arguments about the EDC being the best and safest

[165] For the first set of a long line of papers concerning alternatives to the EDC, see the PPS paper "United States Policy in the Event of Non-Ratification of the EDC and Contractual Agreements," December 3, 1952, PPS Records, box 29. For comments on the study, see Wolf to Moore, December 15, 1952, RG 59, Records of the Office of European Regional Affairs: Files of J. Graham Parsons, box 2, NA.

[166] For an explanation of the EDC's failure which focuses on coalitional politics, see Helen V. Milner, *Interests, Institutions, and Information* (Princeton: Princeton University Press, 1997), 179–202.

[167] Dunn to Secretary of State, May 11, 1952, *FRUS*, 1952–54, vol. 5, 655.

[168] Dunn to Secretary of State, July 3, 1952, *FRUS*, 1952–54, vol. 6, 96–98.

method of rearming Germany could not easily compete with emotional arguments about the EDC leading to the death of the French army and the revival of the Wehrmacht. French nationalism was still a much stronger political force than European supranationalism.[169]

With the Truman presidency about to come to an end, Acheson was well aware of the reality that it would be up to his successors to get the French to ratify the EDC treaty. Threatening or pressuring the French was seen as a counterproductive step that would only reinforce the idea that the EDC was an American invention being forced upon France.[170] Some analysts thought that the prospects for ratification might be improved if the United States were willing to submit to a "species of blackmail" on the part of the French, but Acheson was unwilling and unable to offer the French very much in the way of inducements after May 1952.[171] Although something might be done for the French in North Africa, Indochina, or issues related to offshore production, Acheson told officials at the U.S. embassy in Paris that they should "promptly" disillusion French officials of any thoughts they might have about the prospects of strengthened U.S. guarantees in the event of a German secession from the EDC.[172] Whether any American approach to the French might have helped achieve ratification is questionable, but there was no doubt that the momentum behind the EDC was gone by the end of 1952. In a conversation with Jean Monnet in December 1952, Acheson said that he feared the EDC situation was on "the very verge of complete disaster."[173]

The EDC may well have been on the verge of disaster, but any possibility that the United States would search for other alternatives came to an end once Eisenhower took office with Dulles as his secretary of state in January 1953. Both men truly believed that the EDC was the only possible way for Europe to resolve the German question on a permanent basis. Although they were unconditional supporters of the EDC, their reasons for supporting European unity were not identical. Dulles's primary concern was the *internal* European balance of power and the problems posed

[169] For the best discussion of French arguments over the EDC, see William I. Hitchcock, *France Restored: Cold War Diplomacy and the Quest for Leadership in France, 1944–54* (Chapel Hill: University of North Carolina Press, 1998), 170–76.

[170] See Dunn to Secretary of State, June 20, 1952, *FRUS*, 1952–54, vol. 5, 688–90; Dunn to Draper, "Possible EDC Crisis," November 18, 1952, Paris Embassy Files, Records Pertaining to the EDC, 1951–55, box 14, NA; and Bohlen memo, "EDC in the Paris Meeting of NATO," enclosed in Bohlen to Moore, December 8, 1952, RG 59, Records of Charles E. Bohlen, box 5, NA.

[171] Other analysts, however, were against submitting to French requests because they recognized that no single concession would be enough to guarantee ratification of the EDC. See Knight to Perkins, October 22, 1952, *FRUS*, 1952–54, vol. 6, 1266–67.

[172] Secretary of State to Embassy in France, September 6, 1952, *FRUS*, 1952–54, vol. 5, 690–92.

[173] Memorandum of Convesation by Acheson, December 14, 1952, *FRUS*, 1952–54, vol. 6, 254.

by Germany's inherent superiority over its neighbors. In a system with no restrictions on the sovereignty of individual states, Dulles felt the German problem was insoluble because relations based on treaties such as Versailles were inherently fragile. His lack of any faith in Western Europe's ability to solve the German problem through treaties among sovereign states explains why Dulles never had any great enthusiasm for simply admitting Germany to NATO as an alternative to the EDC. In contrast, Eisenhower's primary concern with European unity was always related to the *external* balance of power. European unity was important to Eisenhower primarily because it was the only way that the states of Western Europe could eventually develop the collective power which would make it possible to defend themselves against the Soviets and allow American troops to return home. These differing motivations for supporting the EDC would become more relevant over time. However, Dulles and Eisenhower were united from the start that the ratification of the EDC was their most important objective. Neither of them were willing to tolerate or accept the idea that there was such a thing as an "alternative" to the EDC. When Livingston Merchant, assistant secretary of state for European affairs, brought up the need to consider alternatives to the EDC due to the strong parliamentary opposition in France, Dulles lashed out at the mere thought that the administration might not be able to bring the EDC into existence:

> That is just the sort of defeatism which the Eisenhower administration is not going to tolerate in any of its representatives in any position of responsibility for foreign affairs at home or abroad. Livy, put out of your mind any concept that there is an alternative or that we're considering one to the EDC. The EDC is going to go into effect, and it will do so by the utilization of the full influence and power of persuasion of the United States government under President Eisenhower and myself.[174]

The limited extent of Dulles's willingness to consider alternatives to the EDC can be seen in one of the first meetings he held with the JCS and high level State Department officials in January 1953. All of the participants in the meeting were told beforehand that the purpose of the meeting was to discuss alternatives to the EDC, but Dulles quickly made it clear that he was not really interested in alternatives and that he was surprised that anyone could view other options as superior to the EDC. What

[174] Livingston Merchant Oral History, Dulles Oral History Project, Princeton University, 36. For a good discussion of Dulles and the EDC, see Rolf Steininger, "John Foster Dulles, the European Defense Community, and the German Question," in *John Foster Dulles and the Diplomacy of the Cold War*, ed. Richard H. Immerman (Princeton: Princeton University Press, 1990), 79–108.

Dulles really wanted was a discussion of alternatives that he could use purely for negotiating purposes during his upcoming trip to Europe. Despite the fact that the option of Germany in NATO was seen as potentially viable and the option of peripheral defense was seen as disastrous, Dulles wanted to convey the idea to the Europeans that there were no alternatives and that America might be forced to adopt a peripheral defense strategy if the EDC was not ratified. In his view, "If the French and Germans should come to see that the military position would be tolerable for us if we could hold Turkey, Spain, etc., that would create pressures on them which would not exist if they think we are so committed that we must carry the entire load in the area."[175] Rather than reassuring Western Europeans that America's commitment to Europe would be maintained in the event that it was impossible to ratify the EDC, Dulles thought that chances for ratification would be enhanced if the EDC were seen as the only option for German rearmament.

Dulles chose the "EDC or else" strategy despite the fact that the new French government of Prime Minister René Mayer was even more beholden to Gaullist support than the Pinay government that he replaced. In order to obtain investiture, Mayer was willing to promise the Gaullists that he would negotiate protocols designed to protect the integrity of the French army, that he would not push for ratification until the other EDC members had agreed to the French protocols, and that he would not pressure the National Assembly for ratification. As the American embassy noted, Gaullists "apparently voted investiture in belief that Mayer showed willingness to surrender the essence of EDC, namely its supranational character."[176] But since Mayer also had to obtain support from the pro-EDC MRP party to obtain investiture, he proclaimed that his stance was fully consistent with the spirit of the EDC treaty. The fact that Mayer removed Robert Schuman from his position as foreign minister and replaced him with Bidault, who had just tried to become premier by wooing the Gaullists, raised very understandable concerns about how vigorously the new government would pursue EDC ratification.[177] Although most

[175] Memorandum of Conversation of State-Mutual Security Agency-JCS, January 28, 1953, *FRUS*, 1952–54, vol. 5, 711–17 (quotation on 713).

[176] The report by Ted Achilles in RG 59, 751.00/1–753, NA, provides an excellent example of how absurd EDC politics had become by this time. After Mayer provided his views on the EDC to the satisfaction of the Gaullists, the MRP asked for its own clarifications. With the help of the main negotiator of the EDC treaty, Herve Alphand, Mayer was able to somehow convince both the anti-EDC Gaullists and the pro-EDC MRP that his stance was consistent with their own.

[177] Dulles raised the question of whether the government spoke approvingly of the EDC to the United States but quite another way to its coalition partners. Despite the fact that Dunn denied this to be the case, the realities of French domestic politics required a certain amount of talking differently to both the United States and political factions within the country. See, for example, Martin Herz, "Conversation between Alphand and General Billotte," June 11, 1953, Records Pertaining to the EDC, 1951–55, box 14, NA.

American observers concluded that the new government was committed to ratification of the EDC and that the protocols were necessary for ratification, other analysts thought that French actions and the new protocols might be designed as a way of killing the EDC by making unacceptable demands of their EDC partners.[178]

Mayer and Bidault may not have been wildly enthusiastic about the EDC, but their initial course of action was to try and make the EDC more acceptable to the various factions of the National Assembly by gaining support for protocols which made France less restricted by the supranational provisions of the treaty. Dulles and some American officials may have been too committed to the EDC solution, but when Dulles gingerly brought up the possibility that Germany might have to be permitted to join NATO if the EDC failed, Mayer bluntly let him know that the French did not consider this an option. If the United States attempted to bring Germany into NATO, Mayer informed Dulles, "France would use its veto power to prevent this and, if the veto was overridden, would destroy the effectiveness of any German national army by being so strongly in opposition that in practical effect the lines of communication between Germany and the Atlantic were broken."[179] Rather than thinking about alternatives, Mayer believed that the EDC could still pass if the protocols were accepted, a Saar settlement worked out, and greater British participation in the EDC obtained. Mayer also said he needed a much greater financial contribution from the United States for the French effort in Indochina, which would enable them to field an army on the continent that could at least equal the Germans. The numerous French conditions for ratification, combined with the less than enthusiastic reaction of the other EDC members to Dulles's pleas for early ratification, indicates that the secretary of state was unable to establish the "rolling bandwagon" of support that he had hoped for prior to his visit. Although he tried to be optimistic about the effects of his trip on European attitudes toward the EDC, even he thought that the prospects of ratification were still only about 60–40.[180]

Dulles's efforts to build momentum behind EDC ratification were dealt a serious setback in March 1953 with the announcement of Stalin's death. The possibility that Stalin's death might make it possible for the West to consider major initiatives to defuse the Cold War was appealing to Eisenhower and some other administration officials, but Dulles was far more concerned with the threats posed to the EDC's ratification prospects than he was by the possible opportunities of a settlement with the Soviets. The conciliatory gestures put out by the new Soviet leadership, as well as

[178] See Morris and Margolies to Riddleberger, RG 59, 662A.00/2–1753, NA.
[179] *FRUS*, 1952–54, vol. 5, 1561.
[180] Ibid., 1580.

Premier Malenkov's and Deputy Premier Beria's apparent willingness to consider the abandonment of East Germany, has led some scholars to suggest that the Eisenhower administration might have missed a real opportunity to reunify Germany on favorable terms.[181] But although Eisenhower was at least willing to contemplate the idea of bold initiatives in the aftermath of Stalin's death, Dulles was unwilling to do anything which might jeopardize the EDC's ratification prospects. Regardless of the new Soviet leadership's willingness to be more accommodating to the West, which he personally did not think very likely, Dulles was convinced that any prolonged negotiations with the Soviets would only help neutralist forces in Europe and hurt pro-EDC forces. In his view, any four-power negotiations with the Soviets at this time would "ruin every prospect of ratification of the European Defense Community. . . . If an attempt were made to create German unity by some other vehicle than the EDC, then certainly the EDC would be finished."[182]

Despite his best efforts, Dulles was unable to prevent the changes in the Soviet leadership from interfering with the EDC ratification process. Dulles could dampen Eisenhower's enthusiasm for major initiatives, but he could not have a similar influence on Churchill. The British leader was not dissuaded by his own Foreign Office, Eisenhower, or Adenauer from thinking that the timing was now right to try and work out some sort of general settlement over Germany with the Soviets.[183] Regardless of the merits of Churchill's stance, his call for four-power talks now became a primary reason for French reluctance to move forward on the ratification of the EDC. Foreign Secretary Bidault was privately opposed to four-power talks, but claimed that it was now impossible for the French to vote

[181] See Deborah Welch Larson, *Anatomy of Mistrust: U.S.–Soviet Relations during the Cold War* (Ithaca, N.Y.: Cornell University Press, 1997), 39–57. Unlike many scholars on the subject of missed opportunities, Larson is very careful in assessing both sides of the debate and modest in her assessment of the possibilities for a settlement. For an examination of the evidence on Beria and the German question in the aftermath of Stalin's death—and one which casts doubt on the missed opportunity thesis—see James Richter, "Reexamining Soviet Policy towards Germany during the Beria Interregnum," Working Paper no. 3, Cold War International History Project (June 1992).

[182] Memorandum of Conversation of NSC Meeting, March 4, 1953, *FRUS, 1952–54*, vol. 8, 1117–25 (quotation on 1121 and 1123). For discussions within the administration over how to respond to Stalin's death, see Robert R. Bowie and Richard H. Immerman, *Waging Peace: How Eisenhower Shaped an Enduring Cold War Strategy* (New York: Oxford University Press, 1998), 109–22; W. W. Rostow, *Europe after Stalin: Eisenhower's Three Decisions of March 11, 1953* (Austin: University of Texas Press, 1982); and Klaus Larres, "Eisenhower and the First Forty Days after Stalin's Death: The Incompatibility of Detente and Political Warfare," *Diplomacy and Statecraft* 6 (July 1995): 431–69.

[183] For Churchill's quest for detente, a German settlement, and his conflict with the Eisenhower administration, see Steininger, *German Question*, 100–12; John W. Young, "Churchill's Bid for Peace with Moscow, 1954," *History* 73 (October 1988): 425–48; and M. Steven Fish, "After Stalin's Death: The Anglo-American Debate over a New Cold War," *Diplomatic History* 10 (fall 1986): 333–55.

on ratification of the EDC until after a four-power meeting.[184] During meetings with the British and the Americans in July 1953, Bidault refused to agree to the British-American position that four-power meetings be postponed until after the ratification of the EDC. Bidault was not swayed by Dulles's impassioned speeches about the EDC or his warning that Europe would return to the "dark ages" if it was not ratified.[185] Indeed, despite Dulles's insistence that the French at least agree to a strong statement supporting the EDC in the final communiqué of the meetings, Bidault refused to go along because he believed that it would further hurt the ratification prospects of the EDC.[186]

The fact that Bidault resisted any enthusiastic endorsement of the EDC spoke volumes about the prospects of the treaty within France. Nevertheless, as PPS analyst Leon Fuller grimly acknowledged, the United States had long since passed the point where it could do anything else but hope against hope that somehow the French would ultimately ratify the EDC. Withdrawing American support from the EDC would be "a diplomatic triumph of the first magnitude for the Soviet Union. . . . For better or worse, our eggs are all in the EDC basket."[187] Serious consideration of alternatives to the EDC within the State Department was rejected because "there is nothing to be gained by considering these clearly less desirable alternatives to the EDC."[188] The complete paralysis that the EDC had placed on all of America's European policies was apparent in the National Security Council document NSC 160, which was intended to be a major review of policy toward Germany. Despite all of the setbacks that had occurred since the beginning of the year, Dulles remained unwilling to support any major change in course. He was particularly unwilling to

[184] For French arguments concerning domestic political reasons for going along with four-power talks in the aftermath of Churchill's speech, see Byington to Merchant, "French Position on Four-Power Talks in Germany," RG 59, 762.00/7–353, NA; and RG 59, 762.0221/7–753, NA.

[185] The records of the Tripartite Meetings can be found in *FRUS, 1952–54*, vol. 5, 1607–1708. The quotation from Dulles about Europe's return to the "dark ages" is on 1623.

[186] Bidault's reluctance to openly support the EDC fully confirmed the suspicions of David Bruce. See Bruce to Dulles, July 7, 1953, General Correspondence and Memoranda Series, Strictly Confidential, box 2, DDEL.

[187] Leon Fuller, "EDC and a German Settlement," March 17, 1953, PPS Records, box 16, NA.

[188] Memorandum by Russell Fessenden, "EDC Ratification Prospects and Consideration of Alternatives," July 21, 1953, *FRUS, 1952–54*, vol. 5, 799. For a similar conclusion by the PPS, see Fuller to Bowie, "Meeting on NSC German Policy Paper," June 24, 1953, enclosing "Statement of Policy on United States Position with Respect to Germany," PPS Records, box 16, NA. For a radical departure from these views, see the report of Task Force A of Project Solarium. Led by George Kennan, Task Force A recommended that the United States abandon the EDC and independently rearm West Germany in order to facilitate unification. Needless to say, Kennan's proposals did not receive any support within the administration. See "A Report to the National Security Council by Task Force 'A' of Project Solarium," July 16, 1953, National Security Council Series, White House Office, Office of the Special Assistant for National Security Affairs: Records, 1952–1961, box 9, DDEL.

accept the Defense Department's request that the United States should insist on a January 1, 1954, deadline for the ratification of the EDC since "it
would be nothing less than catastrophic to destroy the possibility of realizing an integrated Europe." Dulles also rejected the idea that America
should begin preparing the groundwork for rearming Germany, since
even rumors of such a policy would hurt EDC supporters in France.
Thinking about alternatives to the EDC remained an exercise whose sole
purpose was to help generate pressure on France to ratify the treaty.[189]
Since Eisenhower completely backed Dulles's resistance to any arbitrary
deadlines for EDC ratification and bilateral efforts to rearm Germany,
America's German policy remained firmly in place despite the fact that its
crucial piece—the EDC—was in serious jeopardy.[190]

EISENHOWER, DULLES, AND THE
"REDEPLOYMENT" OF AMERICAN FORCES

Neither the possible opportunities offered by Stalin's death nor the
lack of progress on EDC ratification altered Eisenhower's fundamental
conceptions of American national security. The goals of Western
European self-sufficiency and the eventual removal of American forces
from the continent remained central ones for Eisenhower. His vision was
fully reflected in the strategic concepts put forward by the Joint Chiefs of
Staff in August 1953. The JCS emphasized that American military power
was overextended and that much greater attention needed to be paid to
the continental defense of the United States. One of the key conclusions of
the JCS report was that "Military commitments overseas—that is to say,
peripheral military commitments—would cease to have first claim on our
resources."[191] Although the JCS did not spell out exactly how, where, and
when American forces were to be withdrawn, they did make it clear that
they were not speaking of token cuts or ones that would not be noticed by

---

[189] Memorandum of Conversation of NSC Meeting, August 13, 1953, *FRUS, 1952–54*,
vol. 7, 501–8. The text of NSC 160 can be found on pages 510–31. The language of NSC 160
suggested that the United States might begin taking measures to bilaterally rearm Germany
prior to January 1, 1954, if this could be done without alienating France. Dulles made a point
of emphasizing that he alone would make that decision, which suggests that the language in
the text did not have any real authority since Dulles would veto any moves toward the rearmament of Germany without French concurrence.

[190] For Eisenhower's views, see Memorandum by the Special Assistant to the President
(Cutler), *FRUS, 1952–54*, vol. 7, 509–10. Deleted from the version published in *FRUS* is
Eisenhower's statement that if the French failed to ratify the EDC, "perhaps we would have
to build our European defense on U.K., Low Countries, Denmark, and Spain." The full document can be found in NSC Series, box 4, DDEL.

[191] Memorandum by Radford, Ridgway, Carney, and Twining, August 8, 1953. I thank
Marc Trachtenberg for providing me with a copy of this document. For an excellent discussion of the background to the JCS report, see Bowie and Immerman, *Waging Peace*, 183–87.

the NATO allies. That the JCS was proposing a major reduction in American ground forces overseas can be seen in the enthusiastic manner in which the extreme fiscal conservatives within the administration greeted the report. At a meeting of the National Security Council, Treasury Secretary George Humphrey stated that the JCS report "was the most important thing that had happened in this country since January 20."[192] Eisenhower, who was not at the NSC meeting, was also very impressed with the JCS report:

> This concept is a crystallized and clarified statement of this administration's understanding of our national security objectives since World War II. . . . From the beginning, people who have really studied foreign and military problems have considered that the stationing of American troops abroad was a temporary expedient. It was a stop-gap operation to bring confidence and security to our friends overseas, who were desperately exposed to communist aggression. Any thinking individual, in the services or out, always understood that the basic purpose of so stationing American troops was to produce among our friends morale, confidence, economic and military strength in order that they would be able to hold vital areas with indigenous troops until American help could arrive.[193]

Dulles, on the other hand, was terrified by the implications that the JCS report had for America's relations with the NATO allies. Dulles expressed some sympathy for the approach of the JCS but was insistent that it would take a great deal of preparatory work before redeployment could be sold to the NATO allies: "If we do not succeed in selling this interpretation of the proposed redeployment, we can anticipate that the governments and peoples of the free world will dismiss our proposed new policy as simply camouflaged isolation."[194] Dulles was highly conscious of the fact that this was the worst possible time to even talk about the withdrawal of American forces from Europe since the German elections had not yet been held and the French had not even scheduled a vote on the EDC. An

---

[192] Memorandum of Conversation of NSC Meeting, August 27, 1953, *FRUS, 1952–54*, vol. 2, 443–55 (quotation on 447).

[193] Memorandum by Cutler to Dulles, September 3, 1953, *FRUS, 1952–54*, vol. 2, 455–457 (quotation on 456). Cutler would subsequently request that the task forces involved in the Solarium Project rethink their views based on Eisenhower's approval of the JCS report. Eisenhower himself indicated that he wanted the analysts involved in Solarium to incorporate the emphasis on redeployment. See Robert Cutler, "Overall Comment on Policy Paper, Sept 18/53, of Solarium Special Committee," September 20, 1953, White House Office, National Security Staff Papers, 1948–61, Executive Secretary's Subject File Series, box 17, DDEL.

[194] NSC Meeting, August 27, 1953, *FRUS, 1952–54*, vol. 2, 453.

American withdrawal might be possible after the EDC had been established and European fears about Germany diminished; it would be impossible if the EDC failed and Germany and France remained antagonists. It was precisely because Dulles feared that the JCS concept would become known by the allies that he wanted the NSC to place sole responsibility for discussing "redeployment" in his hands.

Dulles's shock over the implications of the JCS report led directly to his curious memorandum to Eisenhower on September 6 calling for a "spectacular effort to relax world tensions on a global basis and execute mutual withdrawals of Red Army and of U.S. forces abroad."[195] Scholars have always thought that such a proposal was out of character for Dulles, but it reflected a fundamental reality that President Roosevelt had understood very well during the Second World War: policies of containment toward the Soviet Union were hard to carry out in the absence of substantial American forces on the continent. Only a general settlement with the Soviet Union in Europe could possibly reconcile the allies to the withdrawal of American forces. As Dulles would later tell the NSC, an American redeployment from Europe could only take place "under the cover of another and larger operation."[196] Despite the fact that some members of the NSC wanted to immediately start taking steps toward redeployment, Eisenhower accepted Dulles's view that the goal of withdrawal had to be subordinate to other goals for the present time. Withdrawal would have to be postponed "as long as we were still desperately trying to add twelve German divisions to the defense forces of Western Europe."[197]

It is remarkable, given the attention that historians have paid to the question of missed opportunities for ending the Cold War, that little attention has been paid to whether September 1953 represented such an opportunity. Unlike the situation that prevailed within the West during the Berlin Blockade and Kennan's Program A, the Stalin Note of March 1952, and the aftermath of Stalin's death in 1953, some Western European leaders were potentially receptive to major initiatives that envisioned large scale withdrawals of American and Soviet forces from the heart of Europe. At the same time that Dulles and Eisenhower were thinking about redeployment, Adenauer and Belgian Foreign Minister Paul van Zeeland actually forwarded to Washington separate but very similar plans for a new European security system.[198] Both the German and Belgian plans envisioned the creation of a broad demilitarized zone in

---

[195] Memorandum by the Secretary of State, September 6, 1953, *FRUS*, 1952–54, vol. 2, 457–60 (quotation on 459).
[196] Memorandum of Conversation of NSC Meeting, October 7, 1953, *FRUS*, 1952–54, vol. 2, 526.
[197] Ibid., 525.
[198] For the German and Belgian proposals, see *FRUS*, 1952–54, vol. 5, 806–7, 813–14.

central Europe in which all British, American, and Soviet forces would be withdrawn. Soviet forces would be withdrawn from most if not all of the satellite states and only troops from EDC members would be allowed into the eastern part of Germany. Although these plans were not as good as getting the Soviets to willingly accept a united Germany in NATO and their complete withdrawal from Eastern Europe, it is hard to imagine a proposal that on balance better served the interests of the United States, Germany, and Western Europe.[199]

Whether the Soviets would have accepted proposals along these lines is certainly debatable, but the ideas behind the Adenauer and van Zeeland plans never even became the subject of diplomatic negotiations. Eisenhower and Dulles asked van Zeeland to refrain from publicizing his plan until the U.S. government had a chance to study it in greater detail; the fact that they did order such studies before meeting with van Zeeland shows that they were willing to consider the idea of a broad demilitarized zone in Europe with American, British, and Soviet withdrawals from Germany.[200] The basic problem with the JCS and Adenauer/van Zeeland plans for troop withdrawals is that they were based on the assumption that the EDC would come into existence. In addition, the French also made it known to the United States that plans such as van Zeeland's should be put on hold until after the EDC was "an accomplished fact." In fact, the French ambassador to the United States indicated that even after the EDC was ratified the West should focus on "modest gestures" rather than ambitious plans such as van Zeeland's.[201] Like every other element of Western strategy and diplomacy, any initiatives for a new security system in Europe would have to be placed on hold until after EDC ratification.

The reluctance of Dulles and Eisenhower to support the Belgian and German proposals was also motivated by the belief that nothing should interfere with the EDC ratification process in France. Adenauer's victory in early September led to a great resurgence of optimism within the U.S. government about the EDC's prospects.[202] French officials, including former pessimists like Bidault, were now seemingly far more enthusiastic

---

[199] For U.S. assessments of the van Zeeland and Adenauer plans, see MacArthur to Dulles, "Van Zeeland Plan for German Unification," RG 59, 762.00/3–2153, NA; and Thurston to MacArthur, "Revised Paper on Van Zeeland and other Plans for Security Guarantees," RG 59, 762.00/9–2353, NA. The latter paper argued that the United States should attempt to retain the right to station forces throughout Western Germany. As one reader noted in the margin, "The Soviets withdraw from where they are and we don't budge in Western Germany. It won't work."

[200] Memorandum of Conversation by Secretary of State, September 29, 1953, *FRUS, 1952–54*, vol. 5, 813–14; and Smith to Wilson, September 21, 1953, RG 59, 762.00/9–2153, NA.

[201] Memorandum of Conversation by MacArthur, RG 59, 762.00/10–953, NA.

[202] The Paris embassy composed a fairly gloomy assessment a week before Adenauer's victory. A week after Adenauer's election, they sent the same report to Washington with a cover letter explaining that the Chancellor's victory had changed everything in a more favorable

about fighting and winning the EDC debate within the National Assembly. French officials also expressed greater optimism than they had in the past. Directly raising a proposal envisioning a U.S. troop withdrawal from Germany would, at best, probably lead the French to delay their consideration of the treaty. At worst, rumors about America's willingness to consider a troop withdrawal might possibly tip the balance within France to de Gaulle and other opponents of the EDC.

Unfortunately for Dulles and Eisenhower, their efforts to keep the question of an American troop withdrawal out of the EDC debate were unsuccessful. Despite the fact that Dulles had insisted on total secrecy about the status of military planning, one or more participants in the ongoing debate over national security strategy obviously let the press know that the administration was considering withdrawing troops from Europe. Subsequent efforts by Dulles and Eisenhower to squelch military officials from talking about an American withdrawal had little effect. First, Secretary of Defense Charles Wilson gave a press conference on October 20, 1953, in which he stated that the development of new weapons would lead to substantial reductions of overseas troops "in the long run."[203] Dulles was willing to openly lie and state to the press that no U.S. troop withdrawals were being contemplated, but the damage was already done.[204] Nowhere was the effect more damaging than in France. Bidault and other French officials sought to contain the controversy, but even the U.S. embassy in Paris reported that the rumors were "leading to major psychological damage to achievement of US policy objectives. . . . An argument against EDC is thus being put into the hands of groups already opposing it on grounds that it will place France at unacceptable disadvantage with respect to German military power."[205] Second, before the controversy over Wilson's remarks had a chance to die down, Admiral Radford made similar off-the-record comments to reporters about how new weapons and German soldiers would make it possible to withdraw American forces. All of the European papers had lengthy discussions of

---

direction. See "The Opposition to the EDC in the French Parliament," September 1, 1953, Records Pertaining to the EDC, 1951–55," box 14, NA; and RG 59, 751.5/9–153, NA.

[203] See Dulles Telephone Conversation with C. D. Jackson, October 21, 1953 with attached transcript of Wilson Press Conference, White House Confidential Memoranda Series, box 8, Dulles Papers, DDEL. See also C. D. Jackson notes of his meeting with Eisenhower, October 20, 1953, box 56, C. D. Jackson Papers, DDEL.

[204] Dulles Telegram, Records Pertaining to the EDC, 1951–55, box 14, NA. Eisenhower expressed his displeasure at the leaks in a letter to Gruenther, but repeated his philosophy about the temporary nature of the American commitment and stated: "we cannot allow anyone to get up and protest that we are going to keep troops in Europe *forever*." Eisenhower to Gruenther, October 27, 1953, Eisenhower Correspondence Series, box 1, Al Gruenther Papers, DDEL.

[205] Hughes to Secretary of State, October 27, 1953, White House Central Files, Confidential File, box 68, DDEL.

the issue.[206] In short, all of the negative consequences that Dulles had feared upon hearing the JCS report in August had occurred despite his efforts to prevent them.

A context in which the French press was regularly featuring stories about the possibility of a coming American withdrawal was not the best atmosphere to begin the process of EDC ratification, but the administration kept the pressure on the government of new Prime Minister Laniel to go ahead with the preliminary debates.[207] Despite the fact that Bidault went all out for the EDC, he could not marshal a majority for the EDC within the National Assembly. The Paris embassy, although not yet willing to write off the EDC, concluded that "while potential pro-EDC majority in Assembly exists, it has been reduced in course of the recent foreign affairs debate."[208] Laniel was furious with Bidault, and probably with the United States too, for forcing a debate over the EDC which put his government's survival in jeopardy. He told Ted Achilles shortly after the debate, "You see I was right. Bidault insisted on his showdown and has got it, but on what? Govt may or may not survive but in any event it is riven by dissension and bitterness. We are no nearer EDC ratification and no one has gained except perhaps Mendès-France."[209]

The setbacks for the EDC in the National Assembly put Bidault and Laniel in an impossible situation prior to the Bermuda Conference of December 1953. Both of them knew that they would be pressed on the EDC question and that they had no truthful answers that would please the British or the Americans. The French were looking for enhanced assurances about American and British commitments to Europe, but neither of the allies were inclined to view these requests sympathetically. The United States issued veiled threats that further support for France's leadership role was dependent on EDC ratification. The British were even less supportive. Rather than preparing for the conference by reading the briefing books prepared by the Foreign Office, Churchill preferred to read a novel entitled *Death to the French*. Talking to the "Bloody Frogs," he told

---

[206] Hughes to Secretary of State, November 4, 1953, White House Central Files, Confidential File, box 68, DDEL. For the extensive European press commentary, see the clippings and telegrams in Paris Embassy Files, Records Pertaining to the EDC, 1951–55, box 13, NA.

[207] Despite the fact that the American ambassador to France, Douglas Dillon, had urged Washington to accept a slower timetable for EDC ratification, Dulles told the Paris embassy to recommend the earliest possible action on the EDC. See Secretary of State to Embassy in France, November 8, 1953, *FRUS*, 1952–54, vol. 5, 838–39.

[208] Achilles to Secretary of State, November 29, 1953, Paris Embassy Files, Records Pertaining to the EDC, 1951–55, box 14, NA.

[209] Achilles to Secretary of State, November 26, 1953, Paris Embassy Files, Records Pertaining to the EDC, 1951–55, box 14, NA. Achilles told Washington that "it is better that battle has begun rather than being longer evaded." The President of France, Vincent Auriol, told a visiting American that the "EDC was dead insofar as France is concerned." See Robertson to Dulles, RG 59, 651.00/11–1853, NA.

his physician, was a job for Eden rather than himself.[210] As C. D. Jackson noted in his diary, the British were "unbelievably rude to the French." On substantive issues, Churchill told the French that if they could not ratify the EDC treaty within two months, it would be necessary to rearm the Germans within NATO. Despite the fact that the French had made it clear that increased British assurances were crucial to EDC ratification, Churchill emphasized that he would not go beyond any assurances already given.[211] Although the French knew they were in for a rough time at the Bermuda Conference, they were probably not aware that Churchill had planned to indict and convict them for several days over the EDC question.

Eisenhower was more receptive than Churchill to French concerns, a fact which can be explained by his much greater skepticism over the feasibility and desirability of rearming Germany within NATO. Nevertheless, he could not give the French what they wanted and needed at Bermuda. In order to counteract all the rumors about an American withdrawal, Bidault argued that the "key of all solutions" was an agreement "that the strength of U.S. and U.K. forces stationed in Europe should represent a definite proportion of total forces and have a definite proportion relationship to the German forces of the couverture."[212] Whether Bidault was correct that such an agreement would have been enough to get the EDC passed—and it is by no means certain that it would have been enough—Eisenhower was unwilling even to discuss the matter of an American commitment that went beyond those embodied in previous declarations. The United States assured France that previous commitments were solid and binding, but the French knew full well that none of them in any way bound the United States to keep any specified number of forces in Europe.[213] The French, of course, knew it too, which is why Bidault wanted definite numbers and proportions placed on the American assurances.

American policy toward the EDC surely needed a reappraisal by the end of 1953, but Eisenhower and Dulles were unwilling to contemplate any major changes. Leaving aside the constitutional question of whether it was possible to guarantee the presence of a certain number of American

---

[210] Lord Moran, *Churchill: The Struggle for Survival, 1940–65* (Boston, Mass.: Houghton Mifflin, 1966), 536–41. See also J. W. Young, "Churchill, the Russians, and the Western Alliance: The Three Power Conference at Bermuda, December 1953," *English Historical Review* (October 1986): 889–912.

[211] C. D. Jackson Diary, December 5–8, 1953, box 56, C. D. Jackson Papers, DDEL.

[212] *FRUS, 1952–54*, vol. 5, 1800.

[213] On the eve of the Bermuda meeting, the State Department compiled a review for Dulles about whether the United States had either the right or obligation under the NATO treaty to commit troops to Europe for any specified length of time. They concluded that Washington had never committed to maintaining any troops in Europe for any length of time. See Phleger to Dulles, December 2, 1953, PPS Records, box 29, NA.

troops in Europe, Eisenhower was philosophically opposed to buying the ratification of the EDC with concrete and specific promises along the lines desired by the French. If Western Europe was going to need the presence of substantial American troops long after the EDC came into being, a crucial component of Eisenhower's entire national security conception would have to be abandoned. Throughout his presidency, Eisenhower was unwilling to give up on the ideas of Western Europe as a third global power and the temporary nature of U.S. forces on the continent; and he was certainly unwilling to do so in 1953. Since a frank admission that the EDC was an essential element toward the goal of removing American forces would have been counterproductive and potentially disastrous, Eisenhower had no choice but to hide the connection between the two. At an NSC meeting held shortly after the conference in Bermuda, Eisenhower reminded his leading advisors that the EDC was "our one great objective" and that until it was ratified "we could not afford to take any step toward redeployment, or even to talk about redeployment, until these objectives have been reached."[214]

Dulles adopted a different approach from the policy of silence recommended by Eisenhower, although it is quite unlikely that this represented any substantial disagreement between the two men. In his famous "agonizing reappraisal" speech to NATO on December 14, 1953, Dulles raised the question of an American withdrawal by stating directly that America would have to reconsider its entire approach toward Europe if France and Germany could not bury their historic rivalry and "move onward to more complete and organic forms of union." The clear implication that Dulles wanted to put in the mind of his audience was that American troops were likely to stay in Europe if the EDC came into being, and less likely to stay if the EDC were rejected. Although Dulles did not openly discuss the option of admitting Germany directly into NATO, he did suggest that it was not a good option and that the steps Europe needed to take "must involve something more than treaties between sovereign states."[215]

Dulles's speech has been described as a "calculated bluff" since America did not ultimately follow through on abandoning European defense after the failure of the EDC.[216] Although the speech was indeed calculated, it is a mistake to see it as a bluff. Every argument that Dulles made in his speech accurately represented his deepest beliefs about the need for Europe to move on toward greater unity as a sheer matter of self-preservation as well as his fears about what would happen in the event

---

[214] Memorandum of Discussion at the 174th Meeting of the NSC, December 10, 1953, *FRUS*, 1952–54, vol. 5, pt. 1, 449–54 (quotation on 451).

[215] The agonizing reappraisal speech is published in *FRUS*, 1952–54, vol.5, 461–68 (quotation on 463).

[216] Brian Durchin, "The Agonizing Reappraisal: Eisenhower, Dulles, and the European Defense Community," *Diplomatic History* 16 (spring 1992): 201–21.

the EDC did not come into being. It is wrong to believe that Dulles was merely engaging in histrionics or bluffing because he knew that the NATO option could always and easily be adopted if the EDC was rejected by France. The NATO option was still perceived to have the same flaws as it did in 1951. From the perspective of Dulles and Eisenhower, as well as State Department policy planners, the NATO option was far from a sure thing because France would continue to insist on restrictive conditions that Germany would never accept.[217] As Eisenhower told Churchill after the latter raised the idea of the NATO option, "any, and I repeat any, projected alternative to EDC will present problems no less acute and difficult to solve."[218] In short, American policymakers certainly hoped they could avoid an agonizing reappraisal of policy toward Western Europe, but they were far from confident that such a reappraisal would not be necessary in the event of the failure of the EDC.

Successful ratification of the EDC would prevent any need for reappraisals, agonizing or otherwise. Eisenhower and Dulles's efforts were still devoted to this objective, and they were not looking ahead to its failure. It is primarily for this reason that they went along with the holding of the four-power conference at Berlin in early 1954. The Berlin Conference had little rationale other than convincing the French people that the Soviet Union did not have acceptable proposals regarding Germany, which would hopefully remove a major obstacle in the way of EDC ratification.[219] Bidault's unwillingness to go along with the Soviets on European questions made a very favorable impression on Dulles and other American officials. According to Livingston Merchant, Bidault was "the only prominent living Frenchman who wants both to get EDC through as soon as possible and continue the war in Indo-China to a successful conclusion."[220] The strong linkage between the European Defense Community and Indochina was revealed at Berlin when Dulles eventu-

---

[217] See Fuller to Bowie, "Alternatives to EDC (Summary)," December 1, 1953, PPS Records, box 29, NA. As Fuller noted in a later memo to Bowie, analysts in Regional Affairs and Western European Affairs were still only willing to come up with alternatives designed to get France to accept EDC. See Fuller to Bowie, December 10, 1953, *FRUS*, 1952–54, vol. 5, 863–65.

[218] Eisenhower to Churchill, December 17, 1953, in *The Churchill-Eisenhower Correspondence*, ed. Peter G. Boyle (Chapel Hill: University of North Carolina Press, 1990), 117.

[219] The Berlin Conference can be followed in *FRUS*, 1952–54, vol. 7, 601–1234.

[220] Livingston Merchant presentation at the National War College, March 12, 1954, RG 59, 762.00/31954, NA. For other favorable assessments of Bidault by C. D. Jackson and Dulles, see *FRUS*, 1952–54, vol. 7, 919–22, 1210. In light of Bidault's emergence as the crucial figure for both the EDC and Indochina, it is interesting to note that less than six weeks before Berlin he had told Joe Alsop that only American troops could save the situation in Indochina. As for EDC, he told Alsop "no, there was not a hope" that it would be ratified. While unwilling to question Alsop's honesty, the counselor of the Paris Embassy refused to accept that the statement reflected Bidault's true beliefs about the EDC. See Robert Joyce to Livingston Merchant, December 31, 1953, RG 59, Office Files of Assistant Secretaries, box 26, NA.

ally agreed to attend a five-power conference later in the year devoted to Indochina. Dulles would have preferred that such a conference not be held at all, but he agreed to support and attend the Geneva Conference because he recognized that Bidault needed to bring something back from Berlin that would be popular at home.[221]

In addition to support for a conference on Indochina, Bidault also informed Dulles that new American assurances on future troop commitments were essential to French ratification of the EDC. Since the U.S. desire to get the EDC completed before the Geneva Conference imposed a very tight deadline for action, there was no time for any great philosophical debate about the meaning of the new assurances.[222] There were clear limits as to how far the United States could go in terms of assurances. Nevertheless, Dulles was willing to go along with Bidault because "we have done far more for lesser causes and that it would be tragic indeed if our own timidity should be a factor in the failure to bring EDC into force. . . . The stakes were far too large for us to be miserly in our approach."[223] Eisenhower was very upset with the French demands, declaring that he was "sick and tired of being blackmailed," but he too was willing to grant the assurances if they were absolutely necessary.[224] At a very heated NSC meeting in early March 1954, Eisenhower defended the granting of assurances before those members of his administration, including Wilson and Humphrey, who thought that appeasing the French would destroy his desire to redeploy American forces. Although Eisenhower was somewhat sympathetic to those who wanted to take a tough line against the French, he rejected their advice that France should be threatened with an American troop withdrawal if it failed to go through with the EDC. Since he did not intend to reduce American forces over the next two years, and because the new assurances were little more than rehashes of past statements, Eisenhower saw no reason not to offer them if they would help get the EDC treaty ratified. Eisenhower rejected the short-sighted views of Humphrey and other officials who failed to appreciate the fact that the desire for redeployment needed to be considered in conjunction with objectives such as the EDC.[225] For both Eisenhower and Dulles, the establishment of the EDC was the necessary condition for an American troop withdrawal. Both men had originally hoped to avoid

[221] See *FRUS*, 1952–54, vol. 7, 1226; and Kevin Ruane, "Anthony Eden, British Diplomacy, and the Origins of the Geneva Conference," *The Historical Journal* 37 (1994): 153–72.

[222] If the debate were to take place before the Geneva Conference, scheduled for late April, American assurances were needed within a matter of days in order for Bidault to set a date for a vote. Jones to Merchant, February 26, 1954, RG 59, 762A.00/22654, NA.

[223] Summary of Meeting, "Assurances to the French on EDC," February 25, 1954, PPS Records, box 87, NA.

[224] NSC Meeting, February 26, 1954, *FRUS*, 1952–54, vol. 7, 1230.

[225] NSC Meeting, March 4, 1954, *FRUS*, 1952–54, vol. 5, 886–90.

giving assurances to the French on this issue but were unwilling to withhold assurances if it would increase the chance of the EDC's ratification.

Had stronger American assurances been provided much more willingly and early, they might have made an impact on the situation in France, but the time had long passed when the EDC could be salvaged by words. The new American assurances were rehashes of old pledges that had been deemed insufficient; they did not represent the "ironclad" guarantees that might have changed negative votes to positive ones. Opponents of the EDC within France might have used the lack of an American guarantee of troops as a reason to oppose the treaty, but groups on both the Right and Left had many other reasons why they were opposed to the EDC. Gaullists were surely not inclined to believe the truthfulness of any American statements regarding the maintenance of forces, but even if they had, the EDC would still be a technocratic "monster" dangerous to French sovereignty because of its supranational basis. French socialists might welcome the American and British assurances, but the party was still strongly divided between those who opposed German rearmament in all circumstances and those who opposed the EDC because of the lack of any democratic controls over the institution. The fact that it was an open secret that the United States had made the setting of a date for debate on the treaty in the National Assembly a condition for the granting of assurances certainly did not help the EDC cause. Marshall Juin's denunciation of the EDC treaty in March 1954 undoubtedly cost the EDC more votes than the new American pledges won.[226]

Any positive effect the American assurances might have had were dwarfed by the impending disaster facing the French garrison at Dienbienphu in northern Vietnam. American policymakers could not believe that the EDC's fortunes rested on the outcome of Dienbienphu, but Laniel made it clear that defeat in Indochina would spell defeat for both his government and the EDC. Laniel's hope was that the United States would use its airpower to save the garrison, and by doing so save the EDC.[227] If American policymakers had truly believed that Dienbienphu was the only remaining obstacle in the way of EDC ratification, it is possible that the administration might have received the French pleas for help more sympathetically. But after years of wrangling with the French over what they needed for EDC ratification, it is quite likely that Eisenhower and Dulles were unconvinced that anything they could do in Indochina would guarantee the success of the EDC.

---

[226] Bidault estimated that Juin's switch cost the EDC fifty votes. See Alfred Gruenther to Eisenhower, April 3, 1954, NSC Series, Administration Subseries, box 16, DDEL.

[227] See Melanie Billings-Yun, *Decision against War* (New York: Columbia University Press, 1988); and George C. Herring and Richard H. Immerman, "Eisenhower, Dulles, and Dienbienphu: 'The Day We Didn't Go to War' Revisited," *The Journal of American History* 71 (September 1984): 343–63.

After the fall of the Laniel government, the EDC treaty was all but dead: but neither Dulles nor Eisenhower were willing to pull the plug. Eisenhower had told the NSC in April that he would back the EDC as long as there was "a shred of hope" that it could be established.[228] The British considered the treaty dead for all intents and purposes after the assumption of power by Pierre Mendès-France, but the United States was unwilling to accept this conclusion. Pro-European but without any firm convictions one way or the other about the merits of the EDC, Mendès-France had a quite reasonable perspective on the treaty.[229] Although convinced that a majority in the National Assembly for the EDC did not exist at the present time, Mendès-France believed that a bitterly divided France could not enter or reject the community with a majority of only a handful of votes. Rather than begging the United States and Great Britain for greater commitments and financial aid to make the EDC more palatable, as past governments had done, Mendès-France hoped that the opponents of the treaty on both the Left and the Right could negotiate changes in the treaty that would enable a large majority to support France's entry into the EDC. Not surprisingly, the main changes that emerged out of France's reassessment of the EDC in the summer of 1954 all involved a watering down of the supranational principle.

In retrospect, whether it was better for the EDC to pass under these circumstances or for it to be rejected because its revolutionary character had been compromised is a debatable question. It was not a debatable question at all for Dulles in the summer of 1954. An EDC in which supranational features had been eliminated was not acceptable. Pointing to the narrow majorities which had passed the United States constitution in the eighteenth century, Dulles argued that even a majority of one vote in favor the EDC should be an acceptable outcome for Mendès-France.[230] Leaving aside the practical difficulties that French revisions of the treaty might have posed for the other members of the EDC, Dulles urged Mendès-France to avoid any changes in the treaty that would compromise its supranational features since these elements represented "the best and last hope for Europe."[231] With full U.S. encouragement, the other members of the EDC rejected the changes in the treaty put forward by Mendès-France. The long agonizing death of the EDC finally came to an end on August 30 when the National Assembly voted down the treaty on a procedural motion.

---

[228] NSC Meeting, April 1, 1954, Ann Whitman File, NSC Series, box 5, DDEL.

[229] See Jean Lacouture, *Pierre Mendes France* (New York: Holmer & Meier, 1984), 265–82; and Irwin Wall, *The United States and the Making of Postwar France* (New York: Cambridge University Press, 1991), 275–96.

[230] Memorandum of Conversation by MacArthur, July 13, 1954, *FRUS*, 1952–54, vol. 5, 1018–23.

[231] Dulles to Mendes-France, August 21, 1954, *FRUS*, 1952–54, vol. 5, 1060.

CONCLUSION

The French rejection of the EDC was the most spectacular defeat of American foreign policy in the early postwar era. In the aftermath of the French action, lower-level officials within the Eisenhower administration were willing to acknowledge that the American approach to the EDC was at least partially to blame for the outcome. Leon Fuller of the Policy Planning Staff argued that American policy had overemphasized the concept of federalism and failed to appreciate the amount of nationalist resistance a project such as the EDC would engender. Although the idea of a European army was devised by the French, Fuller correctly argued that the EDC failed because it came to be seen as "a *US* project to force *premature* federation along *military* lines involving a high risk of *German* predominance in a European union, and with a too apparent concern for realization of EDC as a device for mobilizing German armed forces."[232] Unfortunately, Dulles was in no mood to acknowledge either past American failures or to adopt a more constructive approach to the problems posed by the French. The EDC represented the salvation of Western Europe for Dulles and he lashed out at France for rejecting the supranational path. In a harshly worded statement issued the day after the French vote, Dulles argued that the rejection of the EDC called into question the American assumption that Western Europe would "develop a unity which would make it immune from war as between its members and defensible from aggression from without." The actions of the French National Assembly did not change what he called the "basic and stubborn fact" that warfare in Western Europe could only be prevented if the states of the region merged "certain functions of their government into supranational institutions."[233] Dulles put the burden of finding alternatives to the EDC primarily in the hands of the Western Europeans and he let Anthony Eden know that these alternatives should also be supranational. Furious with the actions of Mendès-Frances and unconvinced about the viability of alternatives not rooted in supranationalism, Dulles was simply unable to play any constructive role in the immediate aftermath of the EDC's defeat.

Fortunately, other Western statesmen were willing and able to work constructively in September 1954. Adenauer, whose own political fortunes had been staked on the EDC, was as furious as Dulles at the actions of Mendès-France, but he made it known that he would voluntarily accept the same restrictions and force levels within NATO that he had been

---

[232] Leon Fuller, "Post-EDC Reappraisal," September 2, 1954, PPS Records, box 82, NA; and "U.S. Policy Toward Europe-Post-EDC," September 10, 1954, *FRUS*, *1952–54*, vol. 5, 1170–77 (quotation on 1170).

[233] Statement by the Secretary of State, August 31, 1954, *FRUS*, *1952–54*, vol. 5, 1120–22.

willing to accept under the EDC.[234] Adenauer's position made it much easier for Mendès-France to accept direct German membership in NATO. More than anyone else, the credit for settling the German rearmament question belongs to Anthony Eden. Realizing that supranational solutions were part of the problem, Eden proposed the creation of the Western European Union (WEU) as a substitute for the EDC. Based firmly on national principles, the WEU would be able to establish controls on Germany without raising all of the complications posed by the European Defense Community. Just as important, Eden was willing to make specific guarantees about the maintenance of British forces on the continent. Dulles was not sympathetic to Eden's approach since it was not based on supranationalism, but he went along since all other countries accepted the new framework.[235] After Dulles indicated a willingness to restate the same assurances that the United States had provided for the EDC, the longest and most fundamental crisis of the Western alliance was for all intents and purposes resolved.

The EDC was a beautiful and noble dream for Eisenhower and Dulles, but in the final analysis it was always just a dream. Even if Mendès-France or any of the preceding French governments had been able to assure the passage of the EDC, it is foolish to believe that this would have ended concerns about German power or lead inexorably to the creation of the political superstructure that would have transformed the states of Western Europe into a United States of Europe capable of acting as a third great power. Although Western Europe had all of the material prerequisites to become a third great power, particularly if aided by the United States, most Western Europeans were unwilling to make the sacrifices of sovereignty that would have been required to eliminate the German problem and balance against the Soviet Union. More important, even the most enthusiastic advocates of the EDC in Western Europe did not share Eisenhower's basic premise that the presence of American forces on the continent should be seen only as a temporary and regrettable necessity. The EDC was based on a false premise from the start; it was unreasonable to expect the Western Europeans to solve and manage the German problem by their own efforts so soon after the Second World War. The EDC, designed as a mechanism to alleviate fears of German power and advance the cause of unity, had exactly the opposite effect because it focused attention on the fact that even a truncated West Germany would still be the

---

[234] See David Clay Large, *Germans to the Front: West German Rearmament in the Adenauer Era* (Chapel Hill: University of North Carolina Press, 1996), 213–20.

[235] For Eden's crucial role in September 1954, see Anne Deighton, "The Last Piece of the Jigsaw: Britain and the Creation of the Western European Union, 1954," *Contemporary European History* 7 (1998): 181–96. For Dulles's criticisms of Eden's abandonment of supranationalism, see Dulles to Eden, September 14, 1954, *FRUS*, 1952–54, vol. 5, 1192–94.

strongest power in the region. Institutional rules and the trappings of supranationalism could not and should not have been expected to temper the realities of power and anarchy in continental Europe less than a decade after the war. In short, much to Eisenhower's regret, there was no substitute for a more or less permanent American military presence as long as Germany was divided and the Soviet Union posed a threat to European peace and stability.

[6]

No Exit: America and the Future of Europe

Out of this question there arises America's vital interest in the settlement of European affairs, and it is plain, I submit, that our grand objective must be a settlement which does not call for a permanent American military intervention in Europe to maintain it.

Walter Lippmann, 1943

When the time arrived for American policymakers to negotiate the final settlement of the Second World War and an end to the Cold War, no one defined America's grand objective even remotely like Walter Lippmann did in 1943. Indeed, ensuring the maintenance of a permanent military presence in Europe after the Cold War was one of the most important goals sought by American policymakers during the process of negotiating German reunification. No matter how much the Soviet Union reduced its own forces in Europe, George Bush informed Mikhail Gorbachev in 1990, "the U.S. intends, within this ceiling and with the consent of our allies, to retain a substantial military presence in Europe for the foreseeable future, regardless of the decisions you take about your own forces."[1] Long after the total collapse and dissolution of the Soviet Union, American policymakers rarely missed an occasion to make it clear that the United States was determined to maintain a permanent military presence in Europe well into the twenty-first century. According to former Secretary of State Warren Christopher, "We will continue to maintain 100,000 American troops on European soil. We will continue to help preserve peace and prosperity for the next fifty years and beyond—this time for the entire continent."[2] In the aftermath of the Cold War, American policymakers,

---

[1] Cited in Philip Zelikow and Condoleeza Rice, *Germany Unified and Transformed: A Study in Statecraft* (Cambridge, Mass.: Harvard University Press, 1995), 172. According to Robert Hutchings, director for European Affairs at the NSC during this period, "No idea was more strongly and deeply held in the upper levels of the administration than the core conviction that the American presence was indispensable to European stability and therefore to vital American interests." See Robert L. Hutchings, *American Diplomacy and the End of the Cold War* (Baltimore: Johns Hopkins University Press, 1997), 157.

[2] Cited in John Mearsheimer, "The Future of America's Continental Commitment," in *No End to Alliance*, ed. Geir Lundestad (New York: St. Martin's Press, 1998), 221.

both Republicans and Democrats, have provided a very clear answer to the question of when all U.S. military forces can safely be returned from Europe: Never.

Whether European peace and prosperity in the twenty-first century requires a permanent American military presence is surely debatable, but what is most striking about contemporary debates over the future of Europe is how few policymakers or scholars on either side of the Atlantic treat the question as one that should even be debated. America's determination to keep its forces in Europe on a permanent basis has been strongly encouraged and warmly welcomed by its NATO allies, as well as by its former Warsaw Pact enemies. The French may complain about American "hyperpower" tendencies in the aftermath of the Cold War, but these complaints fall far short of any demand that America should remove its military forces from Europe. The rest of Europe, including the reunified Germany, where most of these forces are still located, has been emphatic about the inability of the continent to dispense with an American military presence both now and in the future—despite frequent arguments between the United States and its NATO allies.[3]

Scholarly debates among international relations theorists over the future of Europe have been quite contentious, but the scope of the debate has often been quite narrow and highly partisan. Much of the debate has revolved around John Mearsheimer's controversial argument, based heavily on neorealist theory, that the end of bipolarity and the return of multipolarity will lead to a return of deadly balance-of-power politics. A close reading of Mearsheimer's argument, however, reveals that the real trigger for future European instability would be a complete withdrawal of American forces. Many books and articles have been written in the last ten years arguing against the pessimism of the Mearsheimer thesis, but hardly any of his liberal critics have sought to make the argument that the development of European institutions and the pacific nature of democracies renders an American military presence obsolete or superfluous. Liberal theorists, no less than realist theorists, have found it inconceivable to consider how a stable and peaceful European system could be created and maintained without America continuing to serve as both pacifier and protector.[4]

This book has sought to accomplish a number of objectives, but one of the most important has been to demonstrate that at the conclusion of the

[3] For Western European attitudes about the continuing need for U.S. forces in Europe, see Robert J. Art, "Why Western Europe Needs the United States and NATO," *Political Science Quarterly* 111 (1996): 1–39.

[4] Liberal theorists have every reason to believe that the survival of NATO and the continued progress of European integration provide strong support for their theoretical framework. Nevertheless, I find it very curious that within the entire family of liberal theories of international relations, it is very difficult to find a theory which suggests that American military forces are no longer needed in Europe.

Second World War, American strategists could not and did not avoid thinking about how European stability could be maintained after the withdrawal of American forces. Contemporary policymakers and international relations theorists may take it for granted that a permanent American military presence in Europe is desirable and feasible, but even during the darkest days of the Second World War and the early Cold War, it was taken for granted that eventually American forces in Europe would be withdrawn. American foreign policy during the formative period of bipolarity and the Cold War would surely have been vastly different if policymakers had operated under the assumption that the United States would permanently maintain military forces on the continent. Viewing early postwar American foreign policy simply in terms of the triumph of liberal internationalism over the dark forces of nationalistic isolationism is far too simplistic a story, but many international relations theorists and historians continue to write books and articles that omit or barely pay attention to the strong desire to get American troops out of Europe at the earliest possible moment. Neglect of this desire is somewhat understandable since it goes against the main themes of orthodox, revisionist, and post-revisionist scholarship.[5] Furthermore, for the many international relations theorists who still view the postwar world through the lens of Kenneth Waltz's famous thesis about bipolar systems, the American effort to withdraw its forces from Europe—and the general themes stressed in this book—undoubtedly convey a radically different impression of both the nature of American foreign policy and the structure of the early postwar system.

This chapter focuses on three central elements. The first section addresses the question: How and why did the structural problem of latent German power in Europe persist even after the bipolar revolution? The second examines the two "exit strategies" U.S. policymakers and strategists pursued in order to establish a stable Europe that would not be dependent on the permanent presence of American forces. The final section looks at the implications of this study for thinking about the future of Europe "after bipolarity."

AMERICA, GERMANY, AND THE BIPOLAR REVOLUTION

Most contemporary international relations theorists have never felt a great need to rethink the collapse of the Grand Alliance and the origins of

---

[5] For excellent discussions of these three approaches to the study of postwar American foreign policy, see John Lewis Gaddis, "The Emerging Post-Revisionist Synthesis on the Origins of the Cold War," *Diplomatic History* 7 (summer 1983): 171–90; and Howard Jones and Randall B. Woods, "Origins of the Cold War in Europe and the Near East: Recent Historiography and the National Security Imperative," *Diplomatic History* 17 (summer 1993): 251–76.

the Cold War in Europe. For a generation of political scientists whose introduction to the discipline often started with Waltz's arguments about the distinctive nature of bipolar systems, the kinds of questions that historians generally debate and reassess are rather pointless because the Cold War is viewed as a structural inevitability given the emergence of two superpowers. The neorealist perspective on the Cold War is expressed very well by Glenn Snyder and Paul Diesing in their book *Conflict Among Nations*. In their view, "while the *degree* of tension and hostility in the Cold War was undoubtedly increased by incompatible ideologies and specific hostile behavior that tended to confirm initial perceptions of threat, the initial perceptions themselves were a function of the preponderance of these two powers over all others. In short, the rivalry was structurally ordained."[6] After a brief discussion of the major European events leading up to the emergence of NATO in 1949, Snyder and Diesing essentially argue that the events themselves are not all that important since it "may be plausibly contended that something like this would have occurred in any case, whatever the detailed factual circumstances that attended the birth of the bipolar system."[7] Needless to say, a structural explanation of the origins of the Cold War along these lines makes the close study of the history of the late 1940s irrelevant, and the broad generalities of neorealism do not offer all that much insight for diplomatic historians. Although the conflict between the aims of historians and international relations theorists will never disappear, this book hopes to narrow the divide that currently exists between the former's emphasis on the early Cold War period and the latter's focus on bipolarity.[8]

By focusing on American perceptions of the postwar structure, this book has sought to link the bipolar revolution more directly to the origins of the Cold War in Europe and the course of American foreign policy in the 1940s and 1950s. The history of the early Cold War can be fit into the neorealist framework quite easily without taking into account perceptions, but it is also true that a wide range of choices that American policymakers could have made, as well as many alternative outcomes, can just as easily be accommodated within the same theoretical framework. Some of these possible choices actually would have been far more consistent with neorealism than the choices that American policymakers did in fact make. For example, if American officials had accepted the early contain-

---

[6] Glenn Snyder and Paul Diesing, *Conflict Among Nations: Bargaining, Decision Making, and System Structure in International Crises* (Princeton: Princeton University Press, 1977), 420.

[7] Ibid., 421.

[8] John Lewis Gaddis, of course, did popularize Waltz's bipolarity thesis in the 1980s as part of a broader explanation for the linkage between the Cold War and what Gaddis called the "Long Peace." However, as Anne Deighton suggests, the neorealist argument is not very helpful for understanding very much about the early Cold War period. See Anne Deighton, "The Cold War in Europe, 1945–47," in *Explaining International Relations since 1945*, ed. Ngaire Woods (New York: Oxford University Press, 1996), 81–97.

ment arguments put forward by William Bullitt in 1943 or Winston Churchill in the aftermath of Yalta, it would not be difficult in retrospect to view the resulting actions as a natural choice given the anticipated position of power the Soviets would have at the end of the war. An American decision in 1947 to massively increase the defense budget and the production of atomic weapons would have been far more consistent with neorealism's focus on the primacy of internal balancing than was the decision to invest resources in the economic recovery of Western Europe. Similarly, a unilateral American decision to rearm West Germany in 1950, with or without the support of the allies, would have been far more consistent with neorealism's emphasis on the freedom of action enjoyed by bipolar alliance leaders than was the subsequent four-year conflict within the alliance over the European Defense Community. Since a wide variety of American choices during the 1940s and 1950s can be seen legitimately as a reaction to the structural imperatives of bipolarity, it is necessary to link perceptions of the postwar structure more directly to the specific choices made by American policymakers.[9]

What were the implications of the emergence of the bipolar era for American foreign policy? Consideration of this question needs to begin by examining American perceptions during the Second World War and before the emergence of the Cold War. Political scientists sometimes argue that American policymakers did not immediately grasp the emergence of a bipolar structure until 1947 or that their strong ideological commitment to Wilsonianism prevented them from adopting policies of containment sooner than they should have. However, long before the end of the Second World War, American policymakers were well aware that the postwar structure would be dominated by only two great powers. But unlike later neorealists, they simply did not draw the inference that America and the Soviet Union were destined by structure to become bitter rivals who would compete across a divided Germany for decades to come. The explanation usually put forward—that American policymakers did not reach this conclusion because they were either idealistic Wilsonians, extremely naive about Stalin, or did not recognize the extent of British decline—is mistaken. The rise of Soviet power was accepted as an unalterable consequence of the Second World War, and American officials who thought about the future of the postwar world understood it immediately as a revolutionary and unprecedented change in the global distribution of power. Nevertheless, there were many "structural" reasons for rejecting worst case assumptions about the implications of bipolarity for postwar U.S.–Soviet relations.

[9] For a good statement of this argument and an excellent application of it in practice, see Steve Weber, "Shaping the Postwar Balance of Power: Multilateralism in NATO," in *Multilateralism Matters*, ed. John Ruggie (New York: Columbia University Press, 1993), 233–92.

First, American officials recognized the highly skewed distribution of power that would exist between the two superpowers in the immediate aftermath of the war. American policymakers did not believe that the Soviet Union, utterly devastated by the struggle to defeat Nazi Germany, would be in any position to embark on a program of relentless and risky expansion. The period when the Soviet Union would be in a position to act more aggressively in Europe was thought to be fifteen or twenty years away, given an extended period of economic recovery and peace. In his recent book *The Origins of Major War*, Dale Copeland correctly emphasizes how these assessments of future Soviet power played a role after the war in moving the Truman administration toward a policy of containment. However, during the period prior to the end of the war, similar assessments of the postwar distribution of power supported a policy of seeking to find a reasonable accommodation with the Soviet Union.[10] Given the inevitable position of superiority that the Soviet Union would enjoy over the rest of Europe in twenty or thirty years, it made much more sense to try and establish amicable relations with the Soviet Union sooner rather than later. The extent to which Roosevelt was aware of the assessments of the postwar distribution of power produced by the Joint Chiefs of Staff and the Office of Strategic Services is unclear, but his wartime diplomacy of seeking to win Stalin's cooperation and trust was not out of line with analyses emphasizing that the rise of Soviet power presented future rather than immediate problems. As Charles Bohlen argued to George Kennan in the aftermath of the Yalta Conference, there was no point in prematurely assuming hostile relations with the Soviet Union after the war: "Either our pals intend to limit themselves or they don't. I submit, as the British say, that the answer is not yet clear. But what is clear is that the Soyuz (Soviet Union) is here to stay, as one of the major factors of the world. Quarreling with them would be so easy, but we can always come to that."[11] Roosevelt's pursuit of postwar cooperation with the Soviet Union was not, as is so often portrayed, an example of American policymakers ignoring the power realities of a bipolar structure.

The second reason why worst case assumptions about the Soviet Union were avoided during the Second World War can be attributed to the inability of both strategists and policymakers to think about the future of Europe in terms of a "permanent" American military presence on the continent. Scholars often make the assumption that the removal of troops was merely a personal goal of FDR's, but it is hard to find any evidence that it was rejected at lower-levels of the American government or in more academic discussions of the future of Europe. American military forces

---

[10] See Dale Copeland, *The Origins of Major War* (Ithaca: Cornell University Press, 2000), 146–56.

[11] Charles Bohlen, *Witness to History* (New York: W. W. Norton, 1973), 176.

would obviously be in Europe for some time after the war as occupation forces in Germany, but there does not seem to have been any question that the occupation itself would one day end and that U.S. forces would be brought home. The assumption that American forces could not and would not remain in Europe on a permanent basis also inclined policy-makers away from the possibly premature conclusion that the two strongest powers in the system were inevitably fated to be hostile rivals in Europe after the war.

Third, worst case assumptions ignored the very strong incentives for continued cooperation in Europe that would exist because of the German problem. No matter how much Germany was temporarily weakened by the war, the structural problem of German power in Europe would not be eliminated by the outcome of the Second World War and the rise of two superpowers. Germany's power at the end of the war indicated little or nothing about the country's strength in twenty or thirty years, and it was the latter consideration that was most crucial for everyone who thought about the German problem during the Second World War. One of the basic tenets of neorealist theory is that the superpowers in a bipolar world have no strong incentive for close cooperation because "there is no third party powerful enough to provide a sufficient incentive for alliance."[12] But, as William T. R. Fox and many others argued throughout the early postwar period, the problem of controlling postwar Germany provided a very powerful incentive for attempting to preserve postwar cooperation between the superpowers. As Fox argued, the struggle for Germany could not be won by either side because neither the United States nor the Soviet Union could afford to lose such a struggle. Neither side could permit the other to absorb the resources of Germany and include it in an exclusive sphere directed against the other side without running considerable risk of sparking a great power war. An equally ominous prospect was that the breakdown of cooperation among the superpowers would result in Germany becoming a third power nucleus alongside the Western democracies and the Soviet Union. Although the strong incentives for continued postwar cooperation did not guarantee that the superpowers would be able to reach a solution to the German problem, they did argue against prematurely arriving at that conclusion. Even analysts in 1945 who thought there was "no time to lose" in restoring a balance of power in Europe against Russia believed that a nonaligned Germany represented the best and most desirable solution to the inherent dilemmas represented by the structural problem of future German power.[13]

---

[12] Snyder and Diesing, *Conflict Among Nations*, 421.

[13] See William J. Donovan to Truman, May 5, 1945, enclosing Office of Strategic Services, "Problems and Objectives of United States Policy," April 2, 1945, box 15, Rose Conway File, HSTL.

The central argument of this book is that the problem of latent German power made the bipolar system confronted by American policymakers much different and much more complex than the one found in neorealist theory. The bipolar world of neorealist theory is one in which no third power can decisively influence the balance of power, but American policymakers from the start acted on the belief that U.S.–Soviet relations and the future of Europe turned on the resolution of the German question. The rise of Soviet power, combined with the collapse of indigenous European power, was obviously a development of great significance, but it did not initially lead to any fundamental policy conclusions about postwar Europe. It certainly did not lead American policymakers during the Second World War to view the Soviet Union as a future irreconcilable enemy. American policymakers knew that even if the Soviet Union was the second strongest power in the world, its actual and potential power paled in comparison to that of the United States. The neorealist emphasis on the importance of internal balancing and internally generated sources of power is not very useful for understanding the origins of the Cold War in Europe because of the great disparity between American and Soviet power at the end of the war. As Melvyn Leffler argues, "The Soviet Union would become a formidable competitor of the United States only if it could capture or co-opt the industrial infrastructure, natural resources, and skilled labor of more advanced countries."[14] It is for this reason that rather than being relatively unimportant to the bipolar balance of power, as neorealist theory suggests, the future of Germany was viewed by American policymakers as the critical and decisive question of the post-war world. For Soviet policymakers, the question of how powerful and independent Germany would be in the future was undoubtedly of equal or even greater importance.

EMPIRE BY DEFAULT: AMERICAN EXIT STRATEGIES AND THE FUTURE OF EUROPE

The most obvious inference that could be drawn about the future of Europe at the end of the Second World War was that a lengthy American military presence was essential to a peaceful and stable continent. Even before the end of the war, Western European leaders recognized the post-war need for what the historian Geir Lundestad would later describe as an American "empire by invitation."[15] Churchill emphasized the need for a

[14] Melvyn P. Leffler, *A Preponderance of Power* (Stanford: Stanford University Press, 1992), 6.
[15] Geir Lundestad, "Empire by Invitation? The United States and Western Europe, 1945–52," *Journal of Peace Research* 23 (1986): 263–77. For an extended version of this argu-

postwar presence repeatedly to FDR during the war, and even Charles de Gaulle, never particularly known for excessive fondness of the American role in Europe, recognized as early as April 1945 that it was necessary to "link in the future the United States with the security of the European continent and establish through their presence the conditions of a necessary balance of power in Europe."[16] The fact that Churchill and de Gaulle viewed the American role as critical to the stability of Europe might not be all that surprising, but there is also a fair amount of evidence that suggests Stalin himself welcomed the presence of American forces in Europe as a way of restraining Germany. Indeed, there was only one state at the end of the Second World War that vigorously rejected the idea of a lengthy or permanent American military presence in Europe. Unfortunately, the lone dissenting view was held by the United States itself.

American resistance to the acceptance of an "empire by invitation" began during the Second World War and persisted long after the start of the Cold War, which suggests that the American role in postwar Europe can be better thought of as an "empire by default." Lundestad correctly emphasizes the pull exerted by the Western Europeans after the war to keep U.S. troops in Europe permanently, but he underestimates the resistance of the United States to accepting an imperial role.[17] In the short term, American officials had to accept European invitations, but the purpose of accepting the initial invitations was to bring Western Europe to the point where it would no longer need to extend them. There is no greater symbol of NATO and American participation in European defense than Eisenhower, but even Ike vigorously resisted the idea of a lasting imperial relationship between America and Western Europe: "In the long-run, it is not possible—and certainly not desirable—that Europe should be occupied territory defended by legions brought in from abroad, somewhat in the fashion that Rome's territories vainly sought security many hundred years ago."[18] Rather than desiring to maintain political control over the development of Western Europe, American officials

---

ment, see Lundestad, *The American "Empire" and Other Studies of U.S. Foreign Policy in a Comparative Perspective* (New York: Oxford University Press, 1990), 31–115.

[16] De Gaulle cited in Georges-Henri Soutou, "France," in *The Origins of the Cold War in Europe: International Perspectives,* ed. David Reynolds (New Haven: Yale University Press, 1994), 100.

[17] This is particularly true in Lundestad's more recent works. In an essay built around Lord Ismay's famous quip that NATO was formed to "keep the Russians out, the Germans down, and the Americans in," Lundestad argues that the Americans were "genuinely happy" to stay in Europe. If this were really the case, however, it is not exactly clear why the Western Europeans kept inviting the United States to assume an even larger role, or why they were so worried about the United States declining invitations to stay. See Lundestad, "American-European Cooperation and Conflict: Past, Present, and Future," in *No End to Alliance,* ed. Lundestad, 250.

[18] Eisenhower to Edward Hazlett Jr., June 21, 1951, *TPDDE,* 12:369.

throughout the 1940s and early 1950s sought to create the long-term conditions under which Europe could be peaceful and stable without requiring the permanent presence of American forces. It is the inability to achieve the necessary conditions of stability, rather than any independent desire to exert control and influence, that explains why what was widely thought to be a temporary American commitment to Europe eventually became a permanent one.

No one resisted invitations to empire in postwar Europe more than Roosevelt. In contrast to what many scholars still argue about his wartime diplomacy and postwar plans, FDR was far from oblivious to the basic realities of power, and his wartime diplomacy meshed quite well with his fundamental assumptions about the postwar future of Europe. FDR's basic strategic dilemma was rooted in the two major assumptions he made about the postwar world: the Soviet Union was going to be the strongest power on the continent after the war and America was going to withdraw its military forces from Europe within a few years after the end of the war. Starting from these two assumptions, it is not hard to see why Roosevelt chose to pursue policies of reassurance toward Stalin and why he showed little interest in seeing French power revived after the war. Recreating an indigenous balance of power in Europe against the Soviet Union was simply impossible to contemplate without the restoration of German military power, an option which for understandable reasons no one viewed favorably during the Second World War. As shown by his determination to get American forces into Europe as quickly as possible in 1943 if Germany appeared to be on the verge of collapse, Roosevelt was certainly unwilling to allow the Soviet Union to unilaterally determine the postwar fate of Germany. But he was also determined to pursue a postwar German settlement that the Soviet Union could willingly accept and one which would eliminate everyone's fears about the long-term restoration of German power. With the German problem solved, the Soviet Union would not have to maintain an iron grip on Eastern Europe due to legitimate fears about Germany, and American forces would not have to remain in Europe to balance either Germany or the Soviet Union. Preserving friendly relations with the Soviets and eliminating the German problem were the major components of FDR's postwar exit strategy.

Of course, it was much easier to plan for these objectives than it was to accomplish them. Roosevelt's enthusiasm for the Morgenthau Plan and the dismemberment of Germany are clear indications of his desire to fundamentally alter the dynamics of the European balance-of-power system, but it is impossible to say whether he would have followed through on either of these specific policies after the war. None of the allies, including the Soviet Union, was supportive or enthusiastic about the idea of making Germany a predominately agricultural nation, and Roosevelt himself clearly moved away from Morgenthau's influence after the Quebec Conference of September 1944. Less than a month before his death, in a clear reversal of the Morgenthau approach, the president told representatives from the State and War Departments that he wanted to have "German industry maintained to the fullest extent necessary to maintain the Germans so that we don't have the burden of taking care of them."[19] His legacy on the all-important questions of dismemberment and reparations was also ambiguous. FDR was still enthusiastic about dismembering Germany at the Yalta Conference, but the Big Three left this question as a matter to be determined at a later date. On the question of reparations, he was willing to support the idea that the Soviets should receive substantial reparations from Germany, but only if this could be done in a way that did not increase America's own financial burden. Scholars have frequently criticized Secretary of State Byrnes and President Truman for their seemingly harsh stance on reparations at Potsdam, but it is not at all clear that Roosevelt would have pursued a more generous reparations policy given his own determination to avoid the burden of providing for postwar Germany.

More than anything else, the question of reparations poisoned the atmosphere of U.S.–Soviet relations and the prospects of lasting great power cooperation over Germany. The extreme manner in which the Soviets looted their zone prior to the Potsdam Conference and the unilateral cession of German territory to Poland helped convince Byrnes, rightly or wrongly, that it was highly unrealistic to expect America and the Soviet Union to run the postwar German economy as a single unit. The understandable American desire to reduce the financial costs of the occupation conflicted with the equally understandable Soviet desire to extract as much as they possibly could from Germany. The practical resolution that Byrnes came up with was to allow the Soviets to do whatever they wanted in terms of extracting reparations from their zone but to sharply limit what they could expect to receive from the western zones. Despite the fact that he was repeatedly warned by the British that a zonal reparations plan only made sense in the context of a divided Germany, Byrnes persisted in separating the reparations issue from a unified treatment of the German economy. Although it has become common to associate the division of Germany with the breakdown of U.S.–Soviet relations, Byrnes rejected this association at Potsdam. The outcome he was clearly trying to achieve with the reparations settlement was basically a friendly division of Germany, or what Marc Trachtenberg terms an "amicable divorce."[20] By agreeing not to try and run the German economy in intimate

[19] Cited in Carolyn Eisenberg, *Drawing the Line: The American Decision to Divide Germany, 1944–49* (Cambridge: Cambridge University Press, 1996), 65.
[20] Mark Trachtenberg, *A Constructed Peace: The Making of the European Settlement, 1945–63* (Princeton: Princeton University Press, 1999), 15–35.

collaboration with the Soviet Union, Byrnes believed, the United States would greatly reduce the potential for endless discord and conflict between the superpowers. The spirit and goals of the Byrnes plan on reparations were quite consistent with Roosevelt's basic approach to cooperation with the Soviets.

The Byrnes policy failed for a variety of reasons, but none was more significant than the fact that it was no longer politically feasible to advocate the division of Germany. FDR and Stalin had freely and enthusiastically engaged in numerous discussions about how many parts Germany should be divided into after the war, but open advocacy of this solution died between the Yalta and Potsdam Conferences. The State Department had never considered division a desirable or viable long-term solution, and Stalin himself publicly rejected the idea in his initial appeals to the German people after Hitler's defeat. At Potsdam, Byrnes certainly could not openly embrace the idea that Germany would and should be divided permanently, even if the reparations settlement strongly suggests that he viewed this as the best possible outcome. All of the clarity that Byrnes sought to achieve in the reparations settlement was lost in the many provisions of Potsdam that maintained the goals of four-power cooperation and the unified nature of Germany. Rather than approaching the question of Germany from the perspective of an amicable divorce, sincere Rooseveltians such as Lucius Clay viewed their task as one of forging a long-term marriage with the Soviets in managing every aspect of German affairs. One can certainly admire Clay's determination to preserve great power cooperation in Germany and for resisting worst-case assumptions about the Soviets, but "cooperation" as defined by Clay would not have been acceptable to the Soviet Union. The May 1946 reparations stop, formulated by Byrnes and Clay, was a direct message to the Soviets that they would not get reparations from the West unless they agreed to accept common import-export plans and ceased removing whatever they wanted from the eastern zone. Clay's willingness to compromise on questions such as the permissibility of Soviet reparations from current production in the western zone was not based on the idea that the Soviets deserved greater compensation from Germany, but on the belief that current reparations could and should be traded for Soviet political concessions which could eventually eliminate their dominance in the East. Even if Byrnes had given Clay all of the support and backing he requested in 1945–46, which he most certainly did not, it is highly unlikely that Stalin would have accepted the terms of cooperation envisioned by Clay and other officials who opposed the division of Germany.

The structural changes in the distribution of power brought about by the Second World War had opened up two broad possibilities for the future of Europe. Cautious optimists, such as William T. R. Fox, hoped that the strong common interest in controlling German power would provide a powerful incentive for postwar cooperation among the superpowers. The second possibility, best expressed in Hitler's testament of April 1945, predicted that the two superpowers would soon find themselves bidding for the allegiance of the German people.[21] Whether the outcome can be blamed on specific individuals, countries, or the tragic nature of politics in an anarchic international system can be fiercely debated, but by the summer of 1946 it was becoming clear that Hitler was quite correct in anticipating the shape of things to come. Byrnes's Stuttgart speech of September 1946, in which he openly appealed to German nationalism and promised that American troops would stay in Germany as long as the other occupying powers did, marked the unofficial end of Roosevelt's grand design and exit strategy for postwar Europe. The struggle for Germany would now become the central element of great power politics in Europe for nearly the next two decades.

TRANSFORMING THE SYSTEM: AMERICA AND THE UNIFICATION OF WESTERN EUROPE

The tremendous power advantage that America possessed over the Soviet Union, of course, did not suddenly disappear with the breakdown of cooperation over Germany. With the exception of the disparity in conventional forces in Europe, which may not have been as great as most American officials thought at the time, America was still well ahead of the Soviet Union in every measure of power.[22] Nevertheless, in 1947 American policymakers usually spoke in terms of *restoring* a balance of power on the continent. For example, at a cabinet meeting in November 1947, Secretary of State George Marshall argued that "the objective of our policy from this point on would be the restoration of a balance of power in both Europe and Asia and that all actions would be viewed in light of this objective."[23]

Even more curious than the focus on restoration, given Waltz's emphasis on the primacy of internal balancing in bipolar systems, is the way in which American policymakers sought to restore the balance of power in Europe after 1947. Military spending generally remained constant and well below what military officials thought was needed to meet the growing commitments assumed by the Truman administration. The North

---

[21] For Hitler's view on U.S.–Soviet competition, see the epigraph to chapter 2.

[22] For the most recent debate over the size and abilities of Soviet conventional forces, see Philip A. Karber and Jerald A. Combs, "The United States, NATO, and the Soviet Threat to Western Europe: Military Estimates and Policy Options, 1945–1963," *Diplomatic History* 22 (summer 1998): 399–429; and the separate responses in the same issue by John Duffield and Matthew Evangelista, 431–446.

[23] Cited in Walter Millis, ed., *The Forrestal Diaries* (New York: Viking Press, 1951), 341.

Atlantic Treaty was signed in 1949, but there was no expansion of the American troop presence in Europe before or after the signing of the treaty. As Robert Jervis argues, it is not until after the outbreak of the Korean War that America began to balance Soviet power in a manner consistent with theories of bipolarity.[24]

This book argues that America did not act like a bipolar alliance leader is supposed to act because, even after 1947, policymakers continued to perceive the structure of the system in a fundamentally different way than is suggested by neorealism. American policymakers did not originally believe that a world with only two great powers would be inherently antagonistic, and they also did not believe that the structure of bipolarity could only be transformed with the triumph of one superpower over the other or, as eventually happened many decades later, with the internal collapse of one of the superpowers. What most American officials really envisioned when they talked about the restoration of a balance of power was the creation of a politically integrated and unified Western Europe that eventually would be powerful enough to contain the Soviet Union. As a collection of unconnected nation-states, Western Europe faced a future of complete dependence on the United States. However, as a united entity Western Europe could become a third great power on a level comparable with the superpowers. As John Foster Dulles argued, "Disunity alone prevents Western Europe from being a great—perhaps the greatest—distinctive area of spiritual, intellectual, economic, and military power."[25] Waltz acknowledges American aspirations for a united Western Europe several times in *Theory of International Politics,* and he even recognizes that "A united Europe that developed political competence and military power would one day emerge as the third superpower, ranking probably between the United States and the Soviet Union."[26] What Waltz failed to consider, however, is how much the existence of a latent third superpower in Western Europe could influence the way American policymakers chose among competing options of balancing power, or how much the desire to establish Western Europe as a third superpower could alter the dynamics of alliance relations between the United States and Western Europe.

America's desire to establish a united Western Europe after 1947 was primarily driven by three interrelated objectives. The first was to reduce the obvious burdens, both short and long term, of containing Soviet

[24] Robert Jervis, "The Impact of the Korean War on the Cold War," *Journal of Conflict Resolution* 24 (December 1980): 563–92. For a more recent critique of the distinction between internal and external balancing in neorealist theory and its application to American foreign policy during this period, see David Lake, *Entangling Relations: American Foreign Policy in Its Century* (Princeton: Princeton University Press, 1999), 148–65.

[25] John Foster Dulles, *War or Peace* (New York: Macmillan Company, 1950), 213.

[26] Kenneth N. Waltz, *Theory of International Politics* (New York: Random House, 1979), 180.

power in Europe. "It should be a cardinal point of our policy," George Kennan wrote in October 1947, "to see to it that other elements of independent power are developed on the Eurasian land as rapidly as possible in order to take off our shoulders some of the burdens of bi-polarity."[27] The second and more important reason for pursuing the unification of Western Europe, of course, was the need for American policymakers to come up with a long-term solution to the German problem. Regardless of whether Germany was ultimately divided or unified, U.S. policymakers were convinced that the problem of German power in Europe could not be resolved within the context of a system that preserved individual national sovereignties. European unification might not have been necessary for strictly economic reasons, but it was necessary because of Germany. As Kennan argued, "To leave Germany to continue to realize her national ideals and aspirations within the sovereign-national framework would almost inevitably lead to a repetition of the general sequence of development that followed the Versailles settlement; only some sort of a European federation could provide for Germany a place in the European community that would be comfortable and safe for everyone concerned."[28] For Kennan, as well as for John Foster Dulles, the third reason why unification was necessary was the belief that the American military presence in Europe could not become the permanent solution for either the German or the Soviet problem. The unification of Western Europe represented a solution which would ensure a stable Europe and eventually enable American forces to be withdrawn from the continent.[29]

There are many reasons to doubt whether the goal of creating a third global power in Western Europe, one that would make it possible for American forces to be withdrawn from the continent, could have been obtained under any circumstances. The hope that measures such as the Marshall Plan and NATO could lead to progress on European integration was vindicated by the French proposal for the establishment of a European Coal and Steel Community, but the outbreak of the Korean War injected the question of West German rearmament into the picture at the worst possible moment. America's decision to support the European Defense Community as the institutional framework for German rearmament was an attempt to reconcile immediate imperatives with the long-range goal of creating a united Western Europe. Even Dean Acheson, who was deeply skeptical about the feasibility of grand schemes for European

[27] Kennan cited in John Lewis Gaddis, *The Long Peace: Inquiries into the History of the Cold War* (New York: Oxford University Press, 1987), 58.

[28] George F. Kennan, *Memoirs, 1925–50* (New York: Atlantic, Little, Brown, 1967), 452.

[29] As shown in chapter 4, in 1948 Kennan shifted from being resigned to the division of Germany to advocating a negotiated settlement with the Soviets that would accomplish these objectives in the context of an undivided Germany.

unification, came to support the EDC solution because of its possible future importance:

> We favor this solution as a long term approach to problem of Eur[opean] defense as long as it is clearly a part of and under NATO umbrella. We must look forward to a future in which in one manner or another tension between East and West will be at least temporarily ameliorated. From such long term view point it is probably neither practical nor in best interests Eur[ope] or US that there sh[ou]ld be a US Commander in Eur[ope] or substantial numbers of US forces on Continent. We w[ou]ld, however, regret to see concept of internat[iona]l forces that is now accepted ever disintegrate to point where nothing w[ou]ld remain on Continent except nat[iona]l forces solely under nat[iona]l control. This is particularly important as regards Ger[many].[30]

The qualifications and conditions that Acheson placed on American support for the European Defense Community are important, as is his emphasis on setting the EDC permanently within the NATO framework, but it is debatable how much weight should be placed on them. Contrary to the argument of Saki Dockrill in her fine study of West German rearmament, Acheson did not qualify American support for the EDC because he feared it was "a French device to attain the leadership of Western Europe which, if successful, might threaten American interests in the future."[31] What Acheson really feared was that a European army would never get off the ground unless it were set in the framework of NATO and that the EDC and Western Europe ultimately might not be strong enough to contain Germany. Despite all of Eisenhower's and Dulles's later efforts to bring the EDC into existence, which Eisenhower thought was the key step in both the process of unifying Western Europe and making it possible to withdraw U.S. military forces, Acheson was proven correct. There simply was no substitute for the physical presence of American forces in Europe in the first decade after the Second World War.

THE UNIPOLAR MOMENT?
AMERICA AND THE FUTURE OF EUROPE

When the archives for the immediate post-Cold War era are opened several decades from now, historians and international relations theorists

---

[30] Acheson to the Embassy in France, June 28, 1951, *FRUS, 1951*, vol. 3, 802.
[31] Saki Dockrill, *Britain's Policy for West German Rearmament, 1950–55* (Cambridge: Cambridge University Press, 1991), 69.

will undoubtedly have a field day trying to figure out exactly how American strategists perceived the future implications of the revolutionary changes brought about by the collapse of Soviet power. Like the policymakers and strategists of the 1940s, American planners in the 1990s had to contend with structural changes so unique that neither theory nor history offered very much useful guidance. The most revealing glimpse we have had so far into the minds of national security planners came in March 1992 with the leaking of a draft Pentagon guidance plan which suggested that American grand strategy should be devoted to the goal of making sure that new great powers did not arise in either Europe or Asia. By maintaining a strong military and persuading potential competitors that the United States did not threaten their legitimate interests, Pentagon planners essentially argued that America should aspire to maintain and extend for as long as possible the unipolar distribution of power created by the implosion of the Soviet Union. Moreover, the Pentagon plan argued that America must maintain a substantial military presence in Europe and "seek to prevent the emergence of European-only security arrangements which would undermine NATO."[32] Although public criticism of the plan forced officials to back away from defending its basic premises, there can be little doubt that the views expressed captured many of the basic assumptions of American policy planners in the aftermath of the Cold War.[33] However, the belief that America must continue to take overall responsibility for European security and peace, both for reasons of national interest and for the general interests of Europe, is more than just a transparent Pentagon rationale for maintaining large defense budgets: it is also a widely held view among academics and the general public.

This book does not pretend to offer any predictions about the future of Europe or NATO after bipolarity. If American policymakers had a variety of policy options under conditions of bipolarity, they have an even wider range of choice under conditions of unipolarity. Whether America's unipolar moment will be fleeting or enduring will be heavily influenced by the unpredictable choices of policymakers and the responses they receive from other powers. This study of how America came to have a permanent military presence in Europe may help inform future policy choices, but it certainly cannot validate any structural laws or vindicate a particular grand strategy for the twenty-first century. That wise men such as Roosevelt, Kennan, or Eisenhower believed a permanent troop presence

---

[32] Patrick Tyler, "U.S. Strategy Plan Calls for Insuring No Rivals Develop," *New York Times,* March 8, 1992, A1; and "Excerpts From Pentagon's Plan," A14.

[33] For the best criticism of the plan, see Christopher Layne, "The Unipolar Illusion: Why New Great Powers Will Arise," *International Security* 17 (spring 1993): 5–51. For a defense and elaboration of the Pentagon strategy, see Wohlforth, "The Stability of a Unipolar World," *International Security* 24 (summer 1999): 5–41.

in Europe was highly undesirable does not mean that current and future American officials should hold the same view. Conversely, the fact that the presence of American military forces was essential to solving the German problem and furthering the process of European integration in the early postwar period does not mean that these forces should stay in Europe for another century.

The "lessons" of history are never as clear as we would like them to be, and this is particularly true when it comes to drawing lessons from the early history of the Cold War. Nevertheless, in thinking about the future of Europe after the Cold War, policymakers and grand strategists would do well to keep in mind Eisenhower's two basic assumptions about America's goals in Europe at the height of the Cold War. In a letter to Lucius Clay in March 1951, Eisenhower suggested that "the basic assumption of our entire program is that the retention of the European complex in the free world is vital to America's prosperity and safety. The next assumption is that, if Europe is helped sufficiently to regain her own confidence and build her initial forces, she can permanently defend herself."[34]

Eisenhower's two assumptions provide a useful corrective to legitimate—but unsound—views about how America should envision its future role in Europe. The first view, popular among libertarians and some neorealists, is that America has no real need to be concerned anymore about what happens in Europe and that the primary goal of the United States should be "staying out of Europe's wars."[35] Eisenhower's enthusiasm for the removal of American troops was at least as great as those who now argue for a grand strategy of what Christopher Layne calls "offshore balancing," but the president also recognized that this goal needed to be balanced against the equally important interest of the United States in a peaceful and prosperous Europe. It is for this reason that he rejected the short-sighted views of advisors who urged him to place the withdrawal of American troops ahead of goals such as the ratification of the European Defense Community.

Unfortunately, the capacity of the European Union (EU) to independently handle its own security affairs is not all that much greater today than it was in the early 1950s. The inability of the EU to perform even modest security tasks without the full support of NATO has become increasingly obvious over the course of the 1990s. Although the Europeans might develop greater capabilities for dealing with conflict if American

---

[34] Eisenhower to Clay, March 30, 1951, *TPDDE*, 12:171.

[35] Ted Galen Carpenter of the libertarian Cato Institute has made the most forceful arguments along these lines. See Carpenter, *Beyond NATO: Staying Out of Europe's Wars* (Washington, D.C.: Cato Institute, 1994); and Carpenter and Barbara Conry, eds., *NATO Enlargement: Illusions and Reality* (Washington, D.C.: Cato Institute, 1998). Benjamin Schwartz and Christopher Layne have been very compelling critics of American foreign policy from a neorealist perspective.

troops were withdrawn from the continent, it is equally possible that they would not. The prudent course for America to pursue is to help the EU develop the capacity for independent action while NATO continues to serve as a useful safety net in case the goal of European independence in security affairs proves unattainable. Shock therapy and threats of an agonizing reappraisal did not work for Dulles, and such methods are unlikely to be any more successful in the future.

The biggest complication involved in a complete American withdrawal from Europe, of course, involves the question of Germany's nuclear status. As Marc Trachtenberg has shown, a truly stable peace emerged in Europe only after this question was settled in 1963. The price of West Germany's renunciation of nuclear weapons, one well worth paying at the time, was an implicit American commitment to retain military forces on the continent. Even now, the possible consequences of Germany acquiring nuclear weapons may be so great that they outweigh the benefits of an American withdrawal. Nevertheless, although the question of Germany's nuclear status should be postponed for as long as possible, American policymakers should still pay much more attention to the goal of making Europe self-sufficient in military affairs. The extreme dependence on the United States of the European allies in the Kosovo conflict revealed just how far the EU is from having the capability to defend itself.[36] Responsibility for the poor state of the EU's military capability is primarily the fault of its member states, but part of the problem is surely due to the ambivalent American attitude toward European efforts at lessening this dependency.

Reassuring Europe that the United States was not going to abandon NATO in the immediate aftermath of the Cold War was a prudent decision, but American policymakers went much too far in their efforts to discourage European countries from assuming more responsibility for their own security. In a November 1991 statement, President Bush actually warned the Europeans that America would view any attempts at providing for their own defense outside of NATO as a serious threat: "If our premise is wrong—if, my friends, your ultimate aim is to provide independently for your own defense, the time to tell us is today."[37] The idea that an American president would one day view such a goal (which overstates what the European members of NATO have aspired to achieve) as a threat to be deterred rather than an opportunity to be welcomed would have been unthinkable to a Roosevelt, a Kennan, or an Eisenhower. If the Western Europeans are willing in the future to take any steps at all toward

---

[36] For a good symposium on the European reassessments of security in the aftermath of the Kosovo crisis, see the contributions by Francois Heisbourg, Charles Kupchan, Jocelyn Holworth, Hans Maull, and Guillaume Parmentier in *Survival* 42 (summer 2000): 5–112.

[37] Cited in Geir Lundestad, *"Empire" by Integration: The United States and European Integration, 1945–1997* (New York: Oxford University Press, 1998), 115.

a more independent security role in Europe, they should receive all the support and encouragement that America can provide. The Clinton administration was more welcoming toward European security initiatives than the Bush administration, but future administrations should strive even harder to encourage greater self-sufficiency and worry less about the future of NATO and any supposed challenges to American leadership.

America's approach to NATO and European security in the future should be to seek to turn the clock back as much as possible to the period before the Korean War. Prior to the Korean War, America envisioned a much more limited security relationship with its European allies. The creation of a vast security infrastructure and the stationing of additional divisions were necessary at that time to bolster deterrence against the Soviet Union and make the rearmament of West Germany palatable to its former adversaries. The transformation of the American military presence after the Korean War was ultimately necessary to provide proof that the United States would be willing to defend Western Europe against a Soviet invasion, not just liberate the continent after an invasion. Europe obviously still needs some degree of security reassurance from the United States, but the future goal should be to take the O out of NATO. More precisely, while maintaining the basic commitments we assumed in 1949, the U.S. goal should be to let the European members of the alliance run the show as much as possible. The day when the EU can handle future Kosovos and peacekeeping in Europe without American leadership and manpower should be viewed as a victory rather than a defeat.

Sources

MANUSCRIPT COLLECTIONS

Dwight D. Eisenhower Presidential Library, Abilene, Kans.
  John Foster Dulles Papers
  Dwight D. Eisenhower Papers
      National Security Council Series
      Pre-Presidential Correspondence
      White House Central Files
      Ann Whitman File
  Alfred Gruenther Papers
  C. D. Jackson Papers

Franklin D. Roosevelt Presidential Library, Hyde Park, N.Y.
  Henry Morgenthau Diaries
  President's Soviet Protocol Committee Records
  Franklin D. Roosevelt Papers
      Official File
      Personal File

Harry S. Truman Presidential Library, Independence, Mo.
  Dean Acheson Papers
  Matthew J. Connelly Papers
  Harry S. Truman Papers
      Rose Conway File
      National Security Council Files
      President's Secretary File
      White House Central Files
  Stuart Symington Papers

Clemson University, Robert M. Cooper Library, Clemson, S.C.
  James F. Byrnes Papers

Columbia University, Low Library, New York, N.Y.
    John H. Backer Papers

University of Michigan, Bentley Historical Library, Ann Arbor, Mich.
    James K. Pollock Papers

Princeton University, Seeley G. Mudd Library, Princeton, N.J.
    John Foster Dulles Papers
    George F. Kennan Papers

Stanford University, Hoover Institution, Stanford, Calif.
    Robert D. Murphy Papers

NATIONAL ARCHIVES, COLLEGE PARK, MD.

    Paris Embassy Files. Records Pertaining to the European Defense Community,
        1951–55
    RG 59, General Records of the Department of State
        State Department Decimal Files
        Lot Files
            Records of Charles E. Bohlen
            Records of the Bureau of European Affairs
            Records of the Central European Affairs Division
            Records of the French Desk
            Office Files of Philip Jessup
            Records of the Office of the Assistant Secretary of State for Occupied
                Areas
            Records of the Office of European Regional Affairs: Files of J. Graham
                Parsons
            Records of the Policy Planning Staff
            Records of Western European Affairs
    RG 84, U.S. Polad Germany Post Files, 1945–49. Office of the Political Advisor
    RG 330, Secretary of Defense
    RG 349, Records of Joint Commands

PUBLISHED U.S. GOVERNMENT DOCUMENTS

Executive Branch
    Foreign Relations of the United States, diplomatic papers (*FRUS*). Washington,
        D.C.: Government Printing Office.
        1941
            Vol. 1: *General; The Soviet Union* (1958)
            Vol. 3: *The British Commonwealth; The Near East and Africa* (1959)
        1942
            Vol. 1: *General; The British Commonwealth; The Far East* (1960)
            Vol. 2: *Europe* (1962)
            Vol. 3: *Europe* (1961)

Sources

1943
   Vol. 1: *General* (1963)
   Vol. 3: *The British Commonwealth; Eastern Europe; The Far East* (1963)
   The Conferences at Cairo and Teheran (1961)
   The Conferences at Washington and Quebec (1970)
1944
   Vol. 1: *General* (1966)
   The Conference at Quebec (1972)
1945
   Vol. 3: *The European Advisory Commission; Austria; Germany* (1968)
   Vol. 4: *Europe* (1968)
   Vol. 5: *Europe* (1967)
   The Conference of Berlin (The Potsdam Conference), 2 vols. (1960)
   The Conferences at Malta and Yalta (1955)
1946
   Vol. 2: *Council of Foreign Ministers* (1970)
   Vol. 5: *The British Commonwealth; Western and Central Europe* (1969)
1947
   Vol. 2: *Council of Foreign Ministers; Germany and Austria* (1972)
   Vol. 3: *The British Commonwealth; Europe* (1972)
1948
   Vol. 1 (part 1): *General; United Nations* (1975)
   Vol. 2: *Germany and Austria* (1973)
   Vol. 3: *Western Europe* (1974)
1949
   Vol. 1: *National Security Affairs; Foreign Economic Policy* (1976)
   Vol. 3: *Council of Foreign Ministers; Germany and Austria* (1974)
   Vol. 4: *Western Europe* (1975)
1950
   Vol. 1: *National Security Affairs; Foreign Economic Policy* (1977)
   Vol. 3: *Western Europe* (1977)
   Vol. 4: *Central and Eastern Europe; The Soviet Union* (1981)
1951
   Vol. 3 (2 parts): *European Security and the German Question* (1982)
1952–54
   Vol. 5: *Western European Security* (1983)
   Vol. 6: *Western Europe and Canada* (1987)
   Vol. 7: *Germany and Austria* (1986)
Memoranda of Conversation of the Secretary of State 1947–52. Microfiche publication. Washington, D.C.: Department of State, 1988.
Memoranda of the Secretary of State, 1949–51 and Meetings and Visits of Foreign Dignitaries, 1949–52. Microfiche publication. Washington, D.C.: Department of State, 1988.

United States House of Representatives
   Committee on Foreign Affairs. *Military Assistance Programs: Historical Series.* Volume 5, part 1. Washington, D.C.: Government Printing Office, 1976.

United States Senate

    Committee on Foreign Relations. *Convention on Relations with the Federal Republic of Germany and Protocol to the North Atlantic Treaty.* 82d Cong., 2d sess., 1952.

    ——. *European Recovery Program.* 80th Cong., 2d sess., 1948.

    ——. *Military Assistance Program.* 81st Cong., 1st sess., 1949.

    ——. *The North Atlantic Treaty,* 81st Cong., 1st sess., part 2, 1949.

    ——. *Reviews of the World Situation, 1949–50: Historical Series.* Washington, D.C.: Government Printing Office, 1974.

    Committee on Foreign Relations and the Committee on Armed Services. *Assignment of Ground Forces to Duty in the North Atlantic Area.* 82d Cong., 1st sess., 1951.

    ——. *Mutual Security Act of 1951.* 82d Cong., 1st sess., 1951.

MICROFILM DOCUMENT COLLECTIONS

Adolf A. Berle Diary, 1937–71. Franklin D. Roosevelt Library and National Archives and Records Services Administration, Hyde Park, N.Y., 1978.

Minutes of Meetings of the National Security Council. Frederick, Md.: University Publications of America, 1982.

Records of the Joint Chiefs of Staff, Part 1, 1942–45: Meetings. Frederick, Md.: University Publications of America, 1980.

Records of the Joint Chiefs of Staff, Part 1, 1942–45: The Soviet Union. Frederick, Md.: University Publications of America, 1981.

Records of the Joint Chiefs of Staff, Part 2, 1946–53: Europe and NATO. Frederick, Md.: University Publications of America, 1980.

Records of the Joint Chiefs of Staff, Part 2, 1946–53: The Soviet Union. Frederick, Md.: University Publications of America, 1979.

Records of the Office of European Affairs (Matthews-Hickerson File), 1934–1947. Washington, D.C.: National Archives and Record Service, 1982.

O.S.S./State Department Intelligence and Research Reports: The Soviet Union, Part 6. Washington, D.C.: University Publications of America, 1977.

ORAL HISTORIES

Henry Byroade (Truman Library)

John Hickerson (Columbia University Oral History Project)

Charles Kindleberger (Truman Library)

Isador Lubin (Columbia University Oral History Project)

Isador Lubin (Truman Library)

James Riddleberger (Princeton University, Dulles Oral History Project)

PUBLISHED BRITISH DOCUMENTS

Documents on British Policy Overseas. London: Her Majesty's Stationery Office.

    Series 1

        Vol. 1: *The Conference at Potsdam, 1945* (1984)

Vol. 2: *Conferences and Conversations 1945: London, Washington and Moscow* (1985)
Vol. 5: *Germany and Western Europe: 11 August–31 December 1945* (1990)
Series 2
Vol. 1: *The Schuman Plan, the Council of Europe and Western European Integration, May 1950–December 1952* (1986)
Vol. 2: *The London Conferences: Anglo-American Relations and Cold War Strategy January–June 1950* (1987)
Vol. 3: *German Rearmament: September–December 1950* (1989)

UNPUBLISHED MATERIAL

Conover, Denise O'Neal. "James F. Byrnes, Germany, and the Cold War, 1946." Ph.D. diss., Washington State University, 1978.
Converse, Elliot Vanveltner. "United States Plans for a Postwar Overseas Military Base System." Ph.D. diss., Princeton University, 1984.
Egan, Joseph B. "The Struggle for the Soul of Faust: The American Drive for German Rearmament, 1950–55." Ph.D. diss., University of Connecticut, 1985.
Parrish, Scott. "The USSR and the Security Dilemma: Explaining Soviet Self-Encirclement, 1945–85." Ph.D. diss., Columbia University, 1993.
Reed, Laura. "The Roads Not Taken: The U.S. Security Debate over Germany, 1944–49." Ph.D. diss., Massachussets Institute of Technology, 1995.
Sapp, Steven P. "The United States, France, and the Cold War: Jefferson Caffery and American-French Relations, 1944–49." Ph.D. diss., Kent State University, 1978.

Index

CORNELL STUDIES IN SECURITY AFFAIRS

A series edited by
Robert J. Art
Robert Jervis
Stephen M. Walt

Planning the Unthinkable: How New Powers Will Use Nuclear, Biological, and Chemical Weapons
    edited by Peter R. Lavoy, Scott D. Sagan, and James J. Wirtz
Cooperation under Fire: Anglo-German Restraint during World War II
    by Jeffrey W. Legro
Liddell Hart and the Weight of History
    by John J. Mearsheimer
Reputation and International Politics
    by Jonathan Mercer
Undermining the Kremlin: America's Strategy to Subvert the Soviet Bloc, 1947–1956
    by Gregory Mitrovich
Report to JFK: The Skybolt Crisis in Perspective
    by Richard E. Neustadt
The Sacred Cause: Civil-Military Conflict over Soviet National Security, 1917–1992
    by Thomas M. Nichols
Liberal Peace, Liberal War: American Politics and International Security
    by John M. Owen IV
Bombing to Win: Air Power and Coercion in War
    by Robert A. Pape
A Question of Loyalty: Military Manpower in Multiethnic States
    by Alon Peled
Inadvertent Escalation: Conventional War and Nuclear Risks
    by Barry R. Posen
The Sources of Military Doctrine: France, Britain, and Germany between the World Wars
    by Barry Posen
Dilemmas of Appeasement: British Deterrence and Defense, 1934–1937
    by Gaines Post, Jr.
Crucible of Beliefs: Learning, Alliances, and World Wars
    by Dan Reiter
Eisenhower and the Missile Gap
    by Peter J. Roman
The Domestic Bases of Grand Strategy
    edited by Richard Rosecrance and Arthur Stein
Societies and Military Power: India and Its Armies
    by Stephen Peter Rosen
Winning the Next War: Innovation and the Modern Military
    by Stephen Peter Rosen
Fighting to a Finish: The Politics of War Termination in the United States and Japan, 1945
    by Leon V. Sigal
Alliance Politics
    by Glenn H. Snyder
The Ideology of the Offensive: Military Decision Making and the Disasters of 1914
    by Jack Snyder
Myths of Empire: Domestic Politics and International Ambition
    by Jack Snyder
The Militarization of Space: U.S. Policy, 1945–1984
    by Paul B. Stares

Cornell Studies in Security Affairs